THE CRAFT OF PROSE

FOURTH EDITION

ROBERT H. WOODWARD
San Jose State University

H. WENDELL SMITH
Santa Monica College

Wadsworth Publishing Company, Inc.
Belmont, California

English Editor: Randy Cade

© 1977 by Wadsworth Publishing Company, Inc.

© 1963, 1968, 1972 by Wadsworth Publishing Company, Inc., Belmont, California 94002. All rights reserved. No part of this book may be reproduced, stored in a retrieval system, or transcribed, in any form or by any means, electronic, mechanical, photocopying, recording, or otherwise, without the prior written permission of the publisher.

Printed in the United States of America

2 3 4 5 6 7 8 9 10—81 80 79 78 77

Library of Congress Cataloging in Publication Data

Woodward, Robert Hanson
   The craft of prose.

   Includes index.
   1. English language—Rhetoric. 2. College readers.
I. Smith, H. Wendell   joint author. II. Title.
PE1417.W6 1977   808′.04275   76-21000
ISBN 0-534-00487-3

PREFACE

TO THE FOURTH EDITION

Readers of the fourth edition of *The Craft of Prose* will find that the goals which governed the contents and organization of the first edition have not changed. The purpose of this book remains the same: to assist students to increase their writing proficiency by providing them with a collection of prose selections which can be analyzed and can serve as models for writing exercises.

Like the two previous revisions, however, this edition includes more modern and contemporary prose selections. Although a number of selections from the nineteenth century (and even earlier) have been retained, the new selections —almost one-third of the volume—are exclusively from the present century; many, in fact, are from the last decade, and some are from periodicals of the last few years. Thus, writers of today such as Isaac Asimov and Jack Richardson, writing about issues as current as those in the daily newspaper, stand margin to margin with acknowledged masters of English prose style such as Henry David Thoreau, Mark Twain, and Francis Bacon.

The organization of this edition differs somewhat from that of previous editions. Major sections on description, narration, and argumentation have been retained, but the initial section, "Exposition," has been expanded to include classification, comparison and contrast, and cause and effect. All selections in the latter two sub-sections are new to this edition.

PREFACE TO FOURTH EDITION

Each of the sub-sections under "Exposition," as well as each of the other three major sections, now includes a final essay for further analysis. These essays are accompanied by brief headnotes only. They exemplify the rhetorical devices and methods illustrated by the briefer selections that precede them in each section. The omission of questions for analysis is intended to permit the instructor maximum flexibility in their use. Suggestions for writing are grouped at the conclusion of each sub-section under "Exposition" and at the end of each of the other three principal sections.

It is worthwhile to emphasize that this textbook is a collection of complete essays and self-contained excerpts to be read and analyzed; it does not present a formal or systematic writing program. The individual instructor may, of course, range freely throughout the book. The organization, though not arbitrary, does not presume to prescribe an order of study.

We take pleasure in acknowledging with gratitude the suggestions and counsel of Professors James L. Fife, University of Utah; Byron K. Jackson, Fairmont State College; William Raffaniello, New York City Community College; and Fred Tarpley, East Texas State University, who helped to shape the third edition. We also wish to acknowledge Paulette S. Hooper and the entire English Department at the University of New Orleans, as well as John Hanes of Duquesne University, for their helpful comments on this fourth edition. Finally, thanks to Stephen D. Rutter of Wadsworth Publishing Company, who brought about what has been a pleasant collaboration for us and one that we hope proves to be equally pleasant for the instructors and students who use this book.

Robert H. Woodward
H. Wendell Smith

PREFACE

TO THE FIRST EDITION

In his *Autobiography* Benjamin Franklin recalls his use of certain *Spectator* papers to improve his style and fluency, his vocabulary, and his organization of ideas. Franklin's comments on how he learned to write appear as the first selection in this book—as an example of the process theme, but also as a statement of a principle on which this book is based: that a writer learns his craft at least partly through a careful analysis of what he reads. By noting the methods and devices of careful authors, he becomes conscious of the tools of prose and is able to make use of these tools in his own compositions.

With respect to organization and method, then, this book is a collection of models illustrating the four principal forms of prose: exposition, description, narration, and argumentation. All of the materials provided—the selections, the introductions to each section, the questions and suggestions for writing that follow each selection—are designed primarily to promote the student's understanding of various kinds of prose, the basic relationships and differences between them, and the methods by which a workmanlike piece of prose is constructed and developed.

Another fundamental feature of this volume concerns the length of the selections; though self-contained, they are generally only four hundred to a thousand words in length—about the same as the normal length of the student's own papers. No selection is so long that the student will find himself adrift in a sea of words. He will be able to see both shores at all times and therefore can concentrate on the methods of navigation. He will not experience the confusion that frequently comes from the sheer immensity of the broad water that surrounds him in the midst of a long essay.

The selections—for the most part drawn from the works of well-known English and American authors, from Francis Bacon and Thomas Fuller to William Faulkner and Edmund Wilson—were chosen on the basis of several criteria: their literary value, their success in illustrating the methods of prose discussed in the introductions, their combined brevity and completeness, and their intrinsic interest.

Each selection is preceded by a brief commentary, which provides information that the student needs if he is to read the material intelligently: relevant information about the author and the context in which the selection originally appeared.* The questions that follow each selection call attention to organization, the techniques of prose composition, content, and other relevant matters such as style, tone, figurative language, and sentence structure. These questions may be used in various ways: as guides to the student when he reads the selection outside of class, as subjects for written assignments, as a basis for class discussion. They are not exhaustive, certainly. Each teacher will undoubtedly introduce additional questions that he considers important to the selection. The questions, then, are not designed to take the place of the instructor, but rather to provide him with an analytical apparatus that he may use and supplement as he sees fit.

In addition, almost every selection is followed by suggestions for writing: not lists of topics based on the content of the selections, but writing projects that involve the use of techniques illustrated by the preceding material. (Some of these projects, if assigned, will take the student into the library; for these assignments, the teacher will want to see that certain books are placed on reserve for the student's use.) There are more suggested assignments than any student could write, or any teacher read, in a full-year course; thus, for a single semester's work, both student and teacher can select from a wide variety of writing projects. Through experience I have found that it is best to assign and discuss several of the selections illustrating a single form of writing, and then to allow the student a reasonably wide choice among the writing assignments following those selections.

Although the volume can easily provide the necessary reading for a semester's course, teachers who emphasize ideas and content through the reading of full-length works will find the book suitable as a supplemental reader for occasional assignments involving closer analyses of specific writing problems than are available in more general anthologies.

* The titles for many of the selections have been provided by the editor.

CONTENTS

EXPOSITION 1

THE PROCESS 4

Benjamin Franklin, LEARNING TO WRITE 6
Alan Devoe, LIFE AND DEATH OF A WORM 9
Stewart Edward White, ON MAKING CAMP 13
W. S. Merwin, UNCHOPPING A TREE 17

    For Further Analysis:
Isaac Asimov, COLONIZING THE HEAVENS 21
    Suggestions for Writing 29

CLASSIFICATION 30

Thomas Fuller, FOUR TYPES OF STUDENTS 31
Paul Roberts, COLORFUL, COLORED, AND COLORLESS WORDS 33

Francis Bacon, OF STUDIES   37
Max Eastman, PRACTICAL AND POETIC PEOPLE   40
Eric Berne, CAN PEOPLE BE JUDGED BY THEIR APPEARANCE?   43

    For Further Analysis:
William Golding, THINKING AS A HOBBY   47

    Suggestions for Writing   54

COMPARISON AND CONTRAST   55

Maya Pines, OF BABALAWOS AND SHAMANS   57 *[handwritten: Comparison or contrast / list 3 examples]*
Jack Richardson, SIX O'CLOCK PRAYERS   60
Jacob Brackman, THE PUT-ON   65
Susanne K. Langer, THE LORD OF CREATION   67

    For Further Analysis:
Anne Roiphe, CONFESSIONS OF A FEMALE CHAUVINIST SOW   72

    Suggestions for Writing   77

CAUSE AND EFFECT   78

Dan Lacy, MEN'S WORDS; WOMEN'S ROLES   80
Philip Wylie, SCIENCE HAS SPOILED MY SUPPER   85
Henry David Thoreau, ON OWNING A FARM   92

    For Further Analysis:
George Orwell, POLITICS AND THE ENGLISH LANGUAGE   96

    Suggestions for Writing   107

DEFINITION   108

Carl L. Becker, HISTORY   110
Carl L. Becker, DEMOCRACY   113
Edmund Wilson, AMERICANISM   116
E. H. Sturtevant, LANGUAGE   119
Morton W. Bloomfield and Leonard Newmark, SLANG   121
Claude Brown, "BABY"   124

CONTENTS ix

    For Further Analysis:
Mark Van Doren, WHAT IS A POET?   127

    Suggestions for Writing   131

DESCRIPTION 133

DESCRIPTIONS OF PLACES 137

Frank Norris, POLK STREET   139 ✓   Tuesday April 25.
Mark Twain, STEAMBOAT TOWN   143 ✓
Jack London, STUDENT QUARTERS   146
Sinclair Lewis, THE HOUSE OF BABBITT   150
Herb Caen, THE PLASTIC FANTASTIC   152

DESCRIPTIONS OF PERSONS 155

Leonard Shecter, MUHAMMAD ALI   157
Henry James, THE AMERICAN   162
Herman Melville, CAPTAIN AHAB   166
Harold Frederic, THE THREE TRUSTEES and
        PRELIMINARY SKETCHES   169

SIGHTS, SOUNDS, SENSATIONS 173

Mark Twain, STORM ON JACKSON'S ISLAND   174
John Steinbeck, EMPTY HOUSES   176
Chet Huntley, THE SONG OF THE LAND   178
Stephen Crane, FOUR MEN IN A BOAT   182

    For Further Analysis:
H. L. Mencken, THE LIBIDO FOR THE UGLY   185

    Suggestions for Writing   189

NARRATION 193

AUTOBIOGRAPHY AND BIOGRAPHY 196

Langston Hughes, SALVATION   198

William Allen White, "A CHILD WENT FORTH"   202
Piri Thomas, IN BUSINESS   206
Clair Huffaker, PONY BOY   209

FACTUAL AND HISTORICAL NARRATION   215

Alexander Calandra, ANGELS ON A PIN   217
George Orwell, A HANGING   220
Samuel Eliot Morison, THE SALEM WITCHCRAFT FRENZY   226
John Hersey, A NOISELESS FLASH   229

FICTIONAL INCIDENTS AND ANECDOTES   233

John Steinbeck, THE TURTLE   237
Katharine Brush, BIRTHDAY PARTY   240
Benjamin Franklin, THE SPECKLED AX   241

For Further Analysis:
Richard Wright, " . . . AND I HUNGERED FOR BOOKS"   243

Suggestions for Writing   251

ARGUMENTATION   253

LOGICAL ARGUMENT   255

James Thurber, THE CASE AGAINST WOMEN   260
Robert Claiborne, A WASP STINGS BACK   265
Thomas Jefferson, THE DECLARATION OF INDEPENDENCE   269
Henry David Thoreau, GOVERNMENT AND THE MORAL SENSE   274
Ralph Waldo Emerson, THE MIND OF THE PAST   278

EMOTIONAL APPEALS   284

Allan Planz, THE POOL   286
Nathaniel Hawthorne, A GIANT'S DEAD BODY   289
William Faulkner, THE STOCKHOLM ADDRESS   294
George Bernard Shaw, THE DEVIL SPEAKS   297

Martin Luther King, Jr., I HAVE A DREAM   300

   For Further Analysis:
Tom Bethell, DARWIN'S MISTAKE   306

   Suggestions for Writing   314

INDEX   317

EXPOSITION

All writing that is concerned with setting forth facts or ideas is called *exposition,* from the Latin *exponere*—"to put forth" or "expound." Unless you are taking a literature course, most of the reading that you are now doing as a college student is expository prose. The aim of your textbooks is to provide instruction and information about a given course of study. The words that you are reading at this moment are, in fact, expository.

Furthermore, much of your own writing has probably been expository—that required for the fulfilling of assignments in your various classes. Essay examination questions ("What is a block and tackle, and how is one constructed?" "What are the three principal methods of making pottery by hand without a wheel?" "Compare and contrast *Adventures of Huckleberry Finn* and *An American Tragedy* as social criticism." "What were the basic causes of World War I?" "How can you tell the difference between plant and animal microbes?") usually require answers that involve the principles of exposition. An essay on a block and tackle, for example, would require first of all a definition and then a step-by-step explanation of how the system of pulleys, hooks, and rope is arranged. An explanation of the three basic methods of hand-building in clay would require the division of your essay into sections on pinching, coiling, and the use of slabs. A comparison of the two novels by Mark Twain and Theodore Dreiser with respect to social criticism would involve your giving attention to how they are alike and how they are not alike in the comments they make on American society. Any satisfactory discussion of the basic causes of World War I would have to take into account several factors—nationalism, imperialism, militarism—and explain the role of each. An acceptable discussion of the differences between plant and animal microbes would be based upon definitions of bacteria and Protozoa—their respective sizes, cell structures, and the like. The answers to these questions require the use of several types of expository writing: **explanation of a process, classification, comparison and contrast, cause and effect,** and **definition.**

Although these types of expository writing can be clearly distinguished, they may supplement each other in a particular piece of work; and they may be used in conjunction with the three other main types of prose presented in this book. For example, a process explanation may be preceded by a definition of the over-all process. Or analysis and definition may be interrelated: Max Eastman, in his discussion of two types of human nature, simultaneously classifies and defines; similarly, Eric Berne answers the question "Can people be judged by their appearance?" by distinguishing between physical types of human males and defining their mental or social characteristics. As the selections from Franklin and Golding illustrate, process explanations and classifications may appear in works that are primarily narrative; and the selections from Edmund Wilson and Max Eastman show that both analysis and definition may serve the purpose of persuasion.

In addition, all of the four forms of prose may utilize certain basic techniques or **methods of development,** within individual paragraphs as well as within essays as a whole. These various methods do not always exist in isolation. The careful writer chooses the method, or the combination of methods, that will best serve his purpose. Good paragraphs effectively present a coherent body of material in an economical and convincing manner. A good paragraph cannot always be analyzed as an example of a single method of development.

In order to clarify his meaning, or to make a general statement more concrete and specific, a writer may cite actual instances; that is, he uses **examples** to develop his generalization. In his definition of language, Sturtevant illustrates the concept *arbitrary vocal symbols* by giving examples of the German, French, and Latin equivalents of the English word *dog*. In his definition of *history*, Carl Becker provides a number of examples of what he calls *events*. Similarly, in discussing various meanings of the word *Americanism,* Edmund Wilson uses numerous examples—direct quotations from Lincoln, Theodore

EXPOSITION

Roosevelt, and others—to illustrate the different ways in which the word has been used. Dan Lacy begins his discussion of "Men's Words; Women's Roles" by providing numerous examples to support his premise that textbooks and children's books have for generations "depicted girls as passive observers, boys as bold achievers."

Through the use of **comparisons**, a writer may explain one thing (A) by relating it to something else (B) that is more familiar to the reader or at least less difficult to comprehend than A. Carl Becker calls the word *democracy* "a kind of conceptual Gladstone bag," capable of stretching in order to contain "almost any collection of social facts we may wish to carry about in it." Max Eastman, in order to place men into appropriate classes, compares life to a ferryboat ride. Edmund Wilson employs a comparison to the well-known statement by Dr. Samuel Johnson that "patriotism is the last refuge of the scoundrel" to make his final judgment of the word *Americanism*. Comparisons—including figures of speech and analogies of various kinds—appear in virtually all of the selections in this section, as well as in the other sections of this book.

Instead of showing the similarities between A and B, a writer may instead clarify his subject (A) by showing the **contrast** between A and B. Max Eastman emphasizes the differences between so-called practical and so-called poetic men. Carl Becker helps to clarify his definition of democracy by contrasting it with tyranny, dictatorships, and monarchy. Related to contrast is **negation**, or **exclusion**, which explains what one's subject is not: Language, Sturtevant says, is a *system*, not a series of nonsense syllables like *ta-ra-ra-boom-de-ay*.

A **chronological development** is an arrangement of statements on the basis of their time relationship, as in the sixth paragraph of Stewart Edward White's "On Making Camp," in which White gives instruction for making a camp bed. This method is a basic technique in the process essay. The **enumeration of details** is a common method of paragraph development, observable in all types of writing. An excellent example is Henry David Thoreau's list of the characteristics of the Hollowell farm (in "On Owning a Farm") that were "real attractions" to him. The care and fullness in their enumeration clearly reveal the ironic intentions of the author. **Definition** serves Max Eastman in his essay on "Practical and Poetic People" as a means of clarifying what he means by practical people. In addition, paragraphs are built on the principle of **cause and effect**; in his essay "Colonizing the Heavens" Isaac Asimov captures the reader's interest with a paragraph devoted to population facts about earth (cause) and then discusses their implications for the future (effect).

The types of exposition considered in this section—The Process, Classification, Comparison and Contrast, Cause and Effect, and Definition—are distinguished mainly by their primary purpose and manner of organization; in addition, each type presents certain specific problems for the writer. Each type—

with accompanying selections and exercises—is presented and discussed separately on the following pages.

THE PROCESS

The explanation of a process—how something is done or made, how a mechanical device works—is organized according to a time sequence; each step in the process is presented in the order in which it should be performed. The steps are described in a one-two-three manner so that they can be followed easily. When you read the directions on a can of automobile polish, or on a package of lawn seed, or on a home-permanent kit, you are reading the explanation of a process in its most simple form. Cookbooks, repair manuals, and some technical books employ the same techniques. In a less simplified form, many of your textbooks contain process descriptions—for example, your English handbook's explanation of the process of outlining or the steps involved in writing a research paper.

In general, process descriptions for cooking and repairing are objective and impersonal. The personality of the author cannot be inferred by the reader; and imagination, humor, and warmth are lacking. The writer is required only to know his subject thoroughly and to explain it clearly and simply, so that his reader can follow his directions step by step. If, however, the writer is explaining a rather extensive process—or if he is writing an essay and not merely a set of directions on the back of a can or a package—he will want to organize and present his material in an effective and interesting way. But, although the process explanation is the simplest form of exposition, it is not easy to make the explanation interesting. The chronological sequence of steps, as in the following directions for preparing an outline, invites short, imperative sentences that would be monotonous if carried to any great length:

Make a rough list of the points to be covered. Decide which ideas are the main ones. List other topics under appropriate main topics. Discard irrelevant topics.

Even when the writer attempts to provide **transitions** (words or phrases that indicate the relationship of the steps), he can easily become repetitious; for the impulse is strong to say "then" before each step. To resolve this problem somewhat, the writer can vary his transitional words or phrases ("Next," "Second," "After . . . ," "Following . . ."); or he can combine several steps into a longer, complex sentence that shows the relationships of time by subordinating and coordinating the steps:

After making a rough list of the points to be covered, separate them into main topics and their appropriate subtopics. Then discard any points that are not completely relevant.

A longer description of a process should be organized so that the steps related to a single aspect of the entire process are grouped into a single paragraph, with a suitable **topic sentence** that indicates their relationship. The topic sentence, an essential element of all good expository prose, keys the reader to the principal idea of the paragraph and aids clarity and unity. In the following paragraph, the first sentence is the topic sentence; transitional words and phrases are italicized. The paragraph, you will notice, is developed by the use of an extended example.

First of all, by making a rough list of the points you think you wish to cover, you will be able to see your subject more clearly and to eliminate material that does not fully relate to the subject. *After studying this list,* you can more readily determine the main topics and the related subtopics of your paper and can regroup the points accordingly. *In the process,* you should discard any points that no longer seem completely relevant to the subject. *For example,* you might make the following list of points to be covered in a paper on the use of figurative language:

>Purpose
>Triteness
>Simile
>Metaphor
>Personification
>Effect
>Alliteration

By studying this list, you should see that "Purpose" and "Effect" are main topics and that most of the other points are subtopics. *After regrouping the points,* you should *also* see that another main topic, "Types," is necessary to include the three figures of speech listed; that "Triteness" belongs under "Effect" but should be discussed with "Freshness," which should be added; and that "Alliteration" is not a figure of speech and therefore should be discarded.

Another important problem in process writing is that of maintaining a consistent **point of view**—the perspective that the writer adopts toward his subject and his reader. Once he selects an appropriate point of view, the writer should maintain it, in order to avoid the confusion and general lack of focus that result from constant and sudden shifts. In the following passage, for example, the writer shifts from the imperative mood (addressing his reader, directly or indirectly, as "you") to the passive voice (addressing no one in particular, but stressing only the action done), then to the first person ("I") and to the third person ("the student"):

Choose a good desk dictionary. After the dictionary has been chosen, it should be examined carefully. I usually look first at the table of contents. After glancing through the table of contents, the student should read the preface carefully.

In the following selections, Franklin—explaining a process in his own development and writing in the form of autobiography—consistently uses the first-person point of view. White, describing the process of making camp to an inexperienced young man, generally uses the imperative mood—addressing the young man directly. W. S. Merwin, in his instructions on "Unchopping a Tree," also uses the imperative mood in the sections of his essay in which he is supposedly giving instructions, and he addresses the reader as "you." Although authors—Philip Wylie and George Orwell, for example—may make frequent references to themselves, expository writing seldom contains explicit indications of the presence of the writer.

As mentioned previously, in some of the following selections the process explanation is contained in a work that is primarily narrative and descriptive in purpose; that is, the writer's over-all purpose is to relate and describe rather than to explain.

Of the methods of development previously discussed, the process description probably makes most use of *comparison*, or *analogy*, in order to clarify a complicated or difficult step or to make the description generally more vivid to the reader.

Benjamin Franklin

LEARNING TO WRITE

Benjamin Franklin (1706–1790) advocated three principal virtues: industry, frugality, and attention to one's business; and he measured all things by their usefulness to himself and to mankind. With only the barest of formal education, Franklin made himself perhaps the most influential—and certainly the most representative—American of the eighteenth century. The deliberate means he followed in learning to write indicate his industry, his perception, and his pragmatic philosophy. The following passage appears early in his Autobiography, *which he wrote between 1771 and 1789 as a book of instruction—for his son and for young Americans generally. At the time of the literary exercises described, Franklin was in his early teens, working in an elder brother's printing shop. John Collins was a close childhood friend, "another bookish lad in the town" of Boston, according to Franklin. The* Spectator *was a popular English periodical (1711–1712, 1714) written by Joseph Addison and Richard Steele.*

[1]   A question was once, somehow or other, started between Collins and me, of the propriety of educating the female sex in learning, and their abilities for study. He was of the opinion that it was improper, and that they were naturally unequal to it. I took the contrary side, perhaps a little for dispute's sake. He was naturally more eloquent, had a ready plenty of words; and sometimes, as I thought, bore me down more by his fluency than by the strength of his reasons. As we parted without settling the point, and were not to see one another again for some time, I sat down to put my arguments in writing, which I copied fair and sent to him. He answered, and I replied. Three or four letters of a side had passed, when my father happened to find my papers and read them. Without entering into the discussion, he took occasion to talk to me about the manner of my writing; observed that, though I had the advantage of my antagonist in correct spelling and pointing (which I owed to the printing-house), I fell far short in elegance of expression, in method and in perspicuity, of which he convinced me by several instances. I saw the justice of his remarks, and thence grew more attentive to the manner in writing, and determined to endeavor at improvement.

[2]   About this time I met with an odd volume of the *Spectator*. It was the third. I had never before seen any of them. I bought it, read it over and over, and was much delighted with it. I thought the writing excellent, and wished, if possible, to imitate it. With this view I took some of the papers, and, making short hints of the sentiment in each sentence, laid them by a few days, and then, without looking at the book, tried to complete the papers again, by expressing each hinted sentiment at length, and as fully as it had been expressed before, in any suitable words that should come to hand. Then I compared my *Spectator* with the original, discovered some of my faults, and corrected them. But I found I wanted a stock of words, or a readiness in recollecting and using them, which I thought I should have acquired before that time if I had gone on making verses; since the continual occasion for words of the same import, but of different length, to suit the measure, or of different sound for the rhyme, would have laid me under a constant necessity of searching for variety, and also have tended to fix that variety in my mind, and make me master of it. Therefore I took some of the tales and turned them into verse; and, after a time, when I had pretty well forgotten the prose, turned them back again. I also sometimes jumbled my collections of hints into confusion, and after some weeks endeavored to reduce them into the best order, before I began to form the full sentences and complete the paper. This was to teach me method in the arrangement of thoughts. By comparing my work afterwards with the original, I discovered many faults and amended them; but I sometimes had the pleasure of fancying that, in certain particulars of small import, I had been lucky enough to improve the method or the language, and

this encouraged me to think I might possibly in time come to be a tolerable English writer, of which I was extremely ambitious.

VOCABULARY

Define the following words as they are used in the selection: *propriety, eloquent, fluency, antagonist, pointing, elegance, method, perspicuity, instances, thence* [1]; *odd, sentiment, import, measure, tales, reduce, amended, fancying, tolerable* [2].

QUESTIONS FOR STUDY AND DISCUSSION

1. To what characteristics of writing does Franklin refer in paragraph 1? How would you refer to these characteristics? Would you use the same terminology?

2. What three major steps did Franklin follow in his attempt to learn to write by using the *Spectator* models? (There are three major steps, although each of them involves certain substeps.)

3. What did each of the three steps teach him? Do all three steps relate to the requirements for good writing referred to in paragraph 1?

4. What is the topic sentence or topic idea of paragraph 2?

5. What words provide the transition from the topic idea to the first step in the process? How does the first step lead into the second step? Are the two steps related? What word introduces the second step? Does a transitional word or phrase introduce the third step? Does the third step logically follow the second?

6. How successful was Franklin's attempt to learn by imitating? Would you call Franklin "a tolerable English writer"? Does this passage illustrate that he learned to master the requirements for good writing referred to in paragraph 1? Give examples.

7. Franklin elsewhere set down his own requirements for effective style:

> The words used should be the most expressive that the language affords, provided that they are the most generally understood. Nothing should be expressed in two words that can be as well expressed in one; that is, no synonyms should be used, or very rarely, but the whole should be so placed as to be agreeable to the ear in reading; summarily it should be smooth, clear, and short, for the contrary qualities are displeasing.

Does Franklin follow his own advice? Make specific references to the passage to support your comments.

Alan Devoe

LIFE AND DEATH OF A WORM

> *An author, editor, and naturalist, Alan Devoe (1909–1955) wrote of his scientific awareness and perceptions of nature with a poet's language, often building his observations of fact into philosophical speculations. He was a frequent contributor to nature publications, including* The Audubon Magazine, *and the author of several books on nature, among them* Down to Earth (1940), *a collection of essays that originally appeared in his monthly department of that title in* The American Mercury.

[1]   In a damp earth-tunnel under the subsoil a minute cocoon stirs gently with emergent life. Out of it, presently, there issues a tiny ribbon of pink crawling flesh. An earthworm, commonest of all the annelids, has been born.

[2]   The human infant, emerging out of foetal unawareness, comes into a world bright with colors and clamorous with sound. So does a fox-cub, or a new-hatched jay. The earthworm's birth is no such transition. Out of the darkness of the egg, the wriggling fragment of flesh and muscle emerges into a world that is hardly more fraught with awareness, hardly more informed by mind, than was the egg-mass from which it came. The earthworm is unseeing, for it has no eyes. It is unhearing, for it has no ears. The world into which it has been born is only a darkness and a silence.

[3]   But this eyeless and earless morsel of blood and skin is sensible of inner urgings, responsive from the moment of its birth to dim behests. It is stirred by vague restlessness, such as never infected a mushroom or a sumac-root, and which is token of its membership in animal creation. It is blood-brother, this blind, unhearing worm, to the high hawk and the running deer, and is equipped with compulsions even as these are. It is not exempted from the twin necessities which are visited upon every creature of earth: the necessity to eat and the necessity to beget. These things being so, the earthworm stirs and wriggles in its dark earth-chamber, and sets forth presently on the great adventure of existence.

From *Down to Earth* by Alan Devoe. Reprinted by permission.

[4] In obedience to an inner bidding it directs its body upward, toward the topsoil and the outer air. The way of its going is very slow, and it is this: just under the body-skin runs a layer of circular muscles, and just under these a layer of muscles that lie longitudinally; ultimately the earthworm contracts the circular muscles at its anterior end, rendering the body extended and thin, and contracts the longitudinal muscles, rendering the body short again. It is a slow, laborious way of locomotion, and effects movement at all only because of a curious device. On each segment of the earthworm's body are arranged four pairs of tiny spiny hairs, called setae, under the direct control of muscles. They extend obliquely backward from the sides and underparts of the earthworm's body, and the earthworm moves them as though they were little legs. As the worm thrusts upward now, boring blindly toward that outer otherworld which it cannot know exists, the setae press and grip the burrow-wall and translate the worm's muscular churnings into a slow but steady movement.

[5] Unhaltingly the earthworm struggles upward through the soil. Its infinitesimal brain, in an anterior segment above the pharynx, is incapable of harboring the thing that men call Mind; a subtler and a stranger species of impulsion informs the nerve-cords and directs the muscles in their work. Mindless, the earthworm is yet gifted with perceptions and recognitions. The pressures and stresses of the soil against its flesh are intelligible to it; the sensations of dryness or of moisture are somehow meaningful. When now, on its upward voyage, the earthworm reaches a stratum of hard dry soil through which it cannot penetrate by muscular effort alone, there comes to it—perhaps out of the misty realm called Instinct, perhaps out of an otherwhere never to be plumbed—the knowledge of what must be done. The earthworm begins to eat.

[6] Grain by grain it sucks the hard-packed soil into its muscular pharynx, grain by grain reduces the barrier impeding its progress. Millimeter by millimeter, as the obstructing earth is nibbled away, the worm ascends toward outer air. It reaches the surface at last, thrusting its wriggling way through grass-roots and the final crust, and when ultimately its tunneling is completed it deposits on the surface, in the form of castings, the swallowed earth which has passed through its alimentary canal. No man wholly understands the worm's earth-eating, or comprehends the chemistry whereby its body extracts from the eaten soil the bits of humus and vegetable matter which will give it nourishment. The feeding-process of earthworms is a curious thing, and this much is known of it: from the pharynx the food goes to an oesophagus, and is there mixed with gland-secretions which neutralize the acids. Thence it enters a thin-walled crop, and thence a gizzard, where it is ground to bits by spas-

modic muscular contractions—and by the sharp grains of sand that have been swallowed—and is rendered ready for entrance into the worm's intestine. The network of tiny veins and arteries by which the earthworm's blood is circulated carries likewise waste-products of the digested food, and on every segment of the body is a pair of organs, called nephridia, for the excretion of these wastes. Such is the manner of the earthworm's nourishment, and such the processes which have attended its upward voyage through the earth.

II

[7]   The earthworm has attained the outer world now, although no sight or sound can apprise it of that fact. In the damp darkness (for the ascension has been made at night) the earthworm fastens its tail by the setae to the top of the burrow, and, stretching its soft elastic body to full length, explores the neighborhood in which it finds itself. It is in quest of fallen leaves, of minute fragments of weed-stalks and roots and decayed bark. Having no organs of sight, the earthworm is nevertheless able, perhaps by a dim awareness akin to scent, to detect the presence of these morsels and to seize on them; and it is able, further, to single out those foods for which it has a special preference . . . such foods, for instance, as cabbage-leaves and carrots.

[8]   Slowly the earthworm investigates the night, thrusting its blind naked head this way and that. Its recognition of the universe is hardly more complete than the recognition possessed by a burdock-leaf or a floating waterweed. The texture of its awareness is scarcely more complex. From time to time, now, as it forages blindly and deafly in the damp night air, it wriggles suddenly in response to the glinting of a light or the vibrance of a tread upon the nearby earth. These are the things to which its delicate flesh responds— these the limits of the universe it can perceive. Presently, when it has taken in a sufficiency of food, it terminates its explorations for the night and withdraws once more to inner earth.

[9]   There is small variegation in the pattern of the earthworm's succeeding days. During the sunlit hours the worm stays buried in the cool darkness beneath the surface of the soil, for the thin slime of mucus that covers its skin would be dried up by the sun. But when the nights come—or when the sun is hidden and rain falls—the earthworm grows obscurely aware that it is time for seeking the outer world again, and once more the pink flesh thrusts upward. After this fashion does day follow day, unmarked by any incident but the worm's feeding and breathing. Even the breathing is almost as simple as

a plant's. Blind and deaf and unequipped with mind, the earthworm lacks also lungs. It absorbs the oxygen directly through its body-walls into the sluggish blood, and similarly, imperceptibly, the carbon dioxide is expelled.

[10]   Some time before it dies, the worm must beget young. The individual earthworm is both male and female, having the reproductive organs of each sex, and when the time for egg-laying comes it secretes from a thickened place in its body—the clitellum—a cocoon in which the eggs are secured. This done, the eggs are then fertilized by the spermatozoa of another worm, and the most vital of all animal rites has been accomplished. A few days or a few weeks longer the earthworm feeds and forages and pursues its eyeless way, and then the life goes out of it as unknowledgeably as it came, and the briefly animated morsel of blood and sinew reverts to parent earth.

[11]   An earthworm, I suppose, will hardly attract the contemplation of the kind of men who can be stirred by no less gaudy natural marvel than a Grand Canyon or a shooting star. Charles Darwin, though, thought earthworms were worth studying for forty years, and Darwin made some curious discoveries. He found, for instance, that in a single acre of ground there may be 50,000 worms, and he found that they carry to the surface, in a single year, some eighteen tons of earth-castings. The earthworms in an acre, Darwin learned, would in twenty years carry from the subsoil to the surface a layer of soil three inches thick; and it became evident to him that the honeycombing of the earth by its earthworms was what aerated the soil and made it porous and rendered it fit for man's agriculture.

[12]   It is good sometimes to be reminded that the ephemeral shifts of politics and ideologies are not the things on which our human welfare actually depends. The ultimate welfare of our tribe depends on things like worms.

VOCABULARY

Define the following words as they are used in the selection: *annelids* [1]; *foetal, fraught* [2]; *longitudinally, anterior, effects, obliquely* [4]; *infinitesimal* [5]; *apprise* [7]; *ephemeral* [12].

QUESTIONS FOR STUDY AND DISCUSSION

1. Devoe describes the life and death of the earthworm as a single process, predictable and without variation. What are the principal stages in the process?

2. The surfacing of the earthworm is described in detail. What is the role of the two sets of muscles in the process? How are the setae necessary for this process?

3. Trace in detail the earth-eating process from the pharynx to the nephridia. What are the various stages through which the earth passes?

4. Paragraphs 7 and 8 describe the feeding process in a somewhat different manner from the processes of surfacing and earth-eating. What accounts for the difference? Within limits, however, the feeding process is predictable. Point out the verbs that define the principal acts in the process.

5. What is the reproductive process of the earthworm? Is this process clearly described?

6. Devoe describes the earthworm as a mindless creature living in a silent darkness. At the same time, he invests it with almost a personality. How does he accomplish the characterization of the earthworm?

7. What does the earthworm share with all creatures? How does Devoe relate the life process of the earthworm to its animal instincts?

8. How does the function of the earthworm, described in paragraph 11, illuminate the attitude of gentle respect for the earthworm that is evident in the essay?

9. What comment on man's superiority in nature is implicit in the concluding paragraph?

Stewart Edward White

ON MAKING CAMP

Stewart Edward White (1873–1946) was the author of numerous novels and books of essays on travel, the American frontier, and natural history. The following passage is an excerpt from the fourth chapter of his book The Forest *(1903), which combines accounts of his camping experiences with advice about living in the forest. After describing the unsuccessful attempts of a young companion to make camp himself, White says: "The following is, in brief, what during the next six weeks I told the youth, by precept, by homily, and by making the solution so obvious that he could work it out for himself."*

[1] When five or six o'clock draws near, begin to look about you for a good level dry place, elevated some few feet above the surroundings. Drop

your pack or beach your canoe. Examine the location carefully. You will want two trees about ten feet apart, from which to suspend your tent, and a bit of flat ground underneath them. Of course the flat ground need not be particularly unencumbered by brush or saplings, so the combination ought not to be hard to discover. Now return to your canoe. Do not unpack the tent.

[2] With the little axe clear the ground thoroughly. By bending a sapling over strongly with the left hand, clipping sharply at the strained fibers, and then bending it as strongly the other way to repeat the axe stroke on the other side, you will find that treelets of even two or three inches diameter can be felled by two blows. In a very few moments you will have accomplished a hole in the forest, and your two supporting trees will stand sentinel at either end of a most respectable-looking clearing. Do not unpack the tent.

[3] Now, although the ground seems free of all but unimportant growths, go over it thoroughly for little shrubs and leaves. They look soft and yielding, but are often possessed of unexpectedly abrasive roots. Besides, they mask the face of the ground. When you have finished pulling them up by the roots, you will find that your supposedly level plot is knobby with hummocks. Stand directly over each little mound; swing the back of your axe vigorously against it, adze-wise, between your legs. Nine times out of ten it will crumble, and the tenth time means merely a root to cut or a stone to pry out. At length you are possessed of a plot of clean, fresh earth, level and soft, free from projections. But do not unpack your tent.

[4] Lay a young birch or maple an inch or so in diameter across a log. Two clips will produce you a tent-peg. If you are inexperienced, and cherish memories of striped lawn markees, you will cut them about six inches long. If you are wise and old and gray in woods experience, you will multiply that length by four. Then your loops will not slip off, and you will have a real grip on mother earth, than which nothing can be more desirable in the event of a heavy rain and wind squall about midnight. If your axe is as sharp as it ought to be, you can point them more neatly by holding them suspended in front of you while you snip at their ends with the axe, rather than by resting them against a solid base. Pile them together at the edge of the clearing. Cut a crotched sapling eight or ten feet long. Now unpack your tent.

[5] In a wooded country you will not take the time to fool with tent-poles. A stout line run through the eyelets and along the apex will string it successfully between your two trees. Draw the line as tight as possible, but do not be too unhappy if, after your best efforts, it still sags a little. That is what your long crotched stick is for. Stake out your four corners. If you get them in a

THE PROCESS

good rectangle and in such relation to the apex as to form two isosceles triangles of the ends, your tent will stand smoothly. Therefore, be an artist and do it right. Once the four corners are well placed, the rest follows naturally. Occasionally in the North Country it will be found that the soil is too thin, over the rocks, to grip the tent-pegs. In that case drive them at a sharp angle as deep as they will go, and then lay a large flat stone across the slant of them. Thus anchored, you will ride out a gale. Finally, wedge your long sapling crotch under the line—outside the tent, of course—to tighten it. Your shelter is up. If you are a woodsman, ten or fifteen minutes has sufficed to accomplish all this.

[6]   There remains the question of a bed, and you'd better attend to it now, while your mind is still occupied with the shelter problem. Fell a good thrifty young balsam and set to work pulling off the fans. Those you cannot strip off easily with your hands are too tough for your purpose. Lay them carelessly crisscross against the blade of your axe and up the handle. They will not drop off, and when you shoulder that axe you will resemble a walking haystack, and will probably experience a genuine emotion of surprise at the amount of balsam that can be thus transported. In the tent lay smoothly one layer of fans, convex side up, butts toward the foot. Now thatch the rest on top of this, thrusting the butt ends underneath the layer already placed in such a manner as to leave the fan ends curving up and down towards the foot of your bed. Your second emotion of surprise will assail you as you realize how much spring inheres in but two or three layers thus arranged. When you have spread your rubber blanket, you will be possessed of a bed as soft and a great deal more aromatic and luxurious than any you would be able to buy in town.

[7]   Your next care is to clear a living space in front of the tent. This will take you about twenty seconds, for you need not be particular as to stumps, hummocks, or small brush. All you want is room for cooking, and suitable space for spreading out your provisions. But do not unpack anything yet.

[8]   Your fireplace you will build of two green logs laid side by side. The fire is to be made between them. They should converge slightly, in order that the utensils to be rested across them may be of various sizes. If your vicinity yields flat stones, they build up even better than the logs—unless they happen to be of granite. Granite explodes most disconcertingly. Poles sharpened, driven upright into the ground, and then pressed down to slant over the fireplace, will hold your kettles a suitable height above the blaze.

[9]   Fuel should be your next thought. A roll of birch bark first of all. Then some of the small, dry, resinous branches that stick out from the trunks of

medium-sized pines, living or dead. Finally, the wood itself. If you are merely cooking supper, and have no thought for a warmth-fire or a friendship-fire, I should advise you to stick to the dry pine branches, helped out, in the interest of coals for frying, by a little dry maple or birch. If you need more of a blaze, you will have to search out, fell, and split a standing dead tree. This is not at all necessary. I have traveled many weeks in the woods without using a more formidable implement than a one-pound hatchet. Pile your fuel—a complete supply, all you are going to need—by the side of your already improvised fireplace. But, as you value your peace of mind, do not fool with matches.

[10] It will be a little difficult to turn your mind from the concept of fire, to which all these preparations have compellingly led it,—especially as a fire is the one cheerful thing your weariness needs the most at this time of day,—but you must do so. Leave everything just as it is, and unpack your provisions.

[11] First of all, rinse your utensils. Hang your tea-pail, with the proper quantity of water, from one slanting pole, and your kettle from the other. Salt the water in the latter receptacle. Peel your potatoes, if you have any; open your little provision sacks; puncture your tin cans, if you have any; slice your bacon; clean your fish; pluck your birds; mix your dough or batter; spread your table tinware on your tarpaulin or a sheet of birch bark; cut a kettle-lifter; see that everything you are going to need is within direct reach of your hand as you squat on your heels before the fireplace. Now light your fire.

[12] The civilized method is to build a fire and then to touch a match to the completed structure. If well done and in a grate or stove, this works beautifully. Only in the woods you have no grate. The only sure way is as follows: Hold a piece of birch bark in your hand. Shelter your match all you know how. When the bark has caught, lay it in your fireplace, assist it with more bark, and gradually build up, twig by twig, stick by stick, from the first pinpoint of flame, all the fire you are going to need. It will not be much. The little hot blaze rising between the parallel logs directly against the aluminum of your utensils will do the business in very short order. In fifteen minutes at most your meal is ready. And you have been able to attain to hot food thus quickly because you were prepared.

VOCABULARY

Define the following words as they are used in the selection: *hummocks, adze-wise* [3]; *markees (marquees)* [4]; *isosceles* [5]; *convex, assail, inheres* [6]; *converge, disconcertingly* [8]; *compellingly* [10].

QUESTIONS FOR STUDY AND DISCUSSION

1. According to White's directions, making camp involves the camp site, the tent, the fireplace, and the fire. Does White divide his attention equally among these topics? Show where the divisions occur.

2. Which of the paragraphs are clearly transitional in purpose?

3. Prepare a sentence outline of the passage, dividing the outline into the four major topics. If White has developed his paragraphs well, each one will provide a clear topic idea (a subtopic of the outline), though some may be concerned with two related steps. The sentences of your outline will be imperative (the subject *you* will be understood).

4. Make a list of the transitional words and phrases that White uses. Are the transitions varied and effective? Does the passage need more transitional devices?

5. Notice the concluding sentences of the first four paragraphs. What is their effect? What consideration determines when the tent should be unpacked?

6. The passage provides not only the steps in the process of making camp but also the reasons for many of the steps. Are the reasons intrusive? When forming your answer, consider the audience for which White is writing.

7. White employs short, imperative sentences several times at the end of paragraphs. What rules of camping do these sentences emphasize? Why, at the end of paragraph 9, should the camper "not fool with matches" if he values his "peace of mind"?

8. Is the point of view consistent? White is, of course, writing to *you*, the subject of many of the sentences. Where does he shift to first person? Is the shift distracting?

9. This passage is generally objective, but White's personality can be seen at times. Point out passages that reveal the author.

10. What does White imply by "outside the tent, of course" (paragraph 5)?

W. S. Merwin

UNCHOPPING A TREE

W. S. Merwin (b. 1927) has published six books of poetry in addition to a number of major translations from French, Spanish,

From *The Miner's Pale Children* by W. S. Merwin. Copyright © 1969, 1970 by W. S. Merwin. Reprinted by permission of Atheneum Publishers.

Latin, and Portuguese. He has also written articles for The Nation *and radio scripts for the BBC. Among his books of poems are* The Drunk in the Furnace *(1960),* The Moving Target *(1963), and* The Lice *(1974). The essay reprinted here, an imaginative process piece that comes close to poetry in concept and treatment, is from his book* The Miner's Pale Children *(1969).*

[1] Start with the leaves, the small twigs, and the nests that have been shaken, ripped, or broken off by the fall; these must be gathered and attached once again to their respective places. It is not arduous work, unless major limbs have been smashed or mutilated. If the fall was carefully and correctly planned, the chances of anything of the kind happening will have been reduced. Again, much depends upon the size, age, shape, and species of the tree. Still, you will be lucky if you can get through this stage without having to use machinery. Even in the best of circumstances it is a labor that will make you wish often that you had won the favor of the universe of ants, the empire of mice, or at least a local tribe of squirrels, and could enlist their labors and their talents. But no, they leave you to it. They have learned, with time. This is men's work. It goes without saying that if the tree was hollow in whole or in part, and contained old nests of bird or mammal or insect, or hoards of nuts or such structures as wasps or bees build for their survival, the contents will have to be repaired where necessary, and reassembled, insofar as possible, in their original order, including the shells of nuts already opened. With spiders' webs you must simply do the best you can. We do not have the spider's weaving equipment, nor any substitute for the leaf's living bond with its point of attachment and nourishment. It is even harder to simulate the latter when the leaves have once become dry—as they are bound to do, for this is not the labor of a moment. Also it hardly needs saying that this is the time for repairing any neighboring trees or bushes or other growth that may have been damaged by the fall. The same rules apply. Where neighboring trees were of the same species it is difficult not to waste time conveying a detached leaf back to the wrong tree. Practice, practice. Put your hope in that.

[2] Now the tackle must be put into place or the scaffolding, depending on the surroundings and the dimensions of the tree. It is ticklish work. Almost always it involves, in itself, further damage to the area, which will have to be corrected later. But as you've heard, it can't be helped. And care now is likely to save you considerable trouble later. Be careful to grind nothing into the ground.

[3] At last the time comes for the erecting of the trunk. By now it will scarcely be necessary to remind you of the delicacy of this huge skeleton.

THE PROCESS

Every motion of the tackle, every slight upward heave of the trunk, the branches, their elaborately reassembled panoply of leaves (now dead) will draw from you an involuntary gasp. You will watch for a leaf or a twig to be snapped off yet again. You will listen for the nuts to shift in the hollow limb and you will hear whether they are indeed falling into place or are spilling in disorder—in which case, or in the event of anything else of the kind—operations will have to cease, of course, while you correct the matter. The raising itself is no small enterprise, from the moment when the chains tighten around the old bandages until the bole hangs vertical above the stump, splinter above splinter. Now the final straightening of the splinters themselves can take place (the preliminary work is best done while the wood is still green and soft, but at times when the splinters are not badly twisted most of the straightening is left until now, when the torn ends are face to face with each other). When the splinters are perfectly complementary the appropriate fixative is applied. Again we have no duplicate of the original substance. Ours is extremely strong, but it is rigid. It is limited to surfaces, and there is no play in it. However the core is not the part of the trunk that conducted life from the roots up into the branches and back again. It was relatively inert. The fixative for this part is not the same as the one for the outer layers and the bark, and if either of these is involved in the splintered section they must receive applications of the appropriate adhesives. Apart from being incorrect and probably ineffective, the core fixative would leave a scar on the bark.

[4] When all is ready the splintered trunk is lowered onto the splinters of the stump. This, one might say, is only the skeleton of the resurrection. Now the chips must be gathered, and the sawdust, and returned to their former positions. The fixative for the wood layers will be applied to chips and sawdust consisting only of wood. Chips and sawdust consisting of several substances will receive applications of the correct adhesives. It is as well, where possible, to shelter the materials from the elements while working. Weathering makes it harder to identify the smaller fragments. Bark sawdust in particular the earth lays claim to very quickly. You must find your own ways of coping with this problem. There is a certain beauty, you will notice at moments, in the pattern of the chips as they are fitted back into place. You will wonder to what extent it should be described as natural, to what extent manmade. It will lead you on to speculations about the parentage of beauty itself, to which you will return.

[5] The adhesive for the chips is translucent, and not so rigid as that for the splinters. That for the bark and its subcutaneous layers is transparent and

runs into the fibers on either side, partially dissolving them into each other. It does not set the sap flowing again but it does pay a kind of tribute to the preoccupations of the ancient thoroughfares. You could not roll an egg over the joints but some of the mine-shafts would still be passable, no doubt. For the first exploring insect who raises its head in the tight echoless passages. The day comes when it is all restored, even to the moss (now dead) over the wound. You will sleep badly, thinking of the removal of the scaffolding that must begin the next morning. How you will hope for sun and a still day!

[6] The removal of the scaffolding or tackle is not so dangerous, perhaps, to the surroundings, as its installation, but it presents problems. It should be taken from the spot piece by piece as it is detached, and stored at a distance. You have come to accept it there, around the tree. The sky begins to look naked as the chains and struts one by one vacate their positions. Finally the moment arrives when the last sustaining piece is removed and the tree stands again on its own. It is as though its weight for a moment stood on your heart. You listen for a thud of settlement, a warning creak deep in the intricate joinery. You cannot believe it will hold. How like something dreamed it is, standing there all by itself. How long will it stand there now? The first breeze that touches its dead leaves all seems to flow into your mouth. You are afraid the motion of the clouds will be enough to push it over. What more can you do? What more can you do?

[7] But there is nothing more you can do.

[8] Others are waiting.

[9] Everything is going to have to be put back.

VOCABULARY

Define the following words as they are used in the selection: *simulate* [1]; *tackle* [2]; *panoply, bole, inert* [3]; *translucent, subcutaneous* [5].

QUESTIONS FOR STUDY AND DISCUSSION

1. Unlike most expository essays, this one has no "introduction" but depends upon its title to orient the reader to its apparent topic. Ordinarily that kind of beginning would not be successful; why does it work well for this essay?

2. Merwin's essay guides the reader through a process that is purely imaginary; certainly the writer does not expect anyone ever to perform the operation. What, then, is the value of this "process" essay?

3. Does Merwin follow a step-by-step order in explaining the process? Is his order chronological? Explain your answer.

4. What tone pervades the essay? What is the effect of the brief sentence, "This is men's work" (paragraph 1)?

5. "There is a certain beauty, you will notice at moments, in the pattern of the chips. . . . It will lead you on to speculations about the parentage of beauty itself, to which you will return." What is implied in the phrase "the parentage of beauty"? Why will the reader return to such speculations?

6. What is the thesis of the essay? Is it stated, or is it implied? Has the writer chosen an effective way of presenting the thesis? Explain your answer.

7. You may be reminded of Joyce Kilmer's famous lines, "Poems are made by fools like me,/ But only God can make a tree." The Kilmer poem bears a distinctly sentimental tone. How does Merwin manage to avoid sentimentalism while dealing with a topic similar to Kilmer's?

8. In what ways does this essay differ from most of those you have read on the general topic of ecology?

9. Would the essay make a good church sermon? Why—or why not? What suggestions do you find in it of a religious theme?

10. Why does Merwin use three one-sentence paragraphs to end the essay? Is that ending effective? Why?

FOR FURTHER ANALYSIS

Isaac Asimov

COLONIZING THE HEAVENS

Isaac Asimov (b. 1920) has been best known as a writer of science fiction and nonfiction, one of his most recent publications being

From *Saturday Review*, June 28, 1975. Reprinted by permission.

Science Past—Science Future (1975). It was his one hundred sixty-third book, a fact that helps explain why his entry in the International Who's Who *says, "Leisure interests: no leisure." Says Asimov, "I have been fortunate to be born with a restless and efficient brain, with a capacity for clear thought and an ability to put that thought into words." Asimov packs his prose with facts, not with mere words, however. "Colonizing the Heavens" appeared in* Saturday Review, *June 28, 1975. In it Asimov tells how and where new lands in space soon may be built to help ease the population pile-up on Earth.*

[1] The population bomb ticks on steadily . . .

[2] We are 4 billion now, in 1975. Barring catastrophes, we shall be 5 billion in 1986 and 6 billion in 1995 and 7 billion in 2002 and 8 billion in . . . What do we do with all of ourselves when already, with our puny 4 billion, we find that the effort to feed and power the population is destroying the planet that feeds and powers us? We must reduce the birthrate and lower the population, but that will take time. What do we do meanwhile?

[3] One answer is that we do as we have done before. We must take up the trek again and move on to new lands. Since there are no new lands on earth worth the taking, we must move to new worlds and colonize the heavens.

[4] No, not the moon. Prof. Gerard O'Neill of the physics department of Princeton University suggests two other places to begin with—places as far from earth as the moon is, but not the moon. Imagine the moon at zenith, exactly overhead. Trace a line due eastward from the moon down to the horizon. Two-thirds of the way along that line, one-third of the way up from the horizon, is one of those places. Trace another line westward from the moon down to the horizon. Two-thirds of the way along that line, one-third of the way up from the horizon, is another of those places.

[5] Put an object in either place, and it will form an equilateral triangle with the moon and earth. It is 237,000 miles from earth to the moon. It is also 237,000 miles from earth to that place, and from the moon to that place.

[6] What is so special about those places? Back in 1772 the astronomer Joseph Louis Lagrange showed that in those places any object remained stationary with respect to the moon. As the moon moved about the earth, any object in either of those places would also move about the earth in such a way as to keep perfect step with the moon. The competing gravities of earth and

the moon would keep it where it was. If anything happened to push it out of place, it would promptly move back, wobbling back and forth a bit ("librating") as it did so. The two places ideally are merely points in space and are called "Lagrangian points," or "libration points."

[7]   Lagrange discovered five such points altogether, but three of them are of no importance because they don't represent stable conditions. An object in those three points, once pushed out of place, would continue to drift outward and would never return. The two points in which an object remains stable are called "L4" and "L5." L4 is the one that lies toward the eastern horizon, and L5 the one that lies toward the western.

[8]   Professor O'Neill wants to take advantage of that gravitational lock and suggests the building of space colonies there, colonies that would become permanent parts of the earth-moon system. He envisions long cylinders designed to hold human beings plus a complex life-support system, facilities for growing food, maintaining atmospheres, recycling wastes, and so on.

[9]   Such concepts have been used in science fiction. The most memorable example is Robert A. Heinlein's story "Universe," published in 1941, in which a large ship, supporting thousands of people through indefinite numbers of generations, is making its slow way to the stars. The men aboard have forgotten the original purpose of the voyage and consider the ship to be the entire universe (hence the title). A lineal descendant of the story, translated to television, was the recent ill-fated series, "The Starlost."

[10]   In science fiction, though, such enormous, self-contained ships are *ships*, thickly spaced with decks, utterly enclosed with walls—the equivalent of many-layered caverns. O'Neill's vision is of another kind. He sees hollow cylinders with human beings living on the inner surface, a surface that is designed and contoured into a familiar world with all the accoutrements and accompaniments of earth. The cylinder would be composed of long, alternating strips of opaque and transparent material—aluminum and tough plastic. Sunshine, reflected by long mirrors, would enter and illuminate the cylinder and turn what would otherwise be a cave into a daylit world. The entry of light could be controlled by mirror-shifting to allow for alternating day and night.

[11]   The inner surface of the opaque portions of the cylinder would be spread with soil, which could be used for agriculture and, eventually, animal husbandry. All the artificial works of man—his buildings and machines—would be there, too.

[12]   What makes this concept plausible and lifts the vision out of the realm

of science fiction is the careful manner in which O'Neill has analyzed the masses of material necessary, the details of design, the thicknesses and strengths of materials required, the manner of lifting and assembly, and the cost of it all. The conclusion is that the establishment of such space colonies is possible and even practical in terms of present-day technology.

[13] It would be expensive, of course, and getting the process started would require an input equivalent to that spent on the Apollo program. But O'Neill demonstrates clearly that the expense would decline rapidly after that. As the colonies increase in number, they could be expected to grow larger and more elaborate, too. O'Neill conceives the first space colonies (Model 1) to be only as large as is required to be workable—two spinning cylinders, each 3,280 feet long and 328 feet wide, supporting a total of 10,000 people.

[14] The two cylinders, each spinning about its long axis, would turn in opposite directions. When they were held together, the total system would have virtually no spin and the cylinders could be designed in such a way as to have one end of the structure point constantly toward the sun in the course of the orbit about the earth.

[15] It is from the sun that the colony would obtain its energy—a copious, endless, easily handled, non-polluting form of energy. It would be used to smelt the ores, power the factories, grow the food, recycle the wastes. It would serve to start the cylinders spinning and increase the rate of spin to the point where there would be a centrifugal effect sufficient to hold everything within to all parts of the inner surface with the apparent pull of normal gravity. For a cylinder 328 feet wide, this would require a spin of three revolutions a minute.

[16] O'Neill envisions larger cylinder-pairs, too, and has calculated the requirements for some as large as 20 miles long and 2 miles wide (Model 4), spinning once in two minutes. Each cylinder of a pair like that would be as wide as Manhattan and half again as long, would have a total inner surface 10 times as great as that of Manhattan, and could support up to 20 million people if it were exploited to the full, though 5 to 10 million might be a more comfortable population.

[17] With so great a width, the cylinder would have a sufficient depth of air within to allow a blue sky and to support clouds. In a Model 4 colony the end caps of the cylinders could be modeled into mountainous territory—full-sized mountains, not just bas-reliefs.

[18] But where are we to get all the material for the construction of these

THE PROCESS

space colonies? Our groaning planet, sagging under its weight of humanity, with its supply of key resources sputtering and giving out, couldn't possibly afford to give up the colossal quantities of supplies needed for it all. (Over half a million tons of construction is needed for each Model 1, probably a thousand times as much for a Model 4.)

[19] But earth is lucky, for virtually none of the material need come from our planet. As it happens, we are supplied with a moon, an empty and dead world that is one-eightieth the size of the earth. It is close enough for us to reach—we have already reached it over and over—and it is free to be used as a quarry. Lunar material will yield the aluminum, glass, concrete, and other substances needed for constructing the colony. Lunar soil will be spread over the interior surface, and on it agriculture will be practiced. Not only is all that material present on the moon in virtually unlimited quantities, but lifting it off the moon against that body's weak gravity would require only one-twentieth the effort necessary for lifting it off earth. All the smelting and other chemical work would, of course, be done in space. But the lunar material is not perfectly adapted to human needs. It is low in volatile elements, those that vaporize easily when heated. The most serious lack is the volatile element hydrogen (an essential component of water).

[20] O'Neill calculates that setting up a Model 1 colony would require some 5,400 metric tons of liquid hydrogen, and that would have to come from earth. Fortunately, earth can spare that much. We can get it from sea water, and there is an embarrassing oversupply of sea water on earth. We live in comfort only because so much of the earth's water supply is tied up in the ice caps of Greenland and Antarctica. If these ever melt, the sea level will rise 200 feet and drown our population-packed coastal areas. Extracting hydrogen from a little of our oversupply and giving it away will do us no harm.

[21] As colonies multiply, of course, the quantity of hydrogen we would have to give up could become a little painful. Once space colonization swings into high gear, however, hydrogen and other volatile elements of which the moon has insufficient supply can be obtained from farther out. They can come from some of the asteroids or from the occasional comet that blunders past the earth-moon system on its way to wheel about the sun.

[22] The first space colony would be by far the most expensive, even if it were small, for we would have to supply not only the advanced equipment, the machinery, the various life forms, the basic food supply and energy, but even some 2 percent of the raw materials. After that, there would be leapfrogging. Each space colony would help to build up the next, while the facilities

for mining, smelting, shipping, and constructing would be ever improving. In the end, new colonies might be formed with no more trouble than it now takes to put up a new row of houses in the suburbs.

[23] O'Neill thinks that if all were to go optimally, the first space colony could be floating in space by the late Eighties and that several hundred more elaborate colonies would be there by the mid-twenty-first century. These would be comfortable worlds, not, like earth, taken as found, but carefully designed to meet human needs. The temperature and weather would be controlled; energy would be free and non-polluting; weeds, vermin, and pathogenic bacteria would be left back on earth.

[24] Dangers? Difficulties? Yes, some.

[25] The possibility of a meteor strike exists, but that is not very strong. The space of the earth-moon system is full of meteoric dust, which is not likely to be bothersome, and pinhead meteors may pit the aluminum and craze the plastic, but that would be a minor annoyance. A meteorite large enough to cause serious damage to a colony is so rare that the time between strikes could be counted in the millions of years per colony. As the colonies grow more numerous, the chances that *one* will be hit increases—but mankind can live with that. We now live with the knowledge that there is a finite chance that at any moment a large meteorite, or a major earthquake, may strike and demolish a city on earth.

[26] Energetic solar radiation is dangerous but would not be a problem in a cylinder protected by aluminum, plastic, and soil. Cosmic rays are much more serious. They are ever present and ever dangerous and very penetrating. There is some question as to whether O'Neill's original design offered sufficient protection. At the most recent scientific conference held on the subject (at Princeton on May 7–9, 1975) this subject was among those discussed.

[27] Then, too, the centrifugal effect of the cylinder spin does not perfectly duplicate earth's gravitation. On earth the gravitational pull is not perceptibly altered as we rise from the surface. Inside a spinning cylinder the effect weakens rapidly as one rises from the inner surface, falling to zero at the long axis. Is a fluctuating gravitational effect dangerous to the human body in the long run? We have no way of knowing as yet, but if not, a gravitational pull that lessens with height can have its advantages.

[28] The small distances on the space colonies would make it unnecessary to use high-energy systems for transportation. Bicycles would be ideal for the

ground, and with the lowering gravity, gliders would be perfect for air transport—and amusement.

[29] Mountain climbing on the larger colonies would have comforts unknown on earth. As one climbed higher, the downward pull would weaken, it would become easier to climb farther, and, of course, the air would grow neither thinner nor colder. In carefully enclosed areas on the mountaintops, people could fly by their own muscle power when they were outfitted with plastic wings on light frames. Shades of Icarus!

[30] As the space colonies increased in number, the room available for human beings would increase, too, and at an exponential rate. Within a century there could be room for a billion people on the space colonies, and by 2150, perhaps, there would be more people in space than on earth.

[31] This prospect does not obviate the need to lower our birthrate in the long run, for if human beings continue to multiply at their present rate, the total mass of flesh and blood will equal the total mass of the known universe in 6,700 years. Long before then the building of space colonies would not be able to keep up under any conceivable conditions.

[32] The colonies could act as a safety valve; however, that would give humanity a somewhat longer time to accomplish the turnabout without absolute disaster.

[33] It may be that finally, when a stable population is attained (or at very worst, one that is growing only as fast as can be handled by additional colonies), the earth itself will be only thinly populated. It will, perhaps, be devoted, then, to carefully preserved wilderness and park areas. It may serve as a monument to man's origin and to the pre-human ecology, and it would be supported largely by tourism.

[34] Tourism would also exist among the multiplying colonies (which would eventually expand out of the Lagrangian points and take up other and somewhat more difficult-to-handle orbits). Because each colony would have no intrinsic gravitational field to speak of and all are likely to be at about the same distance from the sun, travel from one to another would consume surprisingly little energy. And because each colony is likely to be unique in its way, the result would be worth the effort.

[35] After all, almost as important as the basic fact that room would be found for humanity is the additional fact that it would be found in thousands

of different, isolated, and culturally independent places. Each colony would have its own way of life, and some might be quite a distance off the norm. Among the offbeat colonies we could imagine puritanical ones and hedonistic ones, libertarian ones and authoritarian ones, Orthodox Jewish ones and hardshell Baptist ones.

[36]   You could choose where you wanted to go; and if you were born on one, you might choose to try another—or at least visit one. Human culture would explode in variety, with each colony having its own styles in clothing, music, art, literature. The options for creativity in general and for scientific advance in particular would be unbounded.

[37]   Yet though the advantages of space colonies can be drawn up in a thoroughly lyrical fashion, one has to admit that the chances that the program will be started are, perhaps, not bright.

[38]   These are difficult times. The Apollo program, by its very success, seems to have taken the shine off space ventures; the economy teeters; there is widespread disillusionment with glowing dreams—particularly in the United States (which would have to supply the major portion of what would have to be a global effort) caught in the wake of the Vietnam failure.

[39]   But perhaps mankind will answer to the lure of immediate and high-visibility profit. With that in mind, perhaps, O'Neill is carefully working out the details of an ancillary idea—the practical economics of establishing a structure designed to be a "Satellite Solar Power Station" (SSPS), one that will absorb sunlight and convert it into microwave energy that can be beamed to earth for use as direct electrical current.

[40]   Earth could, in this way, be supplied with copious, nearly pollution-free energy. The amount of land that would have to be devoted to microwave reception would be, by O'Neill's calculations, as little as 5 percent of that required for direct solar-energy reception, because the inefficient part of the operation would be kept out in space.

[41]   The development of power stations at the Lagrangian points is as practical as the development of space colonies, and the benefits of the former to mankind are sure to be seen as more immediately desirable by the public generally. Yet once power stations are built at the Lagrangian points, the expertise and facilities used for that can also be used to build other industrial systems—and space colonies, too. The basic investments having been made, the additional expense will be almost trivial. Why not go on, then?

[42]   It is the energy crisis, then, that may be offering us the opportunity. It is solar energy by way of space that may serve as the bribe. And, if the opportunity is seized and the bribe is accepted, space colonies could follow almost inevitably. With that *might* come the salvation of humanity and its entry into a new and larger scene with overall changes as momentous as those that followed the discovery of fire.

SUGGESTIONS FOR WRITING

1. Write an essay describing a commonly observed process in nature: the formation of a cumulus cloud, the blossoming of a flower, the flight and coming to rest of a gull, the chirping of a cricket, the coming of dawn. Use a library source for information if necessary.

2. Describe the process whereby a simple type of tool is used or a mechanical device operates. Suggestions: a pair of scissors, a saw, an electric grinder, a can opener, a tobacco pipe, a nail file, a toothbrush, a stapler, a lawn mower, a windshield wiper.

3. Giving special attention to verbs suggesting action, write a process paper describing the steps in an ordinary task like setting a dinner table. Take care to divide your essay into appropriate paragraphs. Here are some suitable topics: making a barbecue pit, lubricating a car, refinishing a piece of furniture, developing a roll of film, reroofing a house, planning a party, applying artificial respiration, making a bookcase, making an omelet.

4. Write an explanation of a complicated process. Suitable topics: producing a play, the function of the electoral college, photosynthesis, the germination of seeds, the function of the heart or lungs, the operation of a gyroscope, the principle of flotation, the formation of an atoll, nuclear fission, making phonograph records. You will probably have to use reference material for this essay; to avoid excessive influence by the reference materials, study the process until you understand it thoroughly, prepare an outline based on your reading, put away your references, and then write your essay from your outline.

5. If you can recall details of how you learned a specific skill (such as reading, walking, swimming, skating, using a typewriter, driving a car), write an essay describing the process of your learning. Remember that the essay is about the process of your learning, not about the process of the skill itself.

6. Maintaining a consistent point of view, write an essay giving directions on how to brush teeth effectively, how to write a letter of application, how to organize a car pool, how to play poker, how to shop for groceries, or some other common but often complex process.

7. Take notes while watching several "editions" of your favorite television newscast. You will perhaps find that the same format, or sequence of types of news and presentations, is followed each day. Following your notes, write an essay describing the process of presenting the news via television. (It may be helpful to

read Richardson's "Six O'Clock Prayers" (p. 60) before you begin to write your process paper.)

8. If you can trace the stages of your development in learning to write, you will find it interesting to write an essay on this subject and compare your experience with Franklin's.

9. After rereading W. S. Merwin's "Unchopping a Tree," write an essay of your own in which you deliberately reverse a familiar process. You might, for example, write on undoing a tragic accident, unmaking a hurtful remark, or even unbuilding a freeway. Remember that your essay will probably be more effective if you avoid preaching.

CLASSIFICATION

The analytical essay is concerned with dividing a complex subject into its component parts on the basis of logical relationships, rather than into chronological steps as in the process essay. The analytical process most frequently used in prose writing is classification.

To classify is to sort things, to place them in classes according to their differing qualities. In setting up a classification the writer tries to make a general topic more understandable by sorting types and specimens according to some logical pattern. The writer of a classification essay may, for example, sort according to types, in the manner of Thomas Fuller in his essay on types of students. Using the qualities of aptitude and effort as the criteria for classification, Fuller classifies students as (1) ingenious and industrious, (2) ingenious and idle, (3) dull and diligent, (4) dull and negligent. A writer could, of course, sort students by other factors, such as specialty of interest (art, science, philosophy, and so on) or level of study (undergraduate, graduate, postdoctorate, and so on).

Selecting appropriate sorting factors is one of the main difficulties for the writer of a classification essay. First, *the topic must be divided into categories that are mutually exclusive.* No freshman would be satisfied with a classification of college students as "men, women, and freshmen." A classification of one's favorite books as adventure stories, histories, and entertaining stories would be equally unsatisfactory—since presumably both adventure stories and histories can be entertaining. Second, *the categories must include all of the items in the class being divided.* If the writer divides aircraft into the categories of airplanes, helicopters, and dirigibles, the essay must not include material about spacecraft—unless the writer revises the classification. Finally, *the criterion or criteria for the divisions must be reasonable and useful*. It would probably be neither reasonable nor useful to classify college students by what they eat for breakfast (unless in writing advertising copy for a certain cereal or in making a sociological study).

The actual work of describing the classified categories on paper also presents some difficulty, for the tendency to enumerate is as great as it is with the process paper. A one-two-three procedure ("The first type of college student . . . ," "The second type . . . ," "The third type of student . . .") can make an essay of classification sound like a catalogue. Effective and varied transitions are as important to classification as they are to process. Some topics, moreover, can be analyzed most logically if all of the categories are related to a single principle that gives unity to the entire topic. For example, Francis Bacon in his essay "Of Studies" relates all of the types of books he discusses to the purposes they serve.

In presenting classification as an essay rather than as a mere list, the writer must use methods of development that will make the divisions vivid. The topic sentence, which will limit the category or characteristic type to be discussed in a paragraph, should provide the central idea. The central idea, in turn, may be developed by means of any or all of the previously discussed basic techniques of *example, comparison,* or *contrast*.

Of the essays that follow in this section, only those by Thomas Fuller and Francis Bacon are concerned simply with classifying and enumerating. Paul Roberts, Max Eastman, and Eric Berne simultaneously classify and define. William Golding's "Thinking as a Hobby" classifies three sorts of thinking but also presents narration of incidents to illustrate the two most common types.

Thomas Fuller

FOUR TYPES OF STUDENTS

Thomas Fuller (1608–1661) was a noted churchman and historian, who is remembered today for his brief descriptions of "characters"—examples of some type of personality. This analysis of student types is contained in Fuller's exhaustive discussion of "The Good Schoolmaster," from his The Holy and the Profane State *(1642).*

[1] . . . Experienced schoolmasters may quickly make a grammar of boys' natures, and reduce them all, saving some few exceptions, to these general rules:

[2] Those that are ingenious and industrious. The conjunction of two such planets in a youth presage much good unto him. To such a lad a frown may be a whipping, and a whipping death; yea, where their master whips them once, shame whips them all the week after. Such natures he useth with all gentleness.

[3] Those that are ingenious and idle. These think, with the hare in the fable, that, running with snails (so they count the rest of their schoolfellows), they shall come soon enough to the post, though sleeping a good while before their starting. Oh, a good rod would finely take them napping!

[4] Those that are dull and diligent. Wines, the stronger they be, the more lees they have when they are new. Many boys are muddy-headed till they be clarified with age, and such afterwards prove the best. Bristol diamonds* are both bright and squared and pointed by nature, and yet are soft and worthless; orient ones in India are rough and rugged naturally. Hard, rugged, and dull natures of youth acquit themselves afterwards the jewels of the country, and therefore their dullness at first is to be borne with, if they be diligent. The schoolmaster deserves to be beaten himself who beats nature in a boy for a fault. And I question whether all the whippings in the world can make their parts, which are naturally sluggish, rise one minute before the hour nature hath appointed.

[5] Those that are invincibly dull and negligent also. Correction may reform the latter, not amend the former. All the whetting in the world can never set a razor's edge on that which hath no steel in it. Such boys he consigneth over to other professions. Shipwrights and boatmakers will choose those crooked pieces of timber which other carpenters refuse. Those may make excellent merchants and mechanics who will not serve for scholars.

VOCABULARY

Define the following words as they are used in the selection: *grammar* [1]; *conjunction, presage* [2]; *orient, parts* [4]; *invincibly* [5]. In each instance, indicate whether Fuller's usage is still current or whether it is listed as "obsolete" or "archaic."

* Quartz crystals from Bristol, England.

QUESTIONS FOR STUDY AND DISCUSSION

1. What two qualities of a student does Fuller consider the most important? Are the four categories of students mutually exclusive?

2. Fuller states in paragraph 1 that there are "some few exceptions to these general rules." What exceptions can you name?

3. Notice the symmetrical structure of the paragraphs. Each one (a) indicates the presence or absence of the essential qualities and (b) illustrates the type through the use of one or more analogies. What other information does each one provide? How does this further information relate to the characteristics of a good schoolmaster?

4. Discuss the effectiveness and the aptness of the analogies in the essay. How are schoolboys like (a) hares, (b) wines, (c) diamonds, (d) razors, (e) timber?

5. Fuller makes limited use of transitional words or phrases between paragraphs. In the original essay, the four types of students are even labeled *a*, *b*, *c*, and *d*. Suggest transitional words or phrases that could be employed between paragraphs, or explain why you think the absence of varied transition is in keeping with Fuller's general style.

Paul Roberts

COLORFUL, COLORED, AND COLORLESS WORDS

Formerly Professor of English at San Jose State University and Cornell University, Paul Roberts (1917–1967) was the author of numerous books that have had wide influence in the teaching of English composition and grammar in high schools and colleges. Among them are Understanding Grammar *(1954),* Understanding English *(1958),* English Sentences *(1962), and* English Syntax *(1964). He was also the author of* Cornflakes and Beaujolais *(1958), an account of his experiences with his family while a Fulbright teacher and scholar in Cairo and Rome.*

"Colorful Words," "Colored Words," and "Colorless Words" from *Understanding English*, by Paul Roberts. Copyright © 1958 by Paul Roberts. Reprinted by permission of Harper & Row, Publishers, Inc.

[1]   The writer builds with words, and no builder uses a raw material more slippery and elusive and treacherous. A writer's work is a constant struggle to get the right word in the right place, to find that particular word that will convey his meaning exactly, that will persuade the reader or soothe him or startle or amuse him. He never succeeds altogther—sometimes he feels that he scarcely succeeds at all—but such successes as he has are what make the thing worth doing.

[2]   There is no book of rules for this game. One progresses through everlasting experiment on the basis of ever-widening experience. There are few useful generalizations that one can make about words as words, but there are perhaps a few.

[3]   Some words are what we call "colorful." By this we mean that they are calculated to produce a picture or induce an emotion. They are dressy instead of plain, specific instead of general, loud instead of soft. Thus, in place of "Her heart beat," we may write "Her heart *pounded, throbbed, fluttered, danced*." Instead of "He sat in his chair," we may say, "He *lounged, sprawled, coiled*." Instead of "It was hot," we may say, "It was *blistering, sultry, muggy, suffocating, steamy, wilting*."

[4]   However, it should not be supposed that the fancy word is always better. Often it is as well to write "Her heart beat" or "It was hot" if that is all it did or all it was. Ages differ in how they like their prose. The nineteenth century liked it rich and smoky. The twentieth has usually preferred it lean and cool. The twentieth century writer, like all writers, is forever seeking the exact word, but he is wary of sounding feverish. He tends to pitch it low, to understate it, to throw it away. He knows that if he gets too colorful, the audience is likely to giggle.

[5]   See how this strikes you: "As the rich, golden glow of the sunset died away along the eternal western hills, Angela's limpid blue eyes looked softly and trustingly into Montague's flashing brown ones, and her heart pounded like a drum in time with the joyous song surging in her soul." Some people like that sort of thing, but most modern readers would say, "Good grief," and turn on the television.

[6]   Some words we would call not so much colorful as colored—that is, loaded with associations, good or bad. All words—except perhaps structure words—have associations of some sort. We have said that the meaning of a word is the sum of the contexts in which it occurs. When we hear a word, we hear with it an echo of all the situations in which we have heard it before.

CLASSIFICATION 35

[7] In some words, these echoes are obvious and discussable. The word *mother*, for example, has, for most people, agreeable associations. When you hear *mother* you probably think of home, safety, love, food, and various other pleasant things. If one writes, "She was like a mother to me," he gets an effect which he would not get in "She was like an aunt to me." The advertiser makes use of the associations of *mother* by working it in when he talks about his product. The politician works it in when he talks about himself.

[8] So also with such words as *home, liberty, fireside, contentment, patriot, tenderness, sacrifice, childlike, manly, bluff, limpid.* All of these words are loaded with favorable associations that would be rather hard to indicate in a straightforward definition. There is more than a literal difference between "They sat around the fireside" and "They sat around the stove." They might have been equally warm and happy around the stove, but *fireside* suggests leisure, grace, quiet tradition, congenial company, and *stove* does not.

[9] Conversely, some words have bad associations. *Mother* suggests pleasant things, but *mother-in-law* does not. Many mothers-in-law are heroically lovable and some mothers drink gin all day and beat their children insensible, but these facts of life are beside the point. The thing is that *mother* sounds good and *mother-in-law* does not.

[10] Or consider the word *intellectual*. This would seem to be a complimentary term, but in point of fact it is not, for it has picked up associations of impracticality and ineffectuality and general dopiness. So also with such words as *liberal, reactionary, Communist, socialist, capitalist, radical, schoolteacher, truck driver, undertaker, operator, salesman, huckster, speculator.* These convey meanings on the literal level, but beyond that—sometimes, in some places—they convey contempt on the part of the speaker.

[11] The question of whether to use loaded words or not depends on what is being written. The scientist, the scholar, try to avoid them; for the poet, the advertising writer, the public speaker, they are standard equipment. But every writer should take care that they do not substitute for thought. If you write, "Anyone who thinks that is nothing but a Socialist (or Communist or capitalist)" you have said nothing except that you don't like people who think that, and such remarks are effective only with the most naïve readers. It is always a bad mistake to think your readers are more naïve than they really are.

[12] But probably most student writers come to grief not with words that are colorful or those that are colored but with those that have no color at all. A pet example is *nice*, a word we would find it hard to dispense with in casual

conversation but which is no longer capable of adding much to a description. Colorless words are those of such general meaning that in a particular sentence they mean nothing. Slang adjectives, like *cool* ("That's real cool"), tend to explode all over the language. They are applied to everything, lose their original force, and quickly die.

[13] Beware also of nouns of very general meaning, like *circumstances, cases, instances, aspects, factors, relationships, attitudes, eventualities,* etc. In most circumstances you will find that those cases of writing which contain too many instances of words like these will in this and other aspects have factors leading to unsatisfactory relationships with the reader resulting in unfavorable attitudes on his part and perhaps other eventualities, like a grade of "D." Notice also what "etc." means. It means "I'd like to make this list longer, but I can't think of any more examples."

VOCABULARY

Define the following words as they are used in the selection: *elusive* [1]; *induce* [3]; *wary* [4]; *limpid* [5]; *literal* [8].

QUESTIONS FOR STUDY AND DISCUSSION

1. This selection, from a composition textbook for college freshmen, is three sections of a chapter entitled "How to Say Nothing in Five Hundred Words." In the original form the three sections are titled and numbered. Where would the divisions occur? Is there any logical reason for the arrangement of the discussion of the three types of words?

2. What is the function of paragraphs 1 and 2? Is the topic sentence of the selection stated in these paragraphs? If so, what is it?

3. What is the point of view employed in the selection? Is it completely consistent? Is it effective? Why?

4. In what ways does Roberts clarify what he means by the term "colorful"? Does his own explanation put into practice the advice that he is giving? How? Give examples.

5. In paragraph 4 Roberts states, "Ages differ in how they like their prose." What does Roberts mean by saying that nineteenth-century readers liked their prose "rich and smoky," whereas modern readers usually prefer it "lean and cool," pitched low, understated, and thrown away?

6. Are the differences Roberts gives between tastes of readers in the nine-

CLASSIFICATION   37

teenth and twentieth centuries absolute? May they not be a matter of individual taste in any given century? Discuss.

7. How does Roberts distinguish between colorful words and colored words? Is the explanation clear? He might, in his explanation of colored words, have referred to *connotation* and *denotation*. What do these terms mean? In what contexts would the words in paragraph 10 be denotative only?

8. What is Roberts's basic method of explaining what colored words are?

9. What are the topic sentences for the paragraphs discussing colorful and colored words? What is the topic sentence for the paragraphs about colorless words?

10. Do Roberts's transitional sentences keep the reader aware of where he has been and where he is? What are these sentences? Could they be grouped with the topic sentences into a sequence to produce a well-organized, but undeveloped, paragraph about the three types of words? Try it.

11. What is the purpose of the second sentence of paragraph 13? Of the concluding sentence?

12. Although the basic organization of this selection is analytical, its methods are those of definition and its purpose is that of process. What sentences are primarily definition sentences? What statements are basically concerned with process?

Francis Bacon

OF STUDIES

> By his own criteria, Francis Bacon (1561–1626) was a full man, as well as a ready and an exact one; for his Advancement of Learning (1605) purposed a summary of existing knowledge and indicated the breadth of his reading, his political career under James I (he became Lord High Chancellor of England in 1618) attested his ability at conference, and his pithy Essays or Counsels, Civil and Moral (first edition, 1597) indicated his exactness. "Of Studies" is the fiftieth of his fifty-eight celebrated Essays; the text is from the third edition, 1625. Bacon's prose is commonly praised as the best in early seventeenth-century England; for breadth of idea and compression of statement, it has seldom been equaled.

Studies serve for delight, for ornament, and for ability. Their chief use for delight is in privateness and retiring; for ornament, is in discourse; and for ability, is in the judgment and disposition of business. For expert men can

execute, and perhaps judge of particulars, one by one; but the general counsels, and the plots and marshalling of affairs come best from those that are learned. To spend too much time in studies is sloth; to use them too much for ornament is affectation; to make judgment wholly by their rules is the humour of a scholar. They perfect nature, and are perfected by experience: for natural abilities are like natural plants, that need pruning by study; and studies themselves do give forth directions too much at large, except they be bounded by experience. Crafty men contemn studies, simple men admire them, and wise men use them; for they teach not their own use; but that is a wisdom without them and above them, won by observation. Read not to contradict and confute, nor to believe and take for granted, nor to find talk and discourse, but to weigh and consider. Some books are to be tasted, others to be swallowed, and some few to be chewed and digested; that is, some books are to be read only in parts; others to be read, but not curiously; and some few to be read wholly, and with diligence and attention. Some books also may be read by deputy, and extracts made of them by others; but that would be only in the less important arguments and the meaner sort of books; else distilled books are, like common distilled waters, flashy things. Reading maketh a full man; conference a ready man; and writing an exact man. And, therefore, if a man write little, he had need have a great memory; if he confer little, he had need have a present wit; and if he read little, he had need have much cunning, to seem to know that he doth not. Histories make men wise; poets, witty; the mathematics, subtile; natural philosophy, deep; moral, grave; logic and rhetoric, able to contend. *Abeunt studia in mores.** Nay, there is no stond or impediment in the wit but may be wrought out by fit studies, like as diseases of the body may have appropriate exercises. Bowling is good for the stone and reins, shooting for the lungs and breast, gentle walking for the stomach, riding for the head, and the like. So if a man's wit be wandering, let him study the mathematics; for in demonstrations, if his wit be called away never so little, he must begin again. If his wit be not apt to distinguish or find differences, let him study the schoolmen; for they are *Cymini sectores.*†
If he be not apt to beat over matters, and to call up one thing to prove and illustrate another, let him study the lawyers' cases. So every defect of the mind may have a special receipt.

VOCABULARY

1. This essay illustrates well how words change in meaning. Whereas Bacon says that studies serve for delight, ornament, and ability, we would say that they

---

* Studies form manners.
† Dividers of cuminseed, *i.e.*, hair-splitters; see Matthew 23:23.

provide pleasure, social advantage, and practical knowledge. What words would we substitute for *privateness, retiring, discourse, judgment and disposition, expert*? What other words need to be translated for a twentieth-century reader?

2. A number of words are employed with meanings unusual to a modern reader. What are the particular meanings of the following: *crafty, simple, curiously, deputy, flashy, stond (stand), wrought*?

3. In addition to words that have changed in meaning, there are several words difficult or important in themselves. Define the following words in context: *affectation, humour, admire, natural philosophy, stone, reins, schoolmen, receipt*.

QUESTIONS FOR STUDY AND DISCUSSION

1. Since the essay is clearly one "to be chewed and digested" read it several times with the purpose of dividing it into paragraphs. Where would you suggest that the paragraph divisions fall? What are the topic ideas of the paragraphs? Does the essay have any progression of idea? Are the paragraphs related?

2. Bacon's first topic involves studies, or knowledge, in the largest possible context, though he does not specify what type of knowledge. To what uses may studies be put? Which ones receive Bacon's favor? What is the ultimate use of studies?

3. Next he discusses the several approaches to books, the principal source of knowledge not learned through experience. What specific advice does he give? Where does this topic begin? Where does it end?

4. His final concern is with the specific advantages to be gained from certain types of books. Notice that Bacon begins this section by commenting on the ultimate end of reading and moves to a consideration of other intellectual activities. How does he manage the transition back to a discussion of reading? How does the final statement (in effect, the topic sentence of this third division of the essay) relate to the subject of the first division?

5. What instances of analogy do you find in the essay? Does Bacon use an analogy to develop each of his major topics?

6. Bacon follows the device of dividing his ideas into sets of three. Point out instances of this device. Why is it better, as a general rule, than dividing into sets of two?

7. He is also fond of balanced sentences; that is, he constructs his sentences so that the parts of them are set against each other in order to emphasize contrast in meaning, as in the third sentence. What other examples can you find?

8. Another characteristic of Bacon is his use of parallel structure, as in the first sentence. Point out other examples.

9. Several of his sentences are elliptical: they omit words that may be supplied by the reader through his awareness of the pattern of the sentence. The sec-

ond sentence is an example. What words are omitted but understood? Point out other examples.

10. What would be Bacon's attitude toward condensed books; moving pictures and television shows made from books; "educational" comic books, such as illustrated literary classics?

Max Eastman

PRACTICAL AND POETIC PEOPLE

This discussion of two types of people opens Chapter 1 of The Enjoyment of Poetry, *by Max Eastman (1883–1969). Both a poetic and a practical person himself—he was a poet and critic as well as a teacher and editor (teachers and editors need to be practical)—he challenges in this essay the easy generalizations about the two types. Among Eastman's other books are* The Literary Mind: Its Place in an Age of Science *and* The End of Socialism in Russia.

[1] A simple experiment will distinguish two types of human nature. Gather a throng of people and pour them into a ferry-boat. By the time the boat has swung into the river you will find that a certain proportion have taken the trouble to climb upstairs, in order to be out on deck and see what is to be seen as they cross over. The rest have settled indoors, to think what they will do upon reaching the other side, or perhaps lose themselves in apathy or tobacco smoke. But leaving out those apathetic, or addicted to a single enjoyment, we may divide all the alert passengers on the boat into two classes—those who are interested in crossing the river, and those who are merely interested in getting across. And we may divide all the people on the earth, or all the moods of people, in the same way. Some of them are chiefly occupied with attaining ends, and some with receiving experiences. The distinction of the two will be more marked when we name the first kind practical, and the second poetic, for common knowledge recognizes that a person poetic or in a poetic mood is impractical, and a practical person is intolerant of poetry.

Reprinted with the permission of Charles Scribner's Sons from *The Enjoyment of Poetry* by Max Eastman. Copyright 1913 Charles Scribner's Sons; renewal copyright 1941 Max Eastman.

[2]   We can see the force of this intolerance too, and how deeply it is justified, if we make clear to our minds just what it means to be practical, and what a great thing it is. It means to be controlled in your doings by the consideration of ends yet unattained. The practical man is never distracted by things, or aspects of things, which have no bearing on his purpose, but, ever seizing the significant, he moves with a single mind and a single emotion toward the goal. And even when the goal is achieved you will hardly see him pause to rejoice in it; he is already on his way to another achievement. For that is the irony of his nature. His joy is not in any conquest or destination, but his joy is in going toward it. To which joy he adds the pleasure of being praised as a practical man, and a man who will arrive.

[3]   In a more usual sense, perhaps, a practical man is a man occupied with attaining certain ends that people consider important. He must stick pretty close to the business of feeding and preserving life. Nourishment and shelter, money-making, maintaining respectability, and if possible a family—these are the things that give its common meaning to the word "practical." An acute regard for such features of the scenery, and the universe, as contribute or can be made to contribute to these ends, and a systematic neglect of all other features, are the traits of mind which this word popularly suggests. And it is because of the vital importance of these things to almost all people that the word "practical" is a eulogy, and is able to be so scornful of the word "poetic."

[4]   "It is an earnest thing to be alive in this world. With competition, with war, with disease and poverty and oppression, misfortune and death oncoming, who but fools will give serious attention to what is not significant to the business?"

[5]   "Yes—but what is the *use* of being alive in the world, if life is so oppressive in its moral character that we must always be busy getting somewhere, and never simply realizing where we are? What were the value of your eternal achieving, if we were not here on our holiday to appreciate, among other things, some of the things you have achieved?"

[6]   Thus, if we could discover a purely poetic and a purely practical person, might they reason together. But we can discover nothing so satisfactory to our definitions, and therefore let us conclude the discussion of the difference between them. It has led us to our own end—a clearer understanding of the nature of poetic people, and of all people when they are in a poetic mood. They are lovers of the qualities of things. They are not engaged, as the learned say that all life is, in becoming adjusted to an environment, but they are engaged in becoming acquainted with it. They are possessed by the impulse to

realize, an impulse as deep, and arbitrary, and unexplained as that "will to live" which lies at the bottom of all the explanations. It seems but the manifestation, indeed, of that will itself in a concrete and positive form. It is a wish to experience life and the world. That is the essence of the poetic temper.

VOCABULARY

Define the following words as they are used in the selection: *apathy, addicted* [1]; *irony* [2]; *acute, eulogy* [3]; *arbitrary, essence, temper* [6].

QUESTIONS FOR STUDY AND DISCUSSION

1. Note the ways in which paragraph 1 illustrates the two types of human nature. Identify which group—the practical or the poetic—is described by Eastman as follows:

   a. On deck to see what can be seen.
   b. Inside the boat.
   c. "Interested in crossing."
   d. "Interested in getting across."

2. Are all people on the ferry boat accounted for in the two categories? How does Eastman further classify the people aboard the boat?

3. Paragraph 2 ascribes to the practical man a singleness of purpose. How does the analogy of the people aboard the boat illustrate this characteristic?

4. In paragraph 6 Eastman states that poetic people attempt to become acquainted with life. How does the ferry-boat analogy illustrate this characteristic?

5. What is Eastman's attitude toward the practical person? Does Eastman feel that the practical person is justified in his concerns? What words and phrases of paragraph 2 reveal the author's attitude?

6. Do the statements ascribed to the practical and the poetic in paragraphs 4 and 5 well summarize the differences?

7. With which group does Eastman feel more closely identified? Defend your answer.

8. How does paragraph 6, in its definition of poetic people or of poetic moods of all people, give poetic people more dignity, more understanding of the nature of life, than that ascribed to the practical?

9. What is the difference between "becoming adjusted to an environment" and "becoming acquainted with it"?

10. List the characteristics of poetic people or people in a poetic mood.

11. Which group seems to you to be the more successful in exhausting life of its possibilities?

Eric Berne

CAN PEOPLE BE JUDGED BY THEIR APPEARANCE?

> *Eric Berne (1910–1970) was a psychiatrist who served on the staff of Mount Sinai Hospital in New York City and later was in private practice in California. He wrote extensively on matters of human relationships, making a particular success with his book* Games People Play *(1964). The essay reprinted here is from* The Mind in Action *(1947) and was included also in Berne's* A Layman's Guide to Psychiatry and Psychoanalysis *(1957). His classification of human body-temperament types gave rise to some popular labels.*

[1] Everyone knows that a human being, like a chicken, comes from an egg. At a very early stage, the human embryo forms a three-layered tube, the inside layer of which grows into the stomach and lungs, the middle layer into bones, muscles, joints, and blood vessels, and the outside layer into the skin and nervous system.

[2] Usually these three grow about equally, so that the average human being is a fair mixture of brains, muscles, and inward organs. In some eggs, however, one layer grows more than the others, and when the angels have finished putting the child together, he may have more gut than brain, or more brain than muscle. When this happens, the individual's activities will often be mostly with the overgrown layer.

[3] We can thus say that while the average human being is a mixture, some people are mainly "digestion-minded," some "muscle-minded," and some "brain-minded," and correspondingly digestion-bodied, muscle-bodied, or brain-bodied. The digestion-bodied people look thick; the muscle-bodied people look wide; and the brain-bodied people look long. This does not mean the

From *A Layman's Guide to Psychiatry and Psychoanalysis* by Eric Berne. Copyright 1947, 1957, 1968 by Eric Berne. Reprinted by permission of Simon & Shuster, Inc.

taller a man is the brainier he will be. It means that if a man, even a short man, looks long rather than wide or thick, he will often be more concerned about what goes on in his mind than about what he does or what he eats; but the key factor is slenderness and not height. On the other hand, a man who gives the impression of being thick rather than long or wide will usually be more interested in a good steak than in a good idea or a good long walk.

[4]   Medical men use Greek words to describe these types of bodybuild. For the man whose body shape mostly depends on the inside layer of the egg, they use the word *endomorph*. If it depends mostly upon the middle layer, they call him a *mesomorph*. If it depends upon the outside layer, they call him an *ectomorph*. We can see the same roots in our English words "enter," "medium," and "exit," which might just as easily have been spelled "ender," "mesium," and "ectit."

[5]   Since the inside skin of the human egg, or endoderm, forms the inner organs of the belly, the viscera, the endomorph is usually belly-minded; since the middle skin forms the body tissues, or soma, the mesomorph is usually muscle-minded; and since the outside skin forms the brain, or cerebrum, the ectomorph is usually brain-minded. Translating this into Greek, we have the viscerotonic endomorph, the somatotonic mesomorph, and the cerebrotonic ectomorph.

[6]   Words are beautiful things to a cerebrotonic, but a viscerotonic knows you cannot eat a menu no matter what language it is printed in, and a somatotonic knows you cannot increase your chest expansion by reading a dictionary. So it is advisable to leave these words and see what kinds of people they actually apply to, remembering again that most individuals are fairly equal mixtures and that what we have to say concerns only the extremes. Up to the present, these types have been thoroughly studied only in the male sex.

[7]   *Viscerotonic Endomorph.* If a man is definitely a thick type rather than a broad or long type, he is likely to be round and soft, with a big chest but a bigger belly. He would rather eat than breathe comfortably. He is likely to have a wide face, short, thick neck, big thighs and upper arms, and small hands and feet. He has overdeveloped breasts and looks as though he were blown up a little like a balloon. His skin is soft and smooth, and when he gets bald, as he does usually quite early, he loses the hair in the middle of his head first.

[8]   The short, jolly, thickset, red-faced politician with a cigar in his mouth, who always looks as though he were about to have a stroke, is the best exam-

CLASSIFICATION   45

ple of this type. The reason he often makes a good politician is that he likes people, banquets, baths, and sleep; he is easygoing, soothing, and his feelings are easy to understand.

[9] His abdomen is big because he has lots of intestines. He likes to take in things. He likes to take in food, and affection and approval as well. Going to a banquet with people who like him is his idea of a fine time. It is important for a psychiatrist to understand the natures of such men when they come to him for advice.

[10] *Somatotonic Mesomorph.* If a man is definitely a broad type rather than a thick or long type, he is likely to be rugged and have lots of muscle. He is apt to have big forearms and legs, and his chest and belly are well formed and firm, with the chest bigger than the belly. He would rather breathe than eat. He has a bony head, big shoulders, and a square jaw. His skin is thick, coarse, and elastic, and tans easily. If he gets bald, it usually starts on the front of the head.

[11] Dick Tracy, Li'l Abner, and other men of action belong to this type. Such people make good lifeguards and construction workers. They like to put out energy. They have lots of muscles and they like to use them. They go in for adventure, exercise, fighting, and getting the upper hand. They are bold and unrestrained, and love to master the people and things around them. If the psychiatrist knows the things which give such people satisfaction, he is able to understand why they may be unhappy in certain situations.

[12] *Cerebrotonic Ectomorph.* The man who is definitely a long type is likely to have thin bones and muscles. His shoulders are apt to sag and he has a flat belly with a dropped stomach, and long, weak legs. His neck and fingers are long, and his face is shaped like a long egg. His skin is thin, dry, and pale, and he rarely gets bald. He looks like an absent-minded professor and often is one.

[13] Though such people are jumpy, they like to keep their energy and don't fancy moving around much. They would rather sit quietly by themselves and keep out of difficulties. Trouble upsets them, and they run away from it. Their friends don't understand them very well. They move jerkily and feel jerkily. The psychiatrist who understands how easily they become anxious is often able to help them get along better in the sociable and aggressive world of endomorphs and mesomorphs.

[14] In the special cases where people definitely belong to one type or another, then, one can tell a good deal about their personalities from their ap-

pearance. When the human mind is engaged in one of its struggles with itself or with the world outside, the individual's way of handling the struggle will be partly determined by his type. If he is a viscerotonic he will often want to go to a party where he can eat and drink and be in good company at a time when he might be better off attending to business; the somatotonic will want to go out and do something about it, master the situation, even if what he does is foolish and not properly figured out, while the cerebrotonic will go off by himself and think it over, when perhaps he would be better off doing something about it or seeking good company to try to forget it.

[15] Since these personality characteristics depend on the growth of the layers of the little egg from which the person developed, they are very difficult to change. Nevertheless, it is important for the individual to know about these types, so that he can have at least an inkling of what to expect from those around him, and can make allowances for the different kinds of human nature, and so that he can become aware of and learn to control his own natural tendencies, which may sometimes guide him into making the same mistakes over and over again in handling his difficulties.

QUESTIONS FOR STUDY AND DISCUSSION

1. Which of the patterns of exposition has Berne used as his primary method in developing this essay? Explain your answer.

2. Berne also uses each of the other patterns of exposition in the essay. Locate an example of each.

3. Berne's topic is scientific, but the tone of the essay is far from technical. Locate and cite at least six examples of diction that help to make the essay seem informal rather than technical.

4. Has Berne designed a classification that includes all human beings? How does he justify his system of classification as useful?

5. What is the purpose of the final sentences of paragraphs 9, 11, and 13? Is the essay directed toward an audience of psychiatrists?

6. Berne refers the reader to specific stereotypes: the politician (paragraph 8), the lifeguard and the construction worker (paragraph 11), the absent-minded professor (paragraph 12). Is such stereotyping justified in terms of Berne's purpose? Are the stereotype examples in keeping with the classification of human types itself?

7. After your careful reading of the Berne essay, what is your answer to the question of the title: "Can People Be Judged by Their Appearance?" Explain your answer.

FOR FURTHER ANALYSIS

William Golding

THINKING AS A HOBBY

Novelist William Golding (b. 1911) won international note for his Lord of the Flies (1954) and has since published The Inheritors (1956), Free Fall (1959), The Spire (1964), The Pyramid (1967), and The Scorpion God (1971). In the present essay Golding classifies three types of thinking, providing for each reader some perspective for placing oneself as a thinker. The reader may boggle in attempting to discern what Golding means by saying, at last, "I dropped my hobby and turned professional." The essay first appeared in Holiday, August 1961.

[1]   While I was still a boy, I came to the conclusion that there were three grades of thinking; and since I was later to claim thinking as my hobby, I came to an even stranger conclusion—namely, that I myself could not think at all.

[2]   I must have been an unsatisfactory child for grownups to deal with. I remember how incomprehensible they appeared to me at first, but not, of course, how I appeared to them. It was the headmaster of my grammar school who first brought the subject of thinking before me—though neither in the way, nor with the result he intended. He had some statuettes in his study. They stood on a high cupboard behind his desk. One was a lady wearing nothing but a bath towel. She seemed frozen in an eternal panic lest the bath towel slip down any farther; and since she had no arms, she was in an unfortunate position to pull the towel up again. Next to her, crouched the statuette of a leopard, ready to spring down at the top drawer of a filing cabinet labeled A-AH. My innocence interpreted this as the victim's last, despairing cry. Beyond the leopard was a naked, muscular gentleman, who sat, looking down, with his chin on his fist and his elbow on his knee. He seemed utterly miserable.

From *Holiday*, August 1961. Copyright © 1961 by The Curtis Publishing Company. Reprinted by permission of Curtis Brown, Ltd.

[3]   Some time later, I learned about these statuettes. The headmaster had placed them where they would face delinquent children, because they symbolized to him the whole of life. The naked lady was the Venus of Milo. She was Love. She was not worried about the towel. She was just busy being beautiful. The leopard was Nature, and he was being natural. The naked, muscular gentleman was not miserable. He was Rodin's Thinker, an image of pure thought. It is easy to buy small plaster models of what you think life is like.

[4]   I had better explain that I was a frequent visitor to the headmaster's study, because of the latest thing I had done or left undone. As we now say, I was not integrated. I was, if anything, disintegrated; and I was puzzled. Grownups never made sense. Whenever I found myself in a penal position before the headmaster's desk, with the statuettes glimmering whitely above him, I would sink my head, clasp my hands behind my back and writhe one shoe over the other.

[5]   The headmaster would look opaquely at me through flashing spectacles.

[6]   "What are we going to do with you?"

[7]   Well, what *were* they going to do with me? I would writhe my shoe some more and stare down at the worn rug.

[8]   "Look up, boy! Can't you look up?"

[9]   Then I would look up at the cupboard, where the naked lady was frozen in her panic and the musclar gentleman contemplated the hindquarters of the leopard in endless gloom. I had nothing to say to the headmaster. His spectacles caught the light so that you could see nothing human behind them. There was no possibility of communication.

[10]   "Don't you ever think at all?"

[11]   No, I didn't think, wasn't thinking, couldn't think—I was simply waiting in anguish for the interview to stop.

[12]   "Then you'd better learn—hadn't you?"

[13]   On one occasion the headmaster leaped to his feet, reached up and plonked Rodin's masterpiece on the desk before me.

[14]   "That's what a man looks like when he's really thinking."

CLASSIFICATION

[15]   I surveyed the gentleman without interest or comprehension.

[16]   "Go back to your class."

[17]   Clearly there was something missing in me. Nature had endowed the rest of the human race with a sixth sense and left me out. This must be so, I mused, on my way back to the class, since whether I had broken a window, or failed to remember Boyle's Law, or been late for school, my teachers produced me one, adult answer: "Why can't you think?"

[18]   As I saw the case, I had broken the window because I had tried to hit Jack Arney with a cricket ball and missed him; I could not remember Boyle's Law because I had never bothered to learn it; and I was late for school because I preferred looking over the bridge into the river. In fact, I was wicked. Were my teachers, perhaps, so good that they could not understand the depths of my depravity? Were they clear, untormented people who could direct their every action by this mysterious business of thinking? The whole thing was incomprehensible. In my earlier years, I found even the statuette of the Thinker confusing. I did not believe any of my teachers were naked, ever. Like someone born deaf, but bitterly determined to find out about sound, I watched my teachers to find out about thought.

[19]   There was Mr. Houghton. He was always telling me to think. With a modest satisfaction, he would tell me that he had thought a bit himself. Then why did he spend so much time drinking? Or was there more sense in drinking than there appeared to be? But if not, and if drinking were in fact ruinous to health—and Mr. Houghton was ruined, there was no doubt about that—why was he always talking about the clean life and the virtues of fresh air? He would spread his arms wide with the action of a man who habitually spent his time striding along mountain ridges.

[20]   "Open air does me good, boys—I know it!"

[21]   Sometimes, exalted by his own oratory, he would leap from his desk and hustle us outside into a hideous wind.

[22]   "Now, boys! Deep breaths! Feel it right down inside you—huge draughts of God's good air!"

[23]   He would stand before us, rejoicing in his perfect health, an open-air man. He would put his hands on his waist and take a tremendous breath. You could hear the wind, trapped in the cavern of his chest and struggling

with all the unnatural impediments. His body would reel with shock and his ruined face go white at the unaccustomed visitation. He would stagger back to his desk and collapse there, useless for the rest of the morning.

[24]   Mr. Houghton was given to high-minded monologues about the good life, sexless and full of duty. Yet in the middle of one of these monologues, if a girl passed the window, tapping along on her neat little feet, he would interrupt his discourse, his neck would turn of itself and he would watch her out of sight. In this instance, he seemed to me ruled not by thought but by an invisible and irresistible spring in his nape.

[25]   His neck was an object of great interest to me. Normally it bulged a bit over his collar. But Mr. Houghton had fought in the First World War alongside both Americans and French, and had come—by who knows what illogic?—to a settled detestation of both countries. If either country happened to be prominent in current affairs, no argument could make Mr. Houghton think well of it. He would bang the desk, his neck would bulge still further and go red. "You can say what you like," he would cry, "but I've thought about this—and I know what I think!"

[26]   Mr. Houghton thought with his neck.

[27]   There was Miss Parsons. She assured us that her dearest wish was our welfare, but I knew even then, with the mysterious clairvoyance of childhood, that what she wanted most was the husband she never got. There was Mr. Hands—and so on.

[28]   I have dealt at length with my teachers because this was my introduction to the nature of what is commonly called thought. Through them I discovered that thought is often full of unconscious prejudice, ignorance and hypocrisy. It will lecture on disinterested purity while its neck is being remorselessly twisted toward a skirt. Technically, it is about as proficient as most businessmen's golf, as honest as most politicians' intentions, or—to come near my own preoccupation—as coherent as most books that get written. It is what I came to call grade-three thinking, though more properly, it is feeling, rather than thought.

[29]   True, often there is a kind of innocence in prejudices, but in those days I viewed grade-three thinking with an intolerant contempt and an incautious mockery. I delighted to confront a pious lady who hated the Germans with the proposition that we should love our enemies. She taught me a great truth in dealing with grade-three thinkers; because of her, I no longer dismiss lightly

CLASSIFICATION 51

a mental process which for nine-tenths of the population is the nearest they will ever get to thought. They have immense solidarity. We had better respect them, for we are outnumbered and surrounded. A crowd of grade-three thinkers, all shouting the same thing, all warming their hands at the fire of their own prejudices, will not thank you for pointing out the contradictions in their beliefs. Man is a gregarious animal, and enjoys agreement as cows will graze all the same way on the side of a hill.

[30] Grade-two thinking is the detection of contradictions. I reached grade two when I trapped the poor, pious lady. Grade-two thinkers do not stampede easily, though often they fall into the other fault and lag behind. Grade-two thinking is a withdrawal, with eyes and ears open. It became my hobby and brought satisfaction and loneliness in either hand. For grade-two thinking destroys without having the power to create. It set me watching the crowds cheering His Majesty the King and asking myself what all the fuss was about, without giving me anything positive to put in the place of that heady patriotism. But there were compensations. To hear people justify their habit of hunting foxes and tearing them to pieces by claiming that the foxes liked it. To hear our Prime Minister talk about the great benefit we conferred on India by jailing people like Pandit Nehru and Gandhi. To hear American politicians talk about peace in one sentence and refuse to join the League of Nations in the next. Yes, there were moments of delight.

[31] But I was growing toward adolescence and had to admit that Mr. Houghton was not the only one with an irresistible spring in his neck. I, too, felt the compulsive hand of nature and began to find that pointing out contradiction could be costly as well as fun. There was Ruth, for example, a serious and attractive girl. I was an atheist at the time. Grade-two thinking is a menace to religion and knocks down sects like skittles. I put myself in a position to be converted by her with an hypocrisy worthy of grade three. She was a Methodist—or at least, her parents were, and Ruth had to follow suit. But, alas, instead of relying on the Holy Spirit to convert me, Ruth was foolish enough to open her pretty mouth in argument. She claimed that the Bible (King James Version) was literally inspired. I countered by saying that the Catholics believed in the literal inspiration of Saint Jerome's *Vulgate*, and the two books were different. Argument flagged.

[32] At last she remarked that there were an awful lot of Methodists, and they couldn't be wrong, could they—not all those millions? That was too easy, said I restively (for the nearer you were to Ruth, the nicer she was to be near to) since there were more Roman Catholics than Methodists anyway; and they couldn't be wrong, could they—not all those hundreds of millions? An

awful flicker of doubt appeared in her eyes. I slid my arm round her waist and murmured breathlessly that if we were counting heads, the Buddhists were the boys for my money. But Ruth had *really* wanted to do me good, because I was so nice. She fled. The combination of my arm and those countless Buddhists was too much for her.

[33]   That night her father visited my father and left, red-cheeked and indignant. I was given the third degree to find out what had happened. It was lucky we were both of us only fourteen. I lost Ruth and gained an undeserved reputation as a potential libertine.

[34]   So grade-two thinking could be dangerous. It was in this knowledge, at the age of fifteen, that I remember making a comment from the heights of grade two, on the limitations of grade three. One evening I found myself alone in the school hall, preparing it for a party. The door of the headmaster's study was open. I went in. The headmaster had ceased to thump Rodin's Thinker down on the desk as an example to the young. Perhaps he had not found any more candidates, but the statuettes were still there, glimmering and gathering dust on top of the cupboard. I stood on a chair and rearranged them. I stood Venus in her bath towel on the filing cabinet, so that now the top drawer caught its breath in a gasp of sexy excitement. "A-ah!" The portentous Thinker I placed on the edge of the cupboard so that he looked down at the bath towel and waited for it to slip.

[35]   Grade-two thinking, though it filled life with fun and excitement, did not make for content. To find out the deficiencies of our elders bolsters the young ego but does not make for personal security. I found that grade two was not only the power to point out contradictions. It took the swimmer some distance from the shore and left him there, out of his depth. I decided that Pontius Pilate was a typical grade-two thinker. "What is truth?" he said, a very common grade-two thought, but one that is used always as the end of an argument instead of the beginning. There is a still higher grade of thought which says, "What is truth?" and sets out to find it.

[36]   But these grade-one thinkers were few and far between. They did not visit my grammar school in the flesh though they were there in books. I aspired to them, partly because I was ambitious and partly because I now saw my hobby as an unsatisfactory thing if it went no further. If you set out to climb a mountain, however high you climb, you have failed if you cannot reach the top.

[37]   I *did* meet an undeniably grade-one thinker in my first year at Oxford. I was looking over a small bridge in Magdalen Deer Park, and a tiny mus-

CLASSIFICATION

tached and hatted figure came and stood by my side. He was a German who had just fled from the Nazis to Oxford as a temporary refuge. His name was Einstein.

[38] But Professor Einstein knew no English at that time and I knew only two words of German. I beamed at him, trying wordlessly to convey by my bearing all the affection and respect that the English felt for him. It is possible—and I have to make the admission—that I felt here were two grade-one thinkers standing side by side; yet I doubt if my face conveyed more than a formless awe. I would have given my Greek and Latin and French and a good slice of my English for enough German to communicate. But we were divided; he was as inscrutable as my headmaster. For perhaps five minutes we stood together on the bridge, undeniable grade-one thinker and breathless aspirant. With true greatness, Professor Einstein realized that any contact was better than none. He pointed to a trout wavering in midstream.

[39] He spoke: *"Fisch."*

[40] My brain reeled. Here I was, mingling with the great, and yet helpless as the veriest grade-three thinker. Desperately I sought for some sign by which I might convey that I, too, revered pure reason. I nodded vehemently. In a brilliant flash I used up half of my German vocabulary. *"Fisch. Ja. Ja."*

[41] For perhaps another five minutes we stood side by side. Then Professor Einstein, his whole figure still conveying good will and amiability, drifted away out of sight.

[42] I, too, would be a grade-one thinker. I was irreverent at the best of times. Political and religious systems, social customs, loyalties and traditions, they all came tumbling down like so many rotten apples off a tree. This was a fine hobby and a sensible substitute for cricket, since you could play it all the year round. I came up in the end with what must always remain the justification for grade-one thinking, its sign, seal and charter. I devised a coherent system for living. It was a moral system, which was wholly logical. Of course, as I readily admitted, conversion of the world to my way of thinking might be difficult, since my system did away with a number of trifles, such as big business, centralized government, armies, marriage. . . .

[43] It was Ruth all over again. I had some very good friends who stood by me, and still do. But my acquaintances vanished, taking the girls with them. Young women seemed oddly contented with the world as it was. They valued the meaningless ceremony with a ring. Young men, while willing to concede

the chaining sordidness of marriage, were hesitant about abandoning the organizations which they hoped would give them a career. A young man on the first rung of the Royal Navy, while perfectly agreeable to doing away with big business and marriage, got as red-necked as Mr. Houghton when I proposed a world without any battleships in it.

[44] Had the game gone too far? Was it a game any longer? In those prewar days, I stood to lose a great deal, for the sake of a hobby.

[45] Now you are expecting me to describe how I saw the folly of my ways and came back to the warm nest, where prejudices are so often called loyalties, where pointless actions are hallowed into custom by repetition, where we are content to say we think when all we do is feel.

[46] But you would be wrong. I dropped my hobby and turned professional.

[47] If I were to go back to the headmaster's study and find the dusty statuettes still there, I would arrange them differently. I would dust Venus and put her aside, for I have come to love her and know her for the fair thing she is. But I would put the Thinker, sunk in his desperate thought, where there were shadows before him—and at his back, I would put the leopard, crouched and ready to spring.

SUGGESTIONS FOR WRITING

1. Using Fuller's enumerative method, write an analysis of a subject that can properly be divided into several categories: for example, types of professors, types of television commercials, types of politicians, types of magazines, types of lies.

2. Write an essay classifying college students by groups according to their study habits.

3. Following Roberts's organizational structure, write an essay that distinguishes the categories of a selected topic and discusses the uses of those categories. Some possible topics: surfboards, garden tools, rifles, cooking utensils, paints, power tools, fishing baits. Your own hobbies and specialized knowledge should furnish you with additional topics.

4. Any musical group has something in common with other groups of its type yet is identifiable because of unique features. The same is true of any public park, any baseball team, any campus, or any city intersection. Write an essay classifying a category of things (such as emergency vehicle sirens, popular country-music singers, woodwind instruments, track events, sportscasters) and describing how one member of the category differs from others of its type.

5. Consider Francis Bacon's essay; then make a list of books that you have read or used in classes, as well as of other books you know about. Write an essay classifying those books in the three categories: those that should be tasted, those that should be swallowed, and those that should be chewed and digested. If you wish, you may add a fourth category: those that should be stuffed into a garbage can. In preparing this essay it may be interesting to read George Orwell's essay on p. 96.

6. Distinguish between two very different groups of people: dreamers and doers, scholars and athletes, idealists and materialists, pacifists and militarists, believers and agnostics. Using the method of Eastman, create an analogy that immediately clarifies the distinctions; but further show that the categories are perhaps too rigid, that they are moods rather than ways of life, since each person, to some degree at least, manifests both sets of characteristics.

7. Eastman explains that all people have both practical and poetic moods. Analyze your own experiences, ambitions, and tendencies, and write an essay illustrating these two moods in yourself.

COMPARISON AND CONTRAST

We perceive things most readily by their difference from something else. The words on this page stand out because they are printed in black against a white background; the spoken word is distinguished because its sound differs from the sounds and silences around it. We know winter by its contrast to summer, age by its differences from youth.

But perception is only the beginning of knowledge; it is also important to understand. We understand things most readily by their likeness to something else that we already know about. If you do not know what skydiving is like, you get some understanding from the word itself, which tells you that it's like diving; if the experience were described for you as "like swimming in air," you would understand it better, because you already know what it's like to swim in water.

These connections between contrast and perception, between comparison and understanding, have been remarked for centuries. Both Plato and Aristotle made note of them, Aristotle drawing the conclusion that the ability to see similarities among differences and differences among similarities is the mark of genius. Perhaps these connections with perception and understanding help to explain why "compare and contrast" is such a familiar phrase in college examinations. As you see and explain how two things are alike or how they differ, you are demonstrating your ability to think clearly. And as you write an essay of comparison and contrast, you are helping readers to see and understand.

Often the word *comparison* is used to include contrast, somewhat as the word *day* is used to include night (as in "twenty-four hours a day"). But it is important to recognize that the two terms do not refer to precisely the same way of dealing with a topic. When we compare, we show how two things are alike; when we contrast, we show how they differ.

There are subtle and important facts to remember about these two methods. First, it is meaningless to compare things that most readers will think of as identical or almost the same. There would be little purpose in comparing a psychologist and a psychiatrist. But Maya Pines, in "Of Babalawos and Shamans," presents a comparison between psychiatrists and witch doctors, knowing that most readers will think them different until specific similarities are pointed out. Second, it is meaningless to contrast things that are in no way alike. There would be little purpose in contrasting human beings and lumps of coal. But in "The Lord of Creation" Susanne Langer contrasts human beings and animals, knowing that the two are alike in many ways though they differ in one essential.

Comparison and contrast are useful in many kinds of writing. They can help in setting up a classification, in forming a definition, in drawing a description; they may appear in narration or argumentation. In his description of "Steamboat Town" (p. 143) Mark Twain contrasts the sleepiness of the village before the approach of the steamboat and the bustle of the same scene once the boat is heard "a-comin'." In defining *democracy*, Carl Becker (p. 113) compares the word to a Gladstone bag, but the comparison is not his central purpose in the essay.

Seldom is a comparison or a contrast made for its own sake. Usually the two methods serve some further purpose. Jack Richardson, in "Six O'Clock Prayers," for example, compares television newscasts to religious rituals, but his purpose is to satirize the culture that tolerates, even encourages, shallow and meaningless news reporting.

Though comparison and contrast may differ in method, they aim at essentially the same thing. Both clarify a topic by making a reader see it and understand it more clearly than before because of its likeness to or difference from something the reader already knows about.

Maya Pines

OF BABALAWOS AND SHAMANS

A graduate of Barnard College, with an M.A. from Columbia University in 1949, Maya Pines is a free-lance journalist specializing in science, medicine, and education. From 1950 to 1952 she was a reporter for the Women's National News Service *and from 1952 to 1960 a reporter for* Life *magazine. Among her writings are* Health and Disease *(1965), which she co-authored for the Life Science Library,* Revolution in Learning *(1967), and* The Brain Changers: Scientists and the New Mind Control *(1973). She has contributed to numerous periodicals, including* McCall's, *in which the following essay appeared in 1971. In it Pines uses comparison and contrast to sharp effect in presenting news of a forthcoming book by a psychiatrist.*

[1] Going to a psychiatrist is not too different from going to a witch doctor, Dr. E. Fuller Torrey claims. Dr. Torrey—himself a psychiatrist—is a young, bearded, and sideburned special assistant to the director of the National Institute of Mental Health in Bethesda, Maryland. Every summer he and his wife travel to such distant places as Bali and Siberia and the Amazon Basin in search of witch doctors: *babalawos, curanderos, shamans, mgangas,* or *baroom xam-xams,* as they are called locally.

[2] "We'd like to believe that our therapeutic techniques are 'scientific' while those of non-Western therapists are 'magical,'" he says. "Yet they're on exactly the same scientific plane. If one is science, so is the other. If one is magic, so is the other."

[3] The main difference between psychiatrists and witch doctors, he says, is the names they give to diseases. One may blame a childhood experience as the source of a patient's problem, while the other blames the violation of a taboo. Either way the patient comes to realize that someone "understands," and after confessing, crying, or undergoing some other emotional catharsis, he feels much better.

[4] Dr. Torrey became fascinated with witch doctors while spending two years in Ethiopia as a Peace Corps physician. He points out that most of our

From *McCall's,* August 1971. Reprinted by permission.

present techniques were used centuries ago, in other cultures. Shock therapy, for instance, was used 4,000 years ago, when healers applied electric eels to the heads of their patients. Reserpine, a tranquilizer introduced into Western psychiatry in the 1950s, had been used in India and West Africa for centuries. There it was known as an extract of the rauwolfia root.

[5] What about Freudian analysis?

[6] "Oh, boy, *is* there an equivalent!" Dr. Torrey exclaimed happily. "That's one of my favorite examples!" The Iroquois Indians used dream analysis in almost the same way Freud did, he explained. The patient who came before the witch doctor would describe the dreams that troubled him. Then, though he didn't have to lie down, he'd be asked to free-associate about his dream. Finally, the therapist would give his own interpretation of what was wrong. There is no more difference between the Iroquois' technique and Freud's, Torrey maintains, than between the styles of Freudian and Jungian analysts.

[7] Though his comments infuriate some of his colleagues, Dr. Torrey thinks that it will help Western therapists understand which elements of their work are common to all therapy. He hopes his book, *The Mind Game: Witchdoctors and Psychiatrists,* which will be published in November, will teach the West to be less arrogant. Meanwhile, since "they're just as effective as Western therapists," he would like to see Indian and Eskimo *shamans*—who have been discredited because of their resistance to Western culture—given due respect and the same civil service status as public health psychiatrists.

VOCABULARY

Define the following words as they are used in the selection: *therapeutic* [1]; *taboo, catharsis* [3]; *shock therapy, extract* [4]; *Freudian* [5]; *equivalent, free-associate* [6]; *common, arrogant* [7].

QUESTIONS FOR STUDY AND DISCUSSION

1. Pines wastes no time before identifying the subjects of the comparison and contrast. Does the essay promise to emphasize the likenesses or the differences between psychiatrists and witch doctors?

2. What does the description of Dr. Torrey ("young, bearded, sideburned") add to the essay? Are those facts about him significant in any way? Does his formal

COMPARISON AND CONTRAST 59

position give weight to his contention that psychiatrists and witch doctors are similar?

3. What is implied by the range of distant places and the list of foreign terms in paragraph 1?

4. Discuss the connotations of *scientific* and *magical* in paragraph 2. Why do Westerners put so much faith in science? Would Dr. Torrey's statement in this paragraph be applicable to types of therapy other than mental? How are paragraphs 3 through 6 related to paragraph 2?

5. By what means is the contrast between *scientific* and *magical* developed?

6. How many types of therapy are mentioned in paragraphs 3 through 6? Are they inclusive enough to make a reasonably convincing argument?

7. Paragraph 3 moves from a discussion of differences to a statement about similarities—in other words, from contrast to comparison. What is the value of this paragraph structure in this essay?

8. Sigmund Freud (1856–1939) and Carl Jung (1875–1961) both made use of dream interpretation and free association in their systems of therapy. Whereas Freud used dream analysis as a means of exploring a patient's past to reveal the causes of psychological problems, Jung was interested in dreams as they illuminated a person's present problems and aspirations. Does the statement concluding paragraph 6 seem warranted?

9. Does Pines's article give any indication that Dr. Torrey's hopes for the Indian and Eskimo *shamans* will soon be realized? What now stands in the way of the realization of those hopes?

10. It is clear from paragraph 7 that this essay, in addition to being a news report, is a preview of a book. The author is, therefore, merely reporting, not attempting to express ideas of her own. Is she objective in her reporting? Is her attitude toward Torrey's views ever expressed? What devices does the author use to make it clear that she is merely reporting?

11. This essay appeared in "Right Now," a feature of *McCall's*, a monthly magazine of general interest for women. How might the essay have been different if it had been written for an audience of psychiatrists?

12. Pines (and apparently Dr. Torrey) compares Indian and Eskimo *shamans* to "Western therapists." Since Indians and Eskimos also live in the West, the term *Western* has some special connotations here. What are they?

Jack Richardson

SIX O'CLOCK PRAYERS

Jack Richardson (b. 1935), theater critic for Commentary, *has published many articles on cultural and literary issues. He has written several plays, including* The Prodigal *(1960),* Gallows Humor *(1961), and* Xmas in Las Vegas *(1965); and in 1975 he published a philosophical book,* Gambling. *"Six O'Clock Prayers" appeared in* Harper's *in December 1975. Although the essay on its surface is a criticism of television news, it is more importantly an indictment of American habits of viewing and thinking.*

[1] It has long been fashionable for anthropologists to stress the important function of ritual in primitive cultures and to demonstrate how totems and taboos form a communal liturgy that allows a society to come to terms with itself and its environment. Ritual, we are told, gives Bantu and Eskimo a hold on experience, a method of confronting the flux of nature and the caprices of the human spirit which is denied our secular, scientific point of view. The more didactic the anthropologist, the more sternly he warns us that without such rites we sentence ourselves to a life of fragmented purpose, to an existence patched together with random facts and disjointed opinions.

[2] Well, I believe I've found a solution to this need for ceremony in an age out of touch with the rhythms of nature and the formalities of faith. It is the television newscast, a form of community worship that in the rigidness and constancy of its attitudes deserves comparison with the highest mass or the lowest fertility rite, and in the meagerness of its substance perhaps deserves to be rated above most of its rivals. For the successful ritual, after all, is not meant to burden the mind with facts and information or to shock it with novel observation; rather, it is intended as a respite from individual speculation, a stylized assurance that there is stability and sameness in the world on which the tribe can depend. Gesture and incantation, while providing neither news nor explanation, do offer one the chance to make a comfortable covenant with reality and to rest in the sanctuary of prescribed social duty.

[3] For a long time I didn't understand the true nature of television news,

From *Harper's*, December 1975. Copyright 1975 by *Harper's* Magazine. Reprinted by permission.

and I wasted many hours fussing over the carefully crafted emptiness on the screen. But sometime during one of the many reportorial litanies on the Vietnam war, in which a network shaman stood in the standard sacramental rice paddy and intoned the dogma that war is an unpleasant experience, I became enlightened. I realized that I was not supposed to be receiving from such broadcasts either startling facts or probing explanations; instead, I was being offered a display of sanctified movements and words which turned reality into a tidy, predictable companion. War, the secular world's highest moral dilemma, gradually was purged of all human intrigue and responsibility and became a comfortably vague condition of nature. I and my fellow citizens could look upon the worst techniques of slaughter and, in lieu of any evidence that human intelligence and choice were behind them, could feel that our obligations to human suffering had been discharged simply by our observing it regularly and by our feeling, until the commercial, a deep and righteous melancholy.

[4] When I grasped the idea that television news was more an act of communion than of communication, it became easier to understand why the same categories of events were repeated over and over again, why the sequence of the ceremony rarely altered, and why one was never startled or intrigued by the questions and responses chanted between reporter and his subject. I was being treated to a way of looking at the world that purported to be concerned with the hard data of reality, but which was in fact a carefully constructed design in which nothing untoward or unmanageable could intrude that might cast doubt on the justness of Walter Cronkite's closing statement, "That's the way it is." Feeling painlessly informed, my task as a good member of the community fulfilled, I could go out and meet others who'd attended the same visual observances and discuss with confidence the world the networks had given us to believe in that day.

[5] And what a stable world it was. Mayhem, treachery, disaster, chaos became so smoothly stylized that it mattered little if the pictures on the screen were of a terrorist bombing, a Peruvian earthquake, a malfeasant President, or an urban riot. Such, after all, I learned, is the basic stuff of serious news, and so long as the consequences of these events could be softened by the priestly analyses of an Eric Sevareid or the folksy homiletics of a David Brinkley, I felt more reassured than unnerved by the daily constancy of disaster.

[6] Of course, even the most ceremonial societies need occasional respites from the prescribed order of things, and occasionally the television news would vary the sequence of its secular service. A Super Bowl or World Series might give sports a position of prominence in the scheme of ceremony, or an

election might, like a rowdy harvest festival, infuse the newscast with a giddy sense of change and possibility. Also, lest it ever be felt that the best themes of catastrophe were becoming too generalized and abstract to impress the less imaginative in the audience, there would be occasional human-interest interpolations, short sacrifices of individual dignity in which mothers of murdered sons and victims of terminal diseases were displayed and interviewed. Prodded by reporters until they wailed incoherently or uttered doughty banalities, these pungent examples of ordinary agony were quickly turned by the reporters' earnest observations into pleasant parables of suffering that dissolved any discomfort I might have felt at observing a stranger's private anguish. Soon these little portraits of despair and dispossession came to seem like well-rehearsed liturgical dramas in which members of the community took turns as performers, and my response to them actually became aesthetic, a cultivated appreciation of the artistry with which a senior citizen wept over his Social Security diet of dog food and tuna fish, or a critical disapproval of the overdone pluckiness of the bandaged survivor of an air crash who joked too loudly about his third-degree burns while thanking God that he was chosen out of a passenger list of more than 100 to appear on the six o'clock news.

[7] Day after day, mornings, evenings, and nights, television allowed me to turn on my set and be reassured that the world was still fixed in the same categories of international, domestic, and human-interest calamity, and that the same chiefs and holy men were conferring, legislating, and compromising to ensure that the world stayed the same while it changed for the better. The newspapers, what few there were left, came to seem like disorganized bulletins from a world I less and less recognized. They were cluttered with disconcerting details and attitudes, with bothersome reports on books being written, sciences being expanded and other examples of individual activity that stirred in me disquieting throbs of ambition. But worse than this, they permitted the individual his own variations of worship: if he found the exordium of headlines not to his liking, he could skip immediately to the sports page; if he found his need for individual drama satisfied in the chess column, he might actually toss his paper away before subjecting himself to the lamentations of a rape victim or the philosophy of a mass murderer.

[8] Reading his paper when and where he chose, twisting it in public into antisocial folds so that no one could share the news over his shoulder, the newspaper votary found that, left alone with a printed view of the world, he faced a complex environment in which events such as stock market prices and racing results threatened him with personal harm and involvement. The freedom he had to skim the front-page columns on the Middle, Near, or Far East crises was paid for by a feeling of estrangement from community seriousness,

and if he tried to make up for his lapses he found himself floundering among contradictions, ambiguities, and the subtle shifts of details that television had learned to smooth out of its depictions of the world. But most disconcerting of all for the newspaper reader was the gnawing suspicion that even a single day in the life of this planet could not be grasped and shaped for easy comprehension; indeed, sometimes between the printed lines he seemed to glimpse alternative possibilities to the facts and tone of stories he read, and with no one except himself to rely on as an arbiter of truth, with no "That's the way it is" to signify an authorized version of reality, days passed by in doubtful outline making him feel that some extraordinary personal effort was demanded on his part in order to be fairly confident that a connection existed between the events of his time and the news they were turned into.

[9] Confronted with a choice between this ragged *Weltanschauung* of print and the ceremonial blandness of television, who wouldn't prefer the latter? To be bound at a prescribed time to millions of others, to share with them an identical image and text, to be shown again and again the same polished day divided into the same neat sections of significance, to be assured by the traditional sign-off of the on-the-spot network subaltern who gives his name as testimony to the truth of what we've witnessed, to be convinced by immediate and portentous comment that we have participated in a day of deep and novel events and fully understood their meaning—what more could one ask for in the way of ritual than all this? Well, perhaps one thing more. A reasonable length. When I sought the image of the world in newspapers and worshiped information in my own way, there was no end to the devotional duties demanded of me. Anything less than three hours on the *New York Times* seemed a sin of omission, and, even if three times that amount was spent on the day's Scriptures, I always felt that I'd left undone some important act of devotion, and that I'd no right to cease studying the high deeds of the day and take to the frivolous pleasures of my personal life. But now I am told exactly when devotion has ended. The same voice that speaks the newscast's thematic envoi also grants me permission to enjoy the game show or nature program that will immediately follow. After such a clear dispensation, I can then, in good conscience and with an empty mind, watch a herd of animals threatened with extinction or the hysteria of a housewife as she wins a matching bedroom set.

VOCABULARY

Define the following words as they are used in the selection: *totems, taboos, liturgy, flux, caprices, didactic, rites* [1]; *meagerness, stylized, incanta-*

tion, sanctuary [2]; *litanies, sacramental, sanctified, secular* [3]; *mayhem, malfeasant, urban, homiletics* [5]; *respites, infuse, giddy, interpolations, doughty, banalities, pungent, parables* [6]; *exordium, lamentations, votary, ambiguities, arbiter* [8]; Weltanschauung, *blandness, subaltern, portentous, envoi* [9].

QUESTIONS FOR STUDY AND DISCUSSION

1. In his opening paragraph Richardson establishes a tone, revealing through his choice of words that he does not fully agree with the anthropologists who stress the importance of ritual in societies. What words and phrases reveal his attitude toward such anthropologists?

2. By comparison and contrast Richardson places television newscasts in a category. What category?

3. *Irony* may be defined as the use of words to mean the opposite of their literal effect. Is Richardson serious or ironic in classifying television newscasts as "a form of community worship" comparable to the high mass or the fertility rite?

4. What sort of news report brought Richardson to the "enlightenment" that television news is not intended to probe or inform? Do you believe his experience was a typical one for viewers?

5. Richardson refers in paragraph 3 to a "network shaman." What is a shaman? (Compare his use of the word with that of Maya Pines in "Of Babalawos and Shamans.") How does Richardson's use of the word help him establish his classification of television newscasts?

6. Richardson supports his thesis by using many words such as *liturgy* and *incantation* that suggest the formalities of public worship. Make a list of at least ten other words from the essay that suggest the same comparison.

7. In paragraph 7 Richardson sets up a contrast between television and newspapers as news media. How does this contrast contribute emphasis to his thesis? Is his statement that newspapers "came to seem like disorganized bulletins" a serious charge against the print medium?

8. Considering again your answer to question 3, do you find that Richardson's tone in paragraph 8 is consistent with that of earlier paragraphs? Cite one sentence that convinces you of his intent. What is there about that sentence that makes his tone unmistakable?

9. Paragraph 9 is one of the longest in the essay. Could it effectively be broken into two paragraphs? At what point might it be broken?

10. Richardson has used throughout his essay a technique of turning from the sublime to the ridiculous—and classifying the ridiculous as sublime. How does that technique serve his purpose? How do the two kinds of television shows exemplified in the final sentence show that technique in action?

Jacob Brackman

THE PUT-ON

Jacob Brackman has done extensive critical writing for magazines. His book The Put-On: Modern Fooling and Modern Mistrust *(1971) includes this essay, which was first published in* The New Yorker *in a somewhat different form. The essay uses comparison and contrast as chief means of defining a contemporary form of social (perhaps antisocial?) behavior, a kind of fooling that differs in motive and manner from other kinds of hoaxes.*

[1] Though there are suddenly many more of them, conversational put-ons are related to old-fashioned joshing and kidding, or to the sort of joke that Southerners call "funning" and Englishmen call "taking a mickey out of" someone. Not unlike the put-on, these older cousins depend upon a certain gullibility in the victim. They are like April-fool gags, perpetrated deadpan to get the victim to believe something that isn't so. Miniature hoaxes, their raison d'être is the surprise revelation of truth ("I was only kidding" or "It was just a gag") and laughter at the fall guy's credulity. Naturally, there were, and still are, habitual kidders or practical jokers. But the object of kidding, as of hoaxing, is always manifest: to *pass off* untruth as truth just for the fun of it. Ideally, there's no doubt in anyone's mind. At first, the victim believes the false to be true, whereas the kidder knows the truth. Then, the gulling accomplished, the kidder lets the victim know he's been taken for a ride. This payoff is the kidder's goal. With kidding and other hoax-derived precedents, the perpetrator smooths the rug out, has you stand on it, and then suddenly yanks it out from under you.

[2] The put-on is more like one of those irregularly moving platforms at an amusement park. The victim must constantly struggle to maintain his balance, constantly awkward, even (perhaps especially) when the floor *stops* moving for an instant; i.e., a "straight" moment, which makes the victim feel he has been paranoid. As he readjusts himself to this vision, the floor, so to speak, starts moving again. If conversation with a kidder is spiced by bosh, conversation with a put-on artist is a process of escalating confusion and distrust. He

From *The Put-On: Modern Fooling and Modern Mistrust* by Jacob Brackman. Text copyright © 1967, 1971 by Jacob Brackman. Reprinted by permission of Bantam Books, Inc.

doesn't deal in isolated little tricks; rather, he has developed a pervasive style of relating to others that perpetually casts what he says into doubt. The put-on is an *open-end* form. That is to say, it is rarely climaxed by having the "truth" set straight—when a truth, indeed, exists. "Straight" discussion, when one of the participants is putting the others on, is soon subverted and eventually sabotaged by uncertainty. His intentions, and his opinions, remain cloudy.

[3] We remember the kidder as a good-natured, teasing sort—that moment when he rendered his victim absurd was quickly dissipated in the general laughter that followed. The put-on artist draws out that derisive moment; the gull has time to reflect (What's he up to? . . . He's trying to make a monkey out of me. . . . How should I respond?), and the joke's latent malice wells close to the surface. As the put-on pursues its course (at times while the subject matter shifts), it becomes clear that the victim is the butt of a generalized ridicule. Occasionally, a victim will try to explain away his confusion by assuming that the put-on artist is "just being ironical"—that he really means precisely the reverse of everything he says. This interpretation is hardly more helpful than taking put-ons at face value. Irony properly suggests the *opposite* of what is explicitly stated, by means of peripheral clues—tone of voice, accompanying gestures, stylistic exaggeration, or previous familiarity with the ironist's real opinions. Thus, for "Brutus is an honorable man" we understand "Brutus is a traitor." Irony is unsuccessful when misunderstood. But the put-on, inherently, *cannot* be understood.

VOCABULARY

Define the following words as they are used in the selection: *perpetrated, raison d'être, credulity, gulling* [1]; *paranoid, bosh, pervasive, subverted* [2]; *derisive, latent, peripheral* [3].

QUESTIONS FOR STUDY AND DISCUSSION

1. In this selection Brackman uses the method of comparison and contrast to serve the central purpose of definition. Can you find a third pattern of exposition also put to work in this selection? What is it?

2. As our introduction to the pattern of comparison and contrast has said, it is meaningless to contrast things that are in no way alike. In what ways has Brackman shown that the things he contrasts are in some respects alike?

3. Where does Brackman begin to show the contrast between his topic and

the other sorts of "gulling"? What rhetorical device does he use to introduce that contrast?

4. What, according to Brackman, is the essential difference between the put-on and irony?

5. Much of the literature and popular entertainment of the last decade in America has been loose in form and free-wheeling in manner, suggesting the contemporary belief that life itself is without order, without finish. Is the put-on a reflection of that attitude toward life? How?

6. "We remember the kidder as a good-natured, teasing sort," says Brackman. Does he make this point a feature of his contrast? How? If the *raison d'être* of kidding and hoaxing is "the surprise revelation of truth," what is the *raison d'être* of the put-on?

7. In view of Brackman's definition of the put-on, what evidence do you find to assure you that the essay itself is not a put-on?

8. Nowhere in his three paragraphs has Brackman given a succinct, one-sentence definition of the put-on. Read the introduction on "Definition" (pp. 108–110); then write a one-sentence definition of the put-on, using characteristics established in the Brackman essay.

Susanne K. Langer

THE LORD OF CREATION

To philosopher Susanne K. Langer (b. 1895) human beings have one special advantage that distinguishes them from other intelligent animals: the ability to use language. In this essay, which has been widely reprinted since its first appearance in 1944, she suggests the specific nature of the human advantage. Among Professor Langer's other writings are Philosophy in a New Key (1942), Feeling and Form (1953), Problems of Art (1957), *and the two-volume* Mind: An Essay on Human Feeling (1967–1973).

[1]   A symbol is not the same thing as a sign; that is a fact that psychologists and philosophers often overlook. All intelligent animals use signs; so do we. To them as well as to us sounds and smells and motions are signs of food, danger, the presence of other beings, or of rain or storm. Furthermore, some animals not only attend to signs but produce them for the benefit of others.

Reprinted from the January 1944 issue of *Fortune Magazine* by special permission; © 1944 Time, Inc.

Dogs bark at the door to be let in; rabbits thump to call each other; the cooing of doves and the growl of a wolf defending his kill are unequivocal signs of feelings and intentions to be reckoned with by other creatures.

[2] We use signs just as animals do, though with considerably more elaboration. We stop at red lights and go on green; we answer calls and bells, watch the sky for coming storms, read trouble or promise or anger in each other's eyes. That is animal intelligence raised to the human level. Those of us who are dog lovers can probably all tell wonderful stories of how high our dogs have sometimes risen in the scale of clever sign interpretation and sign using.

[3] A sign is anything that announces the existence or the imminence of some event, the presence of a thing or a person, or a change in a state of affairs. There are signs of the weather, signs of danger, signs of future good or evil, signs of what the past has been. In every case a sign is closely bound up with something to be noted or expected in experience. It is always a part of the situation to which it refers, though the reference may be remote in space and time. In so far as we are led to note or expect the signified event we are making correct use of a sign. This is the essence of rational behavior, which animals show in varying degrees. It is entirely realistic, being closely bound up with the actual objective course of history—learned by experience, and cashed in or voided by further experience.

[4] If man had kept to the straight and narrow path of sign using, he would be like the other animals, though perhaps a little brighter. He would not talk, but grunt and gesticulate and point. He would make his wishes known, give warnings, perhaps develop a social system like that of bees and ants, with such a wonderful efficiency of communal enterprise that all men would have plenty to eat, warm apartments—all exactly alike and perfectly convenient—to live in, and everybody could and would sit in the sun or by the fire, as the climate demanded, not talking, but just basking, with every want satisfied, most of his life. The young would romp and make love, the old would sleep, the middle-aged would do the routine work almost unconsciously and eat a great deal. But that would be the life of a social, superintelligent, purely sign-using animal.

[5] To us who are human, it does not sound very glorious. We want to go places and do things, own all sorts of gadgets that we do not absolutely need, and when we sit down to take it easy we want to talk. Rights and property, social position, special talents and virtues, and above all our ideas, are what we live for. We have gone off on a tangent that takes us far away from the mere biological cycle that animal generations accomplish; and that is because we can use not only signs but symbols.

[6] A symbol differs from a sign in that it does not announce the presence of the object, the being, condition, or whatnot, which is its meaning, but merely *brings this thing to mind*. It is not a mere "substitute sign" to which we react as though it were the object itself. The fact is that our reaction to hearing a person's name is quite different from our reaction to the person himself. There are certain rare cases where a symbol stands directly for its meaning: in religious experience, for instance, the Host is not only a symbol but a Presence. But symbols in the ordinary sense are not mystic. They are the same sort of thing that ordinary signs are; only they do not call our attention to something necessarily present or to be physically dealt with—they call up merely a conception of the thing they "mean."

[7] The difference between a sign and a symbol is, in brief, that a sign causes us to think or act *in face of* the thing signified, whereas a symbol causes us to think *about* the thing symbolized. Therein lies the great importance of symbolism for human life, its power to make this life so different from any other animal biography that generations of men have found it incredible to suppose that they were of purely zoological origin. A sign is always embedded in reality, in a present that emerges from the actual past and stretches to the future; but a symbol may be divorced from reality altogether. It may refer to what is *not* the case, to a mere idea, a figment, a dream. It serves, therefore, to liberate thought from the immediate stimuli of a physically present world; and that liberation marks the essential difference between human and nonhuman mentality. Animals think, but they think *of* and *at* things; men think primarily *about* things. Words, pictures, and memory images are symbols that may be combined and varied in a thousand ways. The result is a symbolic structure whose meaning is a complex of all their respective meanings, and this kaleidoscope of *ideas* is the typical product of the human brain that we call the "stream of thought."

[8] The process of transforming all direct experience into imagery or into that supreme mode of symbolic expression, language, has so completely taken possession of the human mind that it is not only a special talent but a dominant, organic need. All our sense impressions leave their traces in our memory not only as signs disposing our practical reactions in the future but also as symbols, images representing our *ideas* of things; and the tendency to manipulate ideas, to combine and abstract, mix and extend them by playing with symbols, is man's outstanding characteristic. It seems to be what his brain most naturally and spontaneously does. Therefore his primitive mental function is not judging reality, but *dreaming his desires*.

[9] Dreaming is apparently a basic function of human brains, for it is free

and unexhausting like our metabolism, heartbeat, and breath. It is easier to dream than not to dream, as it is easier to breathe than to refrain from breathing. The symbolic character of dreams is fairly well established. Symbol mongering, on this ineffectual, uncritical level, seems to be instinctive, the fulfillment of an elementary need rather than the purposeful exercise of a high and difficult talent.

[10]   The special power of man's mind rests on the evolution of this special activity, not on any transcendently high development of animal intelligence. We are not immeasurably higher than other animals; we are different. We have a biological need and with it a biological gift that they do not share.

[11]   Because man has not only the ability but the constant need of *conceiving* what has happened to him, what surrounds him, what is demanded of him—in short, of symbolizing nature, himself, and his hopes and fears—he has a constant and crying need of *expression*. What he cannot express, he cannot conceive; what he cannot conceive is chaos, and fills him with terror.

[12]   If we bear in mind this all-important craving for expression we get a new picture of man's behavior; for from this trait spring his powers and his weaknesses. The process of symbolic transformation that all our experiences undergo is nothing more nor less than the process of *conception*, which underlies the human faculties of abstraction and imagination.

[13]   When we are faced with a strange or difficult situation, we cannot react directly, as other creatures do, with flight, aggression, or any such simple instinctive pattern. Our whole reaction depends on how we manage to conceive the situation—whether we cast it in a definite dramatic form, whether we see it as a disaster, a challenge, a fulfillment of doom, or a fiat of the Divine Will. In words or dreamlike images, in artistic or religious or even in cynical form, we must *construe* the events of life. There is great virtue in the figure of speech, "I can *make* nothing of it," to express a failure to understand something. Thought and memory are processes of *making* the thought content and the memory image; the pattern of our ideas is given by the symbols through which we express them. And in the course of manipulating those symbols we inevitably distort the original experience, as we abstract certain features of it, embroider and reinforce those features with other ideas, until the conception we project on the screen of memory is quite different from anything in our real history.

[14]   Conception is a necessary and elementary process; what we do with our conceptions is another story. That is the entire history of human culture—of

intelligence and morality, folly and superstition, ritual, language, and the arts —all the phenomena that set man apart from, and above, the rest of the animal kingdom. As the religious mind has to make all human history a drama of sin and salvation in order to define its own moral attitudes, so a scientist wrestles with the mere presentation of "the facts" before he can reason about them. The process of *envisaging* facts, values, hopes, and fears underlies our whole behavior pattern; and this process is reflected in the evolution of an extraordinary phenomenon found always, and only, in human societies—the phenomenon of language.

[15] Language is the highest and most amazing achievement of the symbolistic human mind. The power it bestows is almost inestimable, for without it anything properly called "thought" is impossible. The birth of language is the dawn of humanity. The line between man and beast—between the highest ape and the lowest savage—is the language line. Whether the primitive Neanderthal man was anthropoid or human depends less on his cranial capacity, his upright posture, or even his use of tools and fire, than on one issue we shall probably never be able to settle—whether or not he spoke.

VOCABULARY

Define the following words as they are used in the selection: *symbol, sign, unequivocal, reckoned* [1]; *imminence, essence, voided* [3]; *gesticulate, communal* [4]; *tangent* [5]; *mystic* [6]; *zoological, divorced, figment, stimuli, complex, respective, kaleidoscope* [7]; *imagery, abstract* [8]; *metabolism, mongering* [9]; *transcendently* [10]; *conceiving* [11]; *transformation* [12]; *aggression, fiat, cynical, construe* [13]; *ritual, phenomena, envisaging* [14]; *bestows, inestimable, anthropoid, cranial* [15].

QUESTIONS FOR STUDY AND DISCUSSION

1. Give your attention to the first five paragraphs, which discuss, define, and give examples of the animal and human uses of signs. The opening sentence of paragraph 1 suggests that Langer will discuss primarily the difference between signs and symbols, perhaps to the end of defining them. But symbols are not mentioned again until paragraph 5. What, then, is the principal concern of these paragraphs? What two things are being compared? How does a discussion of signs serve in making the comparison?

2. How do intelligent animals and human beings use signs in the same way? How do their uses of signs differ? What is the significance of that difference?

3. What would human life be like, according to Langer, if man's only means of communication were through signs? What would be lacking?

4. Point out how Langer uses, in paragraphs 4 and 5, both comparison and contrast to lead to the sentence that concludes paragraph 5.

5. Give your attention to paragraphs 6 through 8. Note how they lead to a concluding sentence (beginning with *Therefore*) in much the same way as do paragraphs 1 through 5. What is the subject of paragraphs 6 through 8? What two things are being compared?

6. How, according to Langer, do signs and symbols differ? How does that difference mark "the essential difference" between human and nonhuman mentality?

7. How does language relate to symbols? How is language dependent upon the ability to manipulate symbols?

8. Does Langer's use of the word *dreaming* in the phrase "*dreaming his desires*" [8] seem to be restricted to the dreaming that accompanies sleep? Is the discussion of dreaming in paragraph 9 concerned with sleep dreaming? What is meant by the phrase "symbol mongering"?

9. What biological difference between animals and human beings does "dreaming" signify?

10. Each of paragraphs 11 through 14 contains italicized words. How do these terms relate to the "special activity" [10] of dreaming? Are they synonyms for *dreaming*?

11. How does man's "special activity" define his humanness? How does it make him not only higher than but also different from animals?

12. Is this essay a comparison of signs and symbols or a comparison of animals and humans developed through the distinction between signs and symbols?

FOR FURTHER ANALYSIS

Anne Roiphe

CONFESSIONS OF A FEMALE CHAUVINIST SOW

Anne Roiphe (b. 1935) was graduated from Sarah Lawrence College and later studied in Germany. Herself a mother of five daugh-

From *New York Magazine*, October 30, 1972. Copyright © 1972 by the NYM Corp. Reprinted with the permission of *New York Magazine*.

ters, she has something to say to women who have of late pursued the battle of the sexes with anti-male slogans born of prejudice, and uses comparison and contrast to throw new light upon the attitudes of women toward men. This essay first appeared in the magazine New York *in 1972. Among books by Anne Roiphe are* Digging Out *(1968),* Up the Sandbox *(1971), and* Long Division *(1973).*

[1]   I once married a man I thought was totally unlike my father and I imagined a whole new world of freedom emerging. Five years later it was clear even to me—floating face down in a wash of despair—that I had simply chosen a replica of my handsome daddy-true. The updated version spoke English like an angel but—good God!—underneath he was my father exactly: wonderful, but not the right man for me.

[2]   Most people I know have at one time or another been fouled up by their childhood experiences. Patterns tend to sink into the unconscious only to reappear, disguised, unseen, like marionette strings, pulling us this way or that. Whatever ails people—keeps them up at night, tossing and turning—also ails movements no matter how historically huge or politically important. The women's movement cannot remake consciousness, or reshape the future, without acknowledging and shedding all the unnecessary and ugly baggage of the past. It's easy enough now to see where men have kept us out of clubs, baseball games, graduate schools; it's easy enough to recognize the hidden directions that limit Sis to cake-baking and Junior to bridge-building; it's now possible for even Miss America herself to identify what *they* have done to us, and, of course, *they* have and *they* did and *they* are. . . . But along the way we also developed our own hidden prejudices, class assumptions and an anti-male humor and collection of expectations that gave us, like all oppressed groups, a secret sense of superiority (co-existing with a poor self-image—it's not news that people can believe two contradictory things at once).

[3]   Listen to any group that suffers materially and socially. They have a lexicon with which they tease the enemy: ofay, goy, honky gringo. "Poor pale devils," said Malcolm X loud enough for us to hear, although blacks had joked about that to each other for years. Behind some of the women's liberation thinking lurk the rumors, the prejudices, the defense systems of generations of oppressed women whispering in the kitchen together, presenting one face to their menfolk and another to their card clubs, their mothers and sisters. All this is natural enough but potentially dangerous in a revolutionary situation in which you hope to create a future that does not mirror the past. The hidden anti-male feelings, a result of the old system, will foul us up if they are allowed to persist.

[4] During my teen years I never left the house on my Saturday night dates without my mother slipping me a few extra dollars—mad money, it was called. I'll explain what it was for the benefit of the new generation in which people just sleep with each other: the fellow was supposed to bring me home, lead me safely through the asphalt jungle, protect me from slithering snakes, rapists and the like. But my mother and I knew young men were apt to drink too much, to slosh down so many rye-and-gingers that some hero might well lead me in front of an oncoming bus, smash his daddy's car into Tiffany's window or, less gallantly, throw up on my new dress. Mad money was for getting home on your own, no matter what form of insanity your date happened to evidence. Mad money was also a wallflower's rope ladder; if the guy you came with suddenly fancied someone else, well, you didn't have to stay there and suffer, you could go home. Boys were fickle and likely to be unkind; my mother and I knew that, as surely as we knew they tried to make you do things in the dark they wouldn't respect you for afterwards, and in fact would spread the word and spoil your rep. Boys liked to be flattered; if you made them feel important they would eat out of your hand. So talk to them about their interests, don't alarm them with displays of intelligence—we all knew that, we groups of girls talking into the wee hours of the night in a kind of easy companionship we thought impossible with boys. Boys were prone to have a good time, get you pregnant, and then pretend they didn't know your name when you came knocking on their door for finances or comfort. In short, we believed boys were less moral than we were. They appeared to be hypocritical, self-seeking, exploitative, untrustworthy and very likely to be showing off their precious masculinity. I never had a girl friend I thought would be unkind or embarrass me in public. I never expected a girl to lie to me about her marks or sports skill or how good she was in bed. Altogether—without anyone's directly coming out and saying so—I gathered that men were sexy, powerful, very interesting, but not very nice, not very moral, humane and tender, like us. Girls played fairly while men, unfortunately, reserved their honor for the battlefield.

[5] Why are there laws insisting on alimony and child support? Well, everyone knows that men don't have an instinct to protect their young and, given half a chance, with the moon in the right phase, they will run off and disappear. Everyone assumes a mother will not let her child starve, yet it is necessary to legislate that a father must not do so. We are taught to accept the idea that men are less than decent; their charms may be manifold but their characters are riddled with faults. To this day I never blink if I hear that a man has gone to find his fortune in South America, having left his pregnant wife, his blind mother and taken the family car. I still gasp in horror when I hear of a woman leaving her asthmatic infant for a rock group in Taos because I can't

seem to avoid the assumption that men are naturally heels and women the ordained carriers of what little is moral in our dubious civilization.

[6] My mother never gave me mad money thinking I would ditch a fellow for some other guy or that I would pass out drunk on the floor. She knew I would be considerate of my companion because, after all, I was more mature than the boys that gathered about. Why was I more mature? Women just are people-oriented; they learn to be empathetic at an early age. Most English students (students interested in humanity, not artifacts) are women. Men and boys—so the myth goes—conceal their feelings and lose interest in anybody else's. Everyone knows that even little boys can tell the difference between one kind of a car and another—proof that their souls are mechanical, their attention directed to the non-human.

[7] I remember shivering in the cold vestibule of a famous men's athletic club. Women and girls are not permitted inside the club's door. What are they doing in there, I asked? They're naked, said my mother, they're sweating, jumping up and down a lot, telling each other dirty jokes and bragging about their stock market exploits. Why can't we go in? I asked. Well, my mother told me, they're afraid we'd laugh at them.

[8] The prejudices of childhood are hard to outgrow. I confess that every time my business takes me past that club, I shudder. Images of large bellies resting on massage tables and flaccid penises rising and falling with the Dow Jones average flash through my head. There it is, chauvinism waving its cancerous tentacles from the depths of my psyche.

[9] Minorities automatically feel superior to the oppressor because, after all, they are not hurting anybody. In fact, they feel morally better. The old canard that women need love, men need sex—believed for too long by both sexes—attributes moral and spiritual superiority to women and makes of men beasts whose urges send them prowling into the night. This false division of good and bad, placing deforming pressures on everyone, doesn't have to contaminate the future. We know that the assumptions we make about each other become a part of the cultural air we breathe and, in fact, become social truths. Women who want equality must be prepared to give it and to believe in it, and in order to do that it is not enough to state that you are as good as any man, but also it must be stated that he is as good as you and both will be humans together. If we want men to share in the care of the family in a new way, we must assume them as capable of consistent loving tenderness as we.

[10] I rummage about and find in my thinking all kinds of anti-male prejudices. Some are just jokes and others I will have a hard time abandoning. First,

I share an emotional conviction with many sisters that women given power would not create wars. Intellectually I know that's ridiculous; great queens have waged war before; the likes of Lurleen Wallace, Pat Nixon and Mrs. General Lavelle can be depended upon in the future to guiltlessly condemn to death other people's children in the name of some ideal of their own. Little girls, of course, don't take toy guns out of their hip pockets and say "Pow, pow" to all their neighbors and friends like the average well-adjusted little boy. However, if we gave little girls the six-shooters, we would soon have double the pretend body count.

[11] Aggression is not, as I secretly think, a male-sex-linked characteristic: brutality is masculine only by virtue of opportunity. True, there are 1,000 Jack the Rippers for every Lizzie Borden, but that surely is the result of social forms. Women as a group are indeed more masochistic than men. The practical result of this division is that women seem nicer and kinder, but when the world changes, women will have a fuller opportunity to be just as rotten as men and there will be fewer claims of female moral superiority.

[12] Now that I am entering early middle age, I hear many women complaining of husbands and ex-husbands who are attracted to younger females. This strikes the older woman as unfair, of course. But I remember a time when I thought all boys around my age and grade were creeps and bores. I wanted to go out with an older man: a senior or, miraculously, a college man. I had a certain contempt for my coevals, not realizing that the freshman in college I thought so desirable, was some older girl's creep. Some women never lose that contempt for men of their own age. That isn't fair either and may be one reason why some sensible men of middle years find solace in young women.

[13] I remember coming home from school one day to find my mother's card game dissolved in hysterical laughter. The cards were floating in black rivers of running mascara. What was so funny? A woman named Helen was lying on a couch pretending to be her husband with a cold. She was issuing demands for orange juice, aspirin, suggesting a call to a specialist, complaining of neglect, of fate's cruel finger, of heat, of cold, of sharp pains on the bridge of the nose that might indicate brain involvement. What was so funny? The ladies explained to me that all men behave just like that with colds, they are reduced to temper tantrums by simple nasal congestion, men cannot stand any little physical discomfort—on and on the laughter went.

[14] The point of this vignette is the nature of the laughter—us laughing at them, us feeling superior to them, us ridiculing them behind their backs. If

they were doing it to us we'd call it male chauvinist pigness; if we do it to them, it is inescapably female chauvinist sowness and, whatever its roots, it leads to the same isolation. Boys are messy, boys are mean, boys are rough, boys are stupid and have sloppy handwriting. A cacophony of childhood memories rushes through my head, balanced, of course, by all the well-documented feelings of inferiority and envy. But the important thing, the hard thing, is to wipe the slate clean, to start again without the meanness of the past. That's why it's so important that the women's movement not become anti-male and allow its most prejudiced spokesmen total leadership. The much-chewed-over abortion issue illustrates this. The women's-liberation position, insisting on a woman's right to determine her own body's destiny, leads in fanatical extreme to a kind of emotional immaculate conception in which the father is not judged even half-responsible—he has no rights, and no consideration is to be given to his concern for either the woman or the fetus.

[15] Woman, who once was abandoned and disgraced by an unwanted pregnancy, has recently arrived at a new pride of ownership or disposal. She has traveled in a straight line that still excludes her sexual partner from an equal share in the wanted or unwanted pregnancy. A better style of life may develop from an assumption that men are as human as we. Why not ask the child's father if he would like to bring up the child? Why not share decisions, when possible, with the male? If we cut them out, assuming an old-style indifference on their part, we perpetuate the ugly divisiveness that has characterized relations between the sexes so far.

[16] Hard as it is for many of us to believe, women are not really superior to men in intelligence or humanity—they are only equal.

SUGGESTIONS FOR WRITING

1. Write an essay of comparison and contrast using one of these pairs as topic: football and warfare, music and noise, marriage and slavery, liberal and conservative, theory and practice, fact and opinion, friend and acquaintance, work and play.

2. With Pines's "Of Babalawos and Shamans" as a guide, write an essay comparing two topics that you think may have much in common although they are usually thought of as different. Some suggested topics: science and religion, beauty contests and pagan rituals, political parties and street gangs, professors and preachers, alcoholics and television viewers, shy people and showoffs.

3. To see ourselves as others see us would be a shock—but perhaps a valuable one. Write an essay comparing and contrasting your view of yourself with the view

you believe one other person has of you (a sister, brother, mother, boyfriend, girlfriend, teacher).

4. Said a wise man (or a wag), "I'm not the person I used to be—and I never was." Write an essay of comparison and contrast using as topic yourself today and yourself ten years ago. Be sure to give your essay purpose beyond the mere comparison and contrast; select for it some point, such as the idea that our self-concepts do not always square with realities, or that one should never look back.

5. Most of us have had the experience of reading a book and seeing a movie made from the same story. Consider one such experience of your own and write a comparison or contrast essay making the point that (as you see it) the screen or the printed page is the more effective medium.

6. The phrase "food for thought" is based upon a metaphor comparing abstract ideas, or thinking, to something edible. Francis Bacon bases his essay "Of Studies" (p. 37) on that metaphor, though he considers thinking as embodied in books. Select an abstract idea (such as love, friendship, happiness, hate, poverty, loneliness) and write an essay comparing it to some concrete thing (such as a compass, an acid, the sea, a mountain, a bird, a snake, a candle). Remember that you are trying to make your reader understand more about the abstract idea by putting it in terms of the concrete thing.

7. Write an essay comparing and contrasting the first-hand experience of an event (such as a sports event) and the experience of the same thing via television. Give your essay a thesis, or point, trying to show that the event has different effects and better effects seen (as you prefer) either directly or on television.

CAUSE AND EFFECT

Discovering the causes of things is somewhat more complex than explaining a process. The writer of exposition, turning to questions of cause and effect, faces some of the same problems that a scientist faces in the quest for *why* things are as they are. The writer must guard against too much intrusion of personality, too quick a readiness to accept untested evidence, and too eager a wish to convince.

To ascribe anything to a cause is to draw a conclusion by the method of **inductive reasoning** (see p. 256): A number of specific facts are observed and a generalization is drawn that explains and is supported by all those facts. Since it is seldom possible to observe all facts relevant to anything, a generalization is often reached that is less than perfect: It is a statement of *probable truth* rather than absolute truth. The writer of a cause-effect essay must be aware that the generalization is at best only probable.

To reach an even probable conclusion, the writer must take great care in dealing with the facts, the evidence. The facts must be *accurate*; the writer cannot merely assume the truth of statements, for a conclusion based upon false evidence is unreliable. The facts must be *typical*; the writer cannot select facts that support a conclusion and ignore those that do not. The facts must be *relevant*; the writer cannot base a conclusion upon facts that have nothing to do with the matter. And the facts must be *adequate*; the writer must have enough of them, for a conclusion based upon too little evidence may have thin substance. If the evidence presented is inaccurate, atypical, irrelevant, or inadequate, the conclusion risks attack as a *non sequitur*, a conclusion that does not follow from the evidence presented.

Further difficulty may arise if the writer so wants to believe in the conclusion that he is too easily convinced by the evidence. It must be anticipated that the reader will not be eager to agree; and, if the reader thinks of objections or facts to the contrary, the conclusion goes down as of little worth. The writer of a cause-effect essay should consider these questions: Has my bias, my wish to believe, blinded me to relevant facts? Have I accepted facts because they have been presented to me by some authority? Is the authority genuine, a person who really knows? Is the authority up to date? Is the authority biased?

When ascribing an effect to a cause, determine if that cause is immediate or remote. For example, if a student's dropping out of college is said to be the result of childhood neglect by parents, a remote cause has been assigned. Is there a real link between the immediate and the remote causes? Can that link be established? Especially to be watched in ascribing effect to cause is the habit of believing that any condition that always follows an event must be caused by that event. If the sunrise always occurs just after the rooster crows, it may be assumed that the rooster's crow causes the sun to rise. Are there not other possible causes? Has an effect been mistaken for a cause? The mistake in reasoning here is often referred to as the *post hoc* fallacy, from the Latin *post hoc, ergo propter hoc* (literally, "after this, therefore because of this").

In the actual writing of a cause-effect essay the writer must guard against dogmatic tone. An overpositive way of stating either evidence or conclusion may make readers suspicious. The most effective writer of this kind of exposition keeps in mind the *probability*, not the absolute truth, of the conclusion and establishes a tone of consideration for other possibilities. Words like *all, every, always, never, undoubtedly, certainly, definitely, absolutely* may weaken rather than strengthen the writer's case. Yet the presentation cannot crumble into phrases like *in my opinion, I suppose, it is possible to assume,* and so on. Such hedging shows a wish to be fair, but it also hints that the case has not been thoroughly considered.

Essays of cause and effect usually begin with some presentation of the effect, then continue by marshaling the facts that lead to a conclusion about what has caused the effect. Such a presentation emphasizes the cause. Writers may, of course, work in the other direction, emphasizing the effect by first presenting the cause, then showing how it leads to the effect.

From what we have said about cause-effect writing it appears that there is a close connection between this sort of exposition and another kind of writing, argumentation (see p. 254). In a sense the writer of a cause-effect essay is presenting an argument, trying to convince the reader of the worth of a conclusion. The distinction is one of focus, emphasis, and tone. The cause-effect writer, having prepared his evidence with a scientist's regard for truth and reasoning, presents what is intended primarily to inform rather than to convince; the writer of argumentation, who may be equally careful in preparing evidence and in reasoning, intends primarily to convince.

In the essays that follow in this section the writers may present some convincing arguments, at least by implication; but their essential purpose is to inform. Dan Lacy exposes one of the causes of our tendency to stereotype men and women. Philip Wylie tells why American food is so tasteless. Thoreau says that owning a farm causes people to become enslaved, and George Orwell tells us how rubber-stamp language can have political effects. In reading these essays, all dealing with causes and effects, consider how strikingly they differ in tone.

Dan Lacy

MEN'S WORDS; WOMEN'S ROLES

> *If language guides our thinking, as many linguists have said, then the masculine bias of the English language may have produced some of our attitudes toward women. Dan Lacy suggests that a positive approach by publishers of children's books may reduce the bias. Lacy (b. 1914), senior vice-president of McGraw-Hill, Inc., tells what his company has done to help. He is himself the author of several books, including* The Meaning of the American Revolution (1964), The White Use of Blacks in America (1972), *and* The Lost Colony (1972).

[1] For generations textbooks and readers and children's books used in our schools have depicted girls as passive observers, boys as bold achievers. Boys

From *Saturday Review*, June 14, 1975. Reprinted by permission.

have been shown playing baseball or football while girls watched admiringly, hands clasped behind their backs. Girls were easily frightened; brave boys saved them from danger. Boys made rockets and peered through microscopes; girls played with their dolls and teacups. Boys have been portrayed as tousled and dirty from boisterous contact with life; girls as starched and pinafored, made of sugar and space [spice] and everything nice.

[2]   Thus the schools, through their textbooks and teachings, have been giving official sanction to the subordinate roles that society imposed on women in real life. Girls themselves were being conditioned to accept this circumscribed view of their future, just as their mothers before them had done. And the same societal attitudes and expectations were reflected in the magazines, newspapers, and supplementary books that children read on their own. Stereotyping imposes an arbitrary limit on what a girl (or, for that matter, a boy) may aspire to, and those who oppose such limitations believe that reform might well begin in school reading materials and in the sex roles they portray.

[3]   Some publishers have begun to tackle the problem of sex-role stereotypes by drawing up guidelines for authors and editors of educational and reference books and of children's books designed for school use. Perhaps the most comprehensive of the guidelines, and certainly the most publicized, has been the set issued by McGraw-Hill.

[4]   In many ways the "Guidelines for Equal Treatment of the Sexes in McGraw-Hill Book Company Publications" parallels an earlier set of guidelines that sought to eliminate racial and ethnic stereotypes. The problems were similar; black children, too, had been continually exposed to books, magazines, and films that depicted blacks only as laborers, porters, janitors, and servants, often portraying them as shiftless, Stepin Fetchit-like objects of ridicule. Here, again, the schools and the educational materials used were preparing certain children for the subordinate roles that society would expect them to play in later life. Textbooks in the past also tended to use only Anglo-Saxon names in stories and examples, thus excluding children who belonged to other ethnic groups.

[5]   The anti-sexist guidelines aim at two sorts of problems. One is the way girls and women are portrayed, especially in relation to boys and men. The guidelines recommend that women be shown in the whole range of occupations to which young people may aspire, such as doctors, lawyers, executives, professors, public officials, police officers—not always as nurses, teachers, homemakers, secretaries, maids, and salesclerks. The point is also made that girls should not be characterized as emotional or scatterbrained dependents but that, like boys, they should be shown as bold, self-possessed human beings,

who also achieve success through hard work, logic, and common sense. Situations in which women supervise the work of men are to be shown as normal and acceptable, but demeaning adjectives and timeworn clichés (such as "typical feminine logic," "weaker sex," and "buxom blonde") are to be avoided. Parallel treatment of men and women is urged. It is undesirable, for example, to say: "Henry Harris is a shrewd lawyer, and his wife Ann is a striking brunette"—suggesting that Henry is important because he is competent and can do things; Ann, only because she is pretty. It would be fairer to say: "The Harrises are an attractive couple. Henry is a handsome blond, and Ann is a striking brunette." Or: "The Harrises are an interesting couple. Henry is a shrewd lawyer, and Ann is very active in community affairs."

[6] Boys as well as girls, if in somewhat different ways, suffer from stereotypes. Fear and indecision are "unmanly"; an interest in music or ballet may be "sissy"; tenderness and compassion are not "masculine" virtues; men don't cry. Whole areas of interest, many occupations, even a whole side of emotional life, may be blocked off for boys and men by such assumptions. The guidelines urge an avoidance of many typical male stereotypes as well.

[7] A retired colonel called to denounce McGraw-Hill for imperiling the national security by contributing to the rearing of a generation of young men who would be as useless to the Army as he thought WACs were. But with the exception of an occasional response of this nature, there has been little dispute about the guidelines' sex-role recommendations. Almost everyone whose attention is called to the way girls and women have been traditionally portrayed will recognize its injustice. And the elimination of this sort of stereotyping is not difficult to achieve once an author or editor is aware of it.

[8] In many ways it is more difficult to deal with the other major problem to which the guidelines are addressed: the sexist prejudices built into our language itself. The English tongue was shaped over the centuries in a society in which women were distinctly subordinate. The language reflects the social history in many ways.

[9] Masculine terms are used as though they embrace every human—or every human worth mentioning: "Early *man* discovered the use of stone tools near the beginning of the Ice Age." "Someday *man* will discover a cure for cancer." "It is the duty of the chair*man* of a committee to maintain order." "The invention of printing was a great moment in the history of *man*kind." "All congress*men* face a problem in raising funds for re-elections."

[10] On the other hand (though less frequently now than a generation ago), terms neutral in form are assumed to apply only to men, so that a woman who

has achieved a particular status has to be given a special term: "poetess," "aviatrix," "woman doctor" or "woman lawyer," "lady cop," "woman priest" or "woman minister." It was as though a woman who wrote poetry was not really a poet, one who flew an airplane was not really an aviator, and one who practiced medicine was not really a doctor.

[11] And there are the constant difficulties presented by the absence of a neutral singular personal pronoun in English. Do we say, "Every student must complete his work by Tuesday"—thus assuming that the students are all male —or adopt the expression "his or her work," which can be awkward if too often repeated?

[12] But the avoidance of sexist bias does not require tampering with hallowed terms or using stilted and artificial forms. A decent sense of English style wed to genuine regard for the dignity and equality of both sexes will produce good writing without either sexist bias or artificial distortions.

[13] Some linguists may point out, as did Jacques Barzun in a recent issue of the *Columbia Forum*, that *man* in its distant etymological past really meant "human," and that it and its compounds, such as *mankind*, do properly include females and males alike. According to these linguists, it is being pointlessly, and indeed incorrectly, finicky to seek to avoid the generic use of these male terms. But does *men*, even when generically used, truly mean the same thing as *men and women*? Would the Declaration of Independence have meant the same thing if it said ". . . all men and women are created equal"? Indeed, would the signers have signed it? Would there have been no change in the meaning of the biblical query if it had asked, "What are men and women, that Thou art mindful of them?" *Man* and its compounds when used generically have an ambiguity useful to writers who want to be slippery with their meanings. They can decide for themselves when it will be offered as a noble universality and when and by how much its meaning will be restricted. They can ring out with the universal "All men are created equal" and, in the application, narrow the meaning to males—and indeed, relying further on ambiguity, to white males. If a more precise term had been used—"All humans are created equal," or "All men and women are created equal"—we would have had to confront, generations earlier, problems of racial and sexual discrimination veiled in 1776 by the shifting meaning of *man*.

VOCABULARY

Define the following words as they are used in the selection: *sanction, circumscribed* [2]; *demeaning* [5]; *etymological, generic, ambiguity* [13].

QUESTIONS FOR STUDY AND DISCUSSION

1. Paragraph 1 of Lacy's essay catalogues some examples of a cause, and paragraph 2 asserts the effect. In a single sentence restate the cause-and-effect basis of the essay.

2. In paragraph 3 Lacy turns to the presentation of how "some publishers have begun to tackle the problem of sex-role stereotypes." His assumption seems to be that elimination of the cause will lead to elimination of the effect. Is his assumption reasonable?

3. In paragraph 4 Lacy compares the McGraw-Hill guidelines for equal treatment (in print) of the sexes to "an earlier set of guidelines that sought to eliminate racial and ethnic stereotypes." What purpose does this comparison serve in his essay? Does he claim that the earlier guidelines were successful in eliminating racial and ethnic stereotypes?

4. How do the McGraw-Hill guidelines as described in paragraph 5 help to correct the stereotypes described in paragraphs 1 and 2?

5. If the reader is to accept Lacy's assertion of cause and effect, what must the reader know about Lacy's facts?

6. How (in paragraphs 2 and 6) does Lacy keep his essay from becoming a merely one-sided plea for equal status for women?

7. Lacy reports "a retired colonel called" to say that the publishers' antisexist guidelines may contribute to the rearing of young men who would be useless to the army (paragraph 7). Lacy does not comment upon the colonel's opinion. How does Lacy's tone nevertheless convey his attitude toward the colonel's position in the controversy?

8. In paragraph 8, Lacy says, "The language reflects the social history in many ways." But his article seems to be asserting that the language *affects* rather than merely reflects social behavior. Is he begging the question here? (See your dictionary if you are not sure what "beg the question" means.)

9. In paragraph 12, Lacy asserts that "a decent sense of English style wed to genuine regard for the dignity and equality of both sexes will produce good writing without either sexist bias or artificial distortions." But Lacy does not suggest *how* we may avoid the awkwardness of "his or her" and yet be fair to both sexes. Can you suggest a guideline for avoiding the "his or her" phrasing without presuming male dominance?

Philip Wylie

SCIENCE HAS SPOILED MY SUPPER

> *Philip Wylie (1902–1971) earned his reputation as a caustic essayist when he attacked many aspects of American society in his book* Generation of Vipers *(1942). In many later books and articles he attacked "the gulf between our pretensions and what we really do." In this essay he notes that the food on American tables is tasteless and, like some other aspects of machine-made mediocrity, "is bad for our souls, our minds, and our digestion." He says the cause of such tasteless fare is science coupled with economics. America eats the spoils of "the scientific war against deliciousness."*

[1] I am a fan for Science. My education is scientific and I have, in one field, contributed a monograph to a scientific journal. Science, to my mind, is applied honesty, the one reliable means we have to find out truth. That is why, when error is committed in the name of Science, I feel the way a man would if his favorite uncle had taken to drink.

[2] Over the years, I have come to feel that way about what science has done to food. I agree that America can set as good a table as any nation in the world. I agree that our food is nutritious and that the diet of most of us is well-balanced. What America eats is handsomely packaged; it is usually clean and pure; it is excellently preserved. The only trouble with it is this: year by year it grows less good to eat. It appeals increasingly to the eye. But who eats with his eyes? Almost everything used to taste better when I was a kid. For quite a long time I thought that observation was merely another index of advancing age. But some years ago I married a girl whose mother is an expert cook of the kind called "old-fashioned." This gifted woman's daughter (my wife) was taught her mother's venerable skills. She still buys dairy products from the neighbors and, in so far as possible, she uses the same materials her mother and grandmother did—to prepare meals that are superior. They are just as good, in this Year of Grace, as I recall them from my courtship. After eating for a while at the table of my mother-in-law, it is sad to go back to eating with my friends—even the alleged "good cooks" among them. And it is a gruesome experience to have meals at the best big-city restaurants.

Copyright © 1954 by The Atlantic Monthly Company, Boston, Mass. Reprinted by permission of Harold Ober Associates, Incorporated.

[3] Take cheese, for instance. Here and there, in big cities, small stores and delicatessens specialize in cheese. At such places, one can buy at least some of the first-rate cheeses that we used to eat—such as those we had with pie and macaroni. The latter were sharp but not too sharp. They were a little crumbly. We called them American cheeses, or even rat cheese; actually they were Cheddars. Long ago, this cheese began to be supplanted by a material called "cheese foods." Some cheese foods and "processed" cheese are fairly edible; but not one comes within miles of the old kinds—for flavor.

[4] A grocer used to be very fussy about his cheese. Cheddar was made and sold by hundreds of little factories. Representatives of the factories had particular customers, and cheese was prepared by hand to suit the grocers, who knew precisely what their patrons wanted in rat cheese, pie cheese, American and other cheeses. Some liked them sharper; some liked them yellower; some liked anise seeds in cheese, or caraway.

[5] What happened? Science—or what is called science—stepped in. The old-fashioned cheeses didn't ship well enough. They crumbled, became moldy, dried out. "Scientific" tests disclosed that a great majority of the people will buy a less-good-tasting cheese if that's all they can get. "Scientific marketing" then took effect. Its motto is "Give the people the least quality they'll stand for." In food, as in many other things, the "scientific marketers" regard quality as secondary so long as they can sell most persons anyhow; what they are after is "durability" or "shippability."

[6] It is not possible to make the very best cheese in vast quantities at a low average cost. "Scientific sampling" got in its statistically nasty work. It was found that the largest number of people will buy something that is bland and rather tasteless. Those who prefer a product of a pronounced and individualistic flavor have a variety of preferences. Nobody is altogether pleased by bland foodstuff, in other words; but nobody is very violently put off. The result is that a "reason" has been found for turning out zillions of packages of something that will "do" for nearly all and isn't even imagined to be superlatively good by a single soul!

[7] Economics entered. It is possible to turn out in quantity a bland, impersonal, practically imperishable substance more or less resembling, say cheese—at lower cost than cheese. Chain groceries shut out the independent stores and "standardization" became a principal means of cutting costs.

[8] Imitations also came into the cheese business. There are American duplications of most of the celebrated European cheeses, mass-produced and

cheaper by far than the imports. They would cause European food-lovers to gag or guffaw—but generally, the imitations are all that's available in the supermarkets. People buy them and eat them.

[9] Perhaps you don't like cheese—so the fact that decent cheese is hardly ever served in America any more, or used in cooking, doesn't matter to you. Well, take bread. There has been (and still is) something of a hullabaloo about bread. In fact, in the last few years, a few big bakeries have taken to making a fairly good imitation of real bread. It costs much more than what is nowadays called bread, but it is edible. Most persons, however, now eat as "bread" a substance so full of chemicals and so barren of cereals that it approaches a synthetic.

[10] Most bakers are interested mainly in how a loaf of bread looks. They are concerned with how little stuff they can put in it—to get how much money. They are deeply interested in using chemicals that will keep bread from molding, make it seem "fresh" for the longest possible time, and so render it marketable and shippable. They have been at this monkeyshine for a generation. Today a loaf of "bread" looks deceptively real; but it is made from heaven knows what and it resembles, as food, a solidified bubble bath. Some months ago I bought a loaf of the stuff and, experimentally, began pressing it together like an accordion. With a little effort, I squeezed the whole loaf to a length of about one inch.

[11] Yesterday, at the home of my mother-in-law, I ate with country-churned butter and home-canned wild strawberry jam several slices of actual bread, the same thing we used to have every day at home. People who have eaten actual bread will know what I mean. They will know that the material commonly called bread is not even related to real bread, except in name.

II

[12] For years, I couldn't figure out what had happened to vegetables. I knew, of course, that most vegetables, to be enjoyed in their full deliciousness, must be picked fresh and cooked at once. I knew that vegetables cannot be overcooked and remain even edible, in the best sense. They cannot stand on the stove. That set of facts makes it impossible, of course, for any American restaurant—or, indeed, any city-dweller separated from supply by more than a few hours—to have decent fresh vegetables. The Parisians manage by getting their vegetables picked at dawn and rushed in farmers' carts to market, where no middleman or marketman delays produce on its way to the pot.

[13]   Our vegetables, however, come to us through a long chain of command. There are merchants of several sorts—wholesalers before the retailers, commission men, and so on—with the result that what were once edible products become, in transit, mere wilted leaves and withered tubers.

[14]   Homes and restaurants do what they can with this stuff—which my mother-in-law would discard on the spot. I have long thought that the famed blindfold test for cigarettes should be applied to city vegetables. For I am sure that if you puréed them and ate them blindfolded, you couldn't tell the beans from the peas, the turnips from the squash, the Brussels sprouts from the broccoli.

[15]   It is only lately that I have found how much science of genetics is involved. Agronomists and the like have taken to breeding all sorts of vegetables and fruits—changing their original nature. This sounds wonderful and often is insane. For the scientists have not as a rule taken any interest whatsoever in the taste of the things they've tampered with!

[16]   What they've done is to develop "improved" strains of things for every purpose but eating. They work out, say, peas that will ripen all at once. The farmer can then harvest his peas and thresh them and be done with them. It is extremely profitable because it is efficient. What matter if such peas taste like boiled paper wads?

[17]   Geneticists have gone crazy over such "opportunities." They've developed string beans that are straight instead of curved, and all one length. This makes them easier to pack in cans, even if, when eating them, you can't tell them from tender string. Ripening time and identity of size and shape are, nowadays, more important in carrots than the fact that they taste like carrots. Personally, I don't care if they hybridize onions till they are as big as your head and come up through the snow; but, in doing so, they are producing onions that only vaguely and feebly remind you of onions. We are getting some varieties, in fact, that have less flavor than the water off last week's leeks. Yet, if people don't eat onions because they taste like onions, what in the name of Luther Burbank do they eat them for?

[18]   The women's magazines are about one third dedicated to clothes, one third to mild comment on sex, and the other third to recipes and pictures of handsome salads, desserts, and main courses. "Institutes" exist to experiment and tell housewives how to cook attractive meals and how to turn leftovers into works of art. The food thus pictured looks like famous paintings of still life. The only trouble is it's tasteless. It leaves appetite unquenched and merely serves to stave off famine.

[19] I wonder if this blandness of our diet doesn't explain why so many of us are overweight and even dangerously so. When things had flavor, we knew what we were eating all the while—and it satisfied us. A teaspoonful of my mother-in-law's wild strawberry jam will not just provide a gastronome's ecstasy: it will entirely satisfy your jam desire. But, of the average tinned or glass-packed strawberry jam, you need half a cupful to get the idea of what you're eating. A slice of my mother-in-law's apple pie will satiate you far better than a whole bakery pie.

[20] That thought is worthy of investigation—of genuine scientific investigation. It is merely a hypothesis, so far, and my own. But people—and their ancestors—have been eating according to flavor for upwards of a billion years. The need to satisfy the sense of taste may be innate and important. When food is merely a pretty cascade of viands, with the texture of boiled cardboard and the flavor of library paste, it may be the instinct of genus homo to go on eating in the unconscious hope of finally satisfying the ageless craving of the frustrated taste buds. In the days when good-tasting food was the rule in the American home, obesity wasn't such a national curse.

[21] How can you feel you've eaten if you haven't tasted, and fully enjoyed tasting? Why (science is ever so ready to answer the beck and call of mankind) don't people who want to reduce merely give up eating and get the nourishment they must have in measured doses shot into their arms at hospitals? One ready answer to that question suggests that my theory of overeating is sound: people like to taste! In eating, they try to satisfy that like.

[22] The scientific war against deliciousness has been stepped up enormously in the last decade. Some infernal genius found a way to make biscuit batter keep. Housewives began to buy this premixed stuff. It saved work, of course. But any normally intelligent person can learn, in a short period, how to prepare superb baking powder biscuits. I can make better biscuits, myself, than can be made from patent batters. Yet soon after this fiasco became an American staple, it was discovered that a half-baked substitute for all sorts of breads, pastries, rolls, and the like could be mass-manufactured, frozen—and sold for polishing off in the home oven. None of these two-stage creations is as good as even a fair sample of the thing it imitates. A man of taste, who had eaten one of my wife's cinnamon buns, might use the premixed sort to throw at starlings—but not to eat! Cake mixes, too, come ready-prepared—like cement and not much better-tasting compared with true cake.

[23] It is, however, "deep-freezing" that has really rung down the curtain on American cookery. Nothing is improved by the process. I have yet to taste a

deep-frozen victual that measures up, in flavor, to the fresh, unfrosted original. And most foods, cooked or uncooked, are destroyed in the deep freeze for all people of sense and sensibility. Vegetables with crisp and crackling texture emerge as mush, slippery and stringy as hair nets simmered in Vaseline. The essential oils that make peas peas—and cabbage cabbage—must undergo fission and fusion in freezers. Anyhow, they vanish. Some meats turn to leather. Others to wood pulp. Everything, pretty much, tastes like the mosses of tundra, dug up in mid-winter. Even the appearance changes, oftentimes. Handsome comestibles you put down in the summer come out looking very much like the corpses of woolly mammoths recovered from the last Ice Age.

[24] Of course, all this scientific "food handling" tends to save money. It certainly preserves food longer. It reduces work at home. But these facts, and especially the last, imply that the first purpose of living is to avoid work—at home, anyhow.

[25] Without thinking, we are making an important confession about ourselves as a nation. We are abandoning quality—even, to some extent, the quality of people. The "best" is becoming too good for us. We are suckling ourselves on machine-made mediocrity. It is bad for our souls, our minds, and our digestion. It is the way our wiser and calmer forebears fed, not people, but hogs: as much as possible and as fast as possible, with no standard of quality.

[26] The Germans say, "*Mann ist was er isst*—Man is what he eats." If this be true, the people of the U. S. A. are well on their way to becoming a faceless mob of mediocrities, of robots. And if we apply to other attributes the criteria we apply these days to appetite, that is what would happen! We would not want bright children any more; we'd merely want them to look bright—and get through school fast. We wouldn't be interested in beautiful women—just a good paint job. And we'd be opposed to the most precious quality of man: his individuality, his differentness from the mob.

[27] There are some people—sociologists and psychologists among them—who say that is exactly what we Americans are doing, are becoming. Mass man, they say, is on the increase. Conformity, standardization, similarity—all on a cheap and vulgar level—are replacing the great American ideas of colorful liberty and dignified individualism. If this is so, the process may well begin, like most human behavior, in the home—in those homes where a good meal has been replaced by something-to-eat-in-a-hurry. By something not very

good to eat, prepared by a mother without very much to do, for a family that doesn't feel it amounts to much anyhow.

[28]   I call, here, for rebellion.

VOCABULARY

Define the following words as they are used in the selection: *monograph* [1]; *venerable, gruesome* [2]; *anise, caraway* [4]; *tubers* [13]; *puréed* [14]; *hybridize* [17]; *stave* [18]; *gastronome, satiate* [19]; *innate, viands* [20]; *fiasco* [22]; *comestibles* [23]; *criteria* [26].

QUESTIONS FOR STUDY AND DISCUSSION

1. Wylie's essay has an informal, very personal tone; his attitude toward his material is obvious, and he writes as if he and the reader were allied against the enemy, a coalition of science and economics. How does the tone help him to enlist the reader against that enemy?

2. What distinction does Wylie draw between "Science" (paragraph 1) and "what is called science" (paragraph 5)? What does he gain by pointing out (in paragraph 1) that his own education was scientific?

3. The introduction to Wylie's topic takes two paragraphs. What effect does he gain by explaining that he is "a fan for Science" before getting down to the main topic?

4. The effect of science upon the food industry in America is covered in paragraphs 3 through 17. The material of those paragraphs is broken into three sections; what are they?

5. Since a good cause-and-effect essay should marshal facts that are accurate, typical, revelant, and adequate, we may test Wylie's essay by those standards. Has Wylie overlooked (or deliberately ignored) facts that could weaken his case? Are there any advantages in deep-freezing of foods? Does Wylie point out any advantages? Is it possible that today's facts are different from those he pointed to in 1954?

6. Wylie is careful to establish that he, himself, eats very good food. Why does he point that out?

7. After considering the preparation and growing of foods, Wylie turns (in paragraph 18) to other ways in which science has spoiled American food. What are those ways?

8. One of Wylie's devices of style is *hyperbole*, deliberate exaggeration for effect. It is the effect that counts; hyperbole is not intended to be taken literally.

Nowadays, he says, "peas taste like boiled paper wads." Is the simile effective? Do you suppose Wylie himself ever tasted boiled paper wads? List five or six other examples of hyperbole in the essay.

9. Causes often produce effects that may in turn become causes of other effects. Where does Wylie develop such a vicious chain of cause and effect?

10. Once Wylie has put the reader into the position of one who, like him, blames science and economics for America's bad food, he then turns the attack upon "us." He says, "We are abandoning quality . . . The 'best' is becoming too good for us." He thus suggests that science has spoiled not only our suppers but our standards as well. Is that suggestion reasonable?

11. In his final, emphatic sentence, "I call, here, for rebellion," Wylie uses openly the rhetorical "Are you with me?" technique. It has now been a quarter of a century since publication of his essay; can you cite any evidence that his call for rebellion found many joiners?

Henry David Thoreau

ON OWNING A FARM

Henry David Thoreau (1817–1862) has returned to high favor, especially among the young, more than a century after his death. His writings, especially Walden *(1854), are landmark expressions of American individualism. This excerpt from his most famous book turns everyday values upside down, perhaps so they can be seen right side up. Thoreau finds that commitment, especially to ownership of real property, is a prime cause of the individual's enslavement to things outside himself.*

[1]   At a certain season of our life we are accustomed to consider every spot as the possible site of a house. I have thus surveyed the country on every side within a dozen miles of where I live. In imagination I have bought all the farms in succession, for all were to be bought, and I knew their price. I walked over each farmer's premises, tasted his wild apples, discoursed on husbandry with him, took his farm at his price, at any price, mortgaging it to him in my mind; even put a higher price on it,—took everything but a deed of it,—took his word for his deed, for I dearly love to talk,—cultivated it, and him too to some extent, I trust, and withdrew when I had enjoyed it long enough, leaving him to carry it on. This experience entitled me to be regarded as a sort of real-estate broker by my friends. Whenever I sat, there I might live, and the landscape radiated from me accordingly. What is a house but a *sedes*, a seat?—

better if a country seat. I discovered many a site for a house not likely to be soon improved, which some might have thought too far from the village, but to my eyes the village was too far from it. Well, there I might live, I said; and there I did live, for an hour, a summer and a winter life; saw how I could let the years run off, buffet the winter through, and see the spring come in. The future inhabitants of this region, wherever they may place their houses, may be sure that they have been anticipated. An afternoon sufficed to lay out the land into orchard, woodlot, and pasture, and to decide what fine oaks or pines should be left to stand before the door, and whence each blasted tree could be seen to the best advantage; and then I let it lie, fallow perchance, for a man is rich in proportion to the number of things which he can afford to let alone.

[2] My imagination carried me so far that I even had the refusal of several farms,—the refusal was all I wanted,—but I never got my fingers burned by actual possession. The nearest that I came to actual possession was when I bought the Hollowell place, and had begun to sort my seeds, and collected materials with which to make a wheelbarrow to carry it on or off with; but before the owner gave me a deed of it, his wife—every man has such a wife—changed her mind and wished to keep it, and he offered me ten dollars to release him. Now, to speak the truth, I had but ten cents in the world, and it surpassed my arithmetic to tell, if I was the man who had ten cents, or who had a farm, or ten dollars, or all together. However, I let him keep the ten dollars and the farm too, for I had carried it far enough; or rather, to be generous, I sold him the farm for just what I gave for it, and, as he was not a rich man, made him a present of ten dollars, and still had my ten cents, and seeds, and materials for a wheelbarrow left. I found thus that I had been a rich man without any damage to my poverty. But I retained the landscape, and I have since annually carried off what it yielded without a wheelbarrow. With respect to landscapes,—

> "I am monarch of all I *survey*,
> My right there is none to dispute."

[3] I have frequently seen a poet withdraw, having enjoyed the most valuable part of a farm, while the crusty farmer supposed that he had got a few wild apples only. Why, the owner does not know it for many years when a poet has put his farm in rhyme, the most admirable kind of invisible fence, has fairly impounded it, milked it, skimmed it, and got all the cream, and left the farmer only the skimmed milk.

[4] The real attractions of the Hollowell farm, to me, were: its complete retirement, being about two miles from the village, half a mile from the nearest neighbor, and separated from the highway by a broad field; its bounding on

the river, which the owner said protected it by its fogs from frosts in the spring, though that was nothing to me; the gray color and ruinous state of the house and barn, and the dilapidated fences, which put such an interval between me and the last occupant; the hollow and lichen-covered apple trees, gnawed by rabbits, showing what kind of neighbors I should have; but above all, the recollection I had of it from my earliest voyages up the river, when the house was concealed behind a dense grove of red maples, through which I heard the house-dog bark. I was in haste to buy it, before the proprietor finished getting out some rocks, cutting down the hollow apple trees, and grubbing up some young birches which had sprung up in the pasture, or, in short, had made any more of his improvements. To enjoy these advantages I was ready to carry it on; like Atlas, to take the world on my shoulders,—I never heard what compensation he received for that,—and do all those things which had no other motive or excuse but that I might pay for it and be unmolested in my possession of it; for I knew all the while that it would yield the most abundant crop of the kind I wanted if I could only afford to let it alone. But it turned out as I have said.

[5] All that I could say, then, with respect to farming on a large scale, (I have always cultivated a garden,) was, that I had had my seeds ready. Many think that seeds improve with age. I have no doubt that time discriminates between the good and the bad; and when at last I shall plant, I shall be less likely to be disappointed. But I would say to my fellows, once for all, As long as possible live free and uncommitted. It makes but little difference whether you are committed to a farm or the county jail.

[6] Old Cato, whose "De Re Rusticâ" is my "Cultivator," says, and the only translation I have seen makes sheer nonsense of the passage, "When you think of getting a farm turn it thus in your mind, not to buy greedily; nor spare your pains to look at it, and do not think it enough to go round it once. The oftener you go there the more it will please you, if it is good." I think I shall not buy greedily, but go round and round it as long as I live, and be buried in it first, that it may please me the more at last.

VOCABULARY

Define the following words as they are used in the selection: *fallow* [1]; *crusty, impounded* [3]; *dilapidated, grubbing* [4]; *committed* [5].

QUESTIONS FOR STUDY AND DISCUSSION

1. Because Thoreau's essay is imaginative and personal, a reader may overlook its thesis, which is more implied than stated. What is the cause-effect pattern underlying his essay?

2. Thoreau's prose is near to poetry, its language being more compact and suggestive than that of other essays in this section on exposition. He achieves its compactness, in part, by squeezing words for more of their juice, just as he says we should squeeze life for more of what it has to offer. An example of such word-squeezing is his use of *cultivated* in paragraph 1. What are some of the implications of that word in his sly use of it?

3. It becomes clear, at least upon reflection, that Thoreau uses *farm* as a symbol: a concrete reality that suggests an abstract idea. What abstract idea?

4. A *facetious* mind is one that sees many *facets* of things and ideas. Thoreau's word-squeezing is evidence of his facetious mind. In addition to *farm* and *cultivated*, he uses many other words that force us to consider several facets of their meanings, rather than just one. What are some multiple meanings of *surveyed, premises, deed, real-estate, blasted, rich* [1]; *possession* [2]; *real, hollow* [4]; *seeds, plant, committed* [5]?

5. Anther evidence of Thoreau's facetious mind is his *irony*, his use of words to mean the opposite of their usual meanings. An example is *poverty* [3]; another, *improvements* [4]. Explain why these words are ironic.

6. Thoreau's reference to Atlas (paragraph 4) is an example of his use of *allusion*, or reference to things the reader is expected to know about. Who was Atlas? What makes the allusion especially suitable to Thoreau's purpose?

7. Thoreau mentions "wild apples" in paragraphs 1 and 3 and "apple trees" in paragraph 4. In paragraph 5 he says, "I have always cultivated a garden." These references may be further allusions, for they suggest a well-known garden that bore well-known apples. What garden? Is the allusion suitable to Thoreau's thesis?

8. Notice that Thoreau (in paragraph 5) refers to the apple trees as "lichen-covered" and "hollow." The lichen is a flowerless plant. How do these images tie in with the garden allusion (see question 7)? Why does Thoreau refer to these apparently undesirable apple trees as "these advantages"?

9. What is the cause-effect structure underlying Thoreau's statement (at the end of paragraph 1) that "a man is rich in proportion to the number of things which he can afford to let alone"?

10. Does commitment to ownership of a farm suggest other commitments in life? Thoreau remained uncommitted, saying, "All that I could say, then, . . . was, that I had had my seeds ready." Thoreau died unwedded. What does his remark suggest in the light of that fact? Does the fact weaken his thesis?

11. Keeping in mind Thoreau's allusion to Atlas, reread the final sentence

of the selection. In view of both, does the Hollowell farm epitomize a much larger piece of real-estate? Name it.

FOR FURTHER ANALYSIS

George Orwell

POLITICS AND THE ENGLISH LANGUAGE

George Orwell (1903–1950), English novelist and essayist, published his best-known work, 1984, just before his death. In it he depicted fictionally the workings of a Ministry of Truth, a bureau of government committed to the altering of minds by the control of language. The novel illustrated the thesis of the following essay: that the corruption of language causes the erosion of political morality as well as the decline of thought. This essay, first published in 1945, has become one of the century's most widely read examples of cause and effect.

[1] Most people who bother with the matter at all would admit that the English language is in a bad way, but it is generally assumed that we cannot by conscious action do anything about it. Our civilization is decadent and our language—so the argument runs—must inevitably share in the general collapse. It follows that any struggle against the abuse of language is a sentimental archaism, like preferring candles to electric light or hansom cabs to aeroplanes. Underneath this lies the half-conscious belief that language is a natural growth and not an instrument which we shape for our own purposes.

[2] Now, it is clear that the decline of a language must ultimately have political and economic causes: it is not due simply to the bad influence of this or that individual writer. But an effect can become a cause, reinforcing the original cause and producing the same effect in an intensified form, and so on indefinitely. A man may take to drink because he feels himself to be a failure, and then fail all the more completely because he drinks. It is rather the same

From *Shooting an Elephant and Other Essays* by George Orwell, copyright 1945, 1946, 1949, 1950, by Sonia Brownell Orwell. Reprinted by permission of Harcourt Brace Jovanovich, Inc.

thing that is happening to the English language. It becomes ugly and inaccurate because our thoughts are foolish, but the slovenliness of our language makes it easier for us to have foolish thoughts. The point is that the process is reversible. Modern English, especially written English, is full of bad habits which spread by imitation and which can be avoided if one is willing to take the necessary trouble. If one gets rid of these habits one can think more clearly, and to think clearly is a necessary first step toward political regeneration: so that the fight against bad English is not frivolous and is not the exclusive concern of professional writers. I will come back to this presently, and I hope that by that time the meaning of what I have said here will have become clearer. Meanwhile, here are five specimens of the English language as it is now habitually written.

[3] These five passages have not been picked out because they are especially bad—I could have quoted far worse if I had chosen—but because they illustrate various of the mental vices from which we now suffer. They are a little below the average, but are fairly representative samples. I number them so that I can refer back to them when necessary:

(1) I am not, indeed, sure whether it is not true to say that the Milton who once seemed not unlike a seventeenth-century Shelley had not become, out of an experience ever more bitter in each year, more alien [sic] to the founder of that Jesuit sect which nothing could induce him to tolerate.
Professor Harold Laski (Essay in Freedom of Expression)

(2) Above all, we cannot play ducks and drakes with a native battery of idioms which prescribes such egregious collocations of vocables as the Basic *put up with* for *tolerate* or *put at a loss* for *bewilder*.
Professor Lancelot Hogben (Interglossa)

(3) On the one side we have the free personality: by definition it is not neurotic, for it has neither conflict nor dream. Its desires, such as they are, are transparent, for they are just what institutional approval keeps in the forefront of consciousness; another institutional pattern would alter their number and intensity; there is little in them that is natural, irreducible, or culturally dangerous. But *on the other side*, the social bond itself is nothing but the mutual reflection of these self-secure integrities. Recall the definition of love. Is not this the very picture of a small academic? Where is there a place in this hall of mirrors for either personality or fraternity?
Essay on psychology in Politics (New York)

(4) All the "best people" from the gentlemen's clubs, and all the frantic fascist captains, united in common hatred of Socialism and bestial horror of the rising tide of the mass revolutionary movement, have turned to acts of provocation, to foul incendiarism, to medieval legends of poisoned wells, to legalize their own destruction of proletarian organizations, and rouse the agitated petty-bourgeoisie to chauvinistic fervor on behalf of the fight against the revolutionary way out of the crisis.
Communist pamphlet

(5) If a new spirit *is* to be infused into this old country, there is one thorny and contentious reform which must be tackled, and that is the humanization and galvanization of the B.B.C. Timidity here will bespeak canker and atrophy of the soul. The heart of Britain may be sound and of strong beat, for instance, but the British lion's roar at present is like that of Bottom in Shakespeare's *Midsummer Night's Dream*—as gentle as any sucking dove. A virile new Britain cannot continue indefinitely to be traduced in the eyes or rather ears, of the world by the effete languors of Langham Place, brazenly masquerading as "standard English." When the Voice of Britain is heard at nine o'clock, better far and infinitely less ludicrous to hear aitches honestly dropped than the present priggish, inflated, inhibited, school-ma'amish arch braying of blameless bashful mewing maidens!

Letter in *Tribune*

[4]   Each of these passages has faults of its own, but, quite apart from avoidable ugliness, two qualities are common to all of them. The first is staleness of imagery; the other is lack of precision. The writer either has a meaning and cannot express it, or he inadvertently says something else, or he is almost indifferent as to whether his words mean anything or not. This mixture of vagueness and sheer incompetence is the most marked characteristic of modern English prose, and especially of any kind of political writing. As soon as certain topics are raised, the concrete melts into the abstract and no one seems able to think of turns of speech that are not hackneyed: prose consists less and less of *words* chosen for the sake of their meaning, and more and more of *phrases* tacked together like the sections of a prefabricated henhouse. I list below, with notes and examples, various of the tricks by means of which the work of prose-construction is habitually dodged:

[5]   *Dying metaphors.* A newly invented metaphor assists thought by evoking a visual image, while on the other hand a metaphor which is technically "dead" (e.g. *iron resolution*) has in effect reverted to being an ordinary word and can generally be used without loss of vividness. But in between these two classes there is a huge dump of worn-out metaphors which have lost all evocative power and are merely used because they save people the trouble of inventing phrases for themselves. Examples are: *Ring the changes on, take up the cudgels for, toe the line, ride roughshod over, stand shoulder to shoulder with, play into the hands of, no axe to grind, grist to the mill, fishing in troubled waters, on the order of the day, Achilles' heel, swan song, hotbed.* Many of these are used without knowledge of their meaning (what is a "rift," for instance?), and incompatible metaphors are frequently mixed, a sure sign that the writer is not interested in what he is saying. Some metaphors now current have been twisted out of their original meaning without those who use them even being aware of the fact. For example, *toe the line* is sometimes written *tow the line.* Another example is *the hammer and the anvil,* now always used with the implication that the anvil gets the worst of it. In real life it is always

the anvil that breaks the hammer, never the other way about: a writer who stopped to think what he was saying would be aware of this, and would avoid perverting the original phrase.

[6]   *Operators* or *verbal false limbs.* These save the trouble of picking out appropriate verbs and nouns, and at the same time pad each sentence with extra syllables which give it an appearance of symmetry. Characteristic phrases are *render inoperative, militate against, make contact with, be subjected to, give rise to, give grounds for, have the effect of, play a leading part (role) in, make itself felt, take effect, exhibit a tendency to, serve the purpose of, etc., etc.* The keynote is the elimination of simple verbs. Instead of being a single word, such as *break, stop, spoil, mend, kill,* a verb becomes a *phrase,* made up of a noun or adjective tacked on to some general-purpose verb such as *prove, serve, form, play, render.* In addition, the passive voice is wherever possible used in preference to the active, and noun constructions are used instead of gerunds (*by examination of* instead of *by examining*). The range of verbs is further cut down by means of the *-ize* and *de-* formations, and the banal statements are given an appearance of profundity by means of the *not un-* formation. Simple conjunctions and prepositions are replaced by such phrases as *with respect to, having regard to, the fact that, by dint of, in view of, in the interests of, on the hypothesis that*; and the ends of sentences are saved from anticlimax by such resounding commonplaces as *greatly to be desired, cannot be left out of account, a development to be expected in the near future, deserving of serious consideration, brought to a satisfactory conclusion,* and so on and so forth.

[7]   *Pretentious diction.* Words like *phenomenon, element, individual* (as noun), *objective, categorical, effective, virtual, basic, primary, promote, constitute, exhibit, exploit, utilize, eliminate, liquidate,* are used to dress up simple statement and give an air of scientific impartiality to biased judgments. Adjectives like *epoch-making, epic, historic, unforgettable, triumphant, age-old, inevitable, inexorable, veritable,* are used to dignify the sordid processes of international politics, while writing that aims at glorifying war usually takes on an archaic color its characteristic words being: *realm, throne, chariot, mailed fist, trident, sword, shield, buckler, banner, jackboot, clarion.* Foreign words and expressions such as *cul de sac, ancien régime, deus ex machina, mutatis mutandis, status quo, gleichschaltung, weltanschauung,* are used to give an air of culture and elegance. Except for the useful abbreviations *i.e., e.g.,* and *etc.,* there is no real need for any of the hundreds of foreign phrases now current in English. Bad writers, and especially scientific, political, and sociological writers, are nearly always haunted by the notion that Latin or Greek words are grander than Saxon ones, and unnecessary words like *expedite, ameliorate, pre-*

dict, extraneous, deracinated, clandestine, subaqueous, and hundreds of others constantly gain ground from their Anglo-Saxon opposite numbers.* The jargon peculiar to Marxist writing (*hyena, hangman, cannibal, petty bourgeois, these gentry, lackey, flunkey, mad dog, White Guard,* etc.) consists largely of words and phrases translated from Russian, German, or French; but the normal way of coining a new word is to use a Latin or Greek root with the appropriate affix and, where necessary, the size formation. It is often easier to make up words of this kind (*deregionalize, impermissible, extramarital, nonfragmentary* and so forth) than to think up the English words that will cover one's meaning. The result, in general, is an increase in slovenliness and vagueness.

[8] *Meaningless words.* In certain kinds of writing, particularly in art criticism and literary criticism, it is normal to come across long passages which are almost completely lacking in meaning.† Words like *romantic, plastic, values, human, dead, sentimental, natural, vitality,* as used in art criticism, are strictly meaningless, in the sense that they not only do not point to any discoverable object, but are hardly ever expected to do so by the reader. When one critic writes, "The outstanding feature of Mr. X's work is its living quality," while another writes, "The immediately striking thing about Mr. X's work is its peculiar deadness," the reader accepts this as a simple difference of opinion. If words like *black* and *white* were involved, instead of the jargon words *dead* and *living,* he would see at once that language was being used in an improper way. Many political words are similarly abused. The word *Fascism* has now no meaning except in so far as it signifies "something not desirable." The words *democracy, socialism, freedom, patriotic, realistic, justice,* have each of them several different meanings which cannot be reconciled with one another. In the case of a word like *democracy,* not only is there no agreed definition, but the attempt to make one is resisted from all sides. It is almost universally felt that when we call a country democratic we are praising it: consequently the defenders of every kind of régime claim that it is a democracy, and fear that they might have to stop using the word if it were tied down to any one meaning. Words of this kind are often used in a consciously dishonest way. That is, the person who uses them has his own private definition,

---

* An interesting illustration of this is the way in which the English flower names which were in use till very recently are being ousted by Greek ones, *snapdragon* becoming *antirhinum, forget-me-not* becoming *myosotis,* etc. It is hard to see any practical reason for this change of fashion: it is probably due to an instinctive turning away from the more homely word and a vague feeling that the Greek word is scientific.

† Example: "Comfort's catholicity of perception and image, strangely Whitmanesque in range, almost the exact opposite in aesthetic compulsion, continues to evoke that trembling atmospheric accumulative hinting at a cruel, an inexorably serene timelessness. . . . Wrey Gardiner scores by aiming at simple bull's-eyes with precision. Only they are not so simple, and through this contented sadness runs more than the surface bittersweet of resignation." (*Poetry Quarterly.*)

but allows his hearer to think he means something quite different. Statements like *Marshal Pétain was a true patriot, The Soviet press is the freest in the world, The Catholic Church is opposed to persecution,* are almost always made with intent to deceive. Other words used in variable meanings, in most cases more or less dishonestly, are: *class, totalitarian, science, progressive, reactionary, bourgeois, equality.*

[9] Now that I have made this catalogue of swindles and perversions, let me give another example of the kind of writing that they lead to. This time it must of its nature be an imaginary one. I am going to translate a passage of good English into modern English of the worst sort. Here is a well-known verse from *Ecclesiastes:*

I returned and saw under the sun, that the race is not to the swift, nor the battle to the strong, neither yet bread to the wise, nor yet riches to men of understanding, nor yet favour to men of skill; but time and chance happeneth to them all.

Here it is in modern English:

Objective consideration of contemporary phenomena compels the conclusion that success or failure in competitive activities exhibits no tendency to be commensurate with innate capacity, but that a considerable element of the unpredictable must invariably be taken into account.

[10] This is a parody, but not a very gross one. Exhibit (3), above, for instance, contains several patches of the same kind of English. It will be seen that I have not made a full translation. The beginning and ending of the sentence follow the original meaning fairly closely, but in the middle the concrete illustrations—race, battle, bread—dissolve into the vague phrase "success or failure in competitive activities." This had to be so, because no modern writer of the kind I am discussing—no one capable of using phrases like "objective consideration of contemporary phenomena"—would ever tabulate his thoughts in that precise and detailed way. The whole tendency of modern prose is away from concreteness. Now analyze these two sentences a little more closely. The first contains forty-nine words but only sixty syllables, and all its words are those of everyday life. The second contains thirty-eight words of ninety syllables: eighteen of its words are from Latin roots, and one from Greek. The first sentence contains six vivid images, and only one phrase ("time and chance") that could be called vague. The second contains not a single fresh, arresting phrase, and in spite of its ninety syllables it gives only a shortened version of the meaning contained in the first. Yet without a doubt it is the second kind of sentence that is gaining ground in modern English. I do not want to exaggerate. This kind of writing is not yet universal, and outcrops of simplicity will occur here and there in the worst-written page. Still, if you or I were told to write a few lines on the uncertainty of human fortunes,

we should probably come much nearer to my imaginary sentence than to the one from *Ecclesiastes*.

[11]   As I have tried to show, modern writing at its worst does not consist in picking out words for the sake of their meaning and inventing images in order to make the meaning clearer. It consists in gumming together long strips of words which have already been set in order by someone else, and making the results presentable by sheer humbug. The attraction of this way of writing is that it is easy. It is easier—even quicker, once you have the habit—to say *In my opinion it is not an unjustifiable assumption that* than to say *I think*. If you use ready-made phrases, you not only don't have to hunt about for words; you also don't have to bother with the rhythms of your sentences, since these phrases are generally so arranged as to be more or less euphonious. When you are composing in a hurry—when you are dictating to a stenographer, for instance, or making a public speech—it is natural to fall into a pretentious, Latinized style. Tags like *a consideration which we should do well to bear in mind* or *a conclusion to which all of us would readily assent* will save many a sentence from coming down with a bump. By using stale metaphors, similes, and idioms, you save much mental effort, at the cost of leaving your meaning vague, not only for your reader but for yourself. This is the significance of mixed metaphors. The sole aim of a metaphor is to call up a visual image. When these images clash—as in *The Fascist octopus has sung its swan song, the jackboot is thrown into the melting pot*—it can be taken as certain that the writer is not seeing a mental image of the objects he is naming; in other words he is not really thinking. Look again at the examples I gave at the beginning of this essay. Professor Laski (1) uses five negatives in fifty-three words. One of these is superfluous, making nonsense of the whole passage, and in addition there is the slip—*alien* for akin—making further nonsense, and several avoidable pieces of clumsiness which increase the general vagueness. Professor Hogben (2) plays ducks and drakes with a battery which is able to write prescriptions, and, while disapproving of the everyday phrase *put up with*, is unwilling to look *egregious* up in the dictionary and see what it means; (3), if one takes an uncharitable attitude towards it, is simply meaningless: probably one could work out its intended meaning by reading the whole of the article in which it occurs. In (4), the writer knows more or less what he wants to say, but an accumulation of stale phrases chokes him like tea leaves blocking a sink. In (5), words and meaning have almost parted company. People who write in this manner usually have a general emotional meaning—they dislike one thing and want to express solidarity with another—but they are not interested in the detail of what they are saying. A scrupulous writer, in every sentence that he writes, will ask himself at least four questions, thus: What am I trying to say? What words will express it? What image or idiom will

make it clearer? Is this image fresh enough to have an effect? And he will probably ask himself two more: Could I put it more shortly? Have I said anything that is avoidably ugly? But you are not obliged to go to all this trouble. You can shirk it by simply throwing your mind open and letting the readymade phrases come crowding in. They will construct your sentences for you —even think your thoughts for you, to a certain extent—and at need they will perform the important service of partially concealing your meaning even from yourself. It is at this point that the special connection between politics and the debasement of language becomes clear.

[12] In our time it is broadly true that political writing is bad writing. Where it is not true, it will generally be found that the writer is some kind of rebel, expressing his private opinions and not a "party line." Orthodoxy, of whatever color, seems to demand a lifeless, imitative style. The political dialects to be found in pamphlets, leading articles, manifestoes, White Papers and the speeches of undersecretaries do, of course, vary from party to party, but they are all alike in that one almost never finds in them a fresh, vivid, homemade turn of speech. When one watches some tired hack on the platform mechanically repeating the familiar phrases—*bestial atrocities, iron heel, bloodstained tyranny, free peoples of the world, stand shoulder to shoulder*—one often has a curious feeling that one is not watching a live human being but some kind of dummy: a feeling which suddenly becomes stronger at moments when the light catches the speaker's spectacles and turns them into blank discs which seem to have no eyes behind them. And this is not altogether fanciful. A speaker who uses that kind of phraseology has gone some distance toward turning himself into a machine. The appropriate noises are coming out of his larynx, but his brain is not involved as it would be if he were choosing his words for himself. If the speech he is making is one that he is accustomed to make over and over again, he may be almost unconscious of what he is saying, as one is when one utters the responses in church. And this reduced state of consciousness, if not indispensable, is at any rate favorable to political conformity.

[13] In our time, political speech and writing are largely the defense of the indefensible. Things like the continuance of British rule in India, the Russian purges and deportations, the dropping of the atom bombs on Japan, can indeed be defended, but only by arguments which are too brutal for most people to face, and which do not square with the professed aims of political parties. Thus political language has to consist largely of euphemism, question-begging and sheer cloudy vagueness. Defenseless villages are bombarded from the air, the inhabitants driven out into the countryside, the cattle machine-gunned, the huts set on fire with incendiary bullets: this is called *pacification*. Millions

of peasants are robbed of their farms and sent trudging along the roads with no more than they can carry: this is called *transfer of population* or *rectification of frontiers*. People are imprisoned for years without trial, or shot in the back of the neck or sent to die of scurvy in Arctic lumber camps: this is called *elimination of unreliable elements*. Such phraseology is needed if one wants to name things without calling up mental pictures of them. Consider for instance some comfortable English professor defending Russian totalitarianism. He cannot say outright, "I believe in killing off your opponents when you can get good results by doing so." Probably, therefore, he will say something like this:

"While freely conceding that the Soviet régime exhibits certain features which the humanitarian may be inclined to deplore, we must, I think, agree that a certain curtailment of the right to political opposition is an unavoidable concomitant of transitional periods, and that the rigors which the Russian people have been called upon to undergo have been amply justified in the sphere of concrete achievement."

[14]   The inflated style is itself a kind of euphemism. A mass of Latin words falls upon the facts like soft snow, blurring the outlines and covering up all the details. The great enemy of clear language is insincerity. When there is a gap between one's real and one's declared aims, one turns as it were instinctively to long words and exhausted idioms, like a cuttlefish squirting out ink. In our age there is no such thing as "keeping out of politics." All issues are political issues, and politics itself is a mass of lies, evasions, folly, hatred, and schizophrenia. When the general atmosphere is bad, language must suffer. I should expect to find—this is a guess which I have not sufficient knowledge to verify—that the German, Russian and Italian languages have all deteriorated in the last ten or fifteen years, as a result of dictatorship.

[15]   But if thought corrupts language, language can also corrupt thought. A bad usage can spread by tradition and imitation, even among people who should and do know better. The debased language that I have been discussing is in some ways very convenient. Phrases like *a not unjustifiable assumption, leaves much to be desired, would serve no good purpose, a consideration which we should do well to bear in mind,* are a continuous temptation, a packet of aspirins always at one's elbow. Look back through this essay, and for certain you will find that I have again and again committed the very faults I am protesting against. By this morning's post I have received a pamphlet dealing with conditions in Germany. The author tells me that he "felt impelled" to write it. I open it at random, and here is almost the first sentence that I see: "[The Allies] have an opportunity not only of achieving a radical transformation of Germany's social and political structure in such a way as to avoid a nationalistic reaction in Germany itself, but at the same time of laying the

foundations of a co-operative and unified Europe." You see, he "feels impelled" to write—feels, presumably, that he has something new to say—and yet his words, like cavalry horses answering the bugle, group themselves automatically into the familiar dreary pattern. This invasion of one's mind by ready-made phrases *(lay the foundations, achieve a radical transformation)* can only be prevented if one is constantly on guard against them, and every such phrase anaesthetizes a portion of one's brain.

[16] I said earlier that the decadence of our language is probably curable. Those who deny this would argue, if they produced an argument at all, that language merely reflects existing social conditions, and that we cannot influence its development by any direct tinkering with words and constructions. So far as the general tone or spirit of a language goes, this may be true, but it is not true in detail. Silly words and expressions have often disappeared, not through any evolutionary process but owing to the conscious action of a minority. Two recent examples were *explore every avenue* and *leave no stone unturned,* which were killed by the jeers of a few journalists. There is a long list of flyblown metaphors which could similarly be got rid of if enough people would interest themselves in the job; and it should also be possible to laugh the *not un-* formation out of existence,* to reduce the amount of Latin and Greek in the average sentence, to drive out foreign phrases and strayed scientific words, and, in general, to make pretentiousness unfashionable. But all these are minor points. The defense of the English language implies more than this, and perhaps it is best to start by saying what it does *not* imply.

[17] To begin with it has nothing to do with archaism, with the salvaging of obsolete words and turns of speech, or with the setting up of a "standard English" which must never be departed from. On the contrary, it is especially concerned with the scrapping of every word or idiom which has outworn its usefulness. It has nothing to do with correct grammar and syntax, which are of no importance so long as one makes one's meaning clear, or with the avoidance of Americanisms, or with having what is called a "good prose style." On the other hand it is not concerned with fake simplicity and the attempt to make written English colloquial. Nor does it even imply in every case preferring the Saxon word to the Latin one, though it does imply using the fewest and shortest words that will cover one's meaning. What is above all needed is to let the meaning choose the word, and not the other way about. In prose, the worst thing one can do with words is to surrender to them. When you think of a concrete object, you think wordlessly, and then, if you want to describe the thing you have been visualizing you probably hunt about till you

---

  * One can cure oneself of the *not un-* formation by memorizing this sentence: A *not unblack dog was chasing a not unsmall rabbit across a not ungreen field.*

find the exact words that seem to fit it. When you think of something abstract you are more inclined to use words from the start, and unless you make a conscious effort to prevent it, the existing dialect will come rushing in and do the job for you, at the expense of blurring or even changing your meaning. Probably it is better to put off using words as long as possible and get one's meaning as clear as one can through pictures or sensations. Afterward one can choose—not simply *accept*—the phrases that will best cover the meaning, and then switch round and decide what impression one's words are likely to make on another person. This last effort of the mind cuts out all stale or mixed images, all prefabricated phrases, needless repetitions, and humbug and vagueness generally. But one can often be in doubt about the effect of a word or a phrase, and one needs rules that one can rely on when instinct fails. I think the following rules will cover most cases:

(i)   Never use a metaphor, simile, or other figure of speech which you are used to seeing in print.
(ii) Never use a long word where a short one will do.
(iii) If it is possible to cut a word out, always cut it out.
(iv) Never use the passive where you can use the active.
(v)   Never use a foreign phrase, a scientific word, or a jargon word if you can think of an everyday English equivalent.
(vi) Break any of these rules sooner than say anything outright barbarous.

These rules sound elementary, and so they are, but they demand a deep change of attitude in anyone who has grown used to writing in the style now fashionable. One could keep all of them and still write bad English, but one could not write the kind of stuff that I quoted in those five specimens at the beginning of this article.

[18]   I have not here been considering the literary use of language, but merely language as an instrument for expressing and not for concealing or preventing thought. Stuart Chase and others have come near to claiming that all abstract words are meaningless, and have used this as a pretext for advocating a kind of political quietism. Since you don't know what Fascism is, how can you struggle against Fascism? One need not swallow such absurdities as this, but one ought to recognize that the present political chaos is connected with the decay of language, and that one can probably bring about some improvement by starting at the verbal end. If you simplify your English, you are freed from the worst follies of orthodoxy. You cannot speak any of the necessary dialects, and when you make a stupid remark its stupidity will be obvious, even to yourself. Political language—and with variations this is true of all political parties, from Conservatives to Anarchists—is designed to make lies sound truthful and murder respectable, and to give an appearance of solidity to pure

CAUSE AND EFFECT

wind. One cannot change this all in a moment, but one can at least change one's own habits, and from time to time one can even, if one jeers loudly enough, send some worn-out and useless phrase—some *jackboot, Achilles' heel, hotbed, melting pot, acid test, veritable inferno,* or other lump of verbal refuse —into the dustbin where it belongs.

SUGGESTIONS FOR WRITING

Material for writing comes from experience, reading, and reflection. If some of these assignments call for knowledge that has not come to you through experience, turn to sources beyond the essays offered in this book. You may look up specific topics in the *Reader's Guide to Periodical Literature* or other indexes on the reference shelves of your library.

1. After reading Dan Lacy's "Men's Words; Women's Roles" you may find that people are much affected by words. How is our behavior, our self-image, even our choice of career affected by what people around us say of us? Write a cause-effect essay based upon that consideration.

2. If you have some background in physics, you may know why an automobile horn seems to change in pitch if sounded as we are passing that automobile in an opposite direction. If you do not already know the cause, look up the Doppler effect in a reference book and try to find its cause. Write a cause-effect essay in which you explain the cause and the effect to readers not yet familiar with it.

3. Baseball remains the "great American game" despite many criticisms that it is slow and old-fashioned; professional baseball still plays to more spectators than does any other sport. Try to find factual evidence to support this statement. If you find it true, what do you believe to be the causes of baseball's popularity? Write a cause-effect essay presenting the results of your thinking.

4. It is currently popular to blame science or technology for many of the unfavorable aspects of our environment. After reading Philip Wylie's "Science Is Spoiling My Supper," you may be reminded of other effects of "science" in your daily life. Write a cause-effect paper tracing some effect that science or technology has had upon your life. You need not, of course, limit yourself to what is bad in your environment.

5. What influences us to form our political beliefs? Write a cause-effect essay showing why, in your opinion, we become Republicans, Democrats, Independents, Socialists, or whatever.

6. Many books have been written on the causes of love—and, of course, upon the effects of love. But what causes human beings to hate? Write a cause-effect essay setting forth your ideas on that question.

7. Consider Philip Wylie's contention that obesity is caused by the frustrated need for good taste in food. Do you believe there are other causes of obesity? What are they? Can you find scientific or other authoritative evidence to support

your belief? Write a cause-effect essay presenting the results of your thinking and investigation.

8. Do people rebel against authority for good reasons? What are some of the reasons for rebelliousness in human life? Write a cause-effect essay setting forth your opinions on this question, illustrating your ideas with as much personal experience and observation as possible.

9. Thoreau, in another essay in *Walden*, wrote that "most men lead lives of quiet desperation." Well, what about women? To what extent are American women, especially housewives and mothers, leading lives of quiet desperation? If you believe that many of them are, write a cause-effect paper discussing the causes of that desperation.

10. Could man's hunting of wild animals cause a disruption of earth's ecological balance? Following the lead of Thoreau, write an essay that appears to be more personal experience than discussion of facts, yet one that presents the thesis that hunting may be an affront to nature, a desecration of earth's garden. If you do not agree with this thesis, write a cause-effect essay on the beneficial effects of man's hunting of wild animals. On this point it may be helpful to read still another chapter of Thoreau's *Walden*, titled "Higher Laws," in which he argues in favor of hunting.

DEFINITION

Many subjects do not lend themselves to the methods of analysis. If you want to write about love, for example, you may discuss various types of love—parental love, filial love, love of an ideal, physical love, love of country. You will not, however, have clarified what love is. You will have said something about it; you will have shown that love has many forms. But the term *love* will be almost as vague to the reader as it was before he read your essay. Abstract terms like *love, patriotism, courage* demand the methods of definition. Instead of talking about their component parts, you must talk about their essential natures. Instead of analyzing, you must synthesize—bring the parts together to make a whole. You must limit and exclude. A definition of love does not explain all of the types of love but rather finds a common denominator that will apply to love in any form. The definition will explain that all forms of love embody strong affection, attachment, and devotion.

Definitions are of two main types: logical or formal, and extended or informal. The **logical** or **formal definition** is the dictionary definition and is rigorous and rigid in form. It consists of three essential parts: the **term**, the

genus, and the **differentiae.** The term is the word to be defined, the species. The genus limits the term to a restricted class. The differentiae state the distinguishing characteristics that set the species apart from other members of its genus. Here is a logical definition: "A helmet is a head covering worn for protection." The term is *helmet.* The genus is *head covering.* But there are many types of head coverings: hats, caps, bonnets, berets, etc. What limits the helmet?—its protective purpose. Therefore, the words *worn for protection* provide the differentiae. Any type of head covering worn for protection is a helmet. No other type of head covering is a helmet. The logical definition is restrictive.

But the use of the logical definition is clearly limited. It is effective when used to define a concrete noun like *helmet,* or like *pencil, scissors, telephone, paper.* These things can be seen, touched, or felt. Abstractions, however, are more difficult to define. Since they may be ideals *(freedom, democracy, liberty),* emotions *(love, pity, disgust),* or concepts *(liberal education, literature, poetry),* there is not always full agreement about their nature. They can be discussed most meaningfully when the participants in the discussion have reached some agreement about what they mean, and they can be explained satisfactorily only through **extended** or **informal definitions.** Such definitions are ultimately the same as logical or formal definitions, for they both must necessarily use classification and differentiation. The distinction is merely one of extension. In his extended definition of *democracy,* for example, Carl Becker begins by establishing the word in its class, *government,* and then shows how it differs from other forms of government.

The chronological tracing of the history of a term is another useful method for defining words that have changed in meaning over the years. Becker employs this device in his definition of *democracy,* though his purpose is not an exhaustive chronological survey; he provides enough examples through time, however, to indicate significant changes in meaning. The exhaustive discussion of changes in meaning is illustrated by Edmund Wilson's definition of *Americanism,* a term that not only has changed meaning but, according to Wilson, has developed unfortunate connotations.

Historical tracing is akin to the etymological method, which treats a word in the light of its original meaning. The etymology of the word *exposition* opens the introduction to "Exposition" and is helpful in explaining what the word means. Since words change in their meaning, however, the etymology of a given word is frequently of small use in helping a writer to make a precise definition.

In addition, all of the methods of development discussed in the introduction to "Exposition"—the use of examples, comparisons, analogies, contrast, exclusion, or negation—can be used effectively in the theme of definition. In order to narrow the broad definition of *slang* with which they begin, Bloomfield and Newmark move from a discussion of the occasional use of substandard language by speakers of standard dialect to a narrower sense of the word that defines it in terms of social in-groups, thereby excluding all substandard language that is not intended to identify the speaker socially. In his definition of *language*, Sturtevant excludes—only for convenience, as he says—all forms of nonvocal language. Becker uses comparisons and analogies in his definition of *democracy*.

Essays aiming at definition may follow either of two general methods of development: **deduction** or **induction**. The essay employing deduction begins with a definition and brings in specific examples to support or illustrate the definition. The definition of *language* in this book illustrates this pattern of development. The inductive essay reaches the definition *after* employing any of the methods of development. In his discussion of democracy, for example, Carl Becker arrives at his definition after examining a number of examples.

The goal of the extended definition—the limited, restrictive summary—often appears as a **restatement**, in which the essentials of the definition are repeated or reinforced. In the first paragraph of his essay "What Is a Poet?" Mark Van Doren states his definition: "My only conception of the poet is that he is a person who writes poetry." In the final paragraph of his essay he restates the definition informally, but this time with the force of the numerous examples he has employed by way of illustration.

Carl L. Becker

HISTORY

Carl L. Becker (1873–1945) was for many years professor of European history at Cornell University. His numerous books and articles, such as The Declaration of Independence: A Study in the History of Political Ideas *(1922)* and Everyman His Own Historian *(1935), are distinguished contributions to the literature of history. The following three paragraphs open Professor Becker's essay "Everyman His Own Historian," which he delivered as the presidential address before the American Historical Association in 1931.*

[1]   Once upon a time, long, long ago, I learned how to reduce a fraction to its lowest terms. Whether I could still perform that operation is uncertain;

From "Everyman His Own Historian," by Carl L. Becker, *The American Historical Review*, 37 (January 1932), 221–223. Reprinted by permission of *The American Historical Review*.

DEFINITION

but the discipline involved in early training had its uses, since it taught me that in order to understand the essential nature of anything it is well to strip it of all superficial and irrelevant accretions—in short, to reduce it to its lowest terms. That operation I now venture, with some apprehension and all due apologies, to perform on the subject of history.

[2] I ought first of all to explain that when I use the term history I mean knowledge of history. No doubt throughout all past time there actually occurred a series of events which, whether we know what it was or not, constitutes history in some ultimate sense. Nevertheless, much the greater part of these events we can know nothing about, not even that they occurred; many of them we can know only imperfectly; and even the few events that we think we know for sure we can never be absolutely certain of, since we can never revive them, never observe or test them directly. The event itself once occurred, but as an actual event it has disappeared; so that in dealing with it the only objective reality we can observe or test is some material trace which the event has left—usually a written document. With these traces of vanished events, these documents, we must be content since they are all we have; from them we infer what the event was, we affirm that it is a fact that the event was so and so. We do not say "Lincoln is assassinated"; we say "it is a fact that Lincoln was assassinated." The event *was*, but is no longer; it is only the affirmed fact about the event that *is*, that persists, and will persist until we discover that our affirmation is wrong or inadequate. Let us then admit that there are two histories: the actual series of events that once occurred; and the ideal series that we affirm and hold in memory. The first is absolute and unchanged—it was what it was whatever we do or say about it; the second is relative, always changing in response to the increase or refinement of knowledge. The two series correspond more or less; it is our aim to make the correspondence as exact as possible; but the actual series of events exists for us only in terms of the ideal series which we affirm and hold in memory. This is why I am forced to identify history with knowledge of history. For all practical purposes history is, for us and for the time being, what we know it to be.

[3] It is history in this sense that I wish to reduce to its lowest terms. In order to do that I need a very simple definition. I once read that "History is the knowledge of events that have occurred in the past." That is a simple definition, but not simple enough. It contains three words that require examination. The first is knowledge. Knowledge is a formidable word. I always think of knowledge as something that is stored up in the *Encyclopaedia Britannica* or the *Summa Theologica*; something difficult to acquire, something at all events that I have not. Resenting a definition that denies me the title of historian, I therefore ask what is most essential to knowledge. Well, memory, I should

think (and I mean memory in the broad sense, the memory of events inferred as well as the memory of events observed); other things are necessary too, but memory is fundamental: without memory no knowledge. So our definition becomes, "History is the memory of events that have occurred in the past." But events—the word carries an implication of something grand, like the taking of the Bastille or the Spanish-American War. An occurrence need not be spectacular to be an event. If I drive a motor car down the crooked streets of Ithaca, that is an event—something done; if the traffic cop bawls me out, that is an event—something said; if I have evil thoughts of him for so doing, that is an event—something thought. In truth anything done, said, or thought is an event, important or not as may turn out. But since we do not ordinarily speak without thinking, at least in some rudimentary way, and since the psychologists tell us that we cannot think without speaking, or at least not without having anticipatory vibrations in the larynx, we may well combine thought events and speech events under one term; and so our definition becomes, "History is the memory of things said and done in the past." But the past—the word is both misleading and unnecessary: misleading, because the past, used in connection with history, seems to imply the distant past, as if history ceased before we were born; unnecessary, because after all everything said or done is already in the past as soon as it is said or done. Therefore I will omit that word, and our definition becomes, "History is the memory of things said or done." This is a definition that reduces history to its lowest terms, and yet includes everything that is essential to understanding what it really is.

VOCABULARY

Define the following words as they are used in the selection: *superficial, irrelevant, accretions* [1]; *affirm, absolute, relative* [2]; *formidable, rudimentary* [3].

QUESTIONS FOR STUDY AND DISCUSSION

1. According to Professor Becker in paragraph 1, what is the principal task of the writer of a definition? Is the mathematical analogy a clear and an effective one?

2. Identify the genus and the differentiae of the definition of "history in some ultimate sense" in paragraph 2.

3. What distinction does Becker make between history and the knowledge of history? Why is this distinction important to the logical definition at which Becker arrives in paragraph 3?

4. What methods does Becker use to distinguish between the two types of history in paragraph 2?

5. Identify the parts of the preliminary definition of history in paragraph 3. How does it differ from the definition analyzed in question 2 above? What are the three words in this preliminary definition that require examination?

6. Why does the preliminary definition deny Becker "the title of historian"?

7. Identify the parts of the definition of the word *event* at which Becker finally arrives. What methods of extended definition has he employed in making this definition?

8. Why does Becker omit the phrase "in the past"?

9. Identify the parts of the definition of history with which Becker concludes. In what particulars does it differ from the two other definitions of history in the selection?

10. Compare Becker's definition of history with the one given in your dictionary. How do they differ? In what ways are they the same?

Carl L. Becker

DEMOCRACY

This definition of democracy opens Carl L. Becker's Modern Democracy, *a collection of three lectures delivered at the University of Virginia in 1940. It represents, as Becker says in the final (unquoted) sentence of the third paragraph, "the meaning which I attach to [democracy] in these lectures."*

[1] Democracy, like liberty or science or progress, is a word with which we are all so familiar that we rarely take the trouble to ask what we mean by it. It is a term, as the devotees of semantics say, which has no "referent"—there is no precise or palpable thing or object which we all think of when the word is pronounced. On the contrary, it is a word which connotes different things to different people, a kind of conceptual Gladstone bag which, with a little manipulation can be made to accommodate almost any collection of social

From *Modern Democracy*, by Carl L. Becker. Reprinted by permission of Yale University Press.

facts we may wish to carry about in it. In it we can as easily pack a dictatorship as any other form of government. We have only to stretch the concept to include any form of government supported by a majority of the people, for whatever reasons and by whatever means of expressing assent, and before we know it the empire of Napoleon, the Soviet regime of Stalin, and the Fascist systems of Mussolini and Hitler are all safely in the bag. But if this is what we mean by democracy, then virtually all forms of government are democratic, since virtually all governments, except in times of revolution, rest upon the explicit or implicit consent of the people. In order to discuss democracy intelligently, it will be necessary, therefore, to define it, to attach to the word a sufficiently precise meaning to avoid the confusion which is not infrequently the chief result of such discussions.

[2]   All human institutions, we are told, have their ideal forms laid away in heaven, and we do not need to be told that the actual institutions conform but indifferently to these ideal counterparts. It would be possible then to define democracy either in terms of the ideal or in terms of the real form—to define it as government of the people, by the people, for the people; or to define it as government of the people, by the politicians, for whatever pressure groups can get their interests taken care of. But as a historian I am naturally disposed to be satisfied with the meaning which, in the history of politics, men have commonly attributed to the word—a meaning, needless to say, which derives partly from the experience and partly from the aspirations of mankind. So regarded, the term democracy refers primarily to a form of government, and it has always meant government by the many as opposed to government by the one—government by the people as opposed to government by a tyrant, a dictator, or an absolute monarch. This is the most general meaning of the word as men have commonly understood it.

[3]   In this antithesis there are, however, certain implications, always tacitly understood, which give a more precise meaning to the term. Peisistratus, for example, was supported by a majority of the people, but his government was never regarded as a democracy for all that. Caesar's power derived from a popular mandate, conveyed through established republican forms, but that did not make his government any the less a dictatorship. Napoleon called his government a democratic empire, but no one, least of all Napoleon himself, doubted that he had destroyed the last vestiges of the democratic republic. Since the Greeks first used the term, the essential test of democratic government has always been this: the source of political authority must be and remain in the people and not in the ruler. A democratic government has always meant one in which the citizens, or a sufficient number of them to represent more or less effectively the common will, freely act from time to time, and ac-

DEFINITION

cording to established forms, to appoint or recall the magistrates and to enact or revoke the laws by which the community is governed. This I take to be the meaning which history has impressed upon the term democracry as a form of government.

VOCABULARY

Define the following words as they are used in the selection: *devotees, semantics, palpable, connotes, conceptual, Gladstone bag, explicit, implicit* [1]; *aspirations* [2]; *antithesis, tacitly, mandate, republican, vestiges* [3].

QUESTIONS FOR STUDY AND DISCUSSION

1. What important need for careful definitions does Becker's first paragraph point out?

2. Your dictionary lists several meanings under *democracy*. Does it list the stretched concept that Becker attacks in paragraph 1? Does it list the one with which he concludes? Is the dictionary definition or Becker's definition the more explicit?

3. If the term *democracy* has no referent, how can it be defined? What is the basis of Becker's definition in paragraph 2? Is his source valid?

4. In paragraph 2 Becker paraphrases Lincoln, who himself paraphrased Theodore Parker's definition: "Democracy is direct self-government, over all the people, for all the people, by all the people." Why does Becker call this a definition "in terms of the ideal"? Is Becker's final definition "real" or "ideal"? Is it more or less "real" than the definition "in terms of the real" in paragraph 2? What is the tone (witty, cynical, objective) of this "real" definition in paragraph 2?

5. What is the key part of Becker's definition that excludes from democracy the governments of Napoleon, Stalin, Mussolini, Hitler, Peisistratus, and Caesar?

6. Becker's next-to-last statement is a logical definition. Indicate the term, the genus, the differentiae. Point out how the differentiae are more discriminating and restricting than those in paragraph 2.

7. Becker makes use of many of the methods of extended definition. Point out examples of the following: comparison, contrast, historical tracing, analysis, restatement, example. Which methods are the most effective?

8. What is the analogy in paragraph 1? Does the analogy explain anything about the meaning of *democracy*, or does it indicate the semantic problem?

Edmund Wilson

AMERICANISM

In this complete essay from his book A Piece of My Mind *(1956), Edmund Wilson (1895–1972) explores the changes in the meaning of the word* Americanism. *A highly respected literary critic and commentator on American economic and social opinions, Wilson was also the author of fiction, poetry, plays, and historical studies. His volume* Patriotic Gore *(1962) evaluates the impact of the Civil War upon prominent Americans who were caught up in it.*

It is curious to trace the vicissitudes of the term *Americanism*. The first quotation given in the *Dictionary of Americanisms* published by Chicago University is from a letter of Jefferson's of 1797: "The parties here in debate continually charged each other . . . with being governed by an attachment to this or that of the belligerent nations, rather than the dictates of reason and pure Americanism." This is Americanism in the sense defined by Webster (1806) as "a love of America and preference of her interest." In Jefferson's time, of course, it meant the interests of the revolted colonists. But by the fifties of the following century, the word *Americanism* was to take on a new political meaning. It was used by the American or Know Nothing party to designate its own policy . . . of combating the Roman Catholicism of German and Irish immigrants and of debarring persons of foreign birth from exercising political rights till they had lived here twenty-one years. It is in this sense that Lincoln uses it when, in a letter of May 15, 1858, he speaks of the chances of the Republican party: "I think our prospects gradually, and steadily, grow better; though we are not clear out of the woods by a great deal. There is still some effort to make trouble out of 'Americanism.'" This meaning was soon to lapse with the demise of the Know Nothing party. But the word was to be revived, with quite different implications, by Theodore Roosevelt in the nineties. The first use of it in Roosevelt's correspondence is in a letter of December 8, 1888, to Thomas R. Lounsbury, congratulating him on his *Life of Cooper*: "As a very sincere American myself, I feel like thanking you for the genuine Americanism of your book; which is quite as much displayed in its criticisms as in its praises." Here he is speaking merely of an American point of view; but by the time he writes to William Archer in 1899

From *A Piece of My Mind: Reflections at Sixty*, by Edmund Wilson. Reprinted by permission of the late author.

(August 31), he is giving the word a meaning of his own: "I have exactly the feeling about Americanism you describe. Most important of all is it for this country to treat an American on his worth as a man, and to disregard absolutely whether he be of English, German, Irish or any other nation; whether he be of Catholic or Protestant faith." . . . This is Roosevelt at his best. He has changed the Know Nothings' emphasis: instead of wanting to exclude the immigrant, he wishes to take him in and to propose a common ideal of disinterested public service. He is to talk, from the nineties on, a good deal about Americanism, and to give the word a general currency. He is eventually to make it stand for the whole of his political philosophy. Here is his definition in a letter to S. Stanwood Menken of January 10, 1917: "Americanism means many things. It means equality of rights and therefore equality of duty and of obligation. It means service to our common country. It means loyalty to one flag, to our flag, the flag of all of us. It means on the part of each of us respect for the rights of the rest of us. It means that all of us guarantee the rights of each of us. It means free education, genuinely representative government, freedom of speech and thought, equality before the law for all men, genuine political and religious freedom, and the democratizing of industry so as to give at least a measurable quality of opportunity for all, and so as to place before us, as our ideal in all industries where this ideal is possible of attainment, the system of coöperative ownership and management, in order that the tool-users may, so far as possible, become the tool-owners. Everything is un-American that tends either to government by a plutocracy or government by a mob. To divide along the lines of section or caste or creed is un-American. All privileges based on wealth, and all enmity to honest men merely because they are wealthy, are un-American—both of them equally so. Americanism means the virtues of courage, honor, justice, truth, sincerity, and hardihood—the virtues that made America." The last letter included in his published correspondence —written on January 3, 1919, three days before his death, to be read at a benefit concert of the American Defense Society—has, however, an emphasis that is somewhat different. This was written at the end of the first world war, in the era . . . of the mass deportation of radicals. The old chief in retirement had by this time passed into an apoplectic phase in which he was convinced, for example, that the International Workers of the World were necessarily a criminal organization and that labor leaders were guilty, as a matter of course, of the crimes of which, in that moment of hysteria, they were lavishly being accused. "There must be no sagging back," writes Roosevelt, "in the fight for Americanism merely because the war is over. . . . There can be no divided allegiance here. . . . Any man who says he is an American, but something else also, isn't an American at all. We have room for but one flag, the American flag, and this excludes the red flag which symbolizes all wars against liberty and civilization just as much as it excludes any foreign flag of a nation to which we are hostile." This is the fear of the foreigner again. It was rampant after Roosevelt's death, and anyone with a non-Anglo-Saxon name who ventured to complain about anything or to propose a social reform was likely to be told at once that if he didn't like it here in the United States, he ought to go back where he came from. By this time, the very term "Americanism" had become a black-mailing menace. One remembers reading in the New York *Tribune* of March 3, 1920, that the younger Theodore Roosevelt, chairman of the American Legion's "Americanism Commission," had called a meeting "at which it was decided to thoroughly Americanize all war veterans, then to utilize them in the work of making good citizens of the foreign-born of the State." It may not be true that "Americanism"—like Dr. Johnson's "patriotism"—is invariably "the last refuge of a scoundrel"; but it has been made to serve some very bad causes, and is now a word to avoid.

VOCABULARY

Define the following words as they are used in the selection: *curious, vicissitudes, belligerent, revolted, implications, disinterested, democratizing, plutocracy, apoplectic, hysteria, lavishly, rampant.*

QUESTIONS FOR STUDY AND DISCUSSION

1. This definition of *Americanism* utilizes a method not employed as a major device by any other of the writers of definitions studied thus far. What is the principal method employed by Wilson? Could the method have been used in defining democracy or history?

2. In tracing the "vicissitudes of the term *Americanism*," Wilson touches upon several different meanings of the word. List these meanings in outline form; let Wilson's summaries of the meanings serve as main topics; let his examples serve as subtopics. Provide dates for the examples. Depending upon your interpretation, you will find either five or six main topics.

3. Wilson's essay is concerned with the various differentiae of the term *Americanism*. He does not emphasize the genus of the word. What is the genus?

4. Go through Wilson's essay again and extract the definitions of *Americanism* that he discusses. Write each of these as a formal definition. You will, of course, have to condense some of them.

5. Which of the meanings receive Wilson's apparent approval? Which ones does he criticize, and why?

6. What does Wilson achieve by illustrating three or four meanings of the

term with quotations from the writings of Theodore Roosevelt? What are Wilson's attitudes toward Roosevelt?

7. Examine Roosevelt's definition in his letter to Menken (beginning "Americanism means many things"). What methods of definition does he employ?

8. How does your dictionary define the word *Americanism*? Which of Wilson's examples most closely fits the dictionary definition? What limitations does the dictionary definition have?

9. Wilson has set up his essay as a single paragraph, with a single topic sentence: "It is curious to trace the vicissitudes of the term *Americanism*." The essay could, however, be effectively divided into shorter paragraphs. Suggest where these paragraph divisions might come. What principle governs your suggestions?

E. H. Sturtevant

LANGUAGE

A noted scholar in the field of language study, Edgar H. Sturtevant (1875–1952) held appointments as an instructor in Greek and Latin and Professor of Linguistics at Yale University. He was well known for his instruction and research in Greek grammar and Latin and Greek pronunciation. The following definition of language is drawn from his book An Introduction to Linguistic Science (1947).

[1] A language is a system of arbitrary vocal symbols by which members of a social group cooperate and interact.

[2] The word *system* marks a language off from mere sets of nonsense syllables like *ta-ra-ra-boom-de-ay* or *a-heigh-and-a-ho-and-a-heigh-nonny-no*. With the proper rhythm and intonation these or any other groups of syllables can carry a highly emotional message, but they do not form a part of the systematic structure of the English language. In contrast, the sentence *the dog bites the man* is thoroughly systematic; we can transpose the words *dog* and *man* and still be understood by all English-speaking hearers, although the meaning of the sentence *the man bites the dog* is absurd. In spite of an entirely different mechanism the two Latin sentences *canis hominem mordet* and *homō canem mordet* stand in a similar relative position; it is only the system of the Latin

From *An Introduction to Linguistic Science*, by E. H. Sturtevant. Reprinted by permission of Yale University Press.

language that compels us to take the second sentence in a sense that defies all experience.

[3] The key word of the phrase *arbitrary vocal symbols* is the noun *symbols*. A symbol necessarily involves a dualism; there must be something that stands for or represents something else. This may be indicated by a diagram:

$$\frac{\text{the signifier*}}{\text{the signified}} \quad \text{or better} \quad \frac{\text{form}}{\text{meaning}}$$

In the case before us the *form* is any meaningful segment of an utterance, and the *meaning* is the meaning of that segment. An *arbitrary* symbol is one whose form has no necessary or natural connection with its meaning. English *dog* has roughly the same meaning as German *Hund*, French *chien*, Latin *canis*, and hundreds of other words in as many other languages. The only reason why *dog* carries this meaning is that the speakers of English use it with this meaning. The word *vocal* stands in the definition to exclude the human activities denoted by the phrases *gesture language, sign language, written language,* etc. All of these are important activities and proper subjects of investigation, and besides they have obvious connections with audible speech. The only reason for excluding them from our definition is convenience; they are found not to behave in the same way as audible language, and so they cannot conveniently be treated scientifically at the same time.

[4] The final clause of the definition, *by which the members of a social group cooperate and interact,* designates the chief function of language in society. There are, of course, other means of cooperation between living beings, as witness the wolf pack, the swarm of bees, etc. Even men may cooperate not only by writing or by gesture but by actual physical compulsion or by a smile or by the raising of an eyebrow. All we mean to say is that among men language is by far the commonest and most important means of cooperation. Society as now constituted could not long continue without the use of language. We must not forget, however, that language may also be used to interfere with the action of a group or to oppose one group to another; we cannot end our definition with the word *cooperate*.

[5] A corollary of the final clause of the definition is that a language cannot function normally unless there are at least two speakers of it. When only one speaker remains, the language may be said to be dead.

* The horizontal line may be read, "combined with" or "simultaneous with."

QUESTIONS FOR STUDY AND DISCUSSION

1. Identify the parts of the formal definition of language in paragraph 1.

2. What instances of negation are used in paragraphs 2 and 3?

3. Both the English and Latin languages are systematic. What basic difference in the two systems is illustrated by the examples given?

4. What further examples of formal definitions appear in paragraph 3?

5. Rewrite the third sentence of paragraph 3 without making use of the diagram, but incorporating the explanation provided in Sturtevant's footnote. Is the diagrammatic presentation of information more clear than the statement of it?

6. Are all words in the English language arbitrary symbols? Can you give examples of any that are not?

7. Can you suggest why, in paragraph 4, Sturtevant does not use the word *communicate* in place of *cooperate and interact*?

8. What other examples of cooperation between beings could Sturtevant have named in paragraph 4?

9. What distinction do the two words *cooperate* and *interact* denote?

10. Which definition of *dead* in your dictionary is the one applicable to Sturtevant's use of the word in his final paragraph?

Morton W. Bloomfield and Leonard Newmark

SLANG

Like almost all other writers about slang, Professors Bloomfield and Newmark preface their comments with the remark that slang is interesting, widely used, and difficult to define. By focusing on its social function, however, they are able to show what slang is and why it is, what its appeal is and what its characteristics are. Professor Bloomfield, who teaches in the English Department at Harvard, has written widely on language and literature. Also an author of several books and articles, Professor Newmark teaches linguistics at the University of California, San Diego.

From A *Linguistic Introduction to the History of English*, by Morton W. Bloomfield and Leonard Newmark. Copyright © 1963 by Morton W. Bloomfield and Leonard Newmark. Reprinted by permission of the authors.

[1] . . . A language varies both with the geographic location and with the various complex social positions—including those of status and education, trade and profession, age and sex—of its speakers.

[2] One of the most interesting types of social dialect is *slang*, a phenomenon widely recognized and used, but difficult to define. In its broad sense the word *slang* can designate almost any use of substandard linguistic features by speakers of standard dialects. At times speakers of a standard dialect will deliberately use such features to gain a certain effect—humor, intimacy, irony, and so forth. Every dialect, including standard dialect, binds its speakers together to some extent. But standard speakers may wish on occasion to identify themselves with groups in society who speak special nonstandard dialects and may then use phrases or words or pronunciations from those dialects.

[3] *Slang*, in a narrower sense of the word, refers to the speech of social in-groups, notably adolescents, which aims at excluding outsiders. It is part of the defense which an in-group throws up to isolate itself and give itself a sense of superiority, perhaps the same motive which leads children sometimes to invent languages so as to exclude others, particularly adults. As slang expressions get widely known they lose their feature of exclusiveness, and new slang develops. All this helps to explain the ephemerality of much slang, although some slang words and phrases are long-lived (for example, *booze*), and others get taken into standard dialect (*mob* was eighteenth-century slang). Slang phrases or words are sometimes marked by vivid metaphors or implied metaphors. At other times, they are merely variations of socially acceptable words, as for instance *natch*, which was popular a few years ago for *naturally*.

[4] In some countries, such as England, the socially accepted forms of speech play a large role in social and financial success. In the United States "good" English is not quite so highly regarded, although it would hardly be correct to say that it is ignored.

[5] Many professions and trades have their own jargons or cants which are used naturally by their members and are often not known by outsiders. The cant of jazz has close relations with slang because adolescents, who in their rebellious conformity take to slang, are the chief audience for jazz. Certain exclusive or special activities like hunting and soldiering have their own vocabularies and pronunciations which the participants learn. There is no evidence that the large variety of social dialects is being lessened, although the current extension of education might be expected to lead to a leveling of the differences between them.

[6] On the other hand, regional dialects seem to be losing their hold today, with the growth and extension of the means of communication and general social mobility. In a country like the United States, where a great part of the population is on the move, where radio, television, movies, and records penetrate everywhere, distinctions in speech based on location are gradually being eliminated. They will, however, certainly be with us for a long time yet.

VOCABULARY

1. As part of a longer discussion of language, this definition and discussion of slang employs a few linguistic terms that may be only partially meaningful without further attention. In paragraph 2 slang is described as a type of "social dialect." Look up the word *dialect* in a good college desk dictionary. Which of the definitions of the word explains its meaning as a social phenomenon? The definition of *dialect* will be followed by a synonymy of words with similar meanings. How does *dialect* differ from *jargon* and *cant* [5]? How do *social dialects* differ from *regional dialects* [6]?

2. What definition of *standard* in your dictionary explains its meaning in the phrases *standard speakers* and *standard dialect* [2]?

QUESTIONS FOR STUDY AND DISCUSSION

Note: Do the two vocabulary exercises above before answering the following questions:

1. Paragraph 1 points out two principal variants of a language. Using the information provided in this paragraph, formulate a brief formal definition of *social dialect*.

2. Paragraphs 2 through 5 emphasize an important social function of slang. What is the social function?

3. What characteristics of slang are mentioned in this selection? How are these characteristics related to the social function of slang?

4. In both paragraphs 3 and 5 slang is discussed as a phenomenon of adolescence. What needs of adolescents account for their fondness for slang?

5. In paragraph 4 is a brief mention of " 'good' English." In what sense is this type of English a social dialect? Why is such English less highly regarded in this country than in England?

6. What is the effect of mass communication and social mobility on regional dialects? What effect do these phenomena have on social dialects? Why?

7. A thorough discussion of slang would require far more examples than appear in this selection. Yet examples are readily available to illustrate the characteristics and features of slang mentioned in this selection. What features of slang discussed in the selection are illustrated by the following slang words: *headshrinker, whirlybird, sawbones, squares, eager beaver, cool, hood?*

8. What use do the authors make of comparison, exclusion, and other techniques of extended definition?

Claude Brown

"BABY"

Manchild in the Promised Land (1965) is the brutally candid autobiography of Claude Brown (b. 1937), who grew up in Harlem and spent part of his youth in a reform school. Brown's story points up the difficulties of living in the ghetto and focuses on the author's escape from the street gangs to a new life. He has since gone on to Howard and Rutgers universities.

[1]   The first time I heard the expression "baby" used by one cat to address another was up at Warwick in 1951. Gus Jackson used it. The term had a hip ring to it, a real colored ring. The first time I heard it, I knew right away I had to start using it. It was like saying, "Man, look at me. I've got masculinity to spare." It was saying at the same time to the world, "I'm one of the hippest cats, one of the most uninhibited cats on the scene. I can say 'baby' to another cat, and he can say 'baby' to me, and we can say it with strength in our voices." If you could say it, this meant that you really had to be sure of yourself, sure of your masculinity.

[2]   It seemed that everybody in my age group was saying it. The next thing I knew, older guys were saying it. Then just about everybody in Harlem was saying it, even the cats who weren't so hip. It became just one of those things.

[3]   The real hip thing about the "baby" term was that it was something that only colored cats could say the way it was supposed to be said. I'd heard gray

Reprinted with permission of Macmillan Publishing Co., Inc. from *Manchild in the Promised Land,* by Claude Brown. Copyright © 1965 by Claude Brown.

DEFINITION

boys trying it, but they couldn't really do it. Only colored cats could give it the meaning that we all knew it had without ever mentioning it—the meaning of black masculinity.

[4]   Before the Muslims, before I'd heard about the Coptic or anything like that, I remember getting high on the corner with a bunch of guys and watching the chicks go by, fine little girls, and saying, "Man, colored people must be somethin' else!"

[5]   Somebody'd say, "Yeah. How about that? All those years, man, we was down on the plantation in those shacks, eating just potatoes and fatback and chitterlin's and greens, and look at what happened. We had Joe Louises and Jack Johnsons and Sugar Ray Robinsons and Henry Armstrongs, all that sort of thing."

[6]   Somebody'd say, "Yeah, man. Niggers must be some real strong people who just can't be kept down. When you think about it, that's really something great. Fatback, chitterlin's, greens, and Joe Louis. Negroes are some beautiful people. Uh-huh. Fatback, chitterlin's, greens, and Joe Louis . . . and beautiful black bitches."

[7]   Cats would come along with this "baby" thing. It was something that went over strong in the fifties with the jazz musicians and the hip set, the boxers, the dancers, the comedians, just about every set in Harlem. I think everybody said it real loud because they liked the way it sounded. It was always, "Hey, baby. How you doin', baby?" in every phase of the Negro hip life. As a matter of fact, I went to a Negro lawyer's office once, and he said, "Hey, baby. How you doin'?" I really felt at ease, really felt that we had something in common. I imagine there were many people in Harlem who didn't feel they had too much in common with the Negro professionals, the doctors and lawyers and dentists and ministers. I know I didn't. But to hear one of these people greet you with the street thing, the "Hey, baby"—and he knew how to say it—you felt as though you had something strong in common.

[8]   I suppose it's the same thing that almost all Negroes have in common, the fatback, chitterlings, and greens background. I suppose that regardless of what any Negro in America might do or how high he might rise in social status, he still has something in common with every other Negro. I doubt that they're many, if any, gray people who could ever say "baby" to a Negro and make him feel that "me and this cat have got something going, something strong going."

[9]   In the fifties, when "baby" came around, it seemed to be the prelude to a whole new era in Harlem. It was the introduction to the era of black reflection. A fever started spreading.

VOCABULARY

1. This selection is obviously rich in the use of slang. Which of these slang words are recognized by your dictionary: *hip, cat, gray?*
2. Identify the following proper nouns: *Muslims, Coptic* [4].

QUESTIONS FOR STUDY AND DISCUSSION

1. Without making any overt attempt to define the particular meaning of the word *baby,* Brown provides an autobiographical, dramatic context that illustrates very well the implications of the term. To what regular technique of definition is Brown's method most closely related? Which of the other definitions in this book uses the method? How does that definition differ from Brown's? Why?

2. This selection provides an excellent example of some of the features of slang described by Professors Bloomfield and Newmark in the preceding selection. Which of their statements can be used to place this usage of the word *baby* in the genus of social dialect?

3. Which characteristics of slang are illustrated by this discussion of *baby?*

4. How does this usage of *baby* illustrate the principal purpose of slang?

5. One feature of slang not mentioned by Professors Bloomfield and Newmark is that a slang term has strong connotations in addition to its denotation. In fact, if a word is strictly denotative—that is, if it merely names something—it is not slang. What does Brown say that suggests the connotative value of *baby?*

6. Professors Bloomfield and Newmark mention the reasons that users of standard English sometimes employ slang. Which of these reasons are illustrated by Brown's comments?

7. What purpose do paragraphs 4 through 6 serve in this selection?

8. What is Brown's purpose in this selection? What social phenomenon does the use of *baby* partially explain?

9. Does your dictionary recognize the slang usage of *baby* that Brown describes? If not, what definition is most closely related to the one implicit in this selection?

10. Formulate a formal definition of this use of the word *baby.*

FOR FURTHER ANALYSIS

Mark Van Doren

WHAT IS A POET?

Following the completion of his doctorate at Columbia University, Mark Van Doren (1894–1972) joined the English faculty of Columbia in 1920, where he taught until his retirement in 1959. A distinguished writer, he published extended criticism on Shakespeare, John Dryden, and Thoreau; three novels; an autobiography; several volumes of poetry—including Collected Poems (1939), *for which he was awarded the Pulitzer prize for poetry; and two volumes of his collected short stories.*

[1] Poetry speaks for itself. But poets, curiously enough, do not; and so it is time that someone speak for them and say what they would say if they spoke in prose. It is time that they be defended against the silent charge—all the more damning because it is so silent—that they are a special race of men and women, different from all other creatures of their kind and possessed of faculties which would make them, if we knew them, only too wonderful to live with, not to say too embarrassing. I should like to relieve them from the burden of being queer. Poets are supposed to be a suffering race, but the only thing they suffer from is the misapprehension that they are endowed with a peculiar set of thoughts and feelings—particularly feelings—and that these endowments are of the romantic sort. It consists, to speak for the moment historically, in the notion that the poet has always and must always cut the same figure he has cut during the past hundred years or so. It consists in expecting him to be a Shelley, a Keats, a Byron, a Poe, a Verlaine, a Swinburne, a Dowson. He may be another one of those, to be sure; but he also may be any kind of person under the sun. My only conception of the poet is that he is a person who writes poetry. That may sound absurdly simple, but it is arrived at after reflection upon the innumerable kinds of poetry which poets have written, and upon the baffling variety of temperaments which these poets have revealed.

"What Is a Poet?" by Mark Van Doren. © 1942 by Mark Van Doren. Reprinted by permission.

[2]   Here is the figure we have set up. A pale, lost man with long, soft hair. Tapering fingers at the ends of furtively fluttering arms. An air of abstraction in the delicate face, but more often a look of shy pain as some aspect of reality —a real man or woman, a grocer's bill, a train, a load of bricks, a newspaper, a noise from the street—makes itself manifest. He is generally incompetent. He cannot find his way in a city, he forgets where he is going, he has no aptitude for business, he is childishly gullible and so the prey of human sharks, he cares nothing for money, he is probably poor, he will sacrifice his welfare for a whim, he stops to pet homeless cats, he is especially knowing where children are concerned (being a child himself), he sighs, he sleeps, he wakes to sigh again. The one great assumption from which the foregoing portrait is drawn is an assumption which thousands of otherwise intelligent citizens go on. It is the assumption that the poet is more sensitive than any other kind of man, that he feels more than the rest of us and is more definitely the victim of his feeling.

[3]   I am tempted to assert that the poet is as a matter of fact less sensitive than other men. I shall make no such assertion for the simple reason that to do so would be to imply that I knew what kind of man the poet necessarily was. My whole point is that the poet is not anything necessarily. He may be sensitive, and he may not; the question has nothing directly to do with his being a poet. Certainly there have been poets with very thick hides. We have to account for the fact that Browning looked more like a businessman than he did like a poet—whatever a poet is supposed to look like; that Horace was plump, phlegmatic, easy-going, shrewd, and sensible; that Dryden was an excellent trader in literary affairs; that Pope was so insensitive, at least to the sufferings of others, that he poured an emetic into the tea of a publisher with whom he had quarreled; that Li Po and most of the other great Chinese poets were government officials; that Robert Frost is to all outward appearances— and what other appearances are there?—a New England farmer.

[4]   There is reason for supposing that no artist is as sensitive in one respect as the man who is not an artist. He is not so likely, that is, to be overwhelmed by his own feelings. Consider what he does with his feelings. He uses them, deliberately, for the purposes of his art. The ordinary man—meaning for the moment the man who is not an artist—may be so affected by the death of a parent, for instance, that he becomes dumb. There was Daudet, however, who at the funeral of his mother could not help composing the room where he stood into a room that would be the setting of a new story. He was using his feelings, together with the scene which called them forth, for an ulterior purpose. The artist is callous, and must be so in order to keep his mind clear for the work he has before him. So also the poet must be sensitive to words,

DEFINITION 129

rhythms, ideas, and moods; but in the very act of perceiving them clearly, in realizing them for what they are worth, he distinguishes himself from the race of men who feel and only feel. When we read the poetry of a man like Pope who was extraordinarily, almost abnormally, susceptible to the charms of verbal music we can have no doubt that he was, in that one department of his existence, all sense. We are not justified, however, in going on, as a recent biographer of the little man has done, to attribute to him a sensitive heart. As a matter of fact he had another kind, and in the ordinary man it would be denounced as an ugly one.

[5] From the notion that the poet is deeply affected by life we often proceed to the notion that he cannot stand a great deal of it; we say he dies young. To be sure there are the English romantic poets—Shelley, Keats, and Byron—to support our error, and to be sure they are always conspicuously present in spirit when poetry is under discussion, since it was their generation that gave us our conception of poetry and the poet; we still are in the romantic period. But even as we talk this way we seem to forget their contemporary Wordsworth, who lived in perfect peace till he was eighty. We forget that Dryden lived to seventy, Shakespeare to fifty-two, Browning to seventy-seven, Tennyson to eighty-three, Milton to sixty-six, Herrick to eighty-three, Spenser to almost fifty, and Chaucer to an even sixty. We disregard the great age of Homer when he died, at least if the traditions be true. And anyway the ancient traditions about poets have their significance. For one of them was that poets die old; hence the bust of Homer, wrinkled, composed, resigned, with sunken eyes. The three great tragic poets of Greece died old indeed; Aeschylus at sixty-nine, Sophocles at ninety, and Euripides at seventy-five. Vergil and Horace gave up the struggle in their fifties, Lucretius committed suicide, it is said, at forty-three or forty-four, and Catullus, like Shelley, was extinguished at thirty; but Ovid for all his banishment to a cold, uncomfortable part of the world, and his probable suffering there, lived into his sixtieth year; and Ennius, first of all the known Roman poets, saw seventy. Dante had a hard life, but it lasted fifty-six years. Racine went on to sixty; Goethe expired peacefully, calling for more light, at eighty-three. And what of the greatest English poet in recent times? Thomas Hardy, who did not even begin to be a professional poet until he was more than fifty-five, wrote ten volumes of verse after that, and when he died at eighty-eight was busy with the preparation of a new volume, which appeared posthumously!

[6] Another burden of which I should like to relieve poets is the burden of being strangely wise. They have been called prophets, I believe, and seers; clairvoyants, informers, transformers, and what not. All this, too, in spite of the impracticality attributed to them. Indeed, there seems to be a connection

between the two attributes. The poets know nothing of the world, but they may tell us a good deal about life; not life as we live it, but life—shall we say?—as we ought to live it. Simply by virtue of their stupidity in ordinary affairs they somehow become conversant with extraordinary affairs which we ourselves shall never experience but which it might be rather nice to hear about. So runs another legend, and one as romantic as the rest. For it has no foundation whatever if the whole history of poetry be taken into account. In a primitive tribe the poet is also the medicine man, the priest, and the foreteller of future events, since it is in verse that these functionaries speak. Among savages, then, the poet is a prophet. But nowhere else. The division of labor has gone on; the prophet is the prophet, in verse or in prose as the occasion may be; the poet is the poet, and always in verse. The poet is a sayer, not a seer. Wordsworth brought on a considerable confusion by insisting that the poet is one who goes to Nature for her secrets, which are substantially the secrets of existence, and then comes back with the dew of knowledge on his lips. The poet, in other words, is equipped with a peculiar mind which enables him to plumb—or fathom, or penetrate, or see through, or pierce; the phrase matters not—the world's appearances. For us the mere appearances, for him the reality behind. Thus he not only cursed his successors with the responsibility of being prophets; he cursed them also with the duty of being acquainted with Nature, and of pretending to some sort of mastery over her. The truth, I suspect, is that the poet is no more of a magician in this respect than the scientist is. And think of the poets, long ago and since, who have never been the least bit interested in the out-of-doors. Dr. Johnson said that he was unable to tell the difference between one green field and another. Milton got his flowers and mountains out of old books; Spenser got his landscapes out of sixteenth-century woodcuts; Dante read Nature as a work in theology; Horace was comfortable in the presence of his hills only when a few friends from Rome were with him to drink wine and make remarks about life; Vergil in the country was concerned with husbandry and the diseases of sheep; Ovid would not look at a tree unless it had once contained a nymph.

[7] The poet may think anything, feel anything, do anything; he may or may not be a wanderer; he may or may not love his home better than any other plot of ground; he may love children; he may hate them; he may be restless under the pressure of a domestic establishment; he may get his chief joy out of a wife and kitchen; he may inhabit a palace; he may shiver in a garret; he may be noble; he may be mean. He is not limited, in other words, more than other men. Yet we go on limiting him. And to what? To a simpering, humorless, pious, nervous existence which for all the world we should be unwilling to share with him. No wonder we don't like him, and no wonder we don't really enjoy reading poetry.

DEFINITION

SUGGESTIONS FOR WRITING

1. Select a term like *hero, rebel, professional, statesmanship, religion, ethics, education* and write a definition that reduces it "to its lowest terms, and yet includes everything that is essential to understanding what it really is." Include a point-by-point discussion of how you arrive at the genus and differentiae for your definititon. The term you choose should be one about which there can be some difference of opinion, of course. You may wish to develop your essay in the manner of Becker, disagreeing with a preliminary definition. You will find that small "pocket" dictionaries are limited and therefore less useful than larger dictionaries, where you may find a definition that you can extend or revise until it is satisfactory—at least for yourself.

2. Following either the inductive or deductive method of development, write a definition of a term that can be effectively clarified by the use of analogy. Possible topics: freedom, wealth, science, politics, liberty, security, brutality, independence.

3. Stereotyped conceptions of people in certain occupations or professions have long been popular, such as "the absent-minded professor." Such stereotypes, however, are often destroyed by close analysis. Select as a topic one of these stereotypes: the bearded and sandaled political liberal, the illiterate college athlete, the comedian whose jokes mask his tragic personal life, the superpatriot military officer, the bigoted dockworker (Archie Bunker), the beautiful but dumb secretary, the bookworm student. Following Van Doren's method of defining a type, describing it, and then refuting it by factual examples, write an essay of definition. Be sure that your examples constitute adequate evidence for refuting the stereotyped definition.

4. In the manner of Sturtevant's definition of language, write a definition of a type of music: rock, folk rock, country, jazz, blues, Western, baroque, etc. Devote a separate paragraph to the explanation of each of the three parts of your definition.

5. Bloomfield and Newmark define *slang* by presenting several criteria: its function as social dialect, its purposes, its characteristics. Drawing from your study of their essay, from class discussion, and from your own knowledge of and experience with slang, write an essay defining *slang*. You will very likely want to make greater use of examples than do Bloomfield and Newmark. Your essay will have heightened unity if you draw examples from a single source—a particular age group, social group, or occupation.

6. Write an essay in the manner of Claude Brown describing your awareness of special connotations of a word or phrase of current slang. Some suggestions: *fuzz, cat, trip, old lady, jive, get it on, honky, high, zilch, Wasp, get it together, coming from, it's going down, turkey.* For extra background it may be helpful to consider Bloomfield and Newmark and to read Claiborne's "A Wasp Stings Back" (p. 265).

7. Write an essay defining "soul food," showing how it contrasts with or-

dinary American food. It will be helpful first to read Philip Wylie's essay, "Science Has Spoiled My Supper" (p. 85). Try to state the difference between soul food and what Wylie calls "a pretty cascade of viands, with the texture of boiled cardboard and the flavor of library paste." Can soul food be "mass-manufactured —and sold for polishing off in the home oven"?

8. One of the most famous phrases from American history is Jefferson's "the pursuit of Happiness" from the Declaration of Independence. Read the Declaration (p. 269) and write an essay defining *happiness* as you think Jefferson must have meant it to be understood—or as you yourself would like it to be understood in the famous phrase. Remember that the sort of definition that has become popular since the appearance of the line "Happiness is a warm puppy" (from the "Peanuts" comic strip) will probably not do here; what is needed is a consideration of happiness that can be secured (that is, guaranteed) by a government.

OPTIONAL LIBRARY ASSIGNMENTS

1. In his essay Mark Van Doren alludes to three dozen poets and writers to illustrate one or more of his contentions in support of his definition that the poet "is a person who writes poetry." By referring to the biography of one poet in standard biographical sources or in a reputable biography, discuss the poet in the light of the main points of Van Doren's essay. Your thesis in your essay will be that the poet whom you are writing about is or is not merely "a person who writes poetry." The essay should include the two definitions of a poet in Van Doren's essay, and you should clarify the purpose of your essay with respect to these definitions. (Some of the poets Van Doren mentions will be more rewarding for your essay than others; before writing your essay, have your instructor approve your choice of poet.)

2. By making use of a dictionary based on historical principles (the meanings of a word are listed chronologically and are supported by quotations), such as the one referred to by Wilson, *A Dictionary of Americanisms*, ed. Mitford M. Mathews, 2 vols. (Chicago, 1951), write an essay tracing changes in the meaning of a single word. Words such as those following will provide adequate material: *civilian, communism, freedom, home, morality, patriot, patriotism, philosophy, Puritan, socialist, soldier, toleration.*

You will also find helpful the following dictionaries, which also employ the historical method: *New Dictionary of Quotations on Historical Principles*, ed. H. L. Mencken (New York, 1942); *The Oxford English Dictionary (OED)*, ed. James A. H. Murray *et al.*, 13 vols. (Oxford, 1933); and *A Dictionary of American English on Historical Principles*, ed. William Craigie and James R. Hulbert, 4 vols. (Chicago, 1938–1944). In addition, John Bartlett's *Familiar Quotations* and *The Oxford Dictionary of Quotations* may be useful, although they do not give the dates of the quotations.

When copying the quotations and their sources from the dictionaries, note that the quotations are often fragmentary and must be properly introduced and incorporated grammatically into your essay. The sources are frequently indicated by abbreviated titles, and ellipses in the *OED* are indicated by two dots, rather than by the usual three.

DESCRIPTION

The word *description* is from the Latin *describere*, meaning "to write about." But "writing about" may also refer to exposition, or argumentation, or narration. As one of the four major types of discourse, description involves more than telling "about" a subject. The writer of description transfers his observations and sense impressions to the reader; he conveys mood, images, sensations—communicating experience rather than providing factual information or conducting an argument or telling a story.

Unlike exposition, argumentation, and narration, description is a supporting device, a tool of other forms of prose. In exposition, description is a means for making subjects vivid. For example, in the expository essay "Thinking as a Hobby," William Golding gives extended attention to the physical characteristics of one of his teachers, a Mr. Houghton, but the purpose of the description is to show that "Mr. Houghton thought with his neck." Frequently the difference between exposition and description is slight, primarily a matter of emphasis. If the emphasis of the writer is upon explanation, as in "Thinking as a Hobby," he is writing exposition; if his emphasis is upon communicating

133

impressions, as in Melville's portrayal of Captain Ahab, he is writing description. Similarly, as illustrated in Sinclair Lewis's description of "The House of Babbitt" and Herb Caen's "The Plastic Fantastic," a description of Disneyland, the careful selection of descriptive details may be employed effectively as a device of persuasion, a form of argumentation. Lewis and Caen, through their descriptions, indirectly ask the reader to accept and share their implicit criticism of the people and places they are describing. In narration, either fiction or nonfiction, description is employed to create mood and atmosphere, to make settings—landscapes, houses, rooms, furnishings—seem real, to make characters come alive. Most of the selections in the present section are taken from works that are mainly narrative; and many of the selections in the section on "Narration" (particularly Langston Hughes's "Salvation," William Allen White's "A Child Went Forth," and John Steinbeck's "The Turtle") contain descriptive passages that supplement and enhance and give added meaning to the narrative account.

Every description emphasizes one of two principal approaches to its subject. It is either **realistic** or **impressionistic.** That is, every description either portrays a subject as objectively or scientifically as possible, in the manner of the camera, or subjectively, in the manner of the artist. The camera captures details; the artist is free to interpret the details as he sees them. Yet no description can maintain one approach to the absolute exclusion of the other. A camera must, of course be focused on the subject; and the very act of choosing the angle, of utilizing light and shadow, involves selection or interpretation. Frank Norris, in his realistic description of Polk Street, piles detail upon detail to suggest the color and the almost ceaseless activity of the street. Even so, he has had to exclude from his description details that would have conveyed a different picture of the street. Similarly, no matter how impressionistic a writer wishes to be, he still must work within the confines of the material he has selected. Melville, in his description of Captain Ahab, emphasizes two principal details: Ahab's ivory leg and his livid scar; therefore, Melville must use these details to create an impression of Ahab's tragic dignity.

Effective description, whether primarily realistic or impressionistic, depends in large measure upon the **use of details.** Details provide the authenticity necessary to make descriptions convincing; and details provide the most effective means of conveying a writer's attitude toward his subject. Writers known for the excellence of their description, therefore, have been keenly aware of the importance of *careful selection of details*—sights, sounds, odors, actions. Sinclair Lewis, for instance, uses numerous details in his writings; but he selects only those that most clearly convey his attitude toward his subject. In his novel *Main Street*, as he describes Carol Kennicott on her first walk through Gopher Prairie, he introduces the reader to the objects and sights that spell despair to Carol—the untidy, dirty, tawdry aspects of a small town's business

DESCRIPTION 135

section: the fly-specked store windows, the faded paper lining the shelves of the stores, the odor of onions and lard in the lunchroom. Recognizing the effectiveness of such details in creating a specific impression and an authentic description, Lewis maintained a large notebook in which he carefully recorded his observations so that he would have them available when he needed them.

The problem of **point of view**, which was discussed more fully with reference to the process theme, is also extremely important in description. The writer must enable the reader to see the subject from a particular location. Shifts in point of view blur the picture just as the movement of the camera blurs a photograph. If a street is being described from a specific window, the description should contain nothing that cannot be seen from that window. If a person is being described in a darkened room, any attention to the bright color of his clothes would be jarring. If an individual is being described as he is seated, any reference to his manner of walking should be withheld until he is moving about.

When considering his subject, the writer must also decide what **effect** he wishes to create. Lewis, in "The House of Babbitt," conveys a sense of dissatisfaction with the Babbitts; London, in "Student Quarters," a sense of harried activity and cramped conditions; Mark Twain, in "Steamboat Town," a sense of excitement sandwiched between long periods of ennui. All details should support the desired effect; any details that do not do so must be excluded. The writer's attitude toward his material and his readers—that is, the **tone** he strives to create—contributes greatly to his success in achieving the desired effect. In the passages referred to, Lewis is basically ironic; London is objective, though his admiration for Martin Eden's ingenuity and determination is evident; and Twain is nostalgic.

The use of **figurative language** is a common device of description, though it must be employed carefully. Its purpose is to appeal to the imagination of the reader by creating images that are fresh, vivid, and precise. Those figures of speech that come too quickly to mind are likely to be trite and hackneyed. Unless the figures are fresh, they will not be striking and will be passed over by the reader. The three most common figures of speech are the simile, the metaphor, and personification. All are devices to suggest comparison, to create mood, and to make the unfamiliar clear by describing it in terms of the familiar.

The **simile** employs the words *like* or *as* and makes a direct comparison. Such similes as the following, though descriptive, have become trite and should be avoided (here one must control the temptation to say "avoided like the plague"): *black as pitch, bright as a penny, brown as a berry, flat as a pancake, hard as a rock, high as the sky, sharp as a tack, skinny as a rail, sweet as sugar, tough as nails*. On the other hand, fresh similes—if appropriate—create memorable impressions. Stephen Crane, describing the movement of a small boat in a turbulent sea, writes: "The craft pranced and reared and plunged like an animal. As each wave came, and she rose for it, she seemed like a horse making at a fence outrageously high." Leonard Shecter effectively suggests the mobility of the face of Muhammad Ali by likening it to that of "a rubber puppet."

The **metaphor** accomplishes the same end as the simile but does so indirectly, without the use of a preposition or a conjunction. One object is said to *be* another: "Professor Jones is an old bear"; "The room is an absolute pigpen"; "The company was deluged with orders." These metaphors carry to Professor Jones the traditional grouchiness of the bear, to the room the litter and sloppiness of a pigpen, and to the business concern the overwhelming quantity of orders that can be likened to a flood. In the selections that follow are numerous examples of metaphors—some fresh and exciting, some timeworn but still effective. Frank Norris, for instance, compares school children with bees when he says that they "swarmed the sidewalks." Harold Frederic suggests the wrinkled quality of dried fruit when he speaks of one of his characters as having a "juiceless countenance." Jack London employs appropriate nautical imagery when, in his description of the crowded room of Martin Eden, a sailor, he likens the narrow path between the furniture to a canal that is barely navigable.

Descriptions of inanimate objects or animals may be enhanced by the use of human comparisons, a figure of speech called **personification**. Chet Huntley, in "The Song of the Land," personifies the land when he attributes to it the ability to sing. In his vivid and humorous descriptions of animals in the familiar "The Celebrated Jumping Frog of Calaveras County," Mark Twain makes effective use of this device by giving the animals almost human personalities. The frog, Dan'l Webster, is "modest and straightfor'ard" despite his unusual gifts; and when, with his stomach full of quail-shot, he tries to jump, he heaves and strains, elevating his shoulders "like a Frenchman." So vivid is the image that it is hard not to think of Dan'l as wearing a beret. But personification, when used to endow natural objects with human characteristics and emotions, frequently seems strained and unbelievable.

Like figurative language, four rhetorical devices that concern the sounds of words can be used to enhance the effectiveness of description, as well as other forms of prose, but should be employed cautiously. **Alliteration**, the repetition of sounds at the beginnings of words or of stressed syllables, calls attention to the words and, in addition to pleasing the ear, makes the words more emphatic and consequently more memorable. Mark Twain, for instance, writes of "the *m*ajestic, the *m*agnificent *M*ississippi." Here, as in most instances of alliteration, the repetition of the initial sound helps to create tone and a balanced effect in the phrase. Similar to alliteration in purpose and effect are **assonance** (the repetition of similar vowel sounds) and **consonance** (the repetition of identical consonant sounds). When Twain describes a glimpse of the river as "a sort of sea, and withal a very still and brilliant and lovely one," he is making use of all three devices: alliteration in "a *s*ort of *s*ea"; assonance in "w*i*thal . . . st*i*ll . . . br*i*lliant"; and consonance in "witha*l* . . . sti*ll* . . . bri*ll*iant . . . love*l*y." The smoothness and mellifluous quality of Twain's prose is in part a result of his careful attention to the sounds of words. **Onomatopoeia** is the formation of a word that imitates the sound associated with the action the word denotes. Frank Norris, in "Polk Street," writes of the *whirring* sound of the glass windows as the cable car passes; the word suggests the sound that the jostled windows make. Thus, through the use of a single adjective, Norris economically states that the windows make a sound and describes the sound they make. But all of these devices, decorative, pleasing, and effective when used moderately, are irritating when overused.

In the selection "Colorful, Colored, and Colorless Words" (p. 33) Paul Roberts discusses "colorful" words, those "calculated to produce a picture or induce an emotion"; "colored" words, "loaded with associations, good or bad"; and "colorless" words, "no longer capable of adding much to description." Students may find it useful to consider the Roberts selection before moving forward to the discussions that follow.

The foregoing general discussion of the methods of description has application to all of the examples of descriptive writing in this book. Since different objects of description present different problems, however, some of the most common objects (descriptions of places; of people; and of sights, sounds, and sensations) are discussed separately.

DESCRIPTIONS OF PLACES

Descriptions of places involve four principal considerations: the point of view, the dominant mood, the selection of details, and the order of the presentation of the details. The writer must ask, "Where am I standing as I view this scene? What mood do I wish to suggest?" Drawing upon memory or imagination or, best of all, actual observation, the writer should make a list of significant details about the subject—details that relate to as many of the senses as possible—and then must ask, "Which details should I emphasize? In what order can I best present these details?"

The writers whose descriptions of places appear in this book have answered these questions in various ways. In order to suggest the diversity of activity on San Francisco's Polk Street, Frank Norris places his main character in a window above the street and describes the activity below him in terms both of distance and time of day, using the street's most significant detail, the cable car, to give unity to the observations. Mark Twain, nostalgically describing his boyhood home town, makes effective use of contrast: he describes the scene both before and after its most dramatic moment—the arrival of the steamboat; he emphasizes the contrast by concentrating upon the same details viewed at different times. Both Jack London and Sinclair Lewis use the details of the furnishings of the living quarters of their characters to comment upon the occupants. Jack London works from the large pieces of furniture in the room of Martin Eden—the table, bed, the bureau—to the smaller details such as the mirror on which were lists of vocabulary words for study. The bedroom of the Babbitts is used to typify their home and—through Lewis's use of such loaded adjectives as *standard, almost solid, modern, best*—to illustrate what Lewis considers to be their shallow, materialistic values and their attempt to establish social status. Herb Caen's description of Disneyland focuses on those details that are suggested by the title of the essay—"The Plastic Fantastic"—to emphasize the atmosphere of commercialized magic in the amusement park. Caen conveys more the spirit of the place than a visual image.

Descriptions of places also appear in the following selections in other sections of this book (see the Contents for page numbers):

 Henry David Thoreau, "On Owning a Farm"
 Langston Hughes, "Salvation"
 William Allen White, "A Child Went Forth"
 Clair Huffaker, "Pony Boy"
 George Orwell, "A Hanging"
 John Hersey, "A Noiseless Flash"
 John Steinbeck, "The Turtle"
 Allan Planz, "The Pool"

Frank Norris

POLK STREET

The following passage is from the first chapter of McTeague: A Story of San Francisco *(1899), a book that has been called America's first important naturalistic novel, a type of fiction which generally gives an unusual amount of attention to surface or external realism. As a naturalistic writer, Frank Norris (1870–1902) sought to bring to his descriptions of characters or scenes as much specific and realistic detail as possible. His description of Polk Street in San Francisco provides a particularly good example of the way in which the skillful use of details —sights, sounds, odors, and movements—contributes to the creation of a vivid scene. McTeague, incidentally, is a huge and somewhat stupid dentist, who lives in his small dental office overlooking Polk Street.*

[1]   When he had finished the last of his beer, McTeague slowly wiped his lips and huge yellow mustache with the side of his hand. Bull-like, he heaved himself laboriously up, and, going to the window, stood looking down into the street.

[2]   The street never failed to interest him. It was one of those cross streets peculiar to Western cities, situated in the heart of the residence quarter, but occupied by small tradespeople who lived in the rooms above their shops. There were corner drug stores with huge jars of red, yellow, and green liquids in their windows, very brave and gay; stationers' stores, where illustrated weeklies were tacked upon bulletin boards; barber shops with cigar stands in their vestibules; sad-looking plumbers' offices; cheap restaurants, in whose windows one saw piles of unopened oysters weighted down by cubes of ice, and china pigs and cows knee deep in layers of white beans. At one end of the street McTeague could see the huge power-house of the cable line. Immediately opposite him was a great market; while farther on, over the chimney stacks of the intervening houses, the glass roof of some huge public baths glittered like crystal in the afternoon sun. Underneath him the branch post-office was opening its doors, as was its custom between two and three o'clock on Sunday afternoons. An acrid odor of ink rose upward to him. Occasionally a cable car passed, trundling heavily, with a strident whirring of jostled glass windows.

[3]   On week days the street was very lively. It woke to its work about seven o'clock, at the time when the newsboys made their appearance together with

the day laborers. The laborers went trudging past in a straggling file—plumbers' apprentices, their pockets stuffed with sections of lead pipe, tweezers, and pliers; carpenters, carrying nothing but their little pasteboard lunch baskets painted to imitate leather; gangs of street workers, their overalls soiled with yellow clay, their picks and long-handled shovels over their shoulders; plasterers, spotted with lime from head to foot. This little army of workers, tramping steadily in one direction, met and mingled with other toilers of a different description—conductors and "swing men" of the cable company going on duty; heavy-eyed night clerks from the drug stores on their way home to sleep; roundsmen returning to the precinct police station to make their night report, the Chinese market gardeners teetering past under their heavy baskets. The cable cars began to fill up; all along the street could be seen the shop keepers taking down their shutters.

[annotation: police on foot beat]

[4] Between seven and eight the street breakfasted. Now and then a waiter from one of the cheap restaurants crossed from one sidewalk to the other, balancing on one palm a tray covered with a napkin. Everywhere was the smell of coffee and of frying steaks. A little later, following in the path of the day laborers, came the clerks and shop girls, dressed with a certain cheap smartness, always in a hurry, glancing apprehensively at the powerhouse clock. Their employers followed an hour or so later—on the cable cars for the most part—whiskered gentlemen with huge stomachs, reading the morning papers with great gravity; bank cashiers and insurance clerks with flowers in their buttonholes.

[5] At the same time the school children invaded the street, filling the air with a clamor of shrill voices, stopping at the stationers' shops, or idling a moment in the doorways of the candy stores. For over half an hour they held possession of the sidewalks, then suddenly disappeared, leaving behind one or two stragglers who hurried along with great strides of their little thin legs, very anxious and preoccupied.

[6] Towards eleven o'clock the ladies from the great avenue a block above Polk Street made their appearance, promenading the sidewalks leisurely, deliberately. They were at their morning's marketing. They were handsome women, beautifully dressed. They knew by name their butchers and grocers and vegetable men. From his window McTeague saw them in front of the stalls, gloved and veiled and daintily shod, the subservient provision-men at their elbows, scribbling hastily in the order books. They all seemed to know one another, these grand ladies from the fashionable avenue. Meetings took

DESCRIPTIONS OF PLACES 141

place here and there; a conversation was begun; others arrived; groups were formed; little impromptu receptions were held before the chopping blocks of butchers' stalls, or on the sidewalk, around boxes of berries and fruit.

[7] From noon to evening the population of the street was of a mixed character. The street was busiest at that time; a vast and prolonged murmur arose —the mingled shuffling of feet, the rattle of wheels, the heavy trundling of cable cars. At four o'clock the school children once more swarmed the sidewalks, again disappearing with surprising suddenness. At six the great homeward march commenced; the cars were crowded, the laborers thronged the sidewalks, the newsboys chanted the evening papers. Then all at once the street fell quiet; hardly a soul was in sight; the sidewalks were deserted. It was supper hour. Evening began; and one by one a multitude of lights, from the demoniac glare of the druggists' windows to the dazzling blue whiteness of the electric globes, grew thick from street corner to street corner. Once more the street was crowded. Now there was no thought but for amusement. The cable cars were loaded with theatre-goers—men in high hats and young girls in furred opera cloaks. On the sidewalks were groups and couples—the plumbers' apprentices, the girls of the ribbon counters, the little families that lived on the second stories over their shops, the dressmakers, the small doctors, the harness makers—all the various inhabitants of the street were abroad, strolling idly from shop window to shop window, taking the air after the day's work. Groups of girls collected on the corners, talking and laughing very loud, making remarks upon the young men that passed them. The *tamale* men appeared. A band of Salvationists began to sing before a saloon.

[8] Then, little by little, Polk Street dropped back to solitude. Eleven o'clock struck from the power-house clock. Lights were extinguished. At one o'clock the cable stopped, leaving an abrupt silence in the air. All at once it seemed very still. The only noises were the occasional footfalls of a policeman and the persistent calling of ducks and geese in the closed market. The street was asleep.

VOCABULARY

Define the following words as they are used in the selection: *peculiar, brave, acrid, strident* [2]; *apprehensively, gravity* [4]; *clamor* [5]; *subservient* [6].

QUESTIONS FOR STUDY AND DISCUSSION

1. What is the principle of organization in paragraph 2? What statement do all of the details in the paragraph support?

2. What general impression of the street does the third sentence of paragraph 2 create? How does Norris achieve the effect of scope and vastness in the paragraph?

3. What sentence in paragraph 3 provides the topic idea for the remainder of the passage?

4. What is the principle of organization of paragraphs 3 through 8?

5. Beginning with paragraph 3, make an outline of the activities on Polk Street, using the time of day as the main topic.

6. Your outline will help you to see more clearly how Norris has unified his description. Which people of the street are referred to in the evening as well as in the morning? In effect, Norris's parallel references to these people suggest the major activities of Polk Street. In what way does our awareness of the activities of these people contribute to our understanding of the street?

7. What one feature of the street, alluded to in almost every paragraph, unifies the passage through references to sounds and sights?

8. What later reference to shop windows contrasts with the one at the end of paragraph 3?

9. What specific odors are referred to directly or suggested in the passage?

10. What specific sounds does the passage describe or suggest? What is the effect created by the references to sounds?

11. Malcolm Cowley has observed of naturalism that "Things play an important part in it—not the novelist's impressions of things, but the actual hard, angular, soiled, and smelly objects." In what specific ways does his passage qualify in this respect as naturalistic description?

12. Cowley also says of naturalism, "In practice it is careless about the sound or style of words it uses, being based on the eyes (and the nose) rather than the ears." Note Norris's use of adjectives in the first two paragraphs. Is there a suggestion of carelessness about the sound or style of words? Which adjectives does he overuse? Is the phrase "glittered like crystal" fresh and effective?

13. What examples of particularly effective word choices can you find?

14. At the end of paragraph 2, the word *whirring* is onomatopoetic. Can you find other instances of onomatopoeia in the passage? Do you note any alliteration, assonance, or consonance? Where? How would you describe the effect of these uses of words?

Mark Twain

STEAMBOAT TOWN

This passage opens the nostalgic recollection of Mark Twain (1835–1910) entitled "Old Times on the Mississippi," originally published in 1875 in the Atlantic Monthly. *The text used here is that of the slightly revised version appearing in Chapter 4 of* Life on the Mississippi *(1883). Mark Twain, the pen name of Samuel L. Clemens, is regarded by many as the father of modern narrative style. The town that he describes is Hannibal, Missouri.*

[1] When I was a boy, there was but one permanent ambition among my comrades in our village on the west bank of the Mississippi River. That was, to be a steamboatman. We had transient ambitions of other sorts, but they were only transient. When a circus came and went, it left us all burning to become clowns; the first negro minstrel show that ever came to our section left us all suffering to try that kind of life; now and then we had a hope that, if we lived and were good, God would permit us to be pirates. These ambitions faded out, each in its turn; but the ambition to be a steamboatman always remained.

[2] Once a day a cheap, gaudy packet arrived upward from St. Louis, and another downward from Keokuk. Before these events, the day was glorious with expectancy; after them, the day was a dead and empty thing. Not only the boys, but the whole village, felt this. After all these years I can picture that old time to myself now, just as it was then: the white town drowsing in the sunshine of a summer's morning; the streets empty, or pretty nearly so; one or two clerks sitting in front of the Water street stores, with their splint-bottomed chairs tilted back against the walls, chins on breasts, hats slouched over their faces, asleep—with shingle-shavings enough around to show what broke them down; a sow and a litter of pigs loafing along the sidewalk, doing a good business in water-melon rinds and seeds; two or three lonely little freight piles scattered about the "levee"; a pile of "skids" on the slope of the stone-paved wharf, and the fragrant town drunk asleep in the shadow of them; two or three wood flats at the head of the wharf, but nobody to listen to the peaceful lapping of the wavelets against them; the great Mississippi, the majestic, the magnificent Mississippi, rolling its mile-wide tide along, shining in the sun; the dense forest away on the other side; the "point" above the town, and the "point" below, bounding the river-glimpse and turning it into a sort

of sea, and withal a very still and brilliant and lonely one. Presently a film of dark smoke appears above one of those remote "points"; instantly a negro drayman, famous for his quick eye and prodigious voice, lifts up the cry, "S-t-e-a-m-boat a-comin'!" and the scene changes! The town drunkard stirs, the clerks wake up, a furious clatter of drays follows, every house and store pours out a human contribution, and all in a twinkling the dead town is alive and moving. Drays, carts, men, boys, all go hurrying from many quarters to a common center, the wharf. Assembled there, the people fasten their eyes upon the coming boat as upon a wonder they are seeing for the first time. And the boat *is* rather a handsome sight, too. She is long and sharp and trim and pretty; she has two tall, fancy-topped chimneys, with a gilded device of some kind swung between them; a fanciful pilot-house, all glass and "gingerbread," perched on top of the "texas" deck behind them; the paddleboxes are gorgeous with a picture or with gilded rays above the boat's name; the boiler deck, the hurricane deck, and the texas deck are fenced and ornamented with clean white railings; there is a flag gallantly flying from the jack-staff; the furnace doors are open and the fires glaring bravely; the upper decks are black with passengers; the captain stands by the big bell, calm, imposing, the envy of all; great volumes of the blackest smoke are rolling and tumbling out of the chimneys —a husbanded grandeur created with a bit of pitchpine just before arriving at a town; the crew are grouped on the forecastle; the broad stage is run far out over the port bow, and an envied deck-hand stands picturesquely on the end of it with a coil of rope in his hand; the pent steam is screaming through the gauge-cocks; the captain lifts his hand, a bell rings, the wheels stop; then they turn back, churning the water to foam, and the steamer is at rest. Then such a scramble as there is to get aboard, and to get ashore, and to take in freight and to discharge freight, all at one and the same time; and such a yelling and cursing as the mates facilitate it all with! Ten minutes later the steamer is under way again, with no flag on the jack-staff and no black smoke issuing from the chimneys. After ten more minutes the town is dead again, and the town drunkard asleep by the skids once more.

VOCABULARY

Define the following words as they are used in the selection: *transient* [1]; *cheap, gaudy, packet, levee, point, withal, drayman, gilded, gingerbread, texas deck, boiler deck, hurricane deck, jack-staff, imposing, husbanded, forecastle, pent* [2].

QUESTIONS FOR STUDY AND DISCUSSION

1. What does Twain say in paragraph 1 that contributes to the sense of excitement in paragraph 2?

2. In paragraph 1 three transient ambitions are listed. How does Twain indicate the third ambition is perhaps greater than the other two?

3. Paragraph 2 can be divided into three main sections, based upon the order of time. What are they? Where does each begin?

4. What details does Twain select to create the scene before the arrival of the steamboat? List them. Which details suggest activity? Which ones suggest inactivity?

5. How does Twain let the reader know that the town is isolated? How does the isolation contribute to the drama of the steamboat's arrival?

6. What details of the scene before the arrival are used to indicate the changes caused by the boat's appearance at the town?

7. The boat is described as a "handsome sight." What details does Twain offer to convince the reader of his statement?

8. After the departure of the boat, several details referred to before are mentioned again. Which ones refer back to the beginning of the paragraph?

9. What examples can you find of alliteration, assonance, and consonance? What is the effect of these devices?

10. In the second paragraph, Twain uses the word *thing* in the second sentence. Is the word effective in context?

11. In the original version of paragraph 2, the second sentence reads: "Before these events had transpired, the day was glorious with expectancy; after they had transpired, the day was a dead and empty thing." Why might Twain have made the change?

12. Twain uses several types of series. Is "Drays, carts, men, boys" more effective than "Drays and carts and men and boys" in its context? Why? Is "long and sharp and trim and pretty" better than "long, sharp, trim, and pretty"? Why?

Jack London

STUDENT QUARTERS

In his novel Martin Eden *(1909), Jack London (1876–1916) gives fictional treatment to many of his own early experiences as an ignorant, impoverished, but determined young writer in Oakland, California. Martin Eden is a sailor who is exposed to genteel, affluent people and vows to gain respectability himself through his writing. In many respects Martin Eden and Jack London are the same person: "I am Martin Eden," London wrote near the end of his life. The following selection, a description of Martin Eden's quarters when he was struggling to overcome the deprivations of his childhood, appears in Chapter 23 of the novel.*

[1]   [Martin Eden] paid two dollars and a half a month rent for the small room he got from his Portuguese landlady, Maria Silva, a virago and a widow, hard working and harsher tempered, rearing her large brood of children somehow, and drowning her sorrow and fatigue at irregular intervals in a gallon of the thin, sour wine that she bought from the corner grocery and saloon for fifteen cents. From detesting her and her foul tongue at first, Martin grew to admire her as he observed the brave fight she made. There were but four rooms in the little house—three, when Martin's was subtracted. One of these, the parlor, gay with an ingrain carpet and dolorous with a funeral card and a death-picture of one of her numerous departed babes, was kept strictly for company. The blinds were always down, and her barefooted tribe was never permitted to enter the sacred precinct save on state occasions. She cooked, and all ate, in the kitchen, where she likewise washed, starched, and ironed clothes on all days of the week except Sunday; for her income came largely from taking in washing from her more prosperous neighbors. Remained the bedroom, small as the one occupied by Martin, into which she and her seven little ones crowded and slept. It was an everlasting miracle to Martin how it was accomplished, and from her side of the thin partition he heard nightly every detail of the going to bed, the squalls and squabbles, the soft chattering, and the sleepy, twittering noises as of birds. Another source of income to Maria were her cows, two of them, which she milked night and morning and which gained a surreptitious livelihood from vacant lots and the grass that grew on either side the public walks, attended always by one or more of her

Reprinted by permission of Irving Shepard.

ragged boys, whose watchful guardianship consisted chiefly in keeping their eyes out for the poundmen.

[2] In his own small room Martin lived, slept, studied, wrote, and kept house. Before the one window, looking out on the tiny front porch, was the kitchen table that served as desk, library, and typewriting stand. The bed, against the rear wall, occupied two-thirds of the total space of the room. The table was flanked on one side by a gaudy bureau, manufactured for profit and not for service, the thin veneer of which was shed day by day. This bureau stood in the corner, and in the opposite corner, on the table's other flank, was the kitchen—the oil-stove on a dry-goods box, inside of which were dishes and cooking utensils, a shelf on the wall for provisions, and a bucket of water on the floor. Martin had to carry his water from the kitchen sink, there being no tap in his room. On days when there was much steam to his cooking, the harvest of veneer from the bureau was unusually generous. Over the bed, hoisted by a tackle to the ceiling, was his bicycle. At first he had tried to keep it in the basement; but the tribe of Silva, loosening the bearings and puncturing the tires, had driven him out. Next he attempted the tiny front porch, until a howling southeaster drenched the wheel a night-long. Then he had retreated with it to his room and slung it aloft.

[3] A small closet contained his clothes and the books he had accumulated and for which there was no room on the table or under the table. Hand in hand with reading, he had developed the habit of making notes, and so copiously did he make them that there would have been no existence for him in the confined quarters had he not rigged several clothes-lines across the room on which the notes were hung. Even so, he was crowded until navigating the room was a difficult task. He could not open the door without first closing the closet door, and *vice versa*. It was impossible for him anywhere to traverse the room in a straight line. To go from the door to the head of the bed was a zig-zag course that he was never quite able to accomplish in the dark without collisions. Having settled the difficulty of the conflicting doors, he had to steer sharply to the right to avoid the kitchen. Next, he sheered to the left, to escape the foot of the bed; but this sheer, if too generous, brought him against the corner of the table. With a sudden twitch and lurch, he terminated the sheer and bore off to the right along a sort of canal, one bank of which was the bed, the other the table. When the one chair in the room was at its usual place before the table, the canal was unnavigable. When the chair was not in use, it reposed on top of the bed, though sometimes he sat on the chair when cooking, reading a book while the water boiled, and even becoming skilful enough to manage a paragraph or two while steak was frying. Also, so small was the little corner that constituted the kitchen, he was able, sitting down, to reach

anything he needed. In fact, it was expedient to cook sitting down; standing up, he was too often in his own way.

[4] In conjunction with a perfect stomach that could digest anything, he possessed knowledge of the various foods that were at the same time nutritious and cheap. Pea-soup was a common article in his diet, as well as potatoes and beans, the latter large and brown and cooked in Mexican style. Rice, cooked as American housewives never cook it and can never learn to cook it, appeared on Martin's table at least once a day. Dried fruits were less expensive than fresh, and he had usually a pot of them, cooked and ready at hand, for they took the place of butter on his bread. Occasionally he graced his table with a piece of roundsteak, or with a soup-bone. Coffee, without cream or milk, he had twice a day, in the evening substituting tea; but both coffee and tea were excellently cooked.

[5] There was need for him to be economical. His vacation had consumed nearly all he had earned in the laundry, and he was so far from his market that weeks must elapse before he could hope for the first returns from his hack-work. Except at such times as he saw Ruth, or dropped in to see his sister Gertrude, he lived a recluse, in each day accomplishing at least three days' labor of ordinary men. He slept a scant five hours, and only one with a constitution of iron could have held himself down, as Martin did, day after day, to nineteen consecutive hours of toil. He never lost a moment. On the looking-glass were lists of definitions and pronunciations; when shaving, or dressing, or combing his hair, he conned these lists over. Similar lists were on the wall over the oil-stove, and they were similarly conned while he was engaged in cooking or in washing the dishes. New lists continually displaced the old ones. Every strange or partly familiar word encountered in his reading was immediately jotted down, and later, when a sufficient number had been accumulated, were typed and pinned to the wall or looking-glass. He even carried them in his pockets, and reviewed them at odd moments on the street, or while waiting in butcher shop or grocery to be served.

VOCABULARY

Define the following words as they are used in the selection: *virago, dolorous, surreptitious* [1]; *gaudy* [2]; *traverse, sheer, expedient* [3]; *conjunction* [4]; *hack-work, market, recluse, conned* [5].

DESCRIPTIONS OF PLACES 149

QUESTIONS FOR STUDY AND DISCUSSION

1. Although paragraph 1 does not deal specifically with Martin Eden's room, it suggests the general qualities of the house in which Martin lives. What are the qualities of the Silva home? What details are employed to suggest them?

2. In this passage London uses description not as an end in itself but as an aid to characterizing both the Silvas and Martin Eden. For this reason, some of the details are not particularly relevant to the description of the house or room. What details could be omitted without affecting the reader's visual impression of the Silva home and its surroundings?

3. In what specific ways does the description of the Silva home anticipate some of the features of Martin's room?

4. What sentence serves as the topic sentence of paragraph 2? Does the order of the details in this sentence have any relation to the order of details in the paragraph?

5. What adjectives can properly be applied to Martin's room as it is described in paragraph 2?

6. What device does London use in paragraph 3 to dramatize the closeness of Martin's quarters? Is it an effective device?

7. What is the dominant metaphor in paragraph 3? Point out the specific words and images that support this metaphor. Is the metaphor appropriate to Martin Eden?

8. Paragraph 4, useful in helping to characterize Martin Eden and in showing the nature of his life at the time, interrupts the descriptive nature of the passage. How could London have discussed Martin's food in such a way that it would add to, rather than interrupt, the description of the room?

9. Paragraph 5 has two topic sentences. What are they? Which one is not related to the description of Martin's room?

10. What use does London make of details other than visual ones? Do you see places where he could have heightened the descriptive quality of this passage by bringing in details other than visual ones?

11. In the context of the novel the purpose of this passage is to help characterize Martin Eden. What qualities does Martin have? How does the description of the room help to illustrate these qualities?

12. London is sometimes criticized for his lack of attention to the sound of words, to effective sentence structure, and to his uncritical enthusiasm for his main characters (with whom he can often himself be compared). Do you find any words, sentences, or statements in this passage that support such criticisms?

Sinclair Lewis

THE HOUSE OF BABBITT

This description of the house of George F. Babbitt, "modern business man" and "realtor," occurs as a complete unit at the beginning of Chapter 2 of Babbitt (1922), one of the most popular novels of Sinclair Lewis (1885–1951). An earlier description, of Babbitt's arising and dressing, introduces the reader to a man who has become an American symbol. The reader has already learned that Babbitt is a "Solid Citizen" who worships "Modern Appliances" and that his wife, Myra, is "a good woman, a kind woman, a diligent woman," who is "dully habituated to married life."

[1] [The bedroom] gave on the sleeping-porch. It served both of [the Babbitts] as dressing-room, and on the coldest nights Babbitt luxuriously gave up the duty of being manly and retreated to the bed inside, to curl his toes in the warmth and laugh at the January gale.

[2] The room displayed a modest and pleasant color-scheme, after one of the best standard designs of the decorator who "did the interiors" for most of the speculative-builders' houses in Zenith. The walls were gray, the woodwork white, the rug a serene blue; and very much like mahogany was the furniture —the bureau with its great clear mirror, Mrs. Babbitt's dressing-table with toilet-articles of almost solid silver, the plain twin beds, between them a small table holding a standard electric bedside lamp, a glass for water, and a standard bedside book with colored illustrations—what particular book it was cannot be ascertained, since no one had ever opened it. The mattresses were firm but not hard, triumphant modern mattresses which had cost a great deal of money; the hot-water radiator was of exactly the proper scientific surface for the cubic contents of the room. The windows were large and easily opened, with the best catches and cords, and Holland roller-shades guaranteed not to crack. It was a masterpiece among bedrooms, right out of Cheerful Modern Houses for Medium Incomes. Only it had nothing to do with the Babbitts, nor with any one else. If people had ever lived and loved here, read thrillers at midnight and lain in beautiful indolence on a Sunday morning, there were no signs of it. It had the air of being a very good room in a very good hotel. One expected the chambermaid to come in and make it ready for people who

From *Babbitt* by Sinclair Lewis, copyright, 1922, by Harcourt Brace Jovanovich, Inc.; renewed, 1950, by Sinclair Lewis. Reprinted by permission of the publishers.

DESCRIPTIONS OF PLACES 151

would stay but one night, go without looking back, and never think of it again.

[3] Every second house in Floral Heights had a bedroom precisely like this.

[4] The Babbitts' house was five years old. It was all as competent and glossy as this bedroom. It had the best of taste, the best of inexpensive rugs, a simple and laudable architecture, and the latest conveniences. Throughout, electricity took the place of candles and slatternly hearth-fires. Along the bedroom baseboard were three plugs for electric lamps, concealed by little brass doors. In the halls were plugs for the vacuum cleaner, and in the living-room plugs for the piano lamp, for the electric fan. The trim dining-room (with its admirable oak buffet, its leaded-glass cupboard, its creamy plaster walls, its modest scene of a salmon expiring upon a pile of oysters) had plugs which supplied the electric percolator and the electric toaster.

[5] In fact there was but one thing wrong with the Babbitt house: It was not a home.

VOCABULARY

1. Define the following words as they are used in the selection: *indolence* [2]; *laudable, slatternly* [4].

2. Is Lewis's use of *give* (in the first sentence of paragraph 1) recognized by your dictionary?

3. Is *Babbitt* (or *babbitt*)—other than the metal—listed in your dictionary? What has the word come to mean in the American language?

QUESTIONS FOR STUDY AND DISCUSSION

1. This description of the house of the Babbitts comments on its occupants. What can be inferred about the Babbitts from the first paragraph?

2. In the paragraph preceding this excerpt, Lewis refers to the bedroom's "impersonality." How is the tone set by this word appropriate to the entire description?

3. Paragraph 2 contains description and direct comment. Where does description end and direct comment begin?

4. Which adjectives in paragraph 2 suggest the quality of the features of the Babbitt house? Which words or phrases reveal the tastes and values of the Babbitts?

5. Lewis calls the bedroom "modest and pleasant" and a "masterpiece." Yet he obviously does not approve of it. What is the basis of his criticism?

6. How effective is the comparison that concludes paragraph 2?

7. Underline the words in paragraph 4 that help to express the attitude of Lewis toward the Babbitts.

8. Electric conveniences are taken for granted by contemporary Americans. What is the basis for Lewis's dissatisfaction with the Babbitts' electric home?

9. Which definition of *irony* in your dictionary relates to Lewis's use of the adjective *modest* to describe the picture "of a salmon expiring upon a pile of oysters"?

10. Paragraphs 3 and 5 have only one sentence each. Would these sentences be more effective if they were included in the paragraphs that precede them?

11. What are the specific objects of Lewis's criticism in this passage?

Herb Caen

THE PLASTIC FANTASTIC

Except for eight years with the San Francisco Examiner, *Herb Caen (b. 1916) has been a daily correspondent for the* San Francisco Chronicle *since 1938. His column focuses mostly on the San Francisco scene but, as in the following description of Disneyland, is not limited to it. He is the author of numerous books about San Francisco; among them are* The San Francisco Book *(1948),* Baghdad-by-the-Bay *(1949),* Don't Call It Frisco *(1953), and* San Francisco: City on the Golden Hills *(1967).*

Disneyland, Anaheim, Orange County

[1] What am I doing here? It's a question I asked myself several times over the weekend. The answer, if any, is that I felt this overpowering urge to see the Real America, that mythical land where children are a well-behaved minority, men wear their hair short and their ties and minds narrow, and where

From *The San Francisco Chronicle,* December 22, 1970. Reprinted by permission of Herb Caen.

DESCRIPTIONS OF PLACES

women still know their place, which is in the beauty shop, having their hair pumped up to 40 pounds pressure. It's all here in Uncle Walt's Magic Kingdom, where seldom is heard a discouraging word and the skies are not cloudy except when it rains, which it's doing right now. But don't underestimate Uncle Walt's minions. There's a red, white and blue rainbow arching across the Early American sky, in which you can see large slices of pie (Mom's, apple, M-1). Aside from the large wasps flitting about, an idyllic scene.

[2] The flight down, on a 737 "Fat Albert," was uneventful: no Bircher fanatic attempted to hijack the plane to Knott's Berry Farm. Our little band of Northern Radic-Libs checked into the Disneyland Hotel, where we were treated with wary deference. When I first visited here 15 years ago, it was only a motel; now there are two 12-story towers with 1000 rooms—imagine! We ordered room service breakfast and it arrived in plastic containers on a plastic tray with plastic implements, just like tourist class on a second-rate airline. When we'd finished, my wife called room service: "You can pick up our dishes now." "But honey," came the reply, "you just throw it away!" And you can't even recycle it, like the food.

[3] Disneyland lies somewhere between 1984 and 2001, glittering and gleaming in the rain. We zoomed over on the Disney-Alweg Swiss-made monorail, past parking lots, freeways, motels and franchised food palaces. The constant motion is dizzying: steam train circling, tiny cars racing, bobsleds hurtling in and out of the Matterhorn, "People-Movers" clattering overhead, ski-lifts dangling from wires. It is the world's greatest and most serious amusement park—no barkers—and also the cleanest: 10 million a year for maintenance alone. When you drop a cigarette to the undefiled ground, you expect the heavens to part and Uncle Walt to roar: "This is your Magic Kingdom—keep it clean!"

[4] It is a children's wonderland artfully geared to adult tastes. Significantly, the statistics show five grownups to each child. Along with the calculated sentimentality and efficiency, there are those little touches of "naturalistic" violence that made Disney a sometimes perplexing genius. On the submarine ride, a lobster clamping down on a small fish, an octopus with its tentacles wound around a big fish. On the jungle ride, a lion with a zebra's bloody stump between its teeth, a cannibal holding shrunken heads, your boat's skipper firing his revolver at a threatening hippo. Scary haunted houses, bloodthirsty pirates, giant spiders. On Tom Sawyer's Island, a white pioneer lying dead outside his flaming cabin, an arrow in his chest—the victim of Indians. The adults chuckle, the children are frightened. The generation gasp.

[5] Disneyland is a mechanized marvel of recorded voices and automated

figures (the swans in the lagoon are real and therefore look false). When you take the marvelous ride to the moon, you are briefed by "Dr. Morrow," a mechanical man who wears glasses and a sweet, patient smile. He arises from his control panel, swings around and speaks to you so warmly and kindly you feel like taking him out for a drink later. Next door in the "America the Beautiful" exhibit (a brilliant 360-degree film of the U.S.), you are briefed by a baby-faced blonde of flesh and blood, presumably, who rattles off her lines much more mechanically than "Dr. Morrow." That, in sum, is the disturbing thing about Disneyland: the line between the real and the false keeps disappearing. At the Tiki Room, with its fantastic automated birds, a Marine refuses to take a seat under a fake parrot. "I just had my uniform cleaned," he explained.

[6] Christmas at Disneyland. At dusk on Saturday, the rain stopped—magically, of course—and there ensued a candlelight ceremony featuring 48,736 choristers from 27,986 Southern California church and secular schools singing 107,893 carols, or so it seeemd (I may have lost count). Then came the great annual Christmas parade of Disney characters, which got off to a slow start. The horses drawing the Queen's carriage, unnerved by the music and floodlights, refused to budge. If they'd been mechanized, of course, they'd have worked perfectly. Wait till next year.

[7] Walt Disney, a fascinating study, a remarkable and powerful man. His ever-smiling workers still refer to him as "Walt," as though he were there, as he may well be. Disneyland is his monument, a stunning combination of patriotism, technical expertise, Middle American nostalgia (expressed most brilliantly in his Main Street 1910) and the disturbing undertone of violence overlaid with all that surface cleanliness. As always, I was impressed with Disneyland, where everything works, and relieved to return to San Francisco, where hardly anything does. But if "Dr. Morrow" ever gets up here, I'd still like to buy him that drink. Served in a real nonplastic glass.

VOCABULARY

Define the following words as they are used in the selection: *minions, idyllic* [1]; *undefiled* [3]; *"naturalistic"* [4].

QUESTIONS FOR STUDY AND DISCUSSION

1. What is Caen's attitude toward Disneyland? Is he contemptuous of it,

amused by it, or amazed by it? In paragraph 7 he says that he is always "impressed with Disneyland." What is it that always impresses him?

2. What phrases in the essay best denote Caen's response to Disneyland?

3. What features of Disneyland does Caen emphasize? How do these features relate to the title of his essay?

4. Caen presents Disneyland as a place of paradoxes and contrasts. What ones does he point out?

5. In the opening and concluding paragraphs Caen relates Disneyland to America through the phrases "Real America," "Early American sky," and "Middle American nostalgia." What are the connotations of "America" in these phrases?

6. Caen's columns are rich in allusions—musical, literary, cinematographic, social. Which ones do you find in this essay? How do these allusions serve as a means for commentary upon Disneyland?

7. The essay is unified in part by recurring references to America, magic, plastic, Walt Disney, Dr. Morrow, and mechanical efficiency. Trace these references to show how the final paragraph is an appropriate and effective conclusion to the essay.

8. Caen is fond of word play. Point out examples of alliteration, puns, double meanings. What qualities do these devices or techniques add to Caen's style?

9. Though Caen does not describe Disneyland in graphic detail, do you believe that he succeeds in conveying a sense of what Disneyland is? Are the details sufficient to convey an impression of Disneyland to anyone not familiar with it?

DESCRIPTIONS OF PERSONS

A description of a person should tell what the person is like; but since a person, unlike a place, is a complex, living personality, no description can hope to be complete. At best it will be only suggestive. What a person is like in one situation will present only one facet of him. Each individual lives numerous roles; the image that you have of yourself is probably quite different from the ones that your parents, your teachers, and your friends have of you. The only adequate description of a person would be book-length and would describe the person in many situations and through the eyes of many observers. Yet something, surely, can be suggested in even a brief description, though it must necessarily be limited to a single point of view and to a few highly selective details.

What are the central features of a person, the ones most suggestive of personality? Appearance is revealing but is often deceptive. Bret Harte's description of the gold miners in his short story "The Luck of Roaring Camp" points up the dangers of making glib generalizations about personality stereotypes on the basis of appearance:

Physically they exhibited no indication of their past lives and character. The greatest scamp had a Raphael face, with a profusion of blonde hair; Oakhurst, a gambler, had the melancholy abstraction of a Hamlet; the coolest and most courageous man was scarcely over five feet in height, with a soft voice and an embarrassed, timid manner. . . . The strongest man had but three fingers on his right hand; the best shot had but one eye.

Descriptions of physical appearance—features and dress alike—are generally the most objective, for they depend upon details that any observer might see. But they still entail the selection of those details most revealing of the character's personality as the author sees him. Even physical descriptions, then, offer opportunity for impressionistic techniques; Melville, for instance, immediately suggests the desperate quality of Captain Ahab's appearance by saying, "He looked like a man cut away from the stake."

How does a person move or stand? What are his gestures or mannerisms? These details, too, are significant. What are his individual traits, his peculiarities or eccentricities? These details may be even more important than physical description.

Intellectual activity, indicated by what a person says and the way he says it, marks the person immediately. Leonard Shecter suggests the complexity of the personality of Muhammad Ali by quoting him in both boastful and reflective moods. Similarly, the use of anecdotes or brief stories showing a person in a typical act or situation, a device also employed effectively by Shecter, as well as by Sinclair Lewis in the preceding section, is a useful descriptive device.

The impressions that a person makes upon others are also significant and contribute to the total impression. Herman Melville refers to the superstitions and beliefs that have been inspired by Captain Ahab. Harold Frederic, as he describes the three trustees, alludes to the impressions these men have created upon their townspeople. The complete description of these men is the sum of all of the responses of those who see them.

Descriptions of persons are also contained in the following selections in other sections of this book (see the Contents for page numbers):

William Golding, "Thinking as a Hobby"
Sinclair Lewis, "The House of Babbitt"
Clair Huffaker, "Pony Boy"
George Orwell, "A Hanging"
Katharine Brush, "Birthday Party"
Richard Wright, ". . . And I Hungered for Books"

Leonard Shecter

MUHAMMAD ALI

A native New Yorker, Leonard Shecter (1927–1974) attended New York University and the New School for Social Research and served on the New York Post *from 1945 to 1965 as a reporter and sports columnist. He was the author of numerous articles on sports, politics, Negro history, and travel in such periodicals as* The New York Times Magazine, Look, Sports Illustrated, *and* Esquire. *His books on sports include* The Jocks (1969) *and* Once upon the Polo Grounds: The Mets That Were (1970), *and he collaborated with Jim Bouton on* Ball Four: Life and Hard Times Throwing the Knuckleball in the Big Leagues (1970). *The following selection is an excerpt from "The Passion of Muhammad Ali," which originally appeared in* Esquire *in April 1968.*

[1] It was Chicago, September, 1962, the week of the first Floyd Patterson–Sonny Liston heavyweight championship fight. The nature of the match, evil (Liston) vs. good (Patterson), had attracted an impressive delegation of the nation's literati, among them Norman Mailer and James Baldwin. Gathering place was press headquarters, a windowless meeting room in a Loop hotel full of busy typewriters, empty glasses and chatting groups of reporters from places like Quincy, Illinois, London and Sydney. Into this gabbling scene, one late afternoon, a time when the room was usually filled, walked a large, handsome, collegiate-looking young man dressed in sport shirt, sweater and tight pants. "Gentlemen," he shouted. "Your attention please, gentlemen." His voice was strident, his eyes glittered and he smiled. "Is the A.P. here?" he said. He did not have to stand on his toes in order to see over everybody's head. He just lifted his chin and looked around the crowded room. "Is the U.P.I. here? Very good. Reuters? Anybody here from *Time*? Nobody from *Time*? What about *Newsweek*? Fine. Very good. Gentlemen, I have a poem. But first I

Copyright © 1968 by Esquire, Inc. Reprinted by permission of the author and Raines & Raines.

have to tell you that Mr. Archie Moore shook me up by inventing a new punch which he called 'the lip-buttoner.' I had to invent myself a new punch, too. I call it the old-age pension punch."

[2]   There was a rumble of laughter.

[3]   "Now my poem."

> It was that night in the Coliseum
> That's when I annihilated him,
> I gave him a lot of sand
> The one they call the old man;
> He was old and I was new
> You could tell by the bombs I threw.
> I had left jabs to fire like pistons
> They were twice as rough as Liston's;
> The people cry "Stop the fight!"
> Before Clay put out the light,
> He was trying to remain the great Mr. Moore
> For he knew Clay had predicted four;
> I swept that old man clean out of the ring
> For a good new broom sweeps up anything,
> Some say the greatest was Sugar Ray
> But they haven't seen Cassius Clay.

[4]   He hung around the press room for a while, chatting, shouting, mugging and bragging. And when he left, it was as though somebody had cleaned out the ashtrays, cleared the cigar smoke and left the place with a feeling of open windows. He would do the same for boxing, I thought, and he would have a good time doing it.

[5]   And that's the way it seemed to go. He knocked out old Archie Moore in the predicted four rounds and he went on to win the title. Everywhere he went there was noise and laughter and people. Once he went on television with a new poem:

> Me.
> Wheeeee!

[6]   Then he added: "I'm very modest."

[7]   Before his second fight with Liston he showed up with the largest entourage since King Saud brought his harem to the Waldorf Astoria. There

DESCRIPTIONS OF PERSONS

were four sparring partners, three cooks, a valet, a chauffeur, a personal photographer, a secretary, a masseur and Stepin Fetchit (the only movie star who ever made two million dollars in Hollywood and frivoled away five million; Cassius Clay understood flamboyance). And then, of course, there was always Drew (Bundini) Brown, the man who invented Clay's fighting slogan: *Float like a butterfly, sting like a bee.*

[8]   And the bus. It was fire-engine red and in letters four feet high on both sides was painted the legend: Heavyweight Champion of World. (In this bus, he said, all the white men rode in the back.) Before his fight with George Chuvalo he drove the bus—Big Red, he called it affectionately—up to Chuvalo's Catskill training camp and as he arrived he managed to drive it off the road. This made all the wire services, including Reuters. Anywhere he was, it was like a seventy-five-piece band had arrived.

[9]   Even after he cut back some of the noise, having won his campaign for the title, fun-and-games was all around him. Children followed him wherever he went and all over the world adults adulated him. "The only difference between me and the Pied Piper," he once said, "is he didn't have no Cadillac."

[10]   And another time. "I'm so popular I have to hide. I get everything free, invitations to countries. I get letters from all kinds of kings. They want me to live in their castles. Don't no Negro get better treatment than me. If I retired tomorrow, I can say I've had my fun."

[11]   Muhammad Ali, shirtless, dressed in jeans and chukka boots, sat in the corner of his blue velvet couch. He ran his hand over his milk-chocolate torso, caressing, slapping, pinching the new flesh around his middle. The color television, set into a marble fireplace opposite him in this narrow living room, was tuned to a morning game show. He had used remote-control gadget to turn the sound off but the animated lollipops on the screen continued their mindless charade. His eyes, big and brown, kept drifting back to the screen. He was talking about how busy he was.

[12]   "And tonight they're having this big musical and they want me to say a few words about whatever I want to talk about. Then I got a call from this college in Hartford—I forget the name of it—and they want me up there. And some old Negro lady group in New York is going to give me an award and they want me up there on Sunday to accept that. There's always something. Everybody wants me."

[13]   The expression on his face turned to one of bemused pain. His hand-

some face, unmarked but for a thin white scar in his left eyebrow (the result of a childhood accident), is as mobile as that of a rubber puppet and he tugs and twists at it to underline emotion. When he is surprised, his eyes pop out of his head and show white all around the pupil. When he is sad, his face collapses and one can almost see the tears forming. When he is happy, his face glows like a pinball machine and his even white teeth gleam free games. He uses his voice the way he does his face; he never merely quotes anybody, he imitates. He drops it and whispers, he raises it to sound like a woman. He straightens up and tightens his throat and enunciates his g's and d's and he sounds like a white man. He is a performer and he glances often at the mirrored wall behind the fireplace to see how he's coming across.

[14] "It's impossible for me to dry up and have nothing to do," he is saying. "I mean I just don't represent boxing. I'm taking a stand for what I believe in and being one thousand percent for the freedom of the black people. Naturally those who have the same fight, but on a smaller scale, they come to me," and here he whispers, " 'You speak for me, too, brother, you speak for me too. I make my money from Charley but I'm with you. Man, I just jump and shout every time I see you tell them.' " Now he raises his voice again. "So I got hundreds of places to go and talk and I'll always have them as long as I'm talking for freedom."

[15] Ah, freedom. He now is free to talk. He used to be free to fight and he was something to see, the speed of him and the beauty of his motion, his huge, smooth body gliding in a ballet of boxing, his white ring shoes becoming a furry flurr. He was perhaps the best anybody has even seen, because he had the modern athlete's body, as swift as it was large, and no boxer ever had one like it before. But then a sergeant in a Houston Selective Service office asked him to take a step forward and he refused because, he said, he was a minister of the Muslim faith in the Nation of Islam. The boxing commission revoked his title as heavyweight champion of the world. Rumors started, around the fight business first and then in newspapers. Rumor: he was stony-broke, living on heaven knows what, and what had happened to his money? Rumor: he had earned more than two million dollars in the ring—his gross earnings as a champion were probably twice that, except that fifty percent is conceded to his managers—but his co-religionists had stolen it, extorted it, conned him out of it. Rumor: and guess who put up the $135,000 for a mosque in Miami?

[16] "I'll tell you one thing about that," Muhammad Ali said. Then he told a lot of things. They poured out of him like one of his sermons, most of which he excerpts from *Message to the Blackman* by Elijah Muhammad, the self-anointed Messenger of Allah. "Many reporters and many people ask me,

DESCRIPTIONS OF PERSONS 161

they say, 'Champion, how you gonna live? Champion, how you eating? How you gonna make it?' I have this to say to all the reporters and all the critics who want to know why I don't fall and when I'm gonna fall. They seem to want to see that. The power structure seems to want to starve me out. I mean the punishment, five years in jail, ten-thousand-dollar fine, ain't enough. They want to stop me from working, not only in the country but out of it. Not even a license to fight an exhibition for charity. And that's in this twentieth century. You read about these things in the dictatorship countries where a man don't go along with this thing or that and he is completely not allowed to work or to earn a decent living. So this is my position. I rely on Allah. I leave it up to Allah. I believe that there is no God but Allah and I believe Elijah Muhammad is his own true messenger and I'm standing up for my religion and my salvation. If it means suffer, if it means get out of the house, give up the cars, I'll do it. Just give me a pair of blue jeans and a leather jacket, give me a stick with a rag on the back with some food in it and say, Get on the railroad tracks, and I will do it. I believe that Allah would lead me to a gold mine on the train. I might find a million-dollar bill."

[17] He has been saying this sort of thing for years and finally it is apparent that he believes it. He is burning with fervor. He might even believe that Allah, if not the judicial system, will save him from prison. "I am looking for Allah to do something," he says. "I am his servant. *Allah, they're punishing your servant.*"

VOCABULARY

Define the following words as they are used in the selection: *literati, strident* [1]; *entourage, flamboyance* [7]; *adulated* [9]; *charade* [11]; *Charley* [14]; *flurr* [15]; *fervor* [17].

QUESTIONS FOR STUDY AND DISCUSSION

1. This selection contains a break between paragraphs 10 and 11. What determines the division? How have the situation and attitude of Muhammad Ali changed?

2. The first section (paragraphs 1 through 10) also divides, focusing first on a single episode and then generalizing about Cassius Clay. How does Shecter effect a transition from the specific episode to the general?

3. Although Shecter provides a number of details about Clay's physical ap-

pearance in paragraph 1, several of these details are implied rather than made explicit. How, for example, does Shecter say that Clay was tall? What details in this paragraph and the following two paragraphs imply that Clay was a showman and anything but modest?

4. Note the comparison in paragraph 4. Why is it an apt one?

5. What qualities and characteristics of Clay are illustrated in paragraphs 5 through 10? Is there a topic sentence that governs the content of these paragraphs? What word in paragraph 7 best describes the manner of Clay's life at this time?

6. Compare the details of paragraph 11 with those of paragraph 1. What is the significance of the differences in dress, time of day, and situation?

7. The concluding four paragraphs, in which Muhammad Ali speaks seriously, present a much different view of him than do the earlier paragraphs. How does what he says of his role give added significance to the image he is described as projecting in the first half of the essay?

8. Comment on Shecter's use of figurative and colorful language. Is it appropriate and effective? Which comparisons do you think are the best ones?

9. What is Shecter's attitude toward his subject? Does he express his attitude openly, or is it essentially implicit in his description of Muhammad Ali?

10. Does paragraph 17 present Muhammad Ali favorably or critically? In what significant way does the person speaking in this paragraph differ from the one speaking in paragraph 1?

Henry James

THE AMERICAN

In an essay on the art of writing fiction, Henry James (1843–1916), at the forefront of American novelists, tells the beginning writer that he should "try to be one of the people on whom nothing is lost." James adhered with dedication to his own advice. His short stories and novels, as well as his critical writings, are the work of a man sensitive to the complexities and ambiguities of life and literature. Published in 1877, The American still contains much to interest the student of American culture; for Christopher Newman, the central character, is a fictional creation embodying the enduring virtues and faults that James found in Americans.

[1] On a brilliant day in May, in the year 1868, a gentleman was reclining at his ease on the great circular divan which at that period occupied the center

of the Salon Carré, in the Museum of the Louvre. This commodious ottoman has since been removed, to the extreme regret of all weak-kneed lovers of the fine arts, but the gentleman in question had taken serene possession of its softest spot, and, with his head thrown back and his legs outstretched, was staring at Murillo's beautiful moon-borne Madonna in profound enjoyment of his posture. He had removed his hat, and flung down beside him a little red guide-book and an opera-glass. The day was warm; he was heated with walking, and he repeatedly passed his handkerchief over his forehead, with a somewhat wearied gesture. And yet he was evidently not a man to whom fatigue was familiar; long, lean, and muscular, he suggested the sort of vigor that is commonly known as "toughness." But his exertions on this particular day had been of an unwonted sort, and he had performed great physical feats which left him less jaded than his tranquil stroll through the Louvre. He had looked out all the pictures to which an asterisk was affixed in those formidable pages of fine print in his Bädeker; his attention had been strained and his eyes dazzled, and he had sat down with an aesthetic headache. He had looked, moreover, not only at all the pictures, but at all the copies that were going forward around them, in the hands of those innumerable young women in irreproachable toilets who devote themselves, in France, to the propagation of masterpieces, and if the truth must be told, he had often admired the copy much more than the original. His physiognomy would have sufficiently indicated that he was a shrewd and capable fellow, and in truth he had often sat up all night over a bristling bundle of accounts, and heard the cock crow without a yawn. But Raphael and Titian and Rubens were a new kind of arithmetic, and they inspired our friend, for the first time in his life, with a vague self-mistrust.

[2] An observer with anything of an eye for national types would have had no difficulty in determining the local origin of this undeveloped connoisseur, and indeed such an observer might have felt a certain humorous relish of the almost ideal completeness with which he filled out the national mould. The gentleman on the divan was a powerful specimen of an American. But he was not only a fine American; he was in the first place, physically, a fine man. He appeared to possess that kind of health and strength which, when found in perfection, are the most impressive—the physical capital which the owner does nothing to "keep up." If he was a muscular Christian, it was quite without knowing it. If it was necessary to walk to a remote spot, he walked, but he had never known himself to "exercise." He had no theory with regard to cold bathing or the use of Indian clubs; he was neither an oarsman, a rifleman, nor a fencer—he had never had time for these amusements—and he was quite unaware that the saddle is recommended for certain forms of indigestion. He was by inclination a temperate man; but he had supped the night before his visit to the Louvre at the Café Anglais—some one had told him it was an

experience not to be omitted—and he had slept none the less the sleep of the just. His usual attitude and carriage were of a rather relaxed and lounging kind, but when, under a special inspiration, he straightened himself, he looked like a grenadier on parade. He never smoked. He had been assured—such things are said—that cigars were excellent for the health, and he was quite capable of believing it; but he knew as little about tobacco as about homoeopathy. He had a very well-formed head, with a shapely, symmetrical balance of the frontal and the occipital development, and a good deal of straight, rather dry brown hair. His complexion was brown, and his nose had a bold, well-marked arch. His eye was of a clear, cold gray, and save for a rather abundant mustache he was clean-shaved. He had the flat jaw and sinewy neck which are frequent in the American type; but the traces of national origin are a matter of expression even more than of feature, and it was in this respect that our friend's countenance was supremely eloquent. The discriminating observer we have been supposing might, however, perfectly have measured its expressiveness, and yet have been at a loss to describe it. It had that typical vagueness which is not vacuity, that blankness which is not simplicity, that look of being committed to nothing in particular, of standing in an attitude of general hospitality to the chances of life, of being very much at one's own disposal, so characteristic of many American faces. It was our friend's eye that chiefly told his story; an eye in which innocence and experience were singularly blended. It was full of contradictory suggestions, and though it was by no means the glowing orb of a hero of romance, you could find in it almost anything you looked for. Frigid and yet friendly, frank yet cautious, shrewd yet credulous, positive yet skeptical, confident yet shy, extremely intelligent and extremely good-humored, there was something vaguely defiant in its concessions, and something profoundly reassuring in its reserve. The cut of this gentleman's mustache, with the two premature wrinkles in the cheek above it, and the fashion of his garments, in which an exposed shirt-front and a cerulean cravat played perhaps an obtrusive part, completed the conditions of his identity. We have approached him, perhaps, at a not especially favorable moment; he is by no means sitting for his portrait. But listless as he lounges there, rather baffled on the aesthetic question, and guilty of the damning fault (as we have lately discovered it to be) of confounding the merit of the artist with that of his work (for he admires the squinting Madonna of the young lady with the boyish coiffure, because he thinks the young lady herself uncommonly taking), he is a sufficiently promising acquaintance. Decision, salubrity, jocosity, prosperity, seem to hover within his call; he is evidently a practical man, but the idea, in his case, had undefined and mysterious boundaries, which invite the imagination to bestir itself on his behalf.

VOCABULARY

Define the following words as they are used in the selection: *commodious, serene, unwonted, jaded, Bädeker* [1]; *connoisseur, homoeopathy, occipital, vacuity, credulous, concessions, cerulean, confounding, salubrity, jocosity* [2].

QUESTIONS FOR STUDY AND DISCUSSION

1. James's novel *The American* is in its entirety an extended attempt to characterize Christopher Newman, but the qualities of character and personality developed through the action of the novel are initially introduced in the first two paragraphs of the book. What is the principal quality or feature of Newman's character emphasized in paragraph 1?

2. James writes for the unhurried reader, the one able to enjoy his subtle ironies. Identify the irony in the second sentence of paragraph 1, wherein Newman is described as "staring at Murillo's beautiful moon-borne Madonna in profound enjoyment of his posture." How does this detail contribute to the development of the quality of Newman's character emphasized in this paragraph?

3. What details does James introduce to show that Newman is not a regular frequenter of art galleries? How do these details contribute to the reader's understanding of Newman?

4. What sentence or sentences serve well as the topic statement of paragraph 2? What principal points does James develop in the paragraph?

5. Do the details in paragraph 1 contribute to the depiction of Newman as one who with "almost ideal completeness . . . fill[s] out the national mould" of an American?

6. What does James mean by the phrase "muscular Christian"? What details contribute to the idea that if he was a muscular Christian he was an unintentional one?

7. Are the physical characteristics of Newman well selected for an ideal specimen of "the American type"? Do they individualize Newman—i.e., help to characterize him as an individual American—or make him a stereotype?

8. The description of Newman's expression or countenance is worthy of careful attention. To test your comprehension of the subtleties of the description, try rephrasing James's statements in words of your own.

9. The description of Newman's "eye" makes use of paired contradictory qualities. Find examples of these contradictory features in the expressions of persons in public life such as actors and political figures.

10. Comment on the appropriateness of Christopher Newman's name.

11. James's portrait of Newman, like Newman's eyes, is made up of contradictory qualities. What, on the whole, does James seem to think of Newman? Does he respect him, admire him, praise him, belittle him?

12. Could Christopher Newman sit for a portrait of "the American" today? Which of his qualities are still regarded as typically American qualities? Which ones, if any, are now outdated? Which public person, of the past or present, seems to you best to embody the American qualities and features that James ascribes to Newman?

Herman Melville

CAPTAIN AHAB

Captain Ahab, the central character in Moby-Dick, *by Herman Melville (1819–1891), appears first in Chapter 28, many days after the Pequod has sailed from Nantucket. The first sight of him is described by Ishmael, the narrator of the novel, and has been prepared for by several previous references ("He's a grand, ungodly, godlike man . . . ," for instance), as well as by Ishmael's growing conviction that Ahab's purpose is evil and that the voyage will end in disaster. Ishmael has been told that Ahab, who did not appear on deck until the ship was several days at sea, had perhaps been ill. Tashtego is a harpooner, an Indian from Gay Head, on Martha's Vineyard, an island off the Massachusetts coast.*

[1]   . . . Captain Ahab stood upon his quarter-deck.

[2]   There seemed no sign of common bodily illness about him, nor of the recovery from any. He looked like a man cut away from the stake, when the fire has overrunningly wasted all the limbs without consuming them, or taking away one particle from their compacted aged robustness. His whole high, broad form, seemed made of solid bronze, and shaped in an unalterable mould, like Cellini's cast Perseus. Threading its way out from among his grey hairs, and continuing down one side of his tawny scorched face and neck, till it disappeared in his clothing, you saw a slender rod-like mark, lividly whitish. It resembled that perpendicular seam sometimes made in the straight, lofty trunk of a great tree, when the upper lightning tearingly darts down it, and without wrenching a single twig, peels and grooves out the bark from top to bottom ere running off into the soil, leaving the tree still greenly alive, but branded. Whether that mark was born with him, or whether it was the scar left by some desperate wound, no one could certainly say. By some tacit con-

DESCRIPTIONS OF PERSONS 167

sent, throughout the voyage little or no allusion was made to it, especially by the mates. But once Tashtego's senior, an old Gay-Head Indian among the crew, superstitiously asserted that not till he was full forty years old did Ahab become that way branded, and then it came upon him, not in the fury of any mortal fray, but in an elemental strife at sea. Yet, this wild hint seemed inferentially negatived, by what a grey Manxman insinuated, an old sepulchral man, who, having never before sailed out of Nantucket, had never ere this laid eye upon wild Ahab. Nevertheless, the old sea-traditions, the immemorial credulities, popularly invested this old Manxman with preternatural powers of discernment. So that no white sailor seriously contradicted him when he said that if ever Captain Ahab should be tranquilly laid out—which might hardly come to pass, so he muttered—then, whoever should do that last office for the dead, would find a birthmark on him from crown to sole.

[3] So powerfully did the whole grim aspect of Ahab affect me, and the livid brand which streaked it, that for the first few moments I hardly noted that not a little of this overbearing grimness was owing to the barbaric white leg upon which he partly stood. It had previously come to me that this ivory leg had at sea been fashioned from the polished bone of the sperm whale's jaw. "Aye, he was dismasted off Japan," said the old Gay-Head Indian once; "but like his dismasted craft, he shipped another mast without coming home for it. He has a quiver of 'em."

[4] I was struck with the singular posture he maintained. Upon each side of the Pequod's quarter-deck, and pretty close to the mizzen shrouds, there was an auger hole, bored about half an inch or so, into the plank. His bone leg steadied in that hole; one arm elevated, and holding by a shroud; Captain Ahab stood erect, looking straight out beyond the ship's ever-pitching prow. There was an infinity of firmest fortitude, a determinate, unsurrenderable wilfulness, in the fixed and fearless, forward dedication of that glance. Not a word he spoke; nor did his officers say aught to him; though by all their minutest gestures and expressions, they plainly showed the uneasy, if not painful, consciousness of being under a troubled master-eye. And not only that, but moody stricken Ahab stood before them with a crucifixion in his face; in all the nameless regal overbearing dignity of some mighty woe.

VOCABULARY

1. Define the following words as they are used in the selection: *tawny, lividly, tacit, allusion, mortal, fray, elemental, strife, inferentially, negatived,*

Manxman, sepulchral, immemorial, credulities, preternatural, discernment [2]; *grimness, barbaric* [3]; *fortitude, dedication, stricken, crucifixion, regal, overbearing* [4].

2. Melville makes deliberate use of Biblical allusions in naming some of his characters. For the Biblical Ahab, see I Kings 16:29. What qualities do the two Ahabs share? Is Melville's Ahab well named? Although Ishmael does not emerge as a character in this selection, you may find it interesting to see what Melville is suggesting about him through his name. See Genesis 16:12.

QUESTIONS FOR STUDY AND DISCUSSION

1. What methods does Melville employ in the characterization of Ahab? Which ones are most effective?

2. Is Melville concerned most with realistic details or with general impressions? What specific details about Ahab's appearance does Melville develop?

3. What comparisons are used in paragraph 2 to suggest Ahab's appearance? What words introduce these comparisons? Are all of the comparisons similes? Are they appropriate and effective?

4. Paragraph 2 is divided into two sections. What are they? Where does the second section begin?

5. The hints of the Indian and the Manxman are presented as superstitions or preternatural knowledge. How effectively do they contribute to the description of Ahab?

6. What adjectives, other than those employed by Melville, could be used to describe Ahab?

7. Why (in the sentence beginning "It resembled that perpendicular seam") should Melville stipulate a tree trunk that is "straight, lofty"? Do these adjectives relate to Ahab?

8. In the last sentence of pargaraph 2, would "from head to toe" or "from head to foot" be as effective as "from crown to sole"? Why or why not? What are the connotations of Melville's words?

9. What instances of alliteration or similar devices do you find in the passage? What is their effect?

Harold Frederic

THE THREE TRUSTEES

The Reverend Theron Ware, a young, ambitious minister, has been assigned a new congregation in Octavius, New York, a fictitious town in the central part of the state. His meeting with the three trustees introduces Mr. Ware (as well as the readers of the novel) to the men whom the minister must serve, and please, in his new assignment. The time is about 1870; the setting, Mr. Ware's home. The description of the trustees should be viewed as a comment upon provincialism, rather than upon Methodism. The passage appears in Chapter 3 of The Damnation of Theron Ware *(1896), by Harold Frederic (1856–1898), a New York novelist whose best fiction portrays rural or small-town life in his own state. The story of Theron Ware, his masterpiece, traces the disintegration of a young minister whose thin cultural background has not equipped him to face the intellectual and social challenges that he finds in Octavius.*

[1] When the three trustees had been shown in by the Rev. Mr. Ware, and had taken seats, an awkward little pause ensued. The young minister looked doubtingly from one face to another, the while they glanced with inquiring interest about the room, noting the pictures and appraising the furniture in their minds.

[2] The obvious leader of the party, Loren Pierce, a rich quarryman, was an old man of medium size and mean attire, with a square, beardless face as hard and impassive in expression as one of his blocks of limestone. The irregular, thin-lipped mouth, slightly sunken, and shut with vice-like firmness, the short snub nose, and the little eyes squinting from half-closed lids beneath slightly marked brows, seemed scarcely to attain to the dignity of features, but evaded attention instead, as if feeling that they were only there at all from plain necessity, and ought not to be taken into account. Mr. Pierce's face did not know how to smile,—what was the use of smiles?—but its whole surface radiated secretiveness. Portrayed on canvas by a master brush, with a ruff or a red robe for a masquerade, generations of imaginative amateurs would have seen in it vast-reaching plots, the skeletons of a dozen dynastic cupboards, the guarded mysteries of half a century's international diplomacy. The amateurs would have been wrong again. There was nothing behind Mr. Pierce's juiceless countenance more weighty than a general determination to exact seven per cent for his money, and some specific notions about capturing certain brick-

yards which were interfering with his quarry-sales. But Octavius watched him shamble along its sidewalks quite as the Vienna of dead and forgotten yesterday might have watched Metternich.

[3] Erastus Winch was of a breezier sort,—a florid, stout, and sandy man, who spent most of his life driving over evil country roads in a buggy, securing orders for dairy furniture and certain allied lines of farm utensils. This practice had given him a loud voice and a deceptively hearty manner, to which the other avocation of cheese-buyer, which he pursued at the Board of Trade meetings every Monday afternoon, had added a considerable command of persuasive yet non-committal language. To look at him, still more to hear him, one would have sworn he was a good fellow, a trifle rough and noisy, perhaps, but all right at bottom. But the County Clerk of Dearborn County could have told you of agriculturists who knew Erastus from long and unhappy experience, and who held him to be even a tighter man than Loren Pierce in the matter of a mortgage.

[4] The third trustee, Levi Gorringe, set one wondering at the very first glance what on earth he was doing in that company. Those who had known him longest had the least notion; but it may be added that no one knew him well. He was a lawyer, and had lived in Octavius for upwards of ten years; that is to say, since early manhood. He had an office on the main street, just under the principal photograph gallery. Doubtless he was sometimes in this office; but his fellow-townsmen saw him more often in the street doorway, with the stairs behind him, and the flaring show-cases of the photographer on either side, standing with his hands in his pockets and an unlighted cigar in his mouth, looking at nothing in particular. About every other day he went off after breakfast into the country roundabout, sometimes with a rod, sometimes with a gun, but always alone. He was a bachelor, and slept in a room at the back of his office, cooking some of his meals himself, getting others at a restaurant close by. Though he had little visible practice, he was understood to be well-to-do and even more, and people tacitly inferred that he "shaved notes." The Methodists of Octavius looked upon him as a queer fish, and through nearly a dozen years had never quite outgrown their hebdomadal tendency to surprise at seeing him enter their church. He had never, it is true, professed religion, but they had elected him as a trustee now for a number of terms, all the same,—partly because he was their only lawyer, partly because he, like both his colleagues, held a mortgage on the church edifice and lot. In person, Mr. Gorringe was a slender man, with a skin of a clear, uniform citron tint, black waving hair, and dark gray eyes, and a thin, high-featured face. He wore a mustache and pointed chin-tuft; and, though he was of New England parentage and had never been further south than Ocean Grove, he

presented a general effect of old Mississippian traditions and tastes startlingly at variance with the standards of Dearborn County Methodism. Nothing could convince some of the elder sisters that he was not a drinking man.

PRELIMINARY SKETCHES

The question of how a professional author approaches the problems of writing is always of interest to students, though different writers' methods differ as greatly as do their works. The following sketches of the qualities and features of the three characters provide some insight into Frederic's methods. Obviously, he did not outline his paragraphs sentence by sentence before writing, but he did know what he wanted to put into each paragraph. About the need for knowing his material thoroughly, he once said: "I seek only to know my people through and through. They make the story 'off their own bat' once they have been started. But you must really know them first." Section I comes from a sheet of notes listing and describing several characters who appear in the novel, as well as several whom Frederic chose to omit from the book. Section II appears on a page of notes prepared by Frederic as an outline for Chapter 3. The square brackets enclose material that Frederic deleted.

I

Loren [Potter] Pierce—old man, thin, iron-gray hair, broad mouth, tight shut like vise, squinting eyes—Rich quarryman, doing little in brick-yards too, who dominant in Ware's church. Dull bigot, swindler in petty way—hard-fisted, dictatorial.

[Stephen Sidney] Levi Gorringe—mustache & thin chin whiskers—Money lender, old bachelor, also Trustee, rather better fellow than others, a lawyer, great fisherman, always went out alone—rumors he drinking man.

Erastus [F]Winch—florid, sandy, rather stout, loud voice, drove great deal in buggy. Deceptive genial air, extraordinary meanness, cheese buyer—salesman of dairy furniture, &c. mortgages on farms. Trustee of church.

From the papers of Harold Frederic in the Library of Congress, Washington, D.C. Printed by permission of the late Ruth Keen.

II

After

    Three Trustees been shown in, taken seats, awkward little pause ensued.
Loren [Potter] Pierce—
Erastus Winch—
Levi Gorringe—

VOCABULARY

Define the following words as they are used in the selection: *mean, dynastic, juiceless, countenance, Metternich* [2]; *breezier, florid, sandy, furniture, avocation, non-committal* [3]; *tacitly, inferred, "shaved notes," hebdomadal, edifice, citron* [4]; in the "Preliminary Sketches": *bigot*.

QUESTIONS FOR STUDY AND DISCUSSION

1. Do the sketches indicate that Frederic was familiar not only with the main features but also with the quality of character that he desired to create? What phrases in the sketches indicate the broader qualities of the men? Are these developed in the descriptions in the novel?

2. Section I of the sketches presents, in order, Pierce, Gorringe, Winch; yet the notes for Chapter 3 and the descriptive passage itself place Gorringe last. What reasons might have influenced Frederic to change the order of the trustees' descriptions?

3. What specific details in the preliminary sketch of Pierce are used in the description? Which ones are elaborated? How does the description present a more vivid account of Pierce than the sketch does? What comments are added?

4. The final comments about Pierce in the sketch ("Dull bigot, swindler in petty way—hard-fisted, dictatorial") are only suggested in the description. How does the description allow the reader to infer these qualities of character?

5. What examples of comparison can be found in paragraph 2 of the selection?

6. What quality of Pierce is the one emphasized? Do the comparisons add to the reader's awareness of this quality in Pierce?

7. What quality of Winch is the one emphasized? How does Frederic convince the reader of this quality?

8. Are all of the details in the sketch of Winch used in the description?

Does the description clarify relationships between some of these details? How does it go beyond the sketch in developing the character of Winch?

9. Each paragraph contains both a description of physical features and a comment by Frederic. How does the paragraph describing Gorringe differ in organization from those describing Pierce and Winch? What has Frederic accomplished by changing the organizational pattern of paragraph 4?

10. What methods does Frederic use in the description of Gorringe? What one method does he use to great degree?

11. Do the details in the description of Gorringe differ from those suggested in the sketch? The sketch calls him a "money lender"; how is this detail used? Is he presented as an "old bachelor," as in the sketch? The sketch refers to him as "rather better fellow than others"; how does Frederic suggest this difference in the description?

12. How does the description of Gorringe serve to suggest in a general way the nature of Mr. Ware's congregation? Does this description also reflect on Pierce and Winch?

13. How is the last sentence in paragraph 4 more dramatic than its counterpart in the sketch ("rumors he drinking man")?

14. What quality of Gorringe is the one emphasized?

15. Compare the connotations of the adjective *thin* in paragraph 2 (second sentence) and paragraph 4 (sentence beginning "In person, Mr. Gorringe was a slender man").

16. Which one of the trustees should Mr. Ware look to for advice and understanding? Why? What qualities do this trustee and Mr. Ware share?

17. Attempt to account for Frederic's final choices of names. Note the ones that he deleted in the sketches.

18. Test your own writing methods against Frederic's. Do you attempt to know your material "through and through"? Do you prepare scratch outlines similar to Frederic's before you begin to write?

SIGHTS, SOUNDS, SENSATIONS

Not all descriptions, of course, are of people or places. Scenes, both natural and artificial, group activities, and even inanimate objects are all properly the subjects of descriptive writing. In the selections that follow, four different writers employ descriptive writing toward different ends. Mark Twain, in "Storm on Jackson's Island," communicates to the reader the experience of a violent summer storm, accentuating its violent and dramatic beauty. John Steinbeck, in his account of the deserted houses of the Dust Bowl, employs description as a vehicle of persuasion, carefully selecting details that establish and communicate to the reader the author's opinions. Chet Huntley describes the Montana frontier landscape of his boyhood, not as a place but as an image with a personality affected by each season and by the passing of time. Stephen Crane describes human activities against a natural background; through carefully controlled tone and the selection of details, he communicates his private view about the quality of the natural scenery that encompasses the human activity.

Despite their diverse subjects and purposes, the selections make use of sensory details to a somewhat greater degree than do most of the descriptions in the preceding two sections. Twain and Crane make especially effective use of color in their descriptions of a thunderstorm and the sea. Most of the selections contain references to sounds—the roll of thunder, the flutter of ragged curtains in the wind, "the melody of the grass." Steinbeck also emphasizes odors as an essential feature of his description of the deserted houses.

Mark Twain

STORM ON JACKSON'S ISLAND

When Huckleberry Finn escaped from Pap Finn and civilization to Jackson's Island, "about two mile and a half downstream" from St. Petersburg (i.e., Hannibal), Missouri, he was soon joined by Jim, a slave who had run away from his owner. While taking refuge in a cave, they witnessed a "lovely" storm, described by Huck in Chapter 9 of Adventures of Huckleberry Finn *(1885). Earlier, they had witnessed "some young birds . . ., flying a yard or two at a time and lighting. Jim said it was a sign it was going to rain."*

[1] The door of the cavern was big enough to roll a hogshead in, and on one side of the door the floor stuck out a little bit and was flat and a good place to build a fire on. So we built it there and cooked dinner.

SIGHTS, SOUNDS, SENSATIONS

[2] We spread the blankets inside for a carpet, and eat our dinner in there. We put all the other things handy at the back of the cavern. Pretty soon it darkened up and begun to thunder and lighten; so the birds was right about it. Directly it begun to rain, and it rained like all fury, too, and I never see the wind blow so. It was one of these regular summer storms. It would get so dark that it looked all blue-black outside, and lovely; and the rain would thrash along by so thick that the trees off a little ways looked dim and spider-webby; and here would come a blast of wind that would bend the trees down and turn up the pale underside of the leaves; and then a perfect ripper of a gust would follow along and set the branches to tossing their arms as if they was just wild; and next, when it was just about the bluest and blackest—*fst!* it was as bright as glory and you'd have a glimpse of tree-tops a-plunging about, away off yonder in the storm, hundreds of yards further than you could see before; dark as sin again in a second, and now you'd hear the thunder let go with an awful crash and then go rumbling, grumbling, tumbling down the sky towards the underside of the world, like rolling empty barrels down stairs, where it's long stairs and they bounce a good deal, you know.

[3] "Jim, this is nice," I says. "I wouldn't want to be nowhere else but here. Pass me along another hunk of fish and some hot cornbread."

VOCABULARY

Define the following words as they are used in the selection: *hogshead* [1]; *thrash, glory* [2].

QUESTIONS FOR STUDY AND DISCUSSION

1. How do paragraphs 1 and 3 and the first two sentences of paragraph 2 help to accentuate the violence of the storm?

2. Notice how the violence of the storm is suggested principally by its effect on the trees. What phrases show the effect of the rain on the trees? The effect of the wind? The effect of the lightning?

3. The references to darkness run through the description. Those to thunder enclose it. Why is the closing attention to thunder perhaps more effective than would be attention to any of the other features of the storm?

4. Make a list of the similes Twain uses. Are the similes appropriate to the speaker?

5. Is any description "literary," or does it all ring true? What of the reference to "the pale underside of the leaves"?

6. What instances of effective onomatopoeia can you point out?

7. What is the effect of the phrase "and lovely" (in paragraph 2)?

8. Since Huckleberry Finn, an unschooled, unsophisticated youngster, tells his story in first person, a great deal of the merit of the novel comes from the realism of language, which is necessarily illiterate. Point out Huck's errors in grammar. Also point out words and constructions that are dialectal.

John Steinbeck

EMPTY HOUSES

The depression and droughts of the 1930s resulted in a mass exodus from the Dust Bowl to the Promised Land of California. John Steinbeck (1902–1968) recorded the human drama in The Grapes of Wrath (1939), *a novel chronicling the story of one family, the Joads, as they moved from Oklahoma to the orange groves of the Pacific Coast. Steinbeck not only tells a story; he protests the economic and social conditions of the thirties. Scattered throughout the book are interchapters, which do not carry the story forward but comment upon the social background. Chapter 11, which follows the departure of the Joads, contains the description of the empty houses left behind.*

[1] The doors of the empty houses swung open, and drifted back and forth in the wind. Bands of little boys came out from the towns to break the windows and to pick over the debris, looking for treasures. And here's a knife with half the blade gone. That's a good thing. And—smells like a rat died there. And look what Whitey wrote on the wall. He wrote that in the toilet in school, too, an' teacher made 'im wash it off.

[2] When the folks first left, and the evening of the first day came, the hunting cats slouched in from the fields and mewed on the porch. And when no one came out, the cats crept through the open doors and walked mewing through the empty rooms. And then they went back to the fields and were wild cats from then on, hunting gophers and field mice, and sleeping in ditches in the daytime. When the night came, the bats, which had stopped

From *The Grapes of Wrath*, by John Steinbeck. Copyright 1939, copyright © renewed 1967 by John Steinbeck. Reprinted by permission of The Viking Press, Inc.

SIGHTS, SOUNDS, SENSATIONS

at the doors for fear of light, swooped into the houses and sailed about the empty rooms, and in a little while they stayed in dark room corners during the day, folded their wings high, and hung head-down among the rafters, and the smell of their droppings was in the empty houses.

[3] And the mice moved in and stored weed seeds in corners, in boxes, in the backs of drawers in the kitchens. And weasels came in to hunt the mice, and the brown owls flew shrieking in and out again.

[4] Now there came a little shower. The weeds sprang up in front of the doorstep, where they had not been allowed, and grass grew up through the porch boards. The houses were vacant, and a vacant house falls quickly apart. Splits started up the sheathing from the rusted nails. A dust settled on the floors, and only mouse and weasel and cat tracks disturbed it.

[5] On a night the wind loosened a shingle and flipped it to the ground. The next wind pried into the hole where the shingle had been, lifted off three, and the next, a dozen. The midday sun burned through the hole and threw a glaring spot on the floor. The wild cats crept in from the fields at night, but they did not mew at the doorstep any more. They moved like shadows of a cloud across the moon, into the rooms to hunt the mice. And on windy nights the doors banged, and the ragged curtains fluttered in the broken windows.

QUESTIONS FOR STUDY AND DISCUSSION

1. Steinbeck's intention in this passage is to describe the process of decay. In these five brief paragraphs, Steinbeck manages to create the sense not only of decay but of complete desolation. The passage has a unity not at first obvious. First of all, note the two features of the house touched upon in paragraph 1, the doors and the windows. In the beginning the doors merely "swung open, and drifted back and forth in the wind." What is the final reference to the doors? How does it suggest complete desolation? Also note the unity provided by the two references to the windows.

2. Trace the process of decay through the entire passage.

3. Trace the references to cats. How do these references show a progression to desolation and abandonment?

4. What references are there to odor, explicit or implicit? Are they in keeping with the tone?

5. What references are there to sound, either explicit or suggested?

6. Indicate the shift in point of view in paragraph 4. Is it obtrusive?

7. What is the effect of the Biblical language in paragraph 2? Notice especially the beginning of sentences with *and,* as well as the clause "and the evening of the first day came," reminiscent of "And there was evening and there was morning, one day" (Genesis 1:5).

8. Notice the contrast between the Biblical language and the slang that concludes paragraph 1. The transition from one style to another is abrupt. What does it accomplish?

9. Steinbeck has maintained the tone of the passage partly by his use of verbs. He makes some of the action dramatic: the doors "swung" and "drifted" and "banged," the cats "slouched" and "crept," the bats "swooped" and "sailed." On the other hand, some of the action is understated, though no less vivid: "the mice moved in," "weasels came in," "there came a little shower." What other verbs might have been used? Would they sound flowery?

10. What is the single figure of speech in the entire passage?

Chet Huntley

THE SONG OF THE LAND

Chet Huntley (1911–1974) was born in a railroad depot in frontier Montana and spent his boyhood on ranches and in mining and railroad towns. His love for the country of his boyhood remained undiminished throughout his years as a news broadcaster and commentator, most notably with the National Broadcasting Company in New York from 1955 to 1970; after his retirement from broadcasting he returned to Montana. His book The Generous Years *(1968) is subtitled* Remembrances of a Frontier Boyhood. *In the following paragraphs, which open the book, he describes the land as he first saw it, near Saco, Montana, in March 1913.*

[1] The iron tires of the spring wagon rolled silently along the twin wheel tracks worn into the grass: parallel trails wandering northward and away to their vanishing point on the treeless folds of the benchland. Behind, the rudimentary road dipped and disappeared into the river valley.

[2] As the weight of the wagon eased on their collars, the team of grays, sensing unhitching and feed, blew out their nostrils and swung into an easy, mile-consuming trot, manes flying in the March wind. The muffled thud of

From *The Generous Years,* by Chet Huntley. Copyright © 1968 by Chet Huntley. Reprinted by permission of Random House, Inc.

SIGHTS, SOUNDS, SENSATIONS

the hooves the occasional creak of the wagon, the jangle of the tug chains and bridle snaps were high-spirited rhythmic beats augmenting the melody . . . the melody of the grass . . . the song of the immense and boundless land.

[3] Sha-a-a-a-e-e-e-sha-o-o-o-m-m-m-m.

[4] It rose out of the land, filled it sky to sky; waves of sound, rolling, rolling, building and diminishing. Toward the source of the wind, to the west, the grass sang in shrill sibilance . . . the reed and flute sections. The violins and horns were on the lee side, and their voices were picked up by the wind and carried over the endless sea of grass.

[5] Sha-a-a-a-ae-e-e-e-e-sh-o-o-o-o-o-m-m-m-m-m!

[6] Wind and grass in assonant conversation. The grass . . . the incredible grass! In March it was only the dried remains of the last year's growth, which had borne up and withstood the crushing weight of the winter snow. Indeed, it had carried the weight of the snow crop like a forest of supporting beams and pillars. In places the snow might come only within proximity of the earth, and as it melted, the drops of water trickled down the myriad stems and blades. Then the dead stalks, free of encumbrance, performed their ballet to the wind, before succumbing, as nutrient, to the rush of new growth surging up from the burgeoning soil.

[7] "Buffalo grass" (*Buchloë dactyloides*), it was called, and it had been host to the tremendous herds which had thrived on the broad plateau rolling gently upward and northward from the Milk River, across the Canadian border, and a hundred miles or so into Alberta, Saskatchewan and Manitoba. From east to west, the grass ocean stretched undulating from the base of the Canadian and Montana Rockies, across North Dakota and the lower halves of the Canadian provinces to the fringe of the Minnesota-Manitoba lake country.

[8] From every spring or creek, from every swale and gully where the snow water collected and remained through the hot summers, thousands of buffalo trails radiated out toward the endless pasture land. Millions of sharp hooves had cut deep paths into the earth and carved terraces on the hillsides. A hundred years of domestic grazing, cultivation, and the consequent intensified erosion by wind and water, would not erase the marks which the great beasts had left upon their land.

[9] The buffalo was a restrained and gentle user of the land and the grass . . . his grass, upon which the incredible growth and development of the

herds depended. He ate it sparingly, grazing off only the tops of the stems, which grew as high as his magnificent head. The tops of the tender stalks contained the seedlings, the flavored nut, the storehouse of protein, and they waved there at the level of his maw. It was a reciprocal balance of favor. The buffalo spared the grass roots and left most of the stem for the protection of the new growth. In return, the grass replenished and fed upon itself in a perpetual cycle of abundance.

[10] The great herds had vanished, but not so long ago. Thirty years earlier, there had been a few remnant groups scattered through the Milk River plateau and hidden in the lower folds of the Little Rockies. All over that vast expanse the carcasses and the frequent mounds of bleaching bones gave mute testimony to the destructive efficiency of man. Even the herds of the Milk River country, sometimes filling the horizons, could not endure the slaughter. By pack-train, barge or wagon, mountains of hides had been carried to Williston or Mandan and then by flatboat down the Missouri to the leather factories of St. Louis. No respectable carriage in all America was wanting its buffalo robes. Nor was there anyone to suggest cropping the buffalo with specified kills each year. Americans were preoccupied with the squandering of their inheritance, and they went about it with energy and dispatch.

[11] So the land had been left to the grass and its smaller denizens. The grass thrived and grew taller, forming an endless sea of seasonal green and gold; and in winter, it rose out of the snow to relieve the white monotony. Each blade and each stem, in consort with the winds sweeping down from the Canadian Northwest, sculptured on the snow surface its own minute drift, frosting the winterland with lacy musings of bas relief.

[12] The spring wagon rolled northward through the sea of grass. Imperceptibly, the trail rose up toward the northern horizon. Each grade and rise was an introduction to another; each depression failed to dip as low as its predecessor. The great glacier had been a precise grade-maker, for all its awesome proportions, and a million thaws since had rounded and leveled the edges of the icecap's gougings.

VOCABULARY

Define the following words as they are used in the selection: *benchland* [1]; *augmenting* [2]; *sibilance* [4]; *assonant, burgeoning* [6]; *undulating* [7]; *swale* [8]; *denizens, bas relief* [11].

QUESTIONS FOR STUDY AND DISCUSSION

1. At the time of which Huntley writes, northern Montana had just been opened for settlement under the Homestead Act. Inhabitants were few; they were intruders in "the immence and boundless land." What details does Huntley use to suggest the permanence and timelessness of the land as it contrasts with man-made changes and human activity?

2. Where is the wagon headed? What does it leave behind? Does this detail contribute to the pervasive idea referred to in question 1?

3. What sounds are mentioned in the first two paragraphs? Does a contrast exist between the sounds related to human activity and the sounds of the land? What nouns are used to describe activities related to man? What nouns describe the sounds of the land?

4. Huntley makes much use of alliteration in the first few paragraphs. Identify the examples of alliteration and comment on their effectiveness.

5. Sound out the onomatopoetic word of paragraphs 3 and 5. Does it have the quality attributed to it in paragraph 4?

6. Point out the instances of personification in paragraphs 4, 6, and 11. Do they help to visualize the images and to experience imaginatively the sounds described? Are they effective? Do they seem natural or contrived?

7. Which images in the selection are metaphors? Are they fresh, natural images?

8. From the end of paragraph 6 through paragraph 11 Huntley is more concerned with placing the natural features of the countryside in perspective than with description for its own sake. What descriptive techniques, however, are used in these paragraphs? Notice the evocative quality of some of the nouns and verbs. Which ones are most effective? Note, too, the use of adverbs and adjectives. Do they contribute descriptively?

9. In this same passage—paragraphs 6 through 11—Huntley introduces an argument. What is it? Does it relate to the contrast between man and nature referred to in question 1?

10. What instances of color imagery are in the passage? Is color imagery well used? Can you suggest where color might well have been used to enhance the descriptive effectiveness?

11. In paragraph 7 the grass ocean is described as "undulating." The land itself is also described as having a similar quality of being gently curving. What details contribute to your awareness of this feature of the land?

Stephen Crane

FOUR MEN IN A BOAT

Stephen Crane (1871–1900) became famous at the age of twenty-four with the publication of The Red Badge of Courage, *a Civil War novel praised for its psychological realism. Two years later, in 1897, when Crane was aboard the* Commodore *on his way to Cuba as a war correspondent, the ship sank off St. Augustine. "The Open Boat" (1898), a long short story, was thus based in part on Crane's own experience. The following selection constitutes the opening paragraphs of the story.*

[1]   None of them knew the color of the sky. Their eyes glanced level, and were fastened upon the waves that swept toward them. These waves were of the hue of slate, save for the tops, which were of foaming white, and all of the men knew the colors of the sea. The horizon narrowed and widened, and dipped and rose, and at all times its edge was jagged with waves that seemed thrust up in points like rocks.

[2]   Many a man ought to have a bathtub larger than the boat which here rode upon the sea. These waves were most wrongfully and barbarously abrupt and tall, and each froth-top was a problem in small-boat navigation.

[3]   The cook squatted in the bottom, and looked with both eyes at the six inches of gunwale which separated him from the ocean. His sleeves were rolled over his fat forearms, and the two flaps of his unbuttoned vest dangled as he bent to bail out the boat. Often he said, "Gawd! that was a narrow clip." As he remarked it he invariably gazed eastward over the broken sea.

[4]   The oiler, steering with one of the two oars in the boat, sometimes raised himself suddenly to keep clear of water that swirled in over the stern. It was a thin little oar, and it seemed often ready to snap.

[5]   The correspondent, pulling at the other oar, watched the waves and wondered why he was there.

[6]   The injured captain, lying in the bow, was at this time buried in that profound dejection and indifference which comes, temporarily at least, to even the bravest and most enduring when, willy-nilly, the firm fails, the army loses,

SIGHTS, SOUNDS, SENSATIONS

the ship goes down. The mind of the master of a vessel is rooted deep in the timbers of her, though he command for a day or a decade; and this captain had on him the stern impression of a scene in the grays of dawn of seven turned faces, and later a stump of a topmast with a white ball on it, that slashed to and fro at the waves, went low and lower, and down. Thereafter there was something strange in his voice. Although steady, it was deep with mourning, and of a quality beyond oration or tears.

[7] "Keep 'er a little more south, Billie," said he.

[8] "A little more south, sir," said the oiler in the stern.

[9] A seat in this boat was not unlike a seat upon a bucking broncho, and by the same token a broncho is not much smaller. The craft pranced and reared and plunged like an animal. As each wave came, and she rose for it, she seemed like a horse making at a fence outrageously high. The manner of her scramble over these walls of water is a mystic thing, and, moreover, at the top of them were ordinarily these problems in white water, the foam racing down from the summit of each wave requiring a new leap, and a leap from the air. Then, after scornfully bumping a crest, she would slide and race and splash down a long incline, and arrive bobbing and nodding in front of the next menace.

[10] A singular disadvantage of the sea lies in the fact that after successfully surmounting one wave you discover that there is another behind it just as important and just as nervously anxious to do something effective in the way of swamping boats. In a ten-foot dinghy one can get an idea of the resources of the sea in the line of waves that is not probable to the average experience, which is never at sea in a dinghy. As each slaty wall of water approached, it shut all else from the view of the men in the boat, and it was not difficult to imagine that this particular wave was the final outburst of the ocean, the last effort of the grim water. There was a terrible grace in the move of the waves, and they came in silence, save for the snarling of the crests.

[11] In the wan light the faces of the men must have been gray. Their eyes must have glinted in strange ways as they gazed steadily astern. Viewed from a balcony, the whole thing would, doubtless, have been weirdly picturesque. But the men in the boat had no time to see it, and if they had had leisure, there were other things to occupy their minds. The sun swung steadily up the sky, and they knew it was broad day because the color of the sea changed from slate to emerald-green streaked with amber lights, and the foam was like tum-

bling snow. The process of the breaking day was unknown to them. They were aware only of this effect upon the color of the waves that rolled toward them.

VOCABULARY

Define the following words as they are used in the selection: *barbarously* [2]; *willy-nilly* [6]; *mystic* [9].

QUESTIONS FOR STUDY AND DISCUSSION

1. These paragraphs do not so much describe the four men in the boat as they communicate to the reader the sensations and emotions of the men. Paragraph 1 effectively establishes the point of view of the men. Crane tells us what they see and what they do not see. In what way does the first sentence suggest dejection, perhaps even loss of hope? What qualities of the waves are commented upon? Does the rhythm of the last sentence in paragraph 1 suggest the movement of the waves? How does the simile in the last sentence suggest hostility?

2. From the larger scene (the horizon and the waves) of paragraph 1, Crane moves in paragraph 2 to the more specific boat. He even ventures a comment on the situation of the men. In what sense were the waves "most wrongfully and barbarously abrupt and tall"?

3. The next four paragraphs, moving to the even more specific, introduce, one by one, the four men. The first three of these paragraphs are progressively shorter, less realistic, and more poetic in language, more suggestive of the numbness of the men. Point out how paragraphs 3 through 5 progress from a relatively complete realism of detail to impressionism.

4. What examples of the rhetorical device of alliteration can you find in paragraphs 3 through 5? Which of the paragraphs is most clearly alliterative in sound?

5. What features of the description of the captain in paragraph 6 coincide with the progression described in question 3? Does the fact that it is the captain who lies injured, rather than a crew member or the correspondent, seem particularly significant to the hopelessness of the situation?

6. What features of the shipwreck does Crane emphasize as the memorable ones? Is the brief reference suggestive of the terrible drama of a shipwreck?

7. Comment on the effectiveness of the sentence describing the captain's voice. What is the condition of man when he is "beyond oration or tears"?

8. The progression from the general to the specific culminates in the brief exchange of dialogue between the captain and the oiler. Do the language and

meaning of the dialogue contribute to the sense of repeated and monotonous activity and scene that the preceding paragraphs have created?

9. Paragraphs 9 through 11 return to the larger scene and to comment by the author. What does the comparison of the boat and a broncho suggest about the situation? How effective is the comparison?

10. The final sentence of paragraph 9 contains examples of alliteration and onomatopoeia. Where?

11. Crane is famous for his understatements. Point out the understatements in the first two sentences of paragraph 10 and paragraph 11.

12. What is paradoxical in the phrase "terrible grace" (in the last sentence of paragraph 10)?

13. Paragraph 11 returns to the concern of paragraph 1, with the addition of Crane's comment upon the entire scene that he has created, now more clear to the reader because of the intervening paragraphs. What features would make "the whole thing . . . weirdly picturesque"? From what figurative balcony would one view this scene?

FOR FURTHER ANALYSIS

H. L. Mencken

THE LIBIDO FOR THE UGLY

As a writer of description, H. L. Mencken (1880–1956) leaves no doubt as to his personal attitudes toward the things described. It was his essays, with their biting combination of drollery and disgust, that lured Richard Wright into the enlightenment of books (see ". . . And I Hungered for Books," p. 243). In this selection Mencken describes the architecture of one stretch of American landscape, finds it ugly, and suggests that Americans prefer it that way.

[1]   On a Winter day some years ago, coming out of Pittsburgh on one of the expresses of the Pennsylvania Railroad, I rolled eastward for an hour through the coal and steel towns of Westmoreland county. It was familiar ground; boy

---

"The Libido for the Ugly" copyright 1927 by Alfred A. Knopf, Inc., and renewed 1955 by H. L. Mencken. Reprinted from *A Mencken Chrestomathy*, edited and annotated by H. L. Mencken, by permission of Alfred A. Knopf, Inc.

and man, I had been through it often before. But somehow I had never quite sensed its appalling desolation. Here was the very heart of industrial America, the center of its most lucrative and characteristic activity, the boast and pride of the richest and grandest nation ever seen on earth—and here was a scene so dreadfully hideous, so intolerably bleak and forlorn that it reduced the whole aspiration of man to a macabre and depressing joke. Here was wealth beyond computation, almost beyond imagination—and here were human habitations so abominable that they would have disgraced a race of alley cats.

[2] I am not speaking of mere filth. One expects steel towns to be dirty. What I allude to is the unbroken and agonizing ugliness, the sheer revolting monstrousness, of every house in sight. From East Liberty to Greensburg, a distance of twenty-five miles, there was not one in sight from the train that did not insult and lacerate the eye. Some were so bad, and they were among the most pretentious—churches, stores, warehouses, and the like—that they were downright startling; one blinked before them as one blinks before a man with his face shot away. A few linger in memory, horrible even there: a crazy little church just west of Jeannette, set like a dormer-window on the side of a bare, leprous hill; the headquarters of the Veterans of Foreign Wars at another forlorn town, a steel stadium like a huge rat-trap somewhere further down the line. But most of all I recall the general effect—of hideousness without a break. There was not a single decent house within eyerange from the Pittsburgh suburbs to the Greensburg yards. There was not one that was not misshapen, and there was not one that was not shabby.

[3] The country itself is not uncomely, despite the grime of endless mills. It is, in form, a narrow river valley, with deep gullies running up into the hills. It is thickly settled, but not noticeably overcrowded. There is still plenty of room for building, even in the larger towns, and there are very few solid blocks. Nearly every house, big and little, has space on all four sides. Obviously, if there were architects of any professional sense or dignity in the region, they would have perfected a chalet to hug the hillsides—a chalet with a high-pitched roof, to throw off the heavy Winter snows, but still essentially a low and clinging building, wider than it was tall. But what have they done? They have taken as their model a brick set on end. This they have converted into a thing of dingy clapboards, with a narrow, low-pitched roof. And the whole they have set upon thin, preposterous brick piers. By the hundreds and thousands these abominable houses cover the bare hillsides, like gravestones in some gigantic and decaying cemetery. On their deep sides they are three, four and even five stories high; on their low sides they bury themselves swinishly in the mud. Not a fifth of them are perpendicular. They lean this way and that, hanging on to their bases precariously. And one and all they are

streaked in grime, with dead and eczematous patches of paint peeping through the streaks.

[4]   Now and then there is a house of brick. But what brick! When it is new it is the color of a fried egg. When it has taken on the patina of the mills it is the color of an egg long past all hope or caring. Was it necessary to adopt that shocking color? No more than it was necessary to set all of the houses on end. Red brick, even in a steel town, ages with some dignity. Let it become downright black, and it is still sightly, especially if its trimmings are of white stone, with soot in the depths and the high spots washed by the rain. But in Westmoreland they prefer that uremic yellow, and so they have the most loathsome towns and villages ever seen by mortal eye.

[5]   I award this championship only after laborious research and incessant prayer. I have seen, I believe, all of the most unlovely towns of the world; they are all to be found in the United States. I have seen the mill towns of decomposing New England and the desert towns of Utah, Arizona and Texas. I am familiar with the back streets of Newark, Brooklyn and Chicago, and have made scientific explorations to Camden, N. J. and Newport News, Va. Safe in a Pullman, I have whirled through the gloomy, God-forsaken villages of Iowa and Kansas, and the malarious tidewater hamlets of Georgia. I have been to Bridgeport, Conn., and to Los Angeles. But nowhere on this earth, at home or abroad, have I seen anything to compare to the villages that huddle along the line of the Pennsylvania from the Pittsburgh yards to Greensburg. They are incomparable in color, and they are incomparable in design. It is as if some titantic and aberrant genius, uncompromisingly inimical to man, had devoted all the ingenuity of Hell to the making of them. They show grotesqueries of ugliness that, in retrospect, become almost diabolical. One cannot imagine mere human beings concocting such dreadful things, and one can scarcely imagine human beings bearing life in them.

[6]   Are they so frightful because the valley is full of foreigners—dull, insensate brutes, with no love of beauty in them? Then why didn't these foreigners set up similar abominations in the countries that they came from? You will, in fact, find nothing of the sort in Europe—save perhaps in the more putrid parts of England. There is scarcely an ugly village on the whole Continent. The peasants, however poor, somehow manage to make themselves graceful and charming habitations, even in Spain. But in the American village and small town the pull is always toward ugliness, and in that Westmoreland valley it has been yielded to with an eagerness bordering upon passion. It is incredible that mere ignorance should have achieved such masterpieces of horror.

[7]   On certain levels of the American race, indeed, there seems to be a positive libido for the ugly, as on other and less Christian levels there is a libido for the beautiful. It is impossible to put down the wallpaper that defaces the average American home of the lower middle class to mere inadvertence, or to the obscene humor of the manufacturers. Such ghastly designs, it must be obvious, give a genuine delight to a certain type of mind. They meet, in some unfathomable way, its obscure and unintelligible demands. They caress it as "The Palms" caresses it, or the art of the movie, or jazz. The taste for them is as enigmatical and yet as common as the taste for dogmatic theology and the poetry of Edgar A. Guest.

[8]   Thus I suspect (though confessedly without knowing) that the vast majority of the honest folk of Westmoreland county, and especially the 100% Americans among them, actually admire the houses they live in, and are proud of them. For the same money they could get vastly better ones, but they prefer what they have got. Certainly there was no pressure upon the Veterans of Foreign Wars to choose the dreadful edifice that bears their banner, for there are plenty of vacant buildings along the track-side, and some of them are appreciably better. They might, indeed, have built a better one of their own. But they chose that clapboarded horror with their eyes open, and having chosen it, they let it mellow into its present shocking depravity. They like it as it is: beside it, the Parthenon would no doubt offend them. In precisely the same way the authors of the rat-trap stadium that I have mentioned made a deliberate choice. After painfully designing and erecting it, they made it perfect in their own sight by putting a completely impossible pent-house, painted a staring yellow, on top of it. The effect is that of a fat woman with a black eye. It is that of a Presbyterian grinning. But they like it.

[9]   Here is something that the psychologists have so far neglected: the love of ugliness for its own sake, the lust to make the world intolerable. Its habitat is the United States. Out of the melting pot emerges a race which hates beauty as it hates truth. The etiology of this madness deserves a great deal more study than it has got. There must be causes behind it; it arises and flourishes in obedience to biological laws, and not as a mere act of God. What, precisely, are the terms of those laws? And why do they run stronger in America than elsewhere? Let some honest *Privat Dozent* in pathological sociology apply himself to the problem.

SUGGESTIONS FOR WRITING

1. Using "Polk Street" as a model for organization and use of details, write a theme describing an area in which typical activities differ during the course of a day. Describe a central area of the campus, for instance, which comes alive in the morning, falls into a pattern of activity during the day, and becomes quiet again at night. Attempt to employ at least one unifying idea associated with the area (similar to the cable cars on Polk Street). Perhaps the bell or buzzer announcing the beginning and end of classes could be used.

2. Describe a group of people involved in an everyday situation: shopping, watching a ball game, working at diverse but related activities (such as building a house or painting a building). Focus your attention on the variety of people and activities, rather than on the time element as in the writing assignment above.

3. Write an essay describing a scene in nature—a hilltop, a forest, a clearing, the oceanside, a beach, a valley—in which there are appeals to the eye and also to the ear, either silence or sound but preferably, for contrast, both. Attempt to create in your essay suggestions of the sound of the wind or the surf or the rustling of leaves.

4. Carlos Baker, Ernest Hemingway's biographer, relates that Hemingway sometimes tried to formulate onomatopoetic words to describe various sounds: "tacrong, carong, craang" for rifle fire, for example, and "rong, cararong, rong, rong" for machine guns. (See Baker's *Ernest Hemingway: A Life Story* [New York: Charles Scribner's Sons, 1969], p. 305.) In an essay describing the sounds heard in a single place—an amusement park, a railway station, a race track, a circus, a city street, a factory—make extended use of onomatopoetic words of your own creation to convey the effect and quality of the sounds.

5. The description of Ahab on his first appearance in *Moby-Dick* is merely suggestive. In the remainder of the book, through actions, dialogue, and soliloquies, Ahab emerges as a proud tyrant, bereft of sympathy and compassion for his fellow man, obsessed with a desire that has become a monomania—to kill Moby Dick. He is dominated by the desire for revenge. His portrait suggests that of Satan in John Milton's *Paradise Lost* (1667), an epic relating the fall of Satan from heaven as well as the fall of man in the Garden of Eden. In a notable description of Satan after his descent to Hell (Book I, lines 589–608), Milton pictures him, his face worn with care, but displaying pride, cruelty, and courage:

> He, above the rest
> In shape and gesture proudly eminent,
> Stood like a tower. His form had yet not lost
> All her original brightness, nor appeared
> Less than Archangel ruined, and the excess
> Of glory obscured: as when the sun new-risen
> Looks through the horizontal misty air
> Shorn of his beams, or, from behind the moon,

> In dim eclipse, disastrous* twilight sheds
> On half the nations, and with fear of change
> Perplexes monarchs. Darkened so, yet shone
> Above them all the Archangel: but his face
> Deep scars of thunder had entrenched, and care
> Sat on his faded cheek, but under brows
> Of dauntless courage, and considerate† pride
> Waiting revenge. Cruel his eye, but cast
> Signs of remorse and passion, to behold
> The fellows of his crime, the followers rather
> (Far other once beheld in bliss), condemned
> Forever now to have their lot in pain. . . .

Of this passage William Cullen Bryant has written: "The imagination of the reader is stimulated by the hints in this powerful passage to form to itself an idea of the features in which reside this strong expression of malignity and dejection—the brow, the cheek, the eye of the fallen angel, bespeaking courage, pride, the settled purpose of revenge, anxiety, sorrow for the fate of his followers, and fearfully marked with the wrath of the Almighty."

Write an essay comparing Ahab and Satan. Make special note of the features and characteristics referred to by Bryant, as well as the devices the two authors use to portray their subjects.

6. On the basis of an actual or an imaginary interview, write a descriptive account of a friend or classmate who has distinguished himself in some way or who has some noteworthy characteristic or quality. A little imagination and curiosity will provide a point that can be emphasized, since each person does something a bit better than most people and is different in some way from everyone else. Describe the person in his typical surroundings. Have him talk about his distinguishing characteristic or accomplishment, and try to capture the quality of his speech in your report.

7. Using the approach in the topic above, write a report of an imaginary interview with yourself.

8. Write a description of a person who seems to you typical of those in his occupation, profession, or social role. Place the person in a situation not usually associated with him, so that the incongruity between setting and person is itself a descriptive technique. Examples would be a conservative businessman in a discotheque, an ultra-modern parent at a P.T.A. meeting, an introvert at a sensitivity encounter, a Democrat at a Republican rally (or vice versa). Your own observation will suggest other, and better, possibilities to you.

9. Write a description of a person whom you regard as an ideal example of a contemporary American. Using James's technique, provide a setting that helps to bring out what you consider to be your subject's typically American characteristics.

10. From a single vantage point on campus, describe a scene before a class break, during the break, and after it.

---

* Threatening disaster.
† Meditative.

DESCRIPTION

11. Describe a visit to a fair, carnival, circus, bazaar, or amusement park. Using the technique of Herb Caen, characterize the event as a complete phenomenon by focusing upon its representative individual details and your own response to them.

12. Washington Irving once wrote, "Nothing impresses the mind with a deeper feeling of loneliness than to tread the silent and deserted scene of former throng and pageant." Choose as your subject a football field, a theater, a classroom building, the site of a rally, an amusement center, a fairground, a ghost town, a museum, a historical landmark. Make use of contrast to emphasize present loneliness.

13. Write a description of a place that creates a mood of gloom, melancholy, or tranquility. Suitable subjects would be a cemetery, a church, a shrine, a deserted building.

14. In the nearly six decades since *Babbitt* was published, the furnishings and features of the standard, middle-class American house have slightly changed. Make a list of the furnishings and features that one could expect to find in such a house, and describe one or two rooms with the purpose of indicating that this house is typical, that it lacks personality.

15. On the basis of your understanding of the Babbitts as they are revealed by their house, write a description of the real estate office of George Babbitt or of a room in the Babbitt house that Myra Babbitt might consider her very own.

16. Describe a room and its furnishings in such a manner that they reveal the personality and activities of the occupant. Use your own room if it provides insight into yourself and if you can be reasonably objective about yourself. If possible, write from actual observation rather than from memory.

17. Write a description of what you consider an ideal room for yourself—one that reflects your image of yourself and that contains the furnishings and effects you consider necessary for the well-enjoyed life.

18. As a final review of the methods of description, and especially of figurative language, write one-sentence descriptions of the following, all reasonably common campus scenes or situations:

    a. A student receiving an unexpected "A."
    b. The look on a coed's face after being asked for her first date in college.
    c. A student counting the pages he has yet to read.
    d. The frantic rush to get in before curfew.
    e. A student entering class after the bell.
    f. A student who has asked an obviously foolish question in class.
    g. A professor who talks in a monotone.
    h. The hush before the first lecture of the semester.
    i. The marching band's drum major or majorette.
    j. The last class before a holiday.

Develop one of the above sentences into a descriptive paragraph of from 200 to 300 words, making use of as many sensory details as seem appropriate.

OPTIONAL WRITING ASSIGNMENT

In "Learning to Write," Benjamin Franklin tells of one of his practices for enlarging his vocabulary and increasing his ability to use the words he already knew. He would take passages of prose from the *Spectator* and turn them into verse; for, as he says, "the continual occasion for words of the same import, but of different length, to suit the measure, or of different sound for the rhyme, . . . laid [him] under a constant necessity of searching for variety. . . ." The practice of "collaborating" with good writers is a sound one still.

Seek out a passage of prose—a reasonably brief description or dramatic statement—and turn its essential content into a poem with a fixed form. Attempt to retain the tone, the imagery, and the original language as much as possible.

The important point in this assignment is to adapt the original prose into an established poetic form—a sonnet, iambic tetrameter or iambic pentameter quatrains, or couplets; for it is the discipline of a rigid form that makes demands on your vocabulary for metrical regularity and rhyme.

The following sonnet, as an example, is a first-person account, from the point of view of the correspondent, of the opening paragraphs of Crane's "The Open Boat":

> We did not know the color of the sky.
> Our eyes glanced level, fastened on each wave
> That swept toward us, foaming white and high,
> In points like rocks. The injured captain, brave
> And most enduring, lying in the bow,
> Was buried in dejection. Billie steered
> With one thin little oar and still somehow
> Kept clear of swirling water. Our craft reared
> And pranced, a broncho bucking at a wall.
> The cook, with rolled-up sleeves, bailed out the boat,
> While waves, most wrongfully abrupt and tall,
> Made it a problem to maintain afloat.
> In that wan light our faces were slate-gray.
> We did not know the breaking of the day.*

---

* Robert H. Woodward, "Stephen Crane: The Correspondent," *California English Journal*, 7 (February 1971), 47. Reprinted by permission.

NARRATION

Of the four types of discourse considered in this book, narration is the most difficult to limit and define. The term *narration* is broad and comprehensive. Narratives include such distinctively different types of writing as story poems and journalistic accounts of newsworthy incidents, scholarly histories and short stories, autobiographies and fables, diaries and novels, parables and fairy tales. The characteristic that all share, however, is their attention to *events*—either a single event or a series of events. The selections in this book illustrate some of the ways in which writers of narration have focused their attention on different types of events. As an example of autobiography, the passage from Piri Thomas's *Down These Mean Streets* recounts the author's first venture "in business"—as a shoeshine boy. Clair Huffaker imaginatively recreates the first meeting of his father and his mother. John Hersey narrates a number of true personal experiences at the moment of the bombing of Hiroshima at the end of World War II. John Steinbeck, a novelist, relates the problems encountered by a turtle as it crosses a busy highway.

Whatever the type of event at its focus, narration (like exposition, description, and argumentation) is commonly found in combination with another form of prose. Piri Thomas, for instance, makes passing use of exposition to explain how he shined shoes. John Hersey's report of the explosion, which contains much description, implicitly presents an argument against the use of atomic weapons. Similarly, John Steinbeck's narrative includes detailed descriptions of the highway and the turtle and at the same time suggests a parallel between the turtle and human beings, which can be viewed as a form of argumentation. But despite the fact that these selections combine various types of prose and have purposes beyond interesting and entertaining the reader, their focal attention upon events marks them as primarily narrative in form.

The introductory remarks about description emphasize the importance of selecting details that contribute toward a single mood or effect or purpose. Selection is equally important in narration. Although many diaries, such as those of Samuel Pepys and Anne Frank, are highly regarded as literature because the personalities of their authors are of such interest that even minor events are invested with significance, the diary of the average person is tedious to read because details have not been selected toward the creation of a single purpose. In his biographical account of his parents' first meeting, however, Huffaker is careful to select details that characterize and personalize his parents. John Hersey, as he describes the moment of the explosion of the atomic bomb, is as attentive as a writer of fiction in choosing details that work toward his preconceived design. The writer of narrative must exert control over the details that he brings into his composition. Good narration, whatever its form, is a thoughtful recording of carefully selected details to support or achieve a preconceived purpose.

Depending upon the scope and purpose of his narrative, the writer must decide what narrative method to employ. If he intends to relate a single event, the most effective method is **dramatized narration,** in which dialogue is given fully and the whole experience is recorded in detail. Leonard Shecter's account of Cassius Clay's appearance in a hotel room filled with reporters well illustrates the technique of dramatic narration. Richard Wright's recollection of his first visit to a library is also in the form of dramatized narration.

In longer works, however, some material may best be reported by generalized or summarized narration. The two following paragraphs from Franklin's *Autobiography* illustrate, first, **generalized narration**—an account of typical events and attitudes of Franklin's childhood, signaled by his words *much, commonly, generally, sometimes*; and, second, **summarized narration**—a condensed report of an incident without the full detail of dramatized narration:

> I . . . had a strong inclination for the sea, but my father declared against it; however, living near the water, I was much in and about it, learnt early to swim well, and to manage boats; and when in a boat or canoe with other boys, I was commonly allowed to govern, especially in any case of difficulty; and upon other occasions I was generally a leader among the boys, and sometimes led them into

NARRATION

scrapes, of which I will mention one instance, as it shows an early projecting public spirit, though not then justly conducted.

There was a salt-marsh that bounded part of the mill-pond, on the edge of which, at high water, we used to stand to fish for minnows. By much tramping, we had made it a mere quagmire. My proposal was to build a wharf there fit for us to stand upon, and I showed my comrades a large heap of stones, which were intended for a new house near the marsh, and which would very well suit our purpose. Accordingly, in the evening, when the workmen were gone, I assembled a number of my play-fellows, and working diligently like so many emmets, sometimes two or three to a stone, we brought them all away and built our little wharf. The next morning the workmen were surprised at missing the stones, which were found in our wharf. Inquiry was made after the removers; we were discovered and complained of; several of us were corrected by our fathers; and, though I pleaded the usefulness of the work, mine convinced me that nothing was useful which was not honest.

If Franklin had wished to dramatize this episode, he would have included actual dialogue, named and probably described his companions, and explained his feelings upon being discovered; in short, he would have included numerous details to suggest more completely the actual excitement of the adventure. The interest of the reader would be both in what happened and how it happened. The generalizations about Franklin's boyhood in the first paragraph could also have been elaborated into dramatic incidents recounting his experiences in learning to swim or to manage boats. Since these experiences are not so important to his narrative as, for instance, his learning to write, Franklin relates them in general terms. The importance of an episode to a writer's purpose largely determines the type of narration that he will choose to employ.

Since narrative writing is chronological in form, one of the first problems that the writer must face is that of where to begin. It is too much an oversimplification to say, "Begin at the beginning"—the beginning may be uninteresting. To be effective, the beginning should alert the reader to the importance of the events that follow or should arouse his curiosity. Langston Hughes begins with a statement of fact—that he was saved from sin when he was going on thirteen—but he interests the reader by exciting his curiosity to find out *how* he was saved.

Like the expository essay, narratives must have a beginning, middle, and end. The beginning, or introduction, conveys the necessary information to inform the reader of the situation, the setting, the initial characters, and, in fiction, the conflict; and it normally creates the tone. The middle is the developed description of the event or events, and the conclusion may provide the author's comment or, in fiction, the resolution of the opposing forces. Good narration, in other words, is not simply the telling of what happened in the chronological order of the events. It is the careful ordering of experience—either actual or imagined—in a structural pattern that arouses the reader's interest, keeps his attention, and creates in him a feeling of satisfaction that the events related have a meaning and interest beyond the superficial level of mere story.

The selections in this book illustrate only a few of the many possible forms of narration. Autobiographical accounts are traditional in composition courses. Everyone—almost everyone, anyway—likes to write about himself. What he has done interests him because he did it. Whether it will interest anyone else will depend upon his ability to select those incidents or events that cling together into a meaningful whole. The material of autobiography is as close as one's memory; all that is required is careful selection. So, too, is the material of biography close at hand, in the experiences and careers of the friends and relatives that one knows well. The selections under "Factual and Historical Narration" illustrate the handling of those subjects that demand research in books as well as those that depend only upon close personal observation or interviewing. The two examples of fictional narrative provide the opportunity to look at invented experience. And the example of the anecdote shows how brief narrative interludes can be included to enliven and strengthen other forms of writing.

AUTOBIOGRAPHY AND BIOGRAPHY

Successful autobiographical writing is more than a mere piling up of details of *who*, *where*, and *what*. These details may have a certain interest to the reader—hardly ever, surely, as much to the reader as to the writer—but the final effect will most likely be one of tediousness and boredom. The reader is interested in knowing more than merely what happened. He wants to know what the event meant; he wants to know *why*.

Anyone who has reached maturity has probably known hundreds of people, read numbers of books, had countless experiences—some humorous, some serious, some perhaps tragic, but untold numbers of no apparent consequence. An individual's life is rich in details—most of them forgotten because they seem unimportant. But somewhere amid that myriad of small and large events nestle the experiences that contribute meaningfully to an understanding of a person's life: experiences that explain, for instance, why he decided on his major subject in school, why he has his particular personality, why his ambition is what it is, why he dreams what he dreams and fears what he fears—in short, why he is what he is.

This *why* is properly the main point of autobiography. Perhaps because of a toy microscope an individual received for Christmas when he was nine, an underwater moving picture he saw when he was twelve, and a magazine article on ocean life he read when he was fourteen, that individual decided to become a marine biologist. The fact of his ambition is significant to him; but the record of his growing ambition, well told, is of interest to others. It is a record of experience, selected to show the importance and direction of seemingly unrelated events in his life. Similarly, Benjamin Franklin selected the wharf-building episode to illustrate his early interest in public projects. These instances of the thoughtful record of selected experience are typical of Franklin's book. His *Autobiography* presents a consciously formulated view of himself as an industrious and public-spirited citizen. What he chose to record bears him out. Such records of experience help to illuminate, in however small a way, part of the mystery of human life and experience.

Autobiographical writing, however, need not broach such large subjects. If an experience has been memorable to the writer, it can be made interesting to others. Again, the selection of details is all-important. In the excerpt from *Down These Mean Streets,* Piri Thomas recalls his childhood experiences as a bootblack. Yet by a careful selection of details and both explicit and implicit comment, he makes the experiences not only autobiographically significant but suggestive of how values in a ghetto are developed and strengthened. William Allen White has grouped together several memories of his early childhood to show the mixed emotional states of childhood, security and fear.

The selections illustrating autobiography in this book are examples of **extended autobiographies.** Langston Hughes, William Allen White, and Piri Thomas are able to move at a leisurely pace and to spend time on matters that may seem of small moment. But as they explore and comment upon what are common incidents, they invest them with a significance that is autobiographically revealing. The single example of biography, Huffaker's "Pony Boy," provides an excellent illustration of the manner in which family history may be made a subject of interest.

It should be remembered that what was said of the description of persons applies to autobiography and biography as well as to fiction. Anecdotes, conversation, the opinions of others, appearance—all contribute to making people on paper seem as if they have really lived.

This book contains, in other sections, these further examples of autobiographical writing (see Contents for page number):

Benjamin Franklin, "Learning to Write"
William Golding, "Thinking as a Hobby"

Anne Roiphe, "Confessions of a Female Chauvinist Sow"
Henry David Thoreau, "On Owning a Farm"
Claude Brown, " 'Baby' "
Mark Twain, "Steamboat Town"
Chet Huntley, "The Song of the Land"
Benjamin Franklin, "The Speckled Ax"

Langston Hughes

SALVATION

Langston Hughes (1902–1967) grew up in Lawrence, Kansas, the setting of the reminiscence that follows. In addition to his autobiography, The Big Sea *(1940), in which "Salvation" is the third chapter, he has written poetry, fiction, and plays, conducted a column for the* New York Post, *and become an expert on jazz. He has written much about his race, notably in* The Weary Blues *(1926),* The Negro Mother *(1931), and* Shakespeare in Harlem *(1942).*

[1] I was saved from sin when I was going on thirteen. But not really saved. It happened like this. There was a big revival at my Auntie Reed's church. Every night for weeks there had been much preaching, singing, praying, and shouting, and some very hardened sinners had been brought to Christ, and the membership of the church had grown by leaps and bounds. Then just before the revival ended, they held a special meeting for children, "to bring the young lambs to the fold." My aunt spoke of it for days ahead. That night I was escorted to the front row and placed on the mourners' bench with all the other young sinners, who had not yet been brought to Jesus.

[2] My aunt told me that when you were saved you saw a light, and something happened to you inside! And Jesus came into your life! And God was with you from then on! She said you could see and hear and feel Jesus in your soul. I believed her. I have heard a great many old people say the same thing and it seemed to me they ought to know. So I sat there calmly in the hot, crowded church, waiting for Jesus to come to me.

[3] The preacher preached a wonderful rhythmical sermon, all moans and shouts and lonely cries and dire pictures of hell, and then he sang a song about

Reprinted with the permission of Farrar, Straus & Giroux, Inc. from *The Big Sea* by Langston Hughes, copyright 1940 by Langston Hughes.

the ninety and nine safe in the fold, but one little lamb was left out in the cold. Then he said: "Won't you come? Won't you come to Jesus? Young lambs, won't you come?" And he held out his arms to all us young sinners there on the mourners' bench. And the little girls cried. And some of them jumped up and went to Jesus right away. But most of us just sat there.

[4] A great many old people came and knelt around us and prayed, old women with jet-black faces and braided hair, old men with work-gnarled hands. And the church sang a song about the lower lights are burning, some poor sinners to be saved. And the whole building rocked with prayer and song.

[5] Still I kept waiting to *see* Jesus.

[6] Finally all the young people had gone to the altar and were saved, but one boy and me. He was a rounder's son named Westley. Westley and I were surrounded by sisters and deacons praying. It was very hot in the church, and getting late now. Finally Westley said to me in a whisper: "God damn! I'm tired o' sitting here. Let's get up and be saved." So he got up and was saved.

[7] Then I was left all alone on the mourners' bench. My aunt came and knelt at my knees and cried, while prayers and songs swirled all around me in the little church. The whole congregation prayed for me alone, in a mighty wail of moans and voices. And I kept waiting serenely for Jesus, waiting, waiting—but he didn't come. I wanted to see him, but nothing happened to me. Nothing! I wanted something to happen to me, but nothing happened.

[8] I heard the songs and the minister saying: "Why don't you come? My dear child, why don't you come to Jesus? Jesus is waiting for you. He wants you. Why don't you come? Sister Reed, what is this child's name?"

[9] "Langston," my aunt sobbed.

[10] "Langston, why don't you come? Why don't you come and be saved? Oh, Lamb of God! Why don't you come?"

[11] Now it was really getting late. I began to be ashamed of myself, holding everything up so long. I began to wonder what God thought about Westley, who certainly hadn't seen Jesus either, but who was now sitting proudly on the platform, swinging his knickerbockered legs and grinning down at me, surrounded by deacons and old women on their knees praying. God had not struck Westley dead for taking his name in vain or for lying in the temple.

So I decided that maybe to save further trouble, I'd better lie, too, and say that Jesus had come, and get up and be saved.

[12]   So I got up.

[13]   Suddenly the whole room broke into a sea of shouting, as they saw me rise. Waves of rejoicing swept the place. Women leaped in the air. My aunt threw her arms around me. The minister took me by the hand and led me to the platform.

[14]   When things quieted down, in a hushed silence, punctuated by a few ecstatic "Amens," all the new young lambs were blessed in the name of God. Then joyous singing filled the room.

[15]   That night, for the last time in my life but one—for I was a big boy twelve years old—I cried. I cried, in bed alone, and couldn't stop. I buried my head under the quilts, but my aunt heard me. She woke up and told my uncle I was crying because the Holy Ghost had come into my life, and because I had seen Jesus. But I was really crying because I couldn't bear to tell her that I had lied, that I had deceived everybody in the church, that I hadn't seen Jesus, and that now I didn't believe there was a Jesus any more, since he didn't come to help me.

VOCABULARY

Define the following words as they are used in the selection: *mourners' bench* [1]; *dire* [3]; *rounder* [6]; *wail, serenely* [7]; *knickerbockered* [11]; *punctuated, ecstatic* [14].

QUESTIONS FOR STUDY AND DISCUSSION

1. This autobiographical reminiscence is carefully controlled to extract the maximum amount of emotional meaning from the experience. It divides into three parts: an expository introduction explaining the possibility, even certainty, of salvation, as well as the ways by which salvation could be recognized; the dramatic description of the experience itself; and, by way of anticlimax, the young Hughes's response to the experience. Which paragraphs relate to each of the three sections?

2. What reasons are advanced to support Hughes's expectancy of salvation? Would a boy of twelve years find them convincing? What sentences suggest that Hughes not only found them convincing but looked forward eagerly to the experience?

3. In the middle, dramatically developed section of the reminiscence, several influences were at work on Hughes to lead him to his feigned salvation. Trace through the various influences: (a) the diminishing number of mourners until only Hughes remained; (b) the element of time, which impresses upon Hughes the realization that he is delaying the revival; (c) the expectancy of the preacher and of the congregation; (d) Hughes's own patient watchfulness for the experience that had been described to him. Notice how these influences are integrated into an overpowering force that prevails upon Hughes to feign his own salvation. What was the observation that Hughes made that finally decided him?

4. At the end of paragraph 11 and in paragraph 12 Hughes communicates an almost cynical sense of his resignation to do what was expected of him. At this point in the reminiscence the false salvation seems to be a matter of little importance. How does Hughes suggest, however, that the experience was of great experience to him, perhaps a turning point in his spiritual life?

5. What details does Hughes describe in order to convey a sense of immediacy and realism? Which ones are the most effective?

6. Although most of the narration is summarized, there is an effective use made of dialogue. Are the minister's words or Westley's words the most vivid?

7. Hughes varies the length and pattern of his sentences for various effects. What effects does he achieve through the use of the short sentences concluding paragraph 3 and the long sentence that concludes the selection?

8. What is Hughes's attitudes toward the experience? Is there anything to suggest that he intended the account to be humorous? Explain.

9. Do you believe that there is any implied criticism of revivals, of the view of automatic salvation Hughes's people held, of the religious experiences forced upon young children? Defend your answer.

10. What does the concluding paragraph suggest about the barriers and misunderstandings that exist even between people who are close to each other emotionally?

William Allen White

"A CHILD WENT FORTH"

William Allen White (1868–1944) was born in Emporia, Kansas, and grew up to become the editor of The Emporia Gazette— *a smalltown newspaper but, because of White's fame as an editor and his influence in national affairs, one of the best-known newspapers in the world. Of the limitations of his autobiography (or of any) he wrote: ". . . in all candor, I wish to warn the reader not to confuse this story with reality. For God only knows the truth. I am hereby trying, in my finite way, to set down some facts which seem real and true to me. At best, this is only a tale that is told." The present selection is drawn from Chapter 3 of the book. The doctor referred to in paragraph 4 is White's father, who was a physician as well as a storekeeper.*

[1] The first emotional disturbance in my life came when I was about two years old, probably a little older. A baby brother was born. I cannot now remember why I hated him. Of course it was jealousy; but I hated him with a bitter, terrible hate. And this I am sure I can remember: I sneaked around the corner of the house to the east porch where his crib was, of a summer afternoon, and began pounding him with my little fists. They caught me when his screams called them. I had no remorse that I remember. I cannot bring back any pictures of his early death and recall nothing of his funeral.

[2] I was three years old then and had a sense of my environment. For me it remained a strange and lovely world. Two elderly, devoted and adoring persons, whom I called "Pa" and "Ma," guided me and bowed down before me; and I knew it and ruled them ruthlessly. I was spoiled, as what child born of parents in their late thirties and forties, would not be? I could draw a picture today of my home, the old "foundry," with its long kitchen where the dining table stood, its attached woodshed with the trapdoor into the cellar. And between the woodshed and the kitchen, in a covered corridor, they hung my little swing where I would swing for hours, singing a little bee song—a kind of long *ah-h-h-h* of sheer delight. I was a happy child and found a thousand things to please me. The world was made to bring me delight. There was a living room, ruled in fall and winter by a big, round, sheet-iron stove. On our

Reprinted with permission of Macmillan Publishing Co., Inc. from *The Autobiography of William Allen White.* Copyright 1946 by Macmillan Publishing Co., Inc., renewed 1974 by Macmillan Publishing Co., Inc. and W. L. White.

walnut table the tall lamp sat, and here always newspapers were piled and books strewn. A spare bed filled a far corner. Our very best room, the parlor, I rarely entered; for it was dark there by day, and I was afraid of it. My own little bedroom and my parents' larger bedroom adjoined the living room and the parlor. Of course, I went in and crawled in between them in the morning and seemed to give them much delight. They did not quarrel then, at least not before me. I must have been eight or ten years old before I was conscious of family differences. But in that Elysian childhood where I first opened my conscious eyes to the world about me, I was shielded from pain and sorrow and lived, if ever a human being did live, in a golden age. I must have had an early sense of tune, for one of my childish recollections is that I stood on the grocery scales in my father's store where he had me sing about "the old man who had a wooden leg and had no tobacco; no tobacco could he beg," of which the chorus was:

> Oh, buckle up my shoe, Johnnie,
> Buckle up my shoe.

[3] I also sang a ballad about Barney O'Flynn, who "had no breeches to wear and got him a sheepskin and made him a pair!" The customers enjoyed it. But this I also remember—that my mother came often rushing in and said:

[4] "Now, Doctor, haven't I always told you?"

[5] And she took me in her arms and headed out of the room with me. I did not like this, for I was a born exhibitionist and loved the applause of the multitude. I seemed to turn everything into song. The little bee song of my babyhood became a long cantata which I made up, perhaps—words and tune and all—as I sat, a solitary only child, in the shade of the morning-glories or, best of all, in the barn at the end of our town lot. That barn was my first enchanted palace. Modern childhood has no equivalent to my barn. I don't know how young I was when I invented the story that it was haunted, and scared the daylights out of other children as I pointed to the barn's high rafters, pretending to see faces and fairies which they also pretended to see; and we scared ourselves and wrestled on the hay of the loft and smelled the nice smell of the horses and the cow. Sometimes we sat in the corncrib and watched the pigs beneath, and the chickens. It was all strange and adventurous. The old pig that woofed at us, and that we were sure would eat us if she caught us, made us feel that we were in the presence of a dragon as authentic as that which St. George went forth to slay.

[6] Of Sunday afternoons, Pa and Ma walked with me to the timber between our creek and its junction with the Walnut River. Pa made me hickory whistles and taught me how to tell different trees by their leaves and bark. It

was before they had cut out the buck-brush, the wild raspberries, the blackberries, elderberries, and pokeberries. Above this wood's brush were the one-story trees—the papaws, haws, buckeyes, and the redbuds that I loved. Far above these rose the sycamore, the hickory, the elm, the oak, the walnut, the ash, the coffee-bean tree or locust, and the cottonwoods. Walking with Pa and Ma of a Sunday afternoon, I saw squirrels, rabbits, and once in a while Pa would show me a coon at the river's brim, or a hell-diver. Pa had been born in the Ohio woods and loved timber, and he taught me from earliest childhood to know and love the woods. But the thing that gave the woods their glamour for me was that, only a few years before, the Indians had moved out of this timber onto the prairie lands far to the West and the South. I used to play little games by myself in the woods with mythical little Indian boys. And in some way—I never exactly knew how—I imagined or fancied or dreamed it, and I believed that I had turned into a little Indian boy and indeed was one. So I believed, or most seriously fancied, that some day soon the Indians would come back and take me with them. I was scared and happy at the fantasy, which hung about me a long time—maybe a week, a month or half a year.

[7]   Then, of course, I had the prairies, the wide illimitable stretches of green in their spring and summer verdure, stretching westward from my front door, with not a dozen rivers or important streams, to the Rocky Mountains six hundred miles away. As a child, I did not know how far they went. To me, they were merely illimitable beyond the horizon and nothing could happen to me except the bite of a rattlesnake; and I never heard of a boy being bitten by a rattlesnake in my childhood. So the woods, the little stream, the prairies, and the dusty road by my door were my playgrounds.

VOCABULARY

Define the following words as they are used in the selection: *ruthlessly, foundry, Elysian, golden age* [2]; *exhibitionist, cantata, equivalent* [5]; *illimitable, verdure* [7].

QUESTIONS FOR STUDY AND DISCUSSION

1. White obtained the title of his chapter about early recollections from a well-known poem by Walt Whitman, "There Was a Child Went Forth," which opens:

> There was a child went forth every day,
> And the first object he look'd upon, that object he became,
> And that object became part of him for the day or a certain part of the day,
> Or for many years or stretching cycles of years.

Why is the title an apt one?

2. How would you describe the tone of the selection? How does White achieve this tone?

3. What frustrations and fears does he recall? Almost each paragraph speaks of some source of unhappiness; yet the over-all recollection is pleasant. How does White achieve this effect?

4. The craftsmanship of the selection lies principally in White's ability to bring together many different memories. Do these memories flow together smoothly? Do they have order? To answer these questions (a) make a list of the points he discusses in each paragraph and (b) point out the transitions within and between the paragraphs.

5. How does he move from his statement about his "early sense of tune" (in paragraph 2) to the observation about the pig (in the final sentence of paragraph 5)?

6. How effectively does White fuse generalized, summarized, and dramatized narration? Point out examples of each.

7. What qualities of White as a young child are evident in the passage? Make a list of the adjectives that would apply to him at this period of his life.

8. Do you think that he tends to romanticize himself, or does he seem to be objective?

Piri Thomas

IN BUSINESS

> The streets in the title of the autobiography of Piri Thomas, *Down These Mean Streets (1967), are those of New York City's Spanish Harlem, where Thomas was born of Puerto Rican parents in 1928. In 1956 Thomas was released from prison after serving six years for attempted robbery. A former* drug addict, *he has, since his return, been active in rehabilitation centers for* drug addicts *in both Spanish Harlem and Puerto Rico, has attended the University of Puerto Rico, and has been involved in the making of films about Spanish Harlem. At the time of the experience described in the following selection, Thomas was, as he writes in the "Prologue" to the book, ". . . a skinny, dark-face, curly-haired, intense Porty-Ree-can—/Unsatisfied, hoping, and always reaching."*

[1] Living in number 109 was snap breeze. I knew practically everybody on the block and, if I didn't, they knew me. When I went to the barbershop, José the barber would ask me, "Shape up or trim?" He liked to trim because in three hot minutes he could earn fifty cents. But I always gave him a hard way to shovel and said, "Give me the works with a square back." "Ay coño," he groaned and started to cut hair and breathe bad breath on me, on spite, while I ignored him on spite.

[2] Just being a kid, nothing different from all the other kids, was good. Even when you slept over at some other kid's house, it was almost like being in your own house. They all had kids, rats, and roaches in common. And life was full of happy moments—spitting out of tenement windows at unsuspecting people below, popping off with sling shots, or even better, with Red Ryder BB rifles, watching the neighbors fight through their open windows or make love under half-drawn shades.

[3] The good kick in the hot summer was to sleep on the fire escape. Sometimes I lay awake all night and thought about all the things I would do when I grew up, about the nice duds I'd have like a champ uptown and come back around the block and treat all the kids to *cuchifritos* and pour tons of nickels

---

From *Down These Mean Streets*, by Piri Thomas. Copyright © 1967 by Piri Thomas. Reprinted by permission of Alfred A. Knopf, Inc.

into the jukebox and help anybody that was in trouble, from a junkie to a priest. I dreamed big; it didn't cost anything.

[4] In the morning I stood on Lexington Avenue in Spanish Harlem, one finger poked through my pants pocket, scratching myself, while I droned, "Shine, mister—good shine, only fifteen cents. Shine, mister . . ." It was hard to shine shoes and harder to keep my corner from getting copped by an early-rising shine boy. I had to be prepared to mess a guy up; that corner spot wasn't mine alone. I had to earn it every time I shined shoes there.

[5] When I got a customer, we both played our roles. The customer, tall and aloof, smiled, "Gimme a shine, kid," and I replied, "Sí, señor, sir, I'll give you one that you'll have to put sunglasses on to eat the bright down."

[6] My knees grinding against the gritty sidewalk, I adopted a serious, businesslike air. Carefully, but confidently, I snaked out my rags, polish, and brushes. I gave my cool breeze customer the treatment. I rolled his pants cuff up—"That'll keep shoe polish off"—straightened his socks, patted his shoe, assured him he was in good hands, and loosened and retied his shoes. Then I wiped my nose with a delicate finger, picked up my shoe brush, and scrunched away the first hard crust of dirt. I opened my bottle of black shoe cleaner—dab, rub in, wipe off, pat the shoe down. Then I opened my can of polish—dab on with three fingers, pat-a-pid, pat-a-pid. He's not looking—spit on the shoe, more polish, let it dry, tap the bottom of his sole, smile up at Mr. Big Tip (you hope), "Next, sir."

[7] I repeated the process on the other shoe, then picked up my brush and rubbed the bristles very hard against the palm of my hand, scientific-like, to warm the brush hairs up so they would melt the black shoe wax and give a cool unlumpy shine. I peeked out of the corner of my eye to see if Mr. Big Tip was watching my modern shoeshine methods. The bum *was* looking. I hadn't touched his shoe, forcing him to look.

[8] The shoe began to gleam dully—more spit, more polish, more brush, little more spit, little more polish, and a lotta rag. I repeated on the other shoe. As Mr. Big Tip started digging in his pocket, I prepared for the climax of my performance. Just as he finished saying, "Damn nice shine, kid," I said, "Oh, I ain't finished, sir. I got a special service," and I plunged my wax-covered fingers into a dark corner of my shoe box and brought out a bottle of "Special shoe lanolin cream for better preservation of leather."

[9] I applied a dab, a tiny dab, pausing long enough to say very confidently,

"You can't put on too much or it'll spoil the shine. It gotta be just right." Then I grabbed the shoe rag firmly, like a maestro with a baton, and hummed a rhythm with it, slapping out a beat on the shoes. A final swish here and there, and *mira!*—finished. Sweating from the effort of my creation, I slowly rose from my knees, bent from the stain, my hand casually extended, palm flat up, and murmured, "Fifteen cents, sir," with a look that said, "But it's worth much more, don't you think?" Mr. Big Tip dropped a quarter and a nickel into the offering plate, and I said, "Thanks a mil, sir," thinking, *Take it cool*, as I cast a watchful eye at his retreating back.

[10] But wasn't it great to work for a living? I calculated how long it would take to make my first million shining shoes. Too long. I would be something like 987 years old. Maybe I could steal it faster.

VOCABULARY

In a glossary appended to *Down These Mean Streets* Thomas defines the Spanish terms in his book. *Coño* [1] means "damn." *Cuchifritos* [3] are a "dish made of pigs' ears, tongue, blood sausage, green bananas, etc." *Mira* [9] means "look." Is a translation necessary for these words, or is their intent, if not their specific meaning, available from the context in which they appear?

QUESTIONS FOR STUDY AND DISCUSSION

1. Even though the autobiographical incident central to this passage does not begin until paragraph 5, the first four paragraphs contribute to the significance of the incident by suggesting the attitudes, values, and conditions of life of Spanish Harlem. Implicit in the entire passage is an attitude toward money. In what way is this attitude suggested in paragraph 1? What is the attitude suggested?

2. In paragraph 2 Thomas employs the conventional language of adults nostalgically recalling their childhood. "Just being a kid . . . ," he says, "was *good*. . . . And life was full of *happy* moments. . . ." Discuss the tone of the italicized words. What relationship do these adjectives have to the details that illustrate them?

3. What attitudes and values are suggested in paragraph 3? How do they contribute to the selection?

4. The competitive, even brutal, nature of Thomas's existence as a child is openly expressed in paragraph 4. What statements in the preceding paragraphs make similar suggestions?

5. Paragraphs 5 through 9 are unified by a central metaphor. What is it? What details in these paragraphs are especially important in carrying out this metaphor?

6. Paragraph 9 also has a central figure of speech, an extension of the one in the preceding paragraphs. Is it stated as a metaphor or as a simile? What details contribute to this figure of speech?

7. What is Thomas's attitude toward his customer? How is this attitude suggested? Is it more apparent through Thomas's actions or his statements?

8. What details in the selection reveal Thomas's ability to give maximum satisfaction to his customer with minimum effort and expense on his part?

9. The tone of the selection is breezy and even lighthearted, despite its unpleasant implications. What details contribute to the tone?

10. Is slang overused in the selection? Is the meaning of the slang always clear?

11. Thomas chooses words carefully. Notice, for instance, the use of the words *droned* [4], *snaked* and *delicate* [6], and *plunged* [8]. What more common words, less effective and colorful than these, would convey the same meaning? What other especially effective word choices can you locate?

12. Immediately following this passage Thomas says, "In Harlem stealing was natural," and describes a raid on a store in order to steal the ingredients for lemonade to sell at stands. In the light of Thomas's subsequent prison conviction for attempted armed robbery, what is the importance of the shoe-shining experience for Thomas? How do the values and attitudes implicit in the selection anticipate the kind of dissatisfaction and frustration that could later find an outlet in stealing?

Clair Huffaker

PONY BOY

For every child the world may seem to have begun with that child's own parents, their first meeting having overtones of Eve's first sight of Adam. Clair Huffaker writes in nostalgic remembrance of such a first meeting, of young love too strong for any setting short of paradise. "Pony Boy" is the opening chapter of Huffaker's biographical One Time, I Saw Morning Come Home (1974). *Other works by the same author are* Nobody Loves a Drunken Indian (1967), The Cowboy and the Cossack (1973), *and* Seven Ways from Sundown (1975).

From *One Time, I Saw Morning Come Home.* Copyright © 1975 by Clair Huffaker. Reprinted by permission of Simon & Schuster, Inc.

[1]   In the beginning, there was the earth.

[2]   And then, there was music.

[3]   Orlean knew these two things in much the same easy way that she knew she was sixteen and that it was a hot September day. There are some things you just simply know, and don't have to bother your mind with.

[4]   At the moment, Orlean was quietly involved with both earth and music, sweeping the dusty kitchen floor and singing to herself in a low voice, "Pony boy, pony boy . . ."

[5]   Suddenly there was a shuffling sound and then a thumping from outside the kitchen door.

[6]   The neighbor's brown-and-white spotted cow again! Two days ago it had got loose and eaten two of the three geraniums Orlean had grown in a pot on the back step. It sounded like that cow was back for the third and last one! Luckily, Orlean was armed with her broom, and she started swiftly for the door. That final red geranium was probably the last living flower for a dozen miles around. In her little mining town in the Rocky Mountains, almost no delicate growing thing could survive. Tumbleweeds and sagebrush and stinging nettles and bitter milkweed managed to make it up through the hard earth to the music of the sun. But none of the pretty and gentle things, like a geranium, seemd to be able to hold onto life against the summer heat and the winter cold and the killing taint of arsenic, that was always and always in the air. The mine and the billowing smelter on the hill made the arsenic, and it was as hard on people as it was on flowers.

[7]   The mining smoke made beautiful orange and red and yellow sunsets, and death.

[8]   But Orlean was not going to let her last geranium die without a battle. That cow was about to be clouted on the rump with all the ferocity an avenging broom could muster.

[9]   Orlean jerked the door open wide, her broom raised high.

[10]   But it wasn't a cow.

[11]   It was a young man loaded down with groceries, who was thumping the door with his foot.

AUTOBIOGRAPHY AND BIOGRAPHY 211

[12] He had two bulging brown bags under his arms, and a sack of eggs held between his teeth, and he was trying to smile within slight embarrassment.

[13] "Oh!" she murmured in her own sudden and greater embarrassment, quickly lowering the broom and taking the package of eggs from his mouth. That was the first word she ever said to him.

[14] And it was also the first and only instant that Orlean ever fell in love. That tiny, inner magic took less than the blink of a fleeting second, and yet the magic was so strong that it lasted always. How such a thing could happen so fast, and so forever, she never really understood, or even tried to figure out. It was like all those other things that you just simply know, and don't have to bother your mind with.

[15] The young man was tall, and overwhelmingly handsome, with a jaunty leather cap angled rakishly down over incredibly bright, sparkling blue eyes that seemed filled with silent, mischievous laughter. Yet there was something else deeper in his eyes. Orlean could see that he would understand about earth and music, and about mean spotted cows, and the crucial importance of one last, red geranium.

[16] "I'm from Swenson's Groceries?" He made a question of the words.

[17] She nodded timidly, quickly backing out of his way with the eggs.

[18] He stepped to the kitchen table just as one of the large sacks started to rip slightly, but he got there in time and put them down safely. Relieved, he turned and took off his cap, smiling. "You were holding that broom like a ball bat."

[19] "—I thought you were a cow." As Orlean finished speaking in her shy voice, she wished she'd said it some other way, but the words were already out.

[20] His smile deepened. "One time up in Wyoming a fella mistook me for a mountain lion and took a shot at me, but at least that was at night."

[21] Orlean wanted to explain the whole thing about defending her geranium, and make him understand. But the words she needed just weren't coming to her, and he was already starting back toward the door.

[22] Before going out he looked back once more with his sky-blue, penetrating eyes and said, "My name's Clair. Thank you, Miss Bird."

[23]   And then he was gone.

[24]   But he knew her name! Orlean quickly put the eggs down on the table with the other groceries and hurried to the window. He was pedaling down the dusty street on Swenson's delivery bike with the big, bent, wire basket on the back. Then she realized crushingly that he'd have to know her name, just to know where to make the delivery.

[25]   Ten thousand things she could have said and should have said, and she hadn't said one. Why couldn't she be quick and glib like all those other girls who always seemed to have something to say? Now he turned at the corner and went out of her sight on the bike, still looking handsome, somehow, even from the back. Orlean moved slowly from the window then and silently busied herself sorting the groceries and putting them in the cupboard and icebox.

[26]   While stacking the last cans of beans in the cupboard she finally broke her silence and muttered angrily to herself, "Boy, are you a dumbbell!" Then, in a higher, self-mocking voice, "Ohhh, kind sir, I thought you were a cow! Just what every man has always wanted to hear. Why couldn't I have told him he *did* look more like a mountain lion, or Rudolph Valentino or something?!"

[27]   Then she went out into the small back yard and split some kindling at the woodshed, so that she could get a fire started in the stove.

[28]   By the time Orlean heard the distant clanging of the bell on the Bamburger trolley coming slowly back from Salt Lake, the house was clean, the wash done, and supper was cooking on the glowing hot stove. Her two sisters, Melva and Margaret, had taken the Bamburger to town, and a few minutes later they arrived in the gathering dusk.

[29]   The twenty-mile trolley trip to Salt Lake cost ten cents per person each way, so a trip to town was something special. And Margaret, a red-headed pixie of a girl a little younger than Orlean, was still filled with the excitement of the big city. "We saw a Rin Tin Tin movie that, *honest,* you wouldn't believe!" she said. "Orlean, he jumped a *thousand-*foot cliff to save a little boy in a river!"

[30]   Melva, the oldest of the sisters, shook her head in amused agreement. "Like the man says, I swear that dog's just not human."

[31]   "Oh, Melva!" Margaret laughed.

[32]   There was time before supper, so Melva made some secret coffee and she and Margaret told Orlean all about their day's trip, and how the city was changing and growing right before your very eyes.

[33]   The stern-faced Elders in that Mormon town would have been outraged about the church-forbidden coffee. But the girls were agreed that what the Elders didn't know couldn't hurt them. And besides, in some mysterious way it made the coffee taste better.

[34]   Finally, Orlean mentioned as offhandedly as possible the thing she'd been waiting anxiously to bring up from the beginning. "—Swensons,—has a new delivery man."

[35]   "He clerks there, too," Melva said. "We gave him our order this morning on the way to the Bamburger." And then, looking at Orlean thoughtfully, she added, "He's a nice-looking boy."

[36]   "Boy?" Orlean frowned. "He's a young man."

[37]   "What I meant was," Melva said, "he's only about your age."

[38]   "And that's not all," Orlean went on, taking a sip of coffee. When she was alone with the sisters she'd grown up with, she could sometimes work wonders with words. "He may be kind of young, like you say, but he's been around a whole lot. Why, he was even in some kind of a shooting scrape up in Wyoming, but got out of it okay."

[39]   "That's awful!" Margaret's eyes were wide with delight. "Did he shoot somebody?!"

[40]   "Oh, no.—I guess he just sort of managed to smooth everything all over, finally. I can tell that he's just naturally that kind of a strong, quiet man."

[41]   "Boy, that's swell!" Margaret said. "I'd like to hear all about it!"

[42]   "No!" Orlean said quickly. "I know for sure he wouldn't want to talk about it any more. I was just saying he's a man, not a boy like Melva said."

[43]   Melva began pouring what was left of the coffee, splitting it three ways. "Must have took him most of the afternoon to bring in all those groceries."

VOCABULARY

Define the following words as they are used in the selection: *taint, smelter* [6]; *avenging* [8]; *crucial* [15]; *glib* [25].

QUESTIONS FOR STUDY AND DISCUSSION

1. Huffaker's book, *One Time, I Saw Morning Come Home*, is based on the lives of the author's parents. Subtitled "A Remembrance," the book bears a dedication: "For the waltzing lady,—she of the soft, and sun-swept hair, and the grass green, dew-swept eyes"—presumably the author's mother. Chapter I, "Pony Boy," alludes to a once popular song. What is the cumulative effect of these details of title, dedication, and allusion to the song? What kind of story can the reader expect the book to tell?

2. The selection narrates a simple, wholly commonplace event: the first meeting of two young people who are later to marry. Huffaker's method of investing the commonplace experience with deep significance is worthy of close attention. Note, for instance, the opening paragraph; what well-known sentence does it echo? What is the effect upon the reader of that echo?

3. Once the opening sentence has triggered its associations, other Biblical associations may come to mind. What parallels in Genesis can be drawn for the first meeting of Clair and Orlean, for their personalities, for their bearing, for the setting?

4. The first two paragraphs introduce motifs that help to unify the narration. Where in the narrative do later references to earth and music recur?

5. What specific facts about Orlean are introduced? Are they introduced merely as facts or as aspects of characterization?

6. What adjectives would you use to describe Orlean? How are those qualities dramatized in the passage?

7. What qualities can you infer for Clair? Is the author more explicit in describing Clair than in describing Orlean?

8. The references to the cow serve as another unifying motif. How do they also serve to characterize Orlean and to reveal her state of mind?

9. What details of setting appear in the passage? Are they obtrusive?

10. Are the author's interpretive comments, such as those in the second sentence of paragraph 3 and in paragraphs 14 and 15, wholly necessary? What is their function?

11. Several of the paragraphs are extremely brief, the tenth and twenty-third containing only five words each. To what do those two paragraphs refer? What does their brevity suggest about Orlean's feelings and reactions?

FACTUAL AND HISTORICAL NARRATION

Factual and historical narration bears certain obvious resemblances to autobiography and biography. It, too, is concerned with facts, and with the ordering of those facts into a meaningful pattern of relationships. And, of course, it frequently deals with people. The differences, however, are important. Historical narratives normally focus primarily upon events rather than upon character, upon what people do rather than what the people are like or upon what they do in order to reveal what they are like. This is not to say that the writer of factual and historical narration should not be involved with the explanation of human motives; for the more fully the individuals in the narrative are characterized, the greater will be the reader's interest in what they do. Yet the fundamental distinction exists: autobiography generally focuses upon the revelation of character and the meaning of experience; factual and historical narration focuses upon the actions and events, with or without interpretative analysis by the author.

The narrative of fact is also similar in some ways to the narrative of fiction. Both are concerned with truth and reality. But, again, the differences are even more significant than the similarities. Whereas fiction portrays a universal or general truth—the truth of human experience, factual narration describes a particular truth—a truth of the historical past or present. And whereas fiction is designed to give the illusion of reality, factual narration describes reality itself. Indeed, the value of a narrative of fact is determined by the extent of the writer's adherence to particular truths and to reality. Factual narration must be true not only to human experience, as is good fiction, but to history.

Documentation, therefore, of one kind or another, is essential to factual narration. Sources of information should be included either as part of the text or by means of footnote references. George Orwell, who was present at the execution he describes, writes as an eyewitness observer; his account has the authority and immediacy of a news report. Samuel Eliot Morison, on the other hand, in his scholarly, historical account of Salem, has made occasional use of footnotes to support his statements. Although John Hersey's narrative of the Hiroshima bombing contains no scholarly apparatus, its very style strongly suggests authenticity; it is a type of narrative known as a "documentary." The close attention to facts—names, places, dates, hours, and minutes—and the obvious care that has gone into the interviewing of actual survivors of the bombing fulfill some of the functions of the more academic types of documentation. Whatever the means of documentation in a narrative of fact, it should be clear to the reader that the writer has either carefully authenticated his facts or has been present as an observer or participant at the event he describes.

In organization, the historical narrative is necessarily chronological. The writer of fiction may choose to complicate the chronology of his fictional events for purposes of his art, but the reporter of fact is concerned with clarifying cause-effect relationships that have occurred in a time sequence. He faces the problem of selecting and arranging details, acquired either from books or from observation, into a coherent pattern and reducing them to a form suitable for his intended medium—whether it be a college composition or a two-volume publication.

A final point: while objectivity is naturally a virtue in factual or historical writing, a narrative of fact need not be completely devoid of the writer's personality. In the selections below, some features of the authors' personalities are plainly evident. At the same time, the writer of fact should not allow his prejudices to control his selection of details or the actual relationships of cause and effect. Different interpretations of the meaning of an event are possible to different writers, but the nature of the event itself should be open to no substantial disagreement.

The examples of factual and historical narration in this anthology differ widely in their scope and style. The first one, by Alexander Calandra, relates a personal experience from his teaching to make a philosophical point. George Orwell narrates an execution in vivid detail in order to dramatize his attitude toward capital punishment. Professor Morison's account of the Salem witchcraft panic summarizes the pertinent facts of four years' time and, although it alludes to some of the major individuals involved, is concerned clearly with the significance of the events. John Hersey combines the close observation of a journalist and the dramatic skill of a novelist to invest with emotion and human significance the brief period covered by his report. Collectively, the selections illustrate the breadth of purpose and technique available to the writer of factual narration.

Alexander Calandra

ANGELS ON A PIN

> *Narratives of personal experience are often used to make a philosophical point, as in this essay relating an incident to a principle of teaching and learning. Specializing in statistical techniques in tests and measurements and in integrated courses in elementary science and mathematics, Dr. Calandra (b. 1911) teaches in the Department of Physics at Washington University, St. Louis, and has been editor of the American Chemical Society's Reporter. This narrative first appeared in* Saturday Review, *December 21, 1968.*

[1]   Some time ago, I received a call from a colleague who asked if I would be the referee on the grading of an examination question. He was about to give a student a zero for his answer to a physics question, while the student claimed he should receive a perfect score and would if the system were not set up against the student. The instructor and the student agreed to submit this to an impartial arbiter, and I was selected.

[2]   I went to my colleague's office and read the examination question: "Show how it is possible to determine the height of a tall building with the aid of a barometer."

[3]   The student had answered: "Take the barometer to the top of the building, attach a long rope to it, lower the barometer to the street, and then bring it up, measuring the length of the rope. The length of the rope is the height of the building."

[4]   I pointed out that the student really had a strong case for full credit, since he had answered the question completely and correctly. On the other hand, if full credit were given, it could well contribute to a high grade for the student in his physics course. A high grade is supposed to certify competence in physics, but the answer did not confirm this. I suggested that the student have another try at answering the question. I was not surprised that my colleague agreed, but I was surprised that the student did.

From *Saturday Review*, December 21, 1968. Reprinted by permission.

[5] I gave the student six minutes to answer the question, with the warning that his answer should show some knowledge of physics. At the end of five minutes, he had not written anything. I asked if he wished to give up, but he said no. He had many answers to this problem; he was just thinking of the best one. I excused myself for interrupting him, and asked him to please go on. In the next minute, he dashed off his answer which read:

[6] "Take the barometer to the top of the building and lean over the edge of the roof. Drop the barometer, timing its fall with a stopwatch. Then, using the formula $S = \frac{1}{2}at^2$, calculate the height of the building."

[7] At this point, I asked my colleague if *he* would give up. He conceded, and I gave the student almost full credit.

[8] In leaving my colleague's office, I recalled that the student had said he had other answers to the problem, so I asked him what they were. "Oh, yes," said the student. "There are many ways of getting the height of a tall building with the aid of a barometer. For example, you could take the barometer out on a sunny day and measure the height of the barometer, the length of its shadow, and the length of the shadow of the building, and by the use of a simple proportion, determine the height of the building."

[9] "Fine," I said. "And the others?"

[10] "Yes," said the student. "There is a very basic measurement method that you will like. In this method, you take the barometer and begin to walk up the stairs. As you climb the stairs, you mark off the length of the barometer along the wall. You then count the number of marks, and this will give you the height of the building in barometer units. A very direct method.

[11] "Of course, if you want a more sophisticated method, you can tie the barometer to the end f a string, swing it as a pendulum, and determine the value of 'g' at the street level and at the top of the building. From the difference between the two values of 'g,' the height of the building can, in principle, be calculated."

[12] Finally he concluded, there are many other ways of solving the problem. "Probably the best," he said, "is to take the barometer to the basement and knock on the superintendent's door. When the superintendent answers, you speak to him as follows: 'Mr. Superintendent, here I have a fine barometer. If you will tell me the height of this building, I will give you this barometer.'"

[13] At this point, I asked the student if he really did not know the conventional answer to this question. He admitted that he did, but said that he was fed up with high school and college instructors trying to teach him how to think, to use the "scientific method," and to explore the deep inner logic of the subject in a pedantic way, as is often done in the new mathematics, rather than teaching him the structure of the subject. With this in mind, he decided to revive scholasticism as an academic lark to challenge the Sputnik-panicked classrooms of America.

VOCABULARY

1. Define the following words as they are used in the selection: *barometer* [2]; *calculate* [6]; *conceded* [7]; *proportion* [8]; *sophisticated* [11]; *conventional, pedantic, scholasticism, lark* [13].

2. Identify the meaning of $S = \frac{1}{2}at^2$ [6]; g [11]; *Sputnik* [13].

QUESTIONS FOR STUDY AND DISCUSSION

1. Rudyard Kipling, one of the masters of narrative, once wrote this of his method:

> I keep six honest serving men
> (They taught me all I knew);
> Their names are What and Why and When
> And How and Where and Who.

These "five W's" have served writers of narrative for centuries. Which of the five does Calandra use to begin this essay? Compare this beginning with those of the other essays in this section.

2. Good storytellers usually establish the setting, the characters, the time, the place, and the problem very early in a narrative. Does Calandra do so?

3. Do the characters in this narrative have personality? Does Calandra provide each of them with distinctive traits? How?

4. This essay is one of factual narration. Its subject matter is by no means so momentous as that of George Orwell's "A Hanging" or John Hersey's "A Noiseless Flash," yet it has more than passing interest. What gives it a lasting quality?

5. Though this essay is not quite autobiography, it does have some of the quality of Benjamin Franklin's narrative of his own life (see "The Speckled Ax," p. 241); that is, the writers tell of personal experience from which they learn something. What does Calandra learn from the incident he narrates?

6. In paragraph 13 the author refers to the "conventional answer" to the problem. How does that phrase relate to the student's decision "to revive scholasticism as an academic lark"?

George Orwell

A HANGING

George Orwell (1903–1950) was the pseudonym of Eric Blair, who was born in Bengal and educated in England. For five years he served in Burma with the Indian Imperial Police and drew from his experiences such essays as "A Hanging," which appears in his Shooting an Elephant and Other Essays *(1950). His best work is very likely in his collections of essays, but he is best known for his satirical novels* Animal Farm *(1946) and* 1984 *(1949), both of which describe modern political conditions and tendencies. His writings are characterized by clarity of thought and vision; one critic has referred to him as "the conscience of his generation."*

[1]   It was in Burma, a sodden morning of the rains. A sickly light, like yellow tinfoil, was slanting over the high walls into the jail yard. We were waiting outside the condemned cells, a row of sheds fronted with double bars, like small animal cages. Each cell measured about ten feet by ten and was quite bare within except for a plank bed and a pot for drinking water. In some of them brown silent men were squatting at the inner bars, with their blankets draped round them. These were the condemned men, due to be hanged within the next week or two.

[2]   One prisoner had been brought out of his cell. He was a Hindu, a puny wisp of a man, with a shaven head and vague liquid eyes. He had a thick, sprouting moustache, absurdly too big for his body, rather like the moustache of a comic man on the films. Six tall Indian warders were guarding him and getting him ready for the gallows. Two of them stood by with rifles and fixed bayonets, while the others handcuffed him, passed a chain through his handcuffs and fixed it to their belts, and lashed his arms tight to his sides. They crowded very close about him, with their hands always on him in a careful,

From *Shooting an Elephant and Other Essays* by George Orwell, copyright, 1945, 1946, 1949, 1950, by Sonia Brownell Orwell. Reprinted by permission of Harcourt Brace Jovanovich, Inc.

caressing grip, as though all the while feeling him to make sure he was there. It was like men handling a fish which is still alive and may jump back into the water. But he stood quite unresisting, yielding his arms limply to the ropes, as though he hardly noticed what was happening.

[3]   Eight o'clock struck and a bugle call, desolately thin in the wet air, floated from the distant barracks. The superintendent of the jail, who was standing apart from the rest of us, moodily prodding the gravel with his stick, raised his head at the sound. He was an army doctor, with a grey toothbrush moustache and a gruff voice. "For God's sake hurry up, Francis," he said irritably. "The man ought to have been dead by this time. Aren't you ready yet?"

[4]   Francis, the head jailer, a fat Dravidian in a white drill suit and gold spectacles, waved his black hand. "Yes sir, yes sir," he bubbled. "All iss satisfactorily prepared. The hangman iss waiting. We shall proceed."

[5]   "Well, quick march, then. The prisoners can't get their breakfast till this job's over."

[6]   We set out for the gallows. Two warders marched on either side of the prisoner, with their rifles at the slope; two others marched close against him, gripping him by arm and shoulder, as though at once pushing and supporting him. The rest of us, magistrates and the like, followed behind. Suddenly, when we had gone ten yards, the procession stopped short without any order or warning. A dreadful thing had happened—a dog, come goodness knows whence, had appeared in the yard. It came bounding among us with a loud volley of barks, and leapt round us wagging its whole body, wild with glee at finding so many human beings together. It was a large woolly dog, half Airedale, half pariah. For a moment it pranced round us, and then, before anyone could stop it, it had made a dash for the prisoner and, jumping up, tried to lick his face. Everyone stood aghast, too taken aback even to grab at the dog.

[7]   "Who let that bloody brute in here?" said the superintendent angrily. "Catch it, someone!"

[8]   A warder, detached from the escort, charged clumsily after the dog, but it danced and gambolled just out of his reach, taking everything as part of the game. A young Eurasian jailer picked up a handful of gravel and tried to stone the dog away, but it dodged the stones and came after us again. Its yaps echoed from the jail walls. The prisoner, in the grasp of the two warders, looked on incuriously, as though this was another formality of the hanging. It was several minutes before someone managed to catch the dog. Then we

put my handkerchief through its collar and moved off once more, with the dog still straining and whimpering.

[9]   It was about forty yards to the gallows. I watched the bare brown back of the prisoner marching in front of me. He walked clumsily with his bound arms, but quite steadily, with that bobbing gait of the Indian who never straightens his knees. At each step his muscles slid neatly into place, the lock of hair on his scalp danced up and down, his feet printed themselves on the wet gravel. And once, in spite of the men who gripped him by each shoulder, he stepped slightly aside to avoid a puddle on the path.

[10]   It is curious, but till that moment I had never realized what it means to destroy a healthy, conscious man. When I saw the prisoner step aside to avoid the puddle I saw the mystery, the unspeakable wrongness, of cutting a life short when it is in full tide. This man was not dying, he was alive just as we are alive. All the organs of his body were working—bowels digesting food, skin renewing itself, nails growing, tissues forming—all toiling away in solemn foolery. His nails would still be growing when he stood on the drop, when he was falling through the air with a tenth-of-a-second to live. His eyes saw the yellow gravel and the grey walls, and his brain still remembered, foresaw, reasoned—reasoned even about puddles. He and we were a party of men walking together, seeing, hearing, feeling, understanding the same world; and in two minutes, with a sudden snap, one of us would be gone—one mind less, one world less.

[11]   The gallows stood in a small yard, separate from the main grounds of the prison, and overgrown with tall prickly weeds. It was a brick erection like three sides of a shed, with planking on top, and above that two beams and a crossbar with the rope dangling. The hangman, a grey-haired convict in the white uniform of the prison, was waiting beside his machine. He greeted us with a servile crouch as we entered. At a word from Francis the two warders, gripping the prisoner more closely than ever, half led half pushed him to the gallows and helped him clumsily up the ladder. Then the hangman climbed up and fixed the rope round the prisoner's neck.

[12]   We stood waiting, five yards away. The warders had formed in a rough circle round the gallows. And then, when the noose was fixed, the prisoner began crying out to his god. It was a high, reiterated cry of "Ram! Ram! Ram! Ram!" not urgent and fearful like a prayer or cry for help, but steady, rhythmical, almost like the tolling of a bell. The dog answered the sound with a whine. The hangman, still standing on the gallows, produced a small cotton bag like a flour bag and drew it down over the prisoner's face. But the sound, muffled

by the cloth, still persisted, over and over again: "Ram! Ram! Ram! Ram! Ram!"

[13] The hangman climbed down and stood ready, holding the lever. Minutes seemed to pass. The steady, muffled crying from the prisoner went on and on, "Ram! Ram! Ram!" never faltering for an instant. The superintendent, his head on his chest, was slowly poking the ground with his stick; perhaps he was counting the cries, allowing the prisoner a fixed number—fifty, perhaps, or a hundred. Everyone had changed color. The Indians had gone grey like bad coffee, and one or two of the bayonets were wavering. We looked at the lashed, hooded man on the drop, and listened to his cries—each cry another second of life; the same thought was in all our minds: oh, kill him quickly, get it over, stop that abominable noise!

[14] Suddenly the superintendent made up his mind. Throwing up his head he made a swift motion with his stick. "Chalo!" he shouted almost fiercely.

[15] There was a clanking noise, and then dead silence. The prisoner had vanished, and the rope was twisting on itself. I let go of the dog, and it galloped immediately to the back of the gallows; but when it got there it stopped short, barked, and then retreated into a corner of the yard, where it stood among the weeds, looking timorously out at us. We went round the gallows to inspect the prisoner's body. He was dangling with his toes pointed straight downwards, very slowly revolving, as dead as a stone.

[16] The superintendent reached out with his stick and poked the bare brown body; it oscillated slightly. "*He's* all right," said the superintendent. He backed out from under the gallows, and blew out a deep breath. The moody look had gone out of his face quite suddenly. He glanced at his wrist-watch. "Eight minutes past eight. Well, that's all for this morning, thank God."

[17] The warders unfixed bayonets and marched away. The dog, sobered and conscious of having misbehaved itself, slipped after them. We walked out of the gallows yard, past the condemned cells with their waiting prisoners, into the big central yard of the prison. The convicts, under the command of warders armed with lathis, were already receiving their breakfast. They squatted in long rows, each man holding a tin panikin, while two warders with buckets marched round ladling out rice; it seemed quite a homely, jolly scene, after the hanging. An enormous relief had come upon us now that the job was done. One felt an impulse to sing, to break into a run, to snigger. All at once everyone began chattering gaily.

[18] The Eurasian boy walking beside me nodded towards the way we had

come, with a knowing smile: "Do you know, sir, our friend [he meant the dead man] when he heard his appeal had been dismissed, he pissed on the floor of his cell. From fright. Kindly take one of my cigarettes, sir. Do you not admire my new silver case, sir? From the boxwalah, two rupees eight annas. Classy European style."

[19]   Several people laughed—at what, nobody seemed certain.

[20]   Francis was walking by the superintendent, talking garrulously: "Well, sir, all hass passed off with the utmost satisfactoriness. It was all finished—flick! like that. It is not always so—oah, no! I have known cases where the doctor wass obliged to go beneath the gallows and pull the prissoner's legs to ensure decease. Most disagreeable!"

[21]   "Wriggling about, eh? That's bad," said the superintendent.

[22]   "Ach, sir, it iss worse when they become refractory! One man, I recall, clung to the bars of hiss cage when we went to take him out. You will scarcely credit, sir, that it took six warders to dislodge him, three pulling at each leg. We reasoned with him. 'My dear fellow,' we said, 'think of all the pain and trouble you are causing to us!' But no, he would not listen! Ach, he wass very troublesome!"

[23]   I found that I was laughing quite loudly. Everyone was laughing. Even the superintendent grinned in a tolerant way. "You'd better all come out and have a drink," he said quite genially. "I've got a bottle of whisky in the car. We could do with it."

[24]   We went through the big double gates of the prison into the road. "Pulling at his legs!" exclaimed a Burmese magistrate suddenly, and burst into a loud chuckling. We all began laughing again. At that moment Francis' anecdote seemed extraordinarily funny. We all had a drink together, native and European alike, quite amicably. The dead man was a hundred yards away.

VOCABULARY

Define the following words as they are used in the selection: *sodden* [1]; *wisp* [2]; *desolately* [3]; *pariah, aghast* [6]; *gambolled* [8]; *gait* [9]; *foolery* [10]; *servile* [11]; *reiterated* [12]; *fixed, abominable* [13]; *timorously* [15]; *oscillated* [16]; *lathis, panikin, snigger* [17]; *Eurasian, boxwalah, rupees, annas* [18]; *garrulously* [20]; *refractory, credit* [22]; *amicably* [24].

QUESTIONS FOR STUDY AND DISCUSSION

1. What do you think was Orwell's purpose in writing this essay? Is his attitude toward the event apparent? How? What is it? Does he at any point make a summarizing statement of his attitude?

2. How would you characterize the prisoner? How did he respond to the situation? Are his reactions important in clarifying Orwell's attitude about the event for himself and for the reader? Is it significant that the crime for which the Hindu is being executed is never mentioned?

3. What does the description of the setting contribute to the atmosphere of the essay? Point out the words that are particularly effective in creating the atmosphere. Substitute other words in their places and discuss the effect of the changes.

4. Orwell employs a number of similes (paragraphs 1, 13, 15). Are these similes fresh and vivid? Are they effective? Are they appropriate to the atmosphere? Do they help to create atmosphere and to provide a comment on the execution? How?

5. Notice, too, that the analogies are much like similes ("the condemned cells . . . like small animal cages" in paragraph 1, "like men handling a fish . . ." in paragraph 2). The questions in number 4 above may also be asked about these analogies.

6. Does paragraph 10 seem appropriate to the essay? Is it necessary?

7. What purpose does the dog serve in the essay? Why does Orwell describe its appearance on the scene as "a dreadful thing"? How does it provide a different view of the prisoner than the one presented through the attitudes toward him by the warders and the head jailer?

8. Although the essay is entitled "A Hanging," the actual hanging takes only a brief moment and is narrated in the first two sentences of paragraph 15. Analyze this paragraph carefully. How does the first sentence epitomize the comment on the vast gulf between life and death that has developed to this point? How do the references to the dog and the man's feet contribute to the comment that Orwell is making? It will be helpful to go back through the preceding paragraphs to note the earlier references to the dog and the man's feet.

9. What references to sounds does Orwell employ in the essay? What is their general effect? Why is the prisoner's repeated cry of "Ram! Ram! Ram!" emphasized? What is its effect on the men?

10. What was the reaction of the men after the execution? After the brief story by the Eurasian boy, Orwell said, "Several people laughed—at what, nobody seemed certain." Why do you think that they laughed? Does Orwell know? If so, why doesn't he say?

11. Why should Francis's anecdote seem "extraordinarily funny"? Is it

possible that Orwell, whose attitude toward capital punishment is one of condemnation, could actually have laughed at the time? Why?

12. What is the effect of the contrast in the concluding two sentences of the essay? What comment is implied in the contrast?

Samuel Eliot Morison

THE SALEM WITCHCRAFT FRENZY

>Beginning with Richard Mather, a first-generation Puritan who emigrated to America in 1634, the Mathers have been closely associated in the public mind with American Puritanism. In 1684, Richard's son Increase Mather published An Essay for the Recording of Illustrious Providences, a compilation of remarkable occurrences supposedly illustrating supernatural and preternatural happenings. A product of its age, it reflects the belief that people then held in the power of Satan to intrude into the affairs of men. Cotton Mather, the son of Increase, took no part in the infamous trials of 1692; yet because of his publications (Cases of Conscience Concerning Evil Spirits and Wonders of the Invisible World) and his role as a leading minister, he has achieved in popular history the reputation of a leading witch-hunter. In the following brief summary of the witchcraft delusion, Samuel Eliot Morison (1887–1976), a Boston-born historian and former Harvard University professor, attempts to set straight Mather's part in the proceedings. The Decennium Luctuosum (in paragraph 2) refers to the "sorrowful decade" of the 1690s; it is also the title of one of Mather's books, published in 1699.

[1] In 1688 there occurred a witchcraft case in Boston. Four children of one of the Mathers' parishioners went into fits and accused an old woman with whom they had had an altercation about the family wash of having bewitched them. The poor creature confessed she had made a compact with the devil, and was discovered to have the traditional witch apparatus of rag dolls representing the victims which she stroked or pinched to torment them.[1] The woman was tried, found guilty, and executed for witchcraft, but the children's con-

From *The Intellectual Life of Colonial New England*, by Samuel Eliot Morison (New York: New York University Press, 1956). Reprinted by permission of New York University Press.

[1] Dr. Alice Hamilton in *American Mercury*, X, 71–75, tells of the same apparatus being used by Italian witch-doctors in Chicago, in the present century.

vulsions, ranting, and riding invisible horses, continued. Cotton Mather took the oldest girl, aged thirteen, into his family, soothed her and prayed with her as a Christian psychiatrist might do in a similar case of nerves today, kept secret the names of the persons she accused, and cured her, completely. If the girls who started the trouble at Salem had been similarly dealt with, that frenzy would not have gone so far as it did.[2] Unfortunately Mather's vanity at this favorable outcome of his efforts was such that he rushed into print with his *Memorable Providences Relating to Witchcrafts* (Boston, 1689), describing the Goodwin case, with all its symptoms in detail; and just as newspaper stories of crime seem to stimulate more people to become criminals, so *Memorable Providences* may well have had a pernicious power of suggestion in that troubled era. That it had any such purpose cannot honestly be maintained by anyone who takes the trouble to read the book; but it is always convenient to have a scapegoat to take the guilt of a community after it has gone mad. Robert Calef, who had it in for Cotton Mather, tied a tin can to him after the frenzy was over; and it has rattled and banged through the pages of superficial and popular historians. Even today the generally accepted version of the Salem tragedy is that Cotton Mather worked it up, aided and abetted by his fellow parsons, in order to drive people back to church.

[2] Yet the terrible outbreak at Salem Village in 1692 needed no clerical belief in witchcraft to bring it about. It arose, as witchcraft epidemics had usually arisen in Europe, during a troubled period, the *Decennium Luctuosum* of New England history when the people were uneasy with rebellions, changes of government, and Indian attacks; and in a community that had for several years been torn by factions. Salem Village, now Danvers, was an outlying parish of Salem township. It had no school, the people were poor, and their ministers had been of rather low grade. A group of girls aged from nine to nineteen began early in 1692 to simulate the physical jerks and shrieks that had been manifested by the Goodwin girls in Boston a few years before. They accused Tituba, a half-breed slave in the minister's family, and two poor old women of having bewitched them. At this point a good spanking administered to the younger girls, and lovers provided for the older ones, might have stopped the whole thing. Instead, the slave was flogged by her master into confessing witchcraft; and to save herself accused two ancient goodwives of being her confederates. The vicious circle was started. The 'afflicted children,' finding themselves the object of unusual attention, and with the exhibitionism natural to young girls, persisted in their accusations for fear of being found out; and a state of neurosis developed similar to that of the shell-shocked soldier torn between fear of death and fear of disgrace. Those accused implicated others to

---

[2] Mather, to his credit, proposed to do this; but the local magistrates refused to accept his advice. [Justin Winsor, ed.,] *Memorial History of Boston*, II, 145–46.

escape the gallows, and confessed broomstick rides, witches' sabbaths, copulation with the devil, and anything that was expected of them. Honest folk who declared the whole thing hokum were cried out upon for witches; and in May, 1692, when Governor Sir William Phips arrived in Boston, several dozen alleged witches were in jail awaiting trial.

[3] The Governor appointed a special court composed of worthy magistrates, some of them college graduates, and presided over by William Stoughton, who had also been a fellow of New College, Oxford. This panel of learned magistrates became infected with the panic; they declined to follow the best rules for detecting witches laid down by professional English witch-hunters, and urged on them, collectively and individually, by the ministers.[3] Before they adjourned in September, 1692, nineteen persons and two dogs had been hanged for witches, and one, the brave Giles Corey, was pressed to death according to the English common law, for refusing to plead guilty or not guilty in order to save his property for his family.

VOCABULARY

Define the following words as they are used in the selection: *altercation, pernicious, scapegoat* [1]; *clerical, simulate, goodwives, witches' sabbaths* [2].

QUESTIONS FOR STUDY AND DISCUSSION

1. Although these three paragraphs are only a part of a longer section dealing with the Puritans' interest in science in general and with the witchcraft delusion in particular, Morison is able to summarize the major events from 1688 to 1692 and to organize them into a meaningful, unified order that emphasizes cause and effect. Trace the chronological order of events, noting the references to dates. How does Morison relate the Goodwin case of 1688 to the later Salem frenzy? Does the reference to Robert Calef fit into the pattern of chronology?

2. What evidence does Morison advance to show that Mather is not so guilty as has been assumed? What is the purpose of footnote 3? (Spectral evidence, or the accusation of a person by an alleged victim, was not admitted in English witchcraft trials.)

---

[3] Cotton Mather's letter to one of the judges, John Richards, 'most humbly' begging him not to 'lay more stresse upon pure Spectre testimony than it will bear' is printed in 4 *Coll.* M.H.S., VIII, 392. The date is May 31, 1692. Cf. C. K. Shipton, in *The American Historical Review*, XL (1935), 464–66.

3. Which of Morison's comments suggest that Mather not only was not responsible for the frenzy but maintained one of the most enlightened attitudes of the time?

4. It is to be expected that a modern historian would view the witchcraft frenzy critically, as Morison does. Yet his attitude is expressed indirectly, partially through occasional adjectives. What is the effect of the following adjectives: *poor* creature (paragraph 1); *afflicted* children, *honest* folk, *alleged* witches (paragraph 2); *worthy* magistrates, *learned* magistrates, *brave* Giles Corey (paragraph 3)?

5. Morison's attitude is also evident in the connotative words and images he uses to comment on the events. What are the implications of the italicized portions of the following: "Robert Calef . . . *tied a tin can* to [Mather] . . . and it has *rattled and banged* through the pages of superficial and popular historians." ". . . the generally accepted version of the Salem tragedy is that Cotton Mather *worked it up, aided and abetted* by his fellow parsons. . . ." "Honest folk who declared the whole thing *hokum* were cried out upon for witches." "This panel of learned magistrates became *infected* with the panic." ". . . nineteen persons *and two dogs* had been hanged for witches."

6. Why does Morison emphasize Stoughton's educational background?

7. What is the purpose of footnote 1?

8. Would the footnotes be as useful for Morison's purposes if he had left out the documentary references? Why?

John Hersey

A NOISELESS FLASH

"At exactly fifteen minutes past eight in the morning, on August 6, 1945, Japanese time . . ." These matter-of-fact words begin John Hersey's already classic narrative of the bombing of Hiroshima. Born in China of American parents, Hersey (b. 1914) was educated in England and America. Following his graduation from Yale in 1936, he served as secretary for a short time to Sinclair Lewis and reported from the Orient for Time *and* Life. *Both a journalist and a novelist, he has published several books of fact and fiction. His novel* A Bell for Adano *(1944) was awarded the Pulitzer Prize in 1945. He is also the author of* Men of Bataan *(1942),* The Wall *(1950), and* The Algiers Motel Incident *(1968). The book from which the present selection is taken,* Hiroshima *(1946), is generally regarded as the most moving human document about atomic warfare.*

From *Hiroshima*, by John Hersey. Copyright 1946 and renewed 1974 by John Hersey. Originally appeared in *The New Yorker*. Reprinted by permission of Alfred A. Knopf, Inc.

[1]   At exactly fifteen minutes past eight in the morning, on August 6, 1945, Japanese time, at the moment when the atomic bomb flashed above Hiroshima, Miss Toshiko Sasaki, a clerk in the personnel department of the East Asia Tin Works, had just sat down at her place in the plant office and was turning her head to speak to the girl at the next desk. At that same moment, Dr. Masakuzu Fujii was settling down cross-legged to read the Osaka *Asahi* on the porch of his private hospital, overhanging one of the seven deltaic rivers which divide Hiroshima; Mrs. Hatsuyo Nakamura, a tailor's widow, stood by the window of her kitchen, watching a neighbor tearing down his house because it lay in the path of an air-raid-defense fire lane; Father Wilhelm Kleinsorge, a German priest of the Society of Jesus, reclined in his underwear on a cot on the top floor of his order's three-story mission house, reading a Jesuit magazine, *Stimmen der Zeit*; Dr. Terufumi Sasaki, a young member of the surgical staff of the city's large, modern Red Cross Hospital, walked along one of the hospital corridors with a blood specimen for a Wassermann test in his hand; and the Reverend Mr. Kiyoshi Tanimoto, pastor of the Hiroshima Methodist Church, paused at the door of a rich man's house in Koi, the city's western suburb, and prepared to unload a handcart full of things he had evacuated from town in fear of the massive B-29 raid which everyone expected Hiroshima to suffer. A hundred thousand people were killed by the atomic bomb, and these six were among the survivors. They still wonder why they lived when so many others died. Each of them counts many small items of chance or volition—a step taken in time, a decision to go indoors, catching one streetcar instead of the next—that spared him. And now each knows that in the act of survival he lived a dozen lives and saw more death than he ever thought he would see. At the time, none of them knew anything.

II

[2]   On the train on the way into Hiroshima from the country, where he lived with his mother, Dr. Terufumi Sasaki, the Red Cross Hospital surgeon, thought over an unpleasant nightmare he had had the night before. His mother's home was in Mukaihara, thirty miles from the city, and it took him two hours by train and tram to reach the hospital. He had slept uneasily all night and had wakened an hour earlier than usual, and, feeling sluggish and slightly feverish, had debated whether to go to the hospital at all; his sense of duty finally forced him to go, and he had started out on an earlier train than he took most mornings. The dream had particularly frightened him because it was so closely associated, on the surface at least, with a disturbing actuality. He was only twenty-five years old and had just completed his training at the Eastern Medical University, in Tsing-tao, China. He was something of an idealist and was much distressed by the inadequacy of medical facilities in

FACTUAL AND HISTORICAL NARRATION   231

the country town where his mother lived. Quite on his own, and without a permit, he had begun visiting a few sick people out there in the evenings, after his eight hours at the hospital and four hours' commuting. He had recently learned that the penalty for practicing without a permit was severe; a fellow-doctor whom he had asked about it had given him a serious scolding. Nevertheless, he had continued to practice. In his dream, he had been at the bedside of a country patient when the police and the doctor he had consulted burst into the room, seized him, dragged him outside, and beat him up cruelly. On the train, he just about decided to give up the work in Makaihara, since he felt it would be impossible to get a permit, because the authorities would hold that it would conflict with his duties at the Red Cross Hospital.

[3] A the terminus, he caught a streetcar at once. (He later calculated that if he had taken his customary train that morning, and if he had had to wait a few minutes for the streetcar, as often happened, he would have been close to the center at the time of the explosion and would surely have perished.) He arrived at the hospital at seven-forty and reported to the chief surgeon. A few minutes later, he went to a room on the first floor and drew blood from the arm of a man in order to perform a Wassermann test. The laboratory containing the incubators for the rest was on the third floor. With the blood specimen in his left hand, walking in a kind of distraction he had felt all morning, probably because of the dream and his restless night, he started along the main corridor on his way toward the stairs. He was one step beyond an open window when the light of the bomb was reflected, like a gigantic photographic flash, in the corridor. He ducked down on one knee and said to himself, as only a Japanese would, "Sasaki, *gambare!* Be brave!" Just then (the building was 1,650 yards from the center), the blast ripped through the hospital. The glasses he was wearing flew off his face; the bottle of blood crashed against one wall; his Japanese slippers zipped out from under his feet—but otherwise, thanks to where he stood, he was untouched.

[4] Dr. Sasaki shouted the name of the chief surgeon and rushed around to the man's office and found him terribly cut by glass. The hospital was in horrible confusion: heavy partitions and ceilings had fallen on patients, beds had overturned, windows had blown in and cut people, blood was spattered on the walls and floors, instruments were everywhere, many of the patients were running about screaming, many more lay dead. (A colleague working in the laboratory to which Dr. Sasaki had been walking was dead; Dr. Sasaki's patient, whom he had just left and who a few moments before had been dreadfully afraid of syphilis, was also dead.) Dr. Sasaki found himself the only doctor in the hospital who was unhurt.

[5] Dr. Sasaki, who believed that the enemy had hit only the building he was in, got bandages and began to bind the wounds of those inside the hospital; while outside, all over Hiroshima, maimed and dying citizens turned their unsteady steps toward the Red Cross Hospital to begin an invasion that was to make Dr. Sasaki forget his private nightmare for a long, long time.

QUESTIONS FOR STUDY AND DISCUSSION

1. In its entirety, *Hiroshima* tells of the explosion and its effects as experienced by the six people referred to in paragraph 1. What does Hersey gain by concentrating on the human experience? Does it seem likely from the roles of the six people that Hersey's book provides an adequately broad report of the explosion and its effects?

2. *Hiroshima* is based primarily on interviews with the actual people involved; thus, the details about the whereabouts and actions of the six individuals are factual. Nevertheless, Hersey maintains artistic control over the manner in which these facts are presented, as well as over the facts he wishes to present. Consider the following points in paragraph 1:

   a. The first two sentences amount to nearly three fourths of the paragraph. What is the effect of having so many details crowded into them?
   b. Does there seem to be any purpose in the order in which the individuals are introduced? How does Reverend Tanimoto's situation provide an effective transition to the third sentence?
   c. Note the tenses of the verbs describing the actions: "had just sat down . . . and was turning her head"; "was settling down"; "stood . . . , watching"; "reclined . . . , reading"; "walked along"; "paused . . . , and prepared to unload." How does the movement from past perfect to simple past tend to focus the reader's attention on a single instant?
   d. Note, too, the kinds of actions described. What effect does Hersey achieve by cataloguing simple, quiet activities?
   e. Hersey could have chosen to say merely that Dr. Fujii was settling down to read and that Father Kleinsorge was reading a Jesuit magazine. What effect does he create by pointing out that the doctor was reading a newspaper? Why is it important to know that the German magazine title means *Voices of the Time?*
   f. Two of the six individuals are involved in actions directly related to air attacks. Point out the irony of these two references sandwiched between the early reference to the atomic bomb in sentence 1 and the reference in sentence 3.

3. The fourth and fifth sentences in the first paragraph are quietly anticlimactic, since they emphasize not the horror of the explosion but rather the curiosity of the individuals about why they were spared. The sixth sentence comments on the immensity of the horror in very general terms. Point out how the fifth sentence presents the topic idea for the more detailed narration that follows, illustrated in the present selection by the experiences of Dr. Sasaki. The

sixth sentence, of course, provides the topic idea for the large part of the book, in which the image of a totally devastated city and population emerges.

4. What are the various meanings that can be attached to the concluding sentence of paragraph 1?

5. Part II is typical of the six brief narratives—one for each individual—which immediately follow paragraph 1. Which statements in this section relate to the curiosity referred to in question 3 above?

6. Why does Hersey relate in such detail the dream of Dr. Sasaki? Does the doctor's dream serve dramatically in the same way as the patient's fear of syphilis?

7. What is Hersey's purpose in noting that Sasaki traveled four hours each day to and from the hospital, that he was an idealist, and that he visited sick people on his own time? In considering your answer, give thought to these more general question: What is the attitude of a nation toward its enemy? How did the American people regard the Japanese during World War II?

8. Note the frequent use of pronouns in Part II to avoid the monotony of repeating Dr. Sasaki's name. Why was it necessary to use his name three times in the concluding two sentences of paragraph 4?

9. In what way does paragraph 5 illuminate the meaning of the final sentence in paragraph 1?

10. On the basis of these two sections from the book, what do you think is Hersey's principal purpose? Is it more than simple reporting? What comments on the atomic attack are implicit in the narrative?

FICTIONAL INCIDENTS AND ANECDOTES

Good autobiographical and biographical writing, as we have seen, selects facts and arranges them in such a manner that they illuminate the meaning of experience. Good factual and historical narration arranges chronological details into a coherent cause-effect sequence. The principal difference between factual narration and fictional narration is that the author of fiction invents the facts of his story to illustrate a truth that he has perceived, not necessarily facts as they have ever been present in actual life.

The purpose of the fiction writer is to tell a story, to entertain the reader; he is not primarily concerned with fact for the sake of fact. A piece of historical fiction usually gives a certain amount of attention to life as it was during the period being written about—to the dress, customs, language, settings; and the characters may even be historical characters. But the author is not writing history, and the reader does not turn to historical fiction for authoritative statements of what life was like at that time. The characters, the settings, the dialogue, the action—all are manipulated by the author, all are made to serve a purpose beyond the re-creation of history. That purpose involves truth, but it is the truth of human experience. The furnishings of the story combine to illustrate an insight into life, some implicit comment, or perhaps even explicit comment, on the meaning of man's experience.

This comment is the author's principal concern. It is the idea of the story. It is what the story is *about*. Ernest Hemingway's famous novel A *Farewell to Arms* is not *about* an American soldier in the Italian ambulance corps during World War I. It illustrates the loss of allegiance and the loss of love, leading to spiritual emptiness. The **theme** of the story, then, is what the story is about: war and fate eat at what is valuable in a man's life and deprive him ultimately of everything but his own existence. Every story of any literary value has some argument that unifies the action. Every good story has a theme.

Since the story is not a sermon, however, the theme must be dramatized. The reader will discover for himself what the story is about if the human action in the story illustrates the theme. By thus dramatizing the theme, the author makes the reader understand and sympathize with the characters, so that he is willing to follow their adventures. In this sense, fictional stories are akin to the parables of the Bible, in which moral lessons are dramatized by actors.

The reader's interest in the characters and the story depends to a large degree upon his understanding what is at stake. In A *Farewell to Arms*, the happiness of the main character—indeed, even his meaningful existence—hangs in the balance. Lieutenant Henry is a lonely individual—as is man himself, suggests the author—in conflict with the world about him, a chaos of experience symbolized in the novel by war. In any rewarding story the **conflict** must be significant, but it need not be so all-embracing as man against the world. The principal areas of conflict are between the protagonist and himself, his fellow man, or nature. A father who has lost his child's respect desires to regain it; a woman can no longer bear her sense of guilt; a husband must fight to save his marriage; a married couple engage in a brief clash of interests and personalities; a marshal struggles to maintain law and order in Dodge City; or a hunter caught in a blizzard fights for his survival—each plot must involve a significant and meaningful conflict.

The **plot** of the story is the series of incidents involving the forces in conflict, so arranged that they lead toward the moment when the stronger of the forces is triumphant. Whereas the simple narrative story is based merely upon the chronological relationship of events, the plot story depends upon causal relationships. When we paraphrase a story, we usually are concerned with the narrative details alone. Thus, we may say of *A Farewell to Arms* that Lieutenant Frederic Henry, an American serving in the Italian ambulance corps, is wounded, falls in love, deserts during a retreat, escapes with his lover, and feels desolate when she dies in childbirth. The plot, however, is more complex, for it turns upon the causal relationship between the lieutenant's wound and his falling in love, his falling in love and his desertion, his desertion and the importance of his lover to him, her death and his desolation. The significance, or theme, of the story becomes evident when the relationships between the elements of the plot are clear. The plot of Hemingway's novel is the author's way of showing, in a cause-effect pattern, *how* "war and fate eat at what is valuable in a man's life and deprive him ultimately of everything but his own existence."

The above discussion of theme, characters, conflict, and plot concerns the fictional narrative in the larger sense. There are two important matters of technique that relate to the manner of telling the story. The first, **point of view,** has already been discussed in connection with exposition and description. It concerns the means whereby the writer sees his story, the distance between him and his material. When an author sits down to write a story, he has the choice of several points of view. The story of Lieutenant Henry, for instance, could be told by any of the characters involved: the lieutenant himself; Catherine Barkley, his lover; or one of the minor characters whose knowledge could conceivably extend to the events of the book. The view of each, however, would be limited; any one of the individuals would know what he himself was thinking, but he would know what the others were doing only so far as he could see their actions or hear them reported. Another possibility would be narration from the position of the **omniscient observer,** one who is capable not only of seeing and hearing everything that goes on but also of knowing what each of the characters is thinking at any moment of the action. This omniscient view (often modified to limited omniscience, in which the thoughts of only the major character are related) is a favorite one of fiction writers; Hemingway has himself used it in several of his novels—notably *For Whom the Bell Tolls* and *The Old Man and the Sea.* In actuality, Hemingway best achieves his purpose in *A Farewell to Arms* by narrating the story in the words of Lieutenant Henry; for it is Henry's response to war, to Catherine, to his friends, to the world about him, that is uppermost in importance in the novel.

The selections from fiction in this book illustrate various points of view. Lewis's *Babbitt,* Frederic's *The Damnation of Theron Ware,* and Norris's *McTeague* illustrate the omniscient author at work. Melville's *Moby-Dick* is told from the point of view of a first-person narrator who is a minor character.

The second matter of technique, **consistency of tone**, is especially important in a brief narrative. It was the contention of Edgar Allan Poe, who viewed the literary artist as a conscious and analytical craftsman, that "in the whole composition there should be no word written, of which the tendency, direct or indirect, is not to the one preestablished design." A misplaced note of humor can dispel a carefully wrought atmosphere of gloom. An incongruous comment or image can distract the reader from the intent of the author long enough to destroy whatever effect the author has labored to achieve.

In addition to the examples of fictional narration below, the sections on exposition, description, and argumentation contain several other excerpts from short stories and novels. These selections may be profitably read or reread as examples of narration and analyzed with attention to some of the fundamental problems of fiction, such as characterization, point of view, and, to a limited extent, even theme. (See the Contents for page numbers.)

Frank Norris, "Polk Street"
Jack London, "Student Quarters"
Sinclair Lewis, "The House of Babbitt"
Henry James, "The American"
Herman Melville, "Captain Ahab"
Harold Frederic, "The Three Trustees"
Mark Twain, "Storm on Jackson's Island"
John Steinbeck, "Empty Houses"
Stephen Crane, "Four Men in a Boat"
Nathaniel Hawthorne, "A Giant's Dead Body"

Like fictional narration, the **anecdote**—whether it is fictional or factual—illustrates a single point or theme. It is a short narrative that focuses upon a single, usually simple, incident. It may be employed in a biography or description of a person as a supporting device to illustrate a particular characteristic of the individual. In his description of Cassius Clay, Leonard Shecter describes a typical action of Clay to dramatize the boxer's boastful showmanship. Or the anecdote may be used, like the short story, to dramatize a general truth. The example given in this book, Benjamin Franklin's "The Speckled Ax," is of this type. It provides Franklin in his *Autobiography* the opportunity to make an observation about people's tendency to rationalize.

The particular point to be illustrated by an anecdote may be expressed explicitly, as in Shecter's description of Cassius Clay, Franklin's story of the man who was buying an ax, or Calandra's "Angels on a Pin," which is essentially a long anecdote. Or the point may be made implicitly, as in the parables of Christ in the New Testament. What is important is that a particular point is illustrated; otherwise, of course, the anecdote is to no purpose.

John Steinbeck

THE TURTLE

In their struggle for existence and in their larger struggle for human dignity, the members of the Joad family in The Grapes of Wrath *(see the headnote to "Empty Houses" in this anthology) contended with both man and nature, and with their own human failings. Although at the end of the novel the struggle for existence was unended, that larger struggle had been achieved; for the Joads, despite their poverty and their lack of education, emblemize human dignity through their compassion, their unbending toil, and their acceptance of the life force that underlies the activity of this earth. In Chapter 3 of the novel, a vivid piece of narrative and descriptive writing about a turtle, Steinbeck foreshadows the story of the Joads and the theme of the novel.*

[1] The concrete highway was edged with a mat of tangled, broken, dry grass, and the grass heads were heavy with oat beards to catch on a dog's coat, and foxtails to tangle in a horse's fetlocks, and clover burrs to fasten in sheep's wool; sleeping life waiting to be spread and dispersed, every seed armed with an appliance of dispersal, twisting darts and parachutes for the wind, little spears and balls of tiny thorns, and all waiting for animals and for the wind, for a man's trouser cuff or the hem of a woman's skirt, all passive but armed with appliances of activity, still, but each possessed of the anlage of movement.

[2] The sun lay on the grass and warmed it, and in the shade under the grass the insects moved, ants and ant lions to set traps for them, grasshoppers to jump into the air and flick their yellow wings for a second, sow bugs like little armadillos, plodding restlessly on many tender feet. And over the grass at the roadside a land turtle crawled, turning aside for nothing, dragging his high-domed shell over the grass. His hard legs and yellow-nailed feet threshed slowly through the grass, not really walking, but boosting and dragging his shell along. The barley beards slid off his shell, and the clover burrs fell on him and rolled to the ground. His horny beak was partly open, and his fierce, humorous eyes, under brows like fingernails, stared straight ahead. He came over the grass leaving a beaten trail behind him, and the hill, which was the highway embankment, reared up ahead of him. For a moment he stopped, his head held high. He blinked and looked up and down. At last he started to

From *The Grapes of Wrath*, by John Steinbeck. Copyright 1939, copyright © renewed 1967 by John Steinbeck. Reprinted by permission of The Viking Press, Inc.

climb the embankment. Front clawed feet reached forward but did not touch. The hind feet kicked his shell along, and it scraped on the grass, and on the gravel. As the embankment grew steeper and steeper, the more frantic were the efforts of the land turtle. Pushing hind legs strained and slipped, boosting the shell along, and the horny head protruded as far as the neck could stretch. Little by little the shell slid up the embankment until at last a parapet cut straight across its line of march, the shoulder of the road, a concrete wall four inches high. As though they worked independently the hind legs pushed the shell against the wall. The head upraised and peered over the wall to the broad smooth plain of cement. Now the hands, braced on top of the wall, strained and lifted, and the shell came slowly up and rested its front end on the wall. For a moment the turtle rested. A red ant ran into the shell, into the soft skin inside the shell, and suddenly head and legs snapped in, and the armored tail clamped in sideways. The red ant was crushed between body and legs. And one head of wild oats was clamped into the shell by a front leg. For a long moment the turtle lay still, and then the neck crept out and the old humorous frowning eyes looked about and the legs and tail came out. The back legs went to work, straining like elephant legs, and the shell tipped to an angle so that the front legs could not reach the level cement plain. But higher and higher the hind legs boosted it, until at last the center of balance was reached, the front tipped down, the front legs scratched at the pavement, and it was up. But the head of wild oats was held by its stem around the front legs.

[3] Now the going was easy, and all the legs worked, and the shell boosted along, waggling from side to side. A sedan driven by a forty-year-old woman approached. She saw the turtle and swung to the right, off the highway, the wheels screamed and a cloud of dust boiled up. Two wheels lifted for a moment and then settled. The car skidded back onto the road, and went on, but more slowly. The turtle had jerked into its shell, but now it hurried on, for the highway was burning hot.

[4] And now a light truck approached, and as it came near, the driver saw the turtle and swerved to hit it. His front wheel struck the edge of the shell, flipped the turtle like a tiddly-wink, spun it like a coin, and rolled it off the highway. The truck went back to its course along the right side. Lying on its back, the turtle was tight in its shell for a long time. But at last its legs waved in the air, reaching for something to pull it over. Its front foot caught a piece of quartz and little by little the shell pulled over and flopped upright. The wild oat head fell out and three of the spearhead seeds stuck in the ground. And as the turtle crawled on down the embankment, its shell dragged dirt over the seeds. The turtle entered a dust road and jerked itself along, drawing a wavy shallow trench in the dust with its shell. The old humorous eyes

looked ahead, and the horny beak opened a little. His yellow toenails slipped a fraction in the dust.

VOCABULARY

Define the following words as they are used in the selection: *dispersal, anlage* [1]; *ant lions, threshed* [2].

QUESTIONS FOR STUDY AND DISCUSSION

1. How would you phrase the theme of this chapter?

2. Two conflicts are apparent in the chapter, both of them related to the life force (the instinctive urge to survive and achieve) mentioned in the head-note. What are they? How are they related in the chapter as a kind of plot and sub-plot?

3. Steinbeck suggests that the life force is passive but inevitable. How does the turtle illustrate this idea? How does the wild oat head illustrate it?

4. What adjectives can be applied to nature as described by Steinbeck? What details support these adjectives?

5. Are the details of the narrative clear? Does the turtle reach the opposite side of the road? What clue does Steinbeck offer?

6. Does the narrative seem tedious or engrossing? Defend your answer.

7. What descriptive devices does Steinbeck employ? Explain why you think that the descriptive passages are, or are not, effectively fused into the narrative.

8. What is Steinbeck's attitude toward the turtle? Does he exaggerate the importance of its struggle?

9. What adjectives can be applied to the turtle?

10. What is the point of view of the author? Is this point of view the only one that Steinbeck could have chosen? Discuss.

11. Are the man and the woman drivers, as part of nature, consistent with the view of nature suggested by the chapter?

12. Discuss the following statement about the struggle of the turtle: "It is an act of heroic obstinacy and persistence against heavy odds . . . it inevitably carries the mind by suggestion to the kindred heroisms of men and women." (Joseph Warren Beach, *American Fiction 1920–1940*)

Katharine Brush

BIRTHDAY PARTY

The 500-word limit so frequently imposed upon college composition students need be no hardship. What can be accomplished in only 300 words is demonstrated by Katharine Brush (1902–1959), author of a dozen novels and collections of short stories. Her writings have appeared in most of the popular national magazines of the United States. The following story was first published in The New Yorker *in 1946.*

[1]   They were a couple in their late thirties, and they looked unmistakably married. They sat on the banquette opposite us in a little narrow restaurant, having dinner. The man had a round, self-satisfied face, with glasses on it; the woman was fadingly pretty, in a big hat. There was nothing conspicuous about them, nothing particularly noticeable, until the end of their meal, when it suddenly became obvious that this was an Occasion—in fact, the husband's birthday, and the wife had planned a little surprise for him.

[2]   It arrived, in the form of a small but glossy birthday cake, with one pink candle burning in the center. The headwaiter brought it in and placed it before the husband, and meanwhile the violin-and-piano orchestra played "Happy Birthday to You" and the wife beamed with shy pride over her little surprise, and such few people as there were in the restaurant tried to help out with a pattering of applause. It became clear at once that help was needed, because the husband was not pleased. Instead he was hotly embarrassed, and indignant at his wife for embarrassing him.

[3]   You looked at him and you saw this and you thought, "Oh, now, don't *be* like that!" But he was like that, and as soon as the little cake had been deposited on the table, and the orchestra had finished the birthday piece, and the general attention had shifted from the man and the woman, I saw him say something to her under his breath—some punishing thing, quick and curt and unkind. I couldn't bear to look at the woman then, so I stared at my plate and waited for quite a long time. Not long enough, though. She was still crying when I finally glanced over there again. Crying quietly and heartbrokenly and hopelessly, all to herself, under the gay big brim of her best hat.

Copyright © 1946 Katharine Brush. Originally published in *The New Yorker*. Reprinted by permission of Thomas S. Brush.

QUESTIONS FOR STUDY AND DISCUSSION

1. Brief as it is, "Birthday Party" is complete in itself and has the principal features of narrative fiction. What is the dominant feature of the story: incident, characterization, or mood?

2. What is the nature of the conflict in the story? Is it between the husband and wife, or is it within the wife?

3. What is the point of view? Is it effective? What are the advantages and disadvantages of this point of view for this particular story?

4. Are there any suggestions in the story that the narrator is a woman, other than the fact that her sympathies are with the wife?

5. Characterize both the husband and wife as broadly as possible on the basis of the specific remarks Mrs. Brush makes about each.

6. Are the husband's reactions to the surprise prepared for by the description of him? Is there any justification for his behavior?

7. What does Mrs. Brush accomplish by her two references to the wife's hat? Why does she emphasize its size?

8. Is the title an appropriate one? Comment on the irony of the title.

9. What is the theme of "Birthday Party"? What truths or truths of human behavior does the story illustrate?

Benjamin Franklin

THE SPECKLED AX

As a young man, Benjamin Franklin drew up a list of thirteen virtues that he wished to achieve in his "bold and arduous project," as he termed it, "of arriving at moral perfection." His account of his interesting project is deservedly one of the most famous sections of his Autobiography, from which this excerpt is drawn. Two of the desired virtues caused Franklin special difficulty. One, as he states in this passage, was order. The other was humility. "Even if I could conceive that I had completely overcome [pride]," he wrote, "I should be proud of my humility."

My scheme of *Order* gave me the most trouble; and I found that, though it might be practicable where a man's business was such as to leave him the disposition of his time, that of a journeyman printer, for instance, it was not possible to be exactly observed by a master, who must mix with the world, and often receive people of business at their own hours. *Order*, too, with regard to places for things, papers, etc., I found extremely difficult to acquire. I had not been early accustomed to it, and, having an exceeding good memory, I was not so sensible of the inconvenience attending want of method. This article, therefore, cost me so much painful attention, and my faults in it vexed me so much, and I made so little progress in amendment, and had such frequent relapses, that I was almost ready to give up the attempt, and content myself with a faulty character in that respect, like the man who, in buying an ax of a smith, my neighbor, desired to have the whole of its surface as bright as the edge. The smith consented to grind it bright for him if he would turn the wheel; he turned, while the smith pressed the broad face of the ax hard and heavily on the stone, which made the turning of it very fatiguing. The man came every now and then from the wheel to see how the work went on, and at length would take his ax as it was, without farther grinding. "No," said the smith, "turn on, turn on; we shall have it bright by-and-by; as yet, it is only speckled." "Yes," says the man, "*But I think I like a speckled ax best.*" And I believe this may have been the case with many, who, having, for want of some such means as I employed, found the difficulty of obtaining good and breaking bad habits in other points of vice and virtue, have given up the struggle, and concluded that "*a speckled ax was best*"; for something that pretended to be reason, was every now and then suggesting to me that such extreme nicety as I exacted of myself might be a kind of foppery in morals, which, if it were known, would make me ridiculous; that a perfect character might be attended with the inconvenience of being envied and hated; and that a benevolent man should allow a few faults in himself, to keep his friends in countenance.

VOCABULARY

Define the following words as they are used in the selection: *disposition, journeyman, nicety, foppery, benevolent, countenance.*

QUESTIONS FOR STUDY AND DISCUSSION

These questions should be used in the analysis of any anecdote:
A. Purpose
    1. What point does the anecdote illustrate? Rephrase the point in one sentence.

2. Is the point implicit or explicit? (Which anecdotes most effectively make their point, those that contain or those that explain the point? Or are the methods equally useful?)

B. Context
3. How much of the selection is the actual ancedote?
4. If the anecdote is contained in the selection, how does the remainder of the selection provide a suitable context for the anecdote?
5. Would the anecdote be effective out of context?

C. Characterization
6. To what extent is characterization achieved?
7. Are the characters individualized or typical?
8. Is full characterization necessary?

D. Setting
9. Is the setting (either time or place) important?
10. Are the details of setting adequately provided?

E. Dialogue
11. How useful is the dialogue?
12. Are the persons characterized by dialogue?

F. Tone and Audience
13. What is the tone of the anecdote?
14. Is the tone appropriate to the story?
15. Is the anecdote humorous? If so, what is the source of the humor?
16. Is the anecdote told in a manner suitable for the intended audience?

FOR FURTHER ANALYSIS

Richard Wright

". . . AND I HUNGERED FOR BOOKS"

"*Reading maketh a full man,*" *wrote Sir Francis Bacon. So it was with Richard Wright (1908–1960), who was young and Southern and black—and thus not supposed to read books. This selection, from Wright's autobiography,* Black Boy *(1945), recounts his earliest experiences with books and what they did to him. Other works by Wright include three of particular note:* Uncle Tom's Children *(1938),* Native Son *(1940), and* Twelve Million Black Voices *(1941).*

From *Black Boy*, copyright 1937, 1942, 1944, 1945 by Richard Wright. Reprinted by permission of Harper & Row, Publishers, Inc.

[1]   One morning I arrived early at work and went into the bank lobby where the Negro porter was mopping. I stood at a counter and picked up the Memphis *Commercial Appeal* and began my free reading of the press. I came finally to the editorial page and saw an article dealing with one H. L. Mencken. I knew by hearsay that he was the editor of the *American Mercury,* but aside from that I knew nothing about him. The article was a furious denunciation of Mencken, concluding with one, hot, short sentence: Mencken is a fool.

[2]   I wondered what on earth this Mencken had done to call down upon him the scorn of the South. The only people I had ever heard denounced in the South were Negroes, and this man was not a Negro. Then what ideas did Mencken hold that made a newspaper like the *Commercial Appeal* castigate him publicly? Undoubtedly he must be advocating ideas that the South did not like. Were there, then, people other than Negroes who criticized the South? I knew that during the Civil War the South had hated northern whites, but I had not encountered such hate during my life. Knowing no more of Mencken than I did at that moment, I felt a vague sympathy for him. Had not the South, which had assigned me the role of a non-man, cast at him its hardest words?

[3]   Now, how could I find out about this Mencken? There was a huge library near the riverfront, but I knew that Negroes were not allowed to patronize its shelves any more than they were the parks and playgrounds of the city. I had gone into the library several times to get books for the white men on the job. Which of them would now help me to get books? And how could I read them without causing concern to the white men with whom I worked? I had so far been successful in hiding my thoughts and feelings from them, but I knew that I would create hostility if I went about this business of reading in a clumsy way.

[4]   I weighed the personalities of the men on the job. There was Don, a Jew; but I distrusted him. His position was not much better than mine and I knew that he was uneasy and insecure; he had always treated me in an offhand, bantering way that barely concealed his contempt. I was afraid to ask him to help me to get books; his frantic desire to demonstrate a racial solidarity with the whites against Negroes might make him betray me.

[5]   Then how about the boss? No, he was a Baptist and I had the suspicion that he would not be quite able to comprehend why a black boy would want to read Mencken. There were other white men on the job whose attitudes showed clearly that they were Kluxers or sympathizers, and they were out of the question.

NARRATION

[6] There remained only one man whose attitude did not fit into an anti-Negro category, for I had heard the white men refer to him as a "Pope lover." He was an Irish Catholic and was hated by the white Southerners. I knew that he read books, because I had got him volumes from the library several times. Since he, too, was an object of hatred, I felt that he might refuse me but would hardly betray me. I hesitated, weighing and balancing the imponderable realities.

[7] One morning I paused before the Catholic fellow's desk.

[8] "I want to ask you a favor," I whispered to him.

[9] "What is it?"

[10] "I want to read. I can't get books from the library. I wonder if you'd let me use your card?"

[11] He looked at me suspiciously.

[12] "My card is full most of the time," he said.

[13] "I see," I said and waited, posing my question silently.

[14] "You're not trying to get me into trouble, are you, boy?" he asked, staring at me.

[15] "Oh, no, sir."

[16] "What book do you want?"

[17] "A book by H. L. Mencken."

[18] "Which one?"

[19] "I don't know. Has he written more than one?"

[20] "He has written several."

[21] "I didn't know that."

[22] "What makes you want to read Mencken?"

[23] "Oh, I just saw his name in the newspaper," I said.

[24] "It's good of you to want to read," he said. "But you ought to read the right things."

[25] I said nothing. Would he want to supervise my reading?

[26] "Let me think," he said. "I'll figure out something."

[27] I turned from him and he called me back. He stared at me quizzically.

[28] "Richard, don't mention this to the other white men," he said.

[29] "I understand," I said. "I won't say a word."

[30] A few days later he called me to him.

[31] "I've got a card in my wife's name," he said. "Here's mine."

[32] "Thank you, sir."

[33] "Do you think you can manage it?"

[34] "I'll manage fine," I said.

[35] "If they suspect you, you'll get in trouble," he said.

[36]   That afternoon I addressed myself to forging a note. Now, what were the names of books written by H. L. Mencken? I did not know any of them. I finally wrote what I thought would be a foolproof note: *Dear Madam: Will you please let this nigger boy*—I used the word "nigger" to make the librarian feel that I could not possibly be the author of the note—*have some books by H. L. Mencken?* I forged the white man's name.

[37]   I entered the library as I had always done when on errands for whites, but I felt that I would somehow slip up and betray myself. I doffed my hat, stood a respectful distance from the desk, looked as unbookish as possible, and waited for the white patrons to be taken care of. When the desk was clear of people, I still waited. The white librarian looked at me.

[38] "What do you want, boy?"

[39]   As though I did not possess the power of speech, I stepped forward and simply handed her the forged note, not parting my lips.

NARRATION

[40] "What books by Mencken does he want?" she asked.

[41] "I don't know, ma'am," I said, avoiding her eyes.

[42] "Who gave you this card?"

[43] "Mr. Falk," I said.

[44] "Where is he?"

[45] "He's at work, at the M——— Optical Company," I said. "I've been in here for him before."

[46] "I remember," the woman said. "But he never wrote notes like this."

[47] Oh, God, she's suspicious. Perhaps she would not let me have the books? If she had turned her back at that moment, I would have ducked out the door and never gone back. Then I thought of a bold idea.

[48] "You can call him up, ma'am," I said, my heart pounding.

[49] "You're not using these books, are you?" she asked pointedly.

[50] "Oh, no, ma'am. I can't read."

[51] "I don't know what he wants by Mencken," she said under her breath.

[52] I knew now that I had won; she was thinking of other things and the race question had gone out of her mind. She went to the shelves. Once or twice she looked over her shoulder at me, as though she was still doubtful. Finally she came forward with two books in her hand.

[53] "I'm sending him two books," she said. "But tell Mr. Falk to come in next time, or send me the names of the books he wants. I don't know what he wants to read."

[54] I said nothing. She stamped the card and handed me the books. Not daring to glance at them, I went out of the library, fearing that the woman would call me back for further questioning. A block away from the library I opened one of the books and read a title: *A Book of Prefaces*. I was nearing my nineteenth birthday and I did not know how to pronounce the word "preface." I thumbed the pages and saw strange words and strange names. I

shook my head, disappointed. I looked at the other book; it was called *Prejudices*. I knew what that word meant; I had heard it all my life. And right off I was on guard against Mencken's books. Why would a man want to call a book *Prejudices*? The word was so stained with all my memories of racial hate that I could not conceive of anybody using it for a title. Perhaps I had made a mistake about Mencken? A man who had prejudices must be wrong.

[55] When I showed the books to Mr. Falk, he looked at me and frowned.

[56] "That librarian might telephone you," I warned him.

[57] "That's all right," he said. "But when you're through reading those books, I want you to tell me what you get out of them."

[58] That night in my rented room, while letting the hot water run over my can of pork and beans in the sink, I opened *A Book of Prefaces* and began to read. I was jarred and shocked by the style, the clear, clean, sweeping sentences. Why did he write like that? And how did one write like that? I pictured the man as a raging demon, slashing with his pen, consumed with hate, denouncing everything American, extolling everything European or German, laughing at the weaknesses of people, mocking God, authority. What was this? I stood up, trying to realize what reality lay behind the meaning of the words. . . . Yes, this man was fighting, fighting with words. He was using words as a weapon, using them as one would use a club. Could words be weapons? No. It frightened me. I read on and what amazed me was not what he said, but how on earth anybody had the courage to say it.

[59] Occasionally I glanced up to reassure myself that I was alone in the room. Who were these men about whom Mencken was talking so passionately? Who was Anatole France? Joseph Conrad? Sinclair Lewis, Sherwood Anderson, Dostoevski, George Moore, Gustave Flaubert, Maupassant, Tolstoy, Frank Harris, Mark Twain, Thomas Hardy, Arnold Bennett, Stephen Crane, Zola, Norris, Gorky, Bergson, Ibsen, Balzac, Bernard Shaw, Dumas, Poe, Thomas Mann, O. Henry, Dreiser, H. G. Wells, Gogol, T. S. Eliot, Gide, Baudelaire, Edgar Lee Masters, Stendhal, Turgenev, Huneker, Nietzsche, and scores of others? Were these men real? Did they exist or had they existed? And how did one pronounce their names?

[60] I ran across many words whose meanings I did not know, and I either looked them up in a dictionary or, before I had a chance to do that, encountered the word in a context that made its meaning clear. But what strange world was this? I concluded the book with the conviction that I had somehow overlooked something terribly important in life. I had once tried to

NARRATION

write, had once reveled in feeling, had let my crude imagination roam, but the impulse to dream had been slowly beaten out of me by experience. Now it surged up again and I hungered for books, new ways of looking and seeing. It was not a matter of believing or disbelieving what I read, but of feeling something new, of being affected by something that made the look of the world different.

[61] As dawn broke I ate my pork and beans, feeling dopey, sleepy. I went to work, but the mood of the book would not die; it lingered, coloring everything I saw, heard, did. I now felt that I knew what the white men were feeling. Merely because I had read a book that had spoken of how they lived and thought, I identified myself with that book. I felt vaguely guilty. Would I, filled with bookish notions, act in a manner that would make the whites dislike me?

[62] I forged more notes and my trips to the library became frequent. Reading grew into a passion. My first serious novel was Sinclair Lewis's *Main Street*. It made me see my boss, Mr. Gerald, and identify him as an American type. I would smile when I saw him lugging his golf bags into the office. I had always felt a vast distance separating me from the boss, and now I felt closer to him, though still distant. I felt now that I knew him, that I could feel the very limits of his narrow life. And this had happened because I had read a novel about a mythical man called George F. Babbitt.

[63] The plots and stories in the novels did not interest me so much as the point of view revealed. I gave myself over to each novel without reserve, without trying to criticize it; it was enough for me to see and feel something different. And for me, everything was something different. Reading was like a drug, a dope. The novels created moods in which I lived for days. But I could not conquer my sense of guilt, my feeling that the white men around me knew that I was changing, that I had begun to regard them differently.

[64] Whenever I brought a book to the job, I wrapped it in newspaper—a habit that was to persist for years in other cities and under other circumstances. But some of the white men pried into my packages when I was absent and they questioned me.

[65] "Boy, what are you reading those books for?"

[66] "Oh, I don't know, sir."

[67] "That's deep stuff you're reading, boy."

[68] "I'm just killing time, sir."

[69]   "You'll addle your brains if you don't watch out."

[70]   I read Dreiser's *Jennie Gerhardt* and *Sister Carrie* and they revived in me a vivid sense of my mother's suffering; I was overwhelmed. I grew silent, wondering about the life around me. It would have been impossible for me to have told anyone what I derived from these novels, for it was nothing less than a sense of life itself. All my life had shaped me for the realism, the naturalism of the modern novel, and I could not read enough of them.

[71]   Steeped in new moods and ideas, I bought a ream of paper and tried to write; but nothing would come, or what did come was flat beyond telling. I discovered that more than desire and feeling were necessary to write and I dropped the idea. Yet I still wondered how it was possible to know people sufficiently to write about them? Could I ever learn about life and people? To me, with my vast ignorance, my Jim Crow station in life, it seemed a task impossible of achievement. I now knew what being a Negro meant. I could endure the hunger. I had learned to live with hate. But to feel that there were feelings denied me, that the very breath of life itself was beyond my reach, that more than anything else hurt, wounded me. I had a new hunger.

[72]   In buoying me up, reading also cast me down, made me see what was possible, what I had missed. My tension returned, new, terrible, bitter, surging, almost too great to be contained. I no longer *felt* that the world about me was hostile, killing; I *knew* it. A million times I asked myself what I could do to save myself, and there were no answers. I seemed forever condemned, ringed by walls.

[73]   I did not discuss my reading with Mr. Falk, who had lent me his library card; it would have meant talking about myself and that would have been too painful. I smiled each day, fighting desperately to maintain my old behavior, to keep my disposition seemingly sunny. But some of the white men discerned that I had begun to brood.

[74]   "Wake up there, boy!" Mr. Olin said one day.

[75]   "Sir!" I answered for the lack of a better word.

[76]   "You act like you've stolen something," he said.

[77]   I laughed in the way I knew he expected me to laugh, but I resolved to be more conscious of myself, to watch my every act, to guard and hide the new knowledge that was dawning within me.

NARRATION

[78] If I went north, would it be possible for me to build a new life then? But how could a man build a life upon vague, unformed yearnings? I wanted to write and I did not even know the English language. I bought English grammars and found them dull. I felt that I was getting a better sense of the language from novels than from grammars. I read hard, discarding a writer as soon as I felt that I had grasped his point of view. At night the printed page stood before my eyes in sleep.

[79] Mrs. Moss, my landlady, asked me one Sunday morning: "Son, what is this you keep on reading?"

[80] "Oh, nothing. Just novels."

[81] "What you get out of 'em?"

[82] "I'm just killing time," I said.

[83] "I hope you know your own mind," she said in a tone which implied that she doubted if I had a mind.

[84] I knew of no Negroes who read the books I liked and wondered if Negroes ever thought of them. I knew that there were Negro doctors, lawyers, newspapermen, but I never saw any of them. When I read a Negro newspaper I never caught the faintest echo of my preoccupation in its pages. I felt trapped and occasionally, for a few days, I would stop reading. But a vague hunger would come over me for books, books that opened up new avenues of feeling and seeing, and again I would forge another note to the white librarian. Again I would read and wonder as only the naïve and unlettered can read and wonder, feeling that I carried a secret, criminal burden about with me each day.

SUGGESTIONS FOR WRITING

    1. Following the method used by Hughes in "Salvation," write a narrative account of some experience in your life that has been significant in forming your religious views. Your attitude toward the experience may be either negative (like that of Hughes) or affirmative, but your account should reveal the state of mind you believe you had during and just after the experience.

    2. Write an account of your early recollections of your home, your parents, your fears and pleasures. By their very nature, such recollections are likely to be disjointed. Give great attention to linking them smoothly to achieve a narrative unity and an evenness of tone.

    3. "Modern childhood," says White, "has no equivalent to my barn." If

your own childhood has an equivalent place or experience that you believe children of today are likely to miss, write a narrative that reveals its importance to you.

4. Write an account of a single incident or experience that you have come to regard as a turning point in your life, or one that has illustrated to you some truth about human nature. Try to convey this truth in an indirect rather than a direct manner—by dramatizing the incident rather than by telling about it.

5. Try to discover how your parents (or any other couple you know) met for the first time. Following the pattern set by Clair Huffaker in "Pony Boy," write a narrative including as much dialogue as you can imagine as realistic to convey the feelings of one (not both) of the two parties. Be sure to maintain a single point of view.

6. People in close and frequent contact with human misery and pain generally assume a protective veneer that permits them to go about their business objectively. To the observer, such a veneer often seems to suggest callousness and insensitivity. If you have observed an incident involving such people—in the emergency room of a hospital, in a police station, at the scene of an accident—describe the incident carefully, giving special attention to the details that have made the incident vivid and memorable for you. Your comment about the incident should be implicit, not openly stated. If you feel that you must make an explicit comment, contain it in a single paragraph, as Orwell has done.

7. Orwell, in paragraph 10 of "A Hanging," suspends his narrative briefly to argue against capital punishment. What is your attitude toward capital punishment? If you have any experience or knowledge of a case that has been influential in forming your attitude, support your view in a narrative that relates details of the case and makes your attitude clear.

8. Write a narrative report of an event of some significance that you have either witnessed yourself or have been able to learn about through interviews. As an alternative to first-hand information (if none is available), make notes from the reports in several newspapers concerning a single event and write a narrative report from your own point of view. If possible, follow the example of Hersey in "A Noiseless Flash" and concentrate upon the human aspect of the event rather than upon statistics.

9. Narrate in detail some simple and common incident—a child contending in a game, a robin foraging on the lawn, an elderly person in a park, an ant carrying food, someone shopping in a supermarket. Make your narrative serve some larger purpose by implication. Give particular attention to point of view, and keep your distance as narrator: do not intrude your comment.

10. Human drama, such as that captured by Katherine Brush, poses two strenuous requirements: the observer's being in the right place at the right time and the ability to recognize drama when it occurs. Write a narrative, either imagined or observed, from the point of view of one who can see the incident but cannot hear what is said between the people in the scene. Have you ever watched through a glass-paneled door as an instructor discussed a failing paper with a student? Have you ever watched a child and mother stop in front of a toy display, exchange a few words, then move on? Have you ever looked from a high window upon a street or campus and watched two people meet? Such situations are well suited to this assignment.

ARGUMENTATION

Every day each person in normal contact with the world about him is confronted with many types of argumentation or persuasion designed to sway his opinion, create in him an opinion where there was none before, or motivate him to some action. Some of these persuasive techniques are in the ephemeral form of advertisements in magazines and newspapers, and on signboards, television screens, and the radio. Others appear as editorials and columns by journalists, as well as lectures and political campaign speeches. Circulars, pamphlets, and broadsides, particularly on college campuses, have in the past few years become common media for political and social messages. Still other attempts to argue and persuade are phrased as magazine articles and books—fact, opinion, and fiction. Some appeal to our basic human desires for social acceptance, financial well-being, and comfort; indeed, many advertisements are designed on the basis of these desires. Others touch us where we are equally concerned and appeal to our emotions or sentiments or conventional loyalties. Still others humor us into smiling at the weaknesses of ourselves and our fellow men, with the purpose of correcting these weaknesses. An individual who understands the principles of persuasive techniques will not only be able to protect himself from being persuaded by invalid methods, but he will also be able to make his own persuasive writing more effective.

As one of the four principal types of discourse, **argumentation** is characterized by its aim or purpose rather than its form. The purpose of argumentation is to convince an audience that a proposition is true or false. Since the writer is interested in explaining the proposition as well as defending or attacking it, argumentation is frequently found in combination with exposition; but since the aim is to convince rather than to make an explanation, it is the argument, not the explanation, that is the principal intent. In the first selection, for instance, James Thurber is not primarily interested in *explaining* the characteristics of women; he lists them only so that they may provide a basis for his argument.

Similarly, argumentation often is combined with description and narration. The words George Bernard Shaw places in the mouth of the Devil effectively describe man's capability for destruction; and a dialogue from *The House of the Seven Gables* permits Nathaniel Hawthorne to express through one of his characters some of the arguments against the corrosive effects of rigid tradition. These selections are nevertheless properly considered as arguments because their purpose is to convince the reader of the authors' views. The form of the selections is subservient to the purpose.

Although some of the selections in other sections convey the convictions of their authors, argumentation does not seem to be the principal aim. In his definition of *Americanism,* Edmund Wilson concludes that the reader should disapprove of the current usage of the word; his main intent, however, is to show how the word has changed in meaning and connotation through the years. John Steinbeck's description of the empty houses contains an implicit comment on the plight of the workers who have been forced to leave their homes; and Orwell's narration of an execution communicates to the reader an insightful comment on capital punishment.

Exposition, description, and narration, then, all can serve the purposes of argumentation. In the selections in this section, however, argumentation is the explicit and major purpose of the writers.

Just as other types of discourse are used in combination with argumentation, argumentation itself makes use of several different methods, which are also frequently found in combination in a single work. **Logical argument** emphasizes reasoning, employing such devices as the *syllogism* and *analogy* (terms that will be discussed later) and the use of evidence. Logical arguments are directed to the intellect of the audience and attempt to establish the truth of the author's position. **Emotional persuasion,** which does not necessarily emphasize reasoning, appeals not only to the intellect but also to the heart; it attempts to arouse the audience to action or to a belief that is not essentially based upon logical argument. In the first group of selections, the arguments of the writers are primarily intellectual, though some obviously make use of emotional appeals. The Declaration of Independence, for instance, enforces its logical argument through language that appeals to the reader's sense of right and justice. On the other hand, the selections that illustrate emotional appeals do not discount completely the value of reasoning. Martin Luther King, Jr., in his "I Have a Dream" speech, builds his emotionally effective statement on a foundation of logical reasoning. Logical arguments and emotional appeals are often most effectively used to support each other; the selections included in this book are grouped according to the type of appeal that is dominant.

In addition to the examples that follow, several other selections in this book illustrate the techniques of persuasive writing (see Contents for page numbers):

W. S. Merwin, "Unchopping a Tree"
Isaac Asimov, "Colonizing the Heavens"
Eric Berne, "Can People Be Judged by Their Appearance?"
Maya Pines, "Of Babalawos and Shamans"
Jack Richardson, "Six O'clock Prayers"
Susanne Langer, "The Lord of Creation"
Anne Roiphe, "Confessions of a Female Chauvinist Sow"
Dan Lacy, "Men's Words; Women's Roles"
Philip Wylie, "Science Has Spoiled My Supper"
Henry David Thoreau, "On Owning a Farm"
George Orwell, "Politics and the English Language"
Edmund Wilson, "Americanism"
Sinclair Lewis, "The House of Babbitt"
Herb Caen, "The Plastic Fantastic"
John Steinbeck, "Empty Houses"
H. L. Mencken, "The Libido for the Ugly"
George Orwell, "A Hanging"
Alexander Calandra, "Angels on a Pin"
Samuel Eliot Morison, "The Salem Witchcraft Frenzy"
John Hersey, "A Noiseless Flash"

LOGICAL ARGUMENT

Although logic is a highly specialized and complex discipline, some familiarity with the methods of logic is essential for any writer who hopes to develop sound and convincing arguments. A satisfactory argument is both *true* and *valid;* that is, it is based upon verifiable evidence, and it follows a prescribed pattern of thought. These two considerations will be discussed in some detail.

The truth of an argument depends upon the amount and nature of the **evidence** that is brought to the argument. Working from particular bits of evidence to arrive at a general conclusion is the method called **induction**. In a classic example of induction, Thomas Henry Huxley tells of a man who bit into an apple and found it sour. The man inspected the apple and saw that it was hard and green. He took up another apple and found that it, too, was hard, green, and sour. On the basis of his two experiences with apples that were hard and green, the man reached the generalization that all hard and green apples are sour. Thus, he used the method of induction to work from particulars to a generalization about the taste of hard, green apples. In our everyday lives we use induction without realizing that it is a method of logic, for it seems only common sense.

Knowing something about the nature of apples, Huxley's gentleman was reasonably safe in concluding that if two hard and green apples are sour, then all hard and green apples are sour; and since we have had our own experiences with apples, we are generally willing to agree with his conclusion. The more evidence that one can bring to an argument, however, the more convincing is the generalization. What is known as the **hasty generalization** is the conclusion based upon an insufficient amount of evidence. The generalization that all hard and green *fruit* is sour, for instance, would be a hasty and false generalization.

The amount of evidence that can be considered sufficient will differ according to the specific argument. In the Declaration of Independence, Thomas Jefferson takes pains to enumerate every possible type of injustice committed by George III, so that he can irrefutably prove that George III was tyrannical in his dealings with the American colonies. On the other hand, James Thurber gives evidence from limited observation to support his charges against women. Whether or not this amount of evidence is sufficient is a question that the reader must consider. In any event, the evidence provided must be at least enough to convince the reader that the writer's conclusion is not based primarily on chance or merely personal opinion. Although Huxley's gentleman reached a true conclusion, more than two experiences would have provided a more convincing argument. Yet, obviously, one need not bite into all hard and green apples to be convinced that the conclusion is probably correct. A satisfactory inductive argument is one that is based upon sufficient verifiable evidence and leads to a conclusion that is true. Ideally the evidence should be available to anyone who cares to verify it for himself. If it cannot be verified by everyone, it must at least be verifiable by specialists in the field. Although the **testimony** of experts is not without limitations (since experts are not always in agreement), it is a usfeul device of argumentation.

The deductive method, or **deduction**, is the reverse of induction. It is the application of a general truth—an accepted proposition (such as a generalization reached through inductive reasoning) or a self-evident proposition (such as the truths that are "self-evident," or agreed upon by a large body of people, in the Declaration of Independence)—to an individual case. Let us imagine that Huxley's gentleman is offered another hard, green apple after he has reached his generalization. He will say, "All hard and green apples are sour; this apple is hard and green; therefore, this apple is sour." This set of statements is a **syllogism**: a general statement, called the **major premise**; a particular instance, based upon the general statement, called the **minor premise**; and a **conclusion** based on the preceding statements. A famous example of syllogistic reasoning is the following:

> All men are mortal.
> Socrates is a man.
> Therefore, Socrates is mortal.

The major premise, that all men are mortal, is an acceptable premise because we can establish inductively that all men who have ever lived have also died. There can be no question, either, that Socrates falls within the category of "all men." Hence, it follows that this one particular man will meet the fate of all men.

This syllogism is not only valid (that is, it follows a proper syllogistic form), but its conclusion is also true. It can be supported by the evidence of our senses and of history: we see that men die; we have read that Socrates died. But the conclusions of syllogisms are not always true. A conclusion will be false if both, or even one, of the premises are incorrect:

> All men are women.
> Socrates is a man.
> Therefore, Socrates is a woman.

Although this syllogism is valid, its false major premise leads to a ridiculous conclusion.

Just as valid syllogisms may lead to false conclusions, the conclusion of a syllogism may be unreliable if the minor premise does not follow from the major premise:

> All men are mortal.
> A pig is mortal.
> Therefore, a pig is a man.

In this syllogism, the minor premise does not follow from the major premise —since the major premise does *not* state that "all mortals are men." Therefore, the syllogism is invalid. What has come to be known as **guilt by association** is based upon this form of mistaken logic. For instance:

All Communists oppose the foreign policy of the United States.
Citizen Jones opposes the foreign policy of the United States.
Therefore, Citizen Jones is a Communist.

Again, the minor premise does not follow from the major premise, since the major premise does not state that all who oppose the foreign policy of the United States are Communists. Therefore—even assuming that the premises can be proved, and that the terms "Communist" and "oppose" are clear and unequivocal—the syllogism is invalid, and the line of reasoning does not establish the truth of the conclusion.

In addition to the misuses of logical methods already discussed, one widespread fallacy in particular deserves special attention. Hardly any discussion between opposing political parties fails to make the point (that is, the Republicans never fail to make the point) that every Democratic administration in recent history has been accompanied by war. The facts are present to support the statement. But what logical conclusion can be drawn? The Republican implies that war has followed as a result of the Democratic administration. He has oversimplified the cause-effect inductive relationship in the form of a fallacy known as *post hoc ergo propter hoc* ("after that; therefore, because of that")—usually shortened to "the *post hoc* fallacy." He has failed to consider *all* of the possible causes—world situations over which the government had no possible control—and has created a chronological rather than a logical line of reasoning. It is true that war followed the Democratic administrations; it is not necessarily true that it came as a direct result of the political party in power. Superstitions are generally the result of *post hoc* reasoning. Perhaps someone who had moles on his back did have money by the sack. The relationship between the two facts, however, is by no means clear. In all likelihood many a well-moled back has found its final resting place in a pauper's grave.

The **non sequitur** ("it does not follow") is also a spurious form of logical argument based upon a false cause-effect relationship. If we know of people who wear long hair, sandals, and outlandish clothes and receive low marks in school, we are perhaps inclined to believe that there is a relationship between their dress and their performance in school. It should follow, then, that if they dress more conservatively and have their hair cut, their grades will improve. But experience proves that the relationship between grades and dress is incidental, not causal. It would be a *non sequitur* to say, "She dresses very strangely; she must get poor grades." Unusual garb and low grades both may result from a defiant or nonconformist attitude, but they are not causally related.

In the Declaration of Independence Jefferson carefully guarded against another error in logic by avoiding arguments *ad hominem*—attacking the opponent personally rather than restricting the argument to the subject under discussion. George III is regarded only in his titular role as king, not as a person. Shaw's Devil, on the other hand, is not above such methods of argument —as when he speaks of the Italian poet Dante (though not by name) as an "ass" because of his characterization of Satan in his *Inferno*. Although the Devil's—or Shaw's—methods are effective with an audience predisposed to agree with him, they are not always those we associate with irrefutable logic. Jefferson's inevitable logic was directed to "mankind" to convince it of the validity of his arguments; it was a public statement to king and colonist alike, not an appeal to men who already agreed with Jefferson.

Another method of argumentation is the **analogy**. Analogy is useful as a method of exposition, for it helps us to understand what is complex by seeing it related to something simple or familiar. In argumentation, however, it is used to lead to a conclusion on the basis of similarities. It can be argued that since A is true, and since B is like A, B is also true. But analogy is frequently misused as a method of argument, for few objects or ideas are the same except in somewhat superficial ways. In his essay "Darwin's Mistake," Tom Bethell points out that Darwin's famous theory of evolution was based upon a fallacious analogy—that the artifical breeding for desirable characteristics in animals is a process that also occurs in nature—and that present scientific thought has undermined the basis of Darwin's theory of natural selection. The **false analogy** which is based upon a false contention, leads to an unreliable conclusion. On the other hand, Thoreau, who argues that the purpose of government is to permit men to "succeed in letting one another alone," draws an analogy between legislators who regulate trade and commerce and revolutionists who block railroads—both of whom intrude on the rights of the individual. Given the purpose of government advanced by Thoreau, the analogy is a clear and convincing one. In order to be effective, analogical arguments must be based upon numerous and significant similarities.

This discussion of logical arguments has been concerned primarily with an explanation of the methods of logic and with some of the possible misuses of the methods. Much of what has been said is as applicable to you in your role as writer as in your role as reader. In presenting your own arguments, as well as in evaluating the arguments of others, you will need to consider both form and content. Every effective argument is based upon sufficient evidence stated in correct form. **Assertions** are not evidence. As a human being you have every right to an opinion, but you have no right to expect to convince others you are right simply because you voice what you believe. Perhaps the furtive behavior of one of your classmates during an examination period leads you to suspect that he is cheating. If you say, "I think he is a cheater," you are making an assertion. But if you see him pull a small piece of paper from inside his shoe, open his book when the instructor is not looking, and read what his neighbor has written, you have found some evidence that presents an effective argument. If you define a cheater as an individual who behaves dishonestly on examinations, and if you can prove that this person has behaved dishonestly on an examination, the deductive conclusion is that he is a cheater. Your argument that makes use of verifiable evidence for believing as you do will convince others; unsupported assertions will generally carry very little weight.

In presenting any argument you will do well to assume that the audience does not agree with you. You must state your argument fully, offering well-considered evidence for each major issue of the argument. You must consider the opposing arguments and answer them or, if they cannot be answered, concede them and proceed to demonstrate that your arguments are stronger.

Each of the authors of the following selections has his own point to prove: Thurber, that he hates women; Claiborne, that the denunciation of "Wasps" is not based upon facts; Jefferson, that the United States should not continue its alliance with Great Britain; Thoreau, that the best citizen is one who follows his conscience; and Emerson, that thoughtful persons should not be dominated by the past. You will be asked to analyze the effectiveness of the arguments that the writers provide. You will be able to strengthen your own argumentative writing by using the best of their methods, and you will be able to see where some of their arguments are weakened by insufficient evidence or invalid reasoning.

James Thurber

THE CASE AGAINST WOMEN

With the publication of his first book, Is Sex Necessary? *(1929), which he wrote in collaboration with E. B. White, James Thurber (1894–1961) established himself as a leading American humorist. In the pages of* The New Yorker *magazine, for which he was a staff writer for several years, he published numerous short stories, fables, cartoons, and essays, later collecting the best of them in many volumes. Like all important humorists, he viewed the language and situations of humor as media in which to couch serious observations. The unhappy lot of the American male faced with a domineering wife was one of his favorite topics.*

Copyright © 1937 James Thurber. Copyright © 1965 Helen W. Thurber and Rosemary Thurber Sauers. From *Let Your Mind Alone*, published by Harper & Row, Publishers, Inc. Originally printed in *The New Yorker*.

LOGICAL ARGUMENT

[1] A bright-eyed woman, whose sparkle was rather more of eagerness than of intelligence, approached me at a party one afternoon and said, "Why do you hate women, Mr. Thurberg?" I quickly adjusted my fixed grin and denied that I hated women; I said I did not hate women at all. But the question remained with me, and I discovered when I went to bed that night that I had been subconsciously listing a number of reasons I do hate women. It might be interesting—at least it will help pass the time—to set down these reasons, just as they came up out of my subconscious.

[2] In the first place, I hate women because they always know where things are. At first blush, you might think that a perverse and merely churlish reason for hating women, but it is not. Naturally, every man enjoys having a woman around the house who knows where his shirt studs and his briefcase are, and things like that, but he detests having a woman around who knows where *everything* is, even things that are of no importance at all, such as, say, the snapshots her husband took three years ago at Elbow Beach. The husband has never known where these snapshots were since the day they were developed and printed; he hopes, in a vague way, if he thinks about them at all, that after three years they have been thrown out. But his wife knows where they are, and so do his mother, his grandmother, his great-grandmother, his daughter, and the maid. They could put their fingers on them in a moment, with that quiet air of superior knowledge which makes a man feel that he is out of touch with all the things that count in life.

[3] A man's interest in old snapshots, unless they are snapshots of himself in action with a gun, a fishing rod, or a tennis racquet, languishes in about two hours. A woman's interest in old snapshots, particularly of groups of people, never languishes; it is always there, as the years roll on, as strong and vivid as it was right at the start. She remembers the snapshots when people come to call, and just as the husband, having mixed drinks for everybody, sits down to sip his own, she will say, "George, I wish you would go and get those snapshots we took at Elbow Beach and show them to the Murphys." The husband, as I have said, doesn't know where the snapshots are; all he knows is that Harry Murphy doesn't want to see them; Harry Murphy wants to talk, just as he himself wants to talk. But Grace Murphy says that she wants to see the pictures; she is crazy to see the pictures; for one thing, the wife, who has brought the subject up, wants Mrs. Murphy to see the photo of a certain costume that the wife wore at Elbow Beach in 1933. The husband finally puts down his drink and snarls, "Well, where are they, then?" The wife, depending on her mood, gives him either the look she reserves for spoiled children or the one she reserves for drunken workmen, and tells him he knows perfectly well where they are. It turns out, after a lot of give and take, the slightly bitter

edge of which is covered by forced laughs, that the snapshots are in the upper right-hand drawer of a certain desk, and the husband goes out of the room to get them. He comes back in three minutes with the news that the snapshots are not in the upper right-hand drawer of the certain desk. Without stirring from her chair, the wife favors her husband with a faint smile (the one that annoys him most of all her smiles) and reiterates that the snapshots *are* in the upper right-hand drawer of the desk. He simply didn't look, that's all. The husband knows that he looked; he knows that he prodded and dug and excavated in that drawer and that the snapshots simply are not there. The wife tells him to go look again and he will find them. The husband goes back and looks again—the guests can hear him growling and cursing and rattling papers. Then he shouts out from the next room. "They are *not* in this *drawer*, just as I told you, Ruth!" The wife quietly excuses herself and leaves the guests and goes into the room where her husband stands, hot, miserable, and defiant—and with a certain nameless fear in his heart. He has pulled the desk drawer out so far that it is about to fall on the floor, and he points at the disarray of the drawer with bitter triumph (still mixed with that nameless fear). "Look for yourself!" he snarls. The wife does not look. She says with quiet coldness, "What is that you have in your hand?" What he has in his hand turns out to be an insurance policy and an old bankbook—and the snapshots. The wife gets off the old line about what it would have done if it had been a snake, and the husband is upset for the rest of the evening; in some cases he cannot keep anything on his stomach for twenty-four hours.

[4] Another reason I hate women (and I am speaking, I believe, for the American male generally) is that in almost every case where there is a sign reading "Please have exact change ready," a woman never has anything smaller than a ten-dollar bill. She gives ten-dollar bills to bus conductors and change men in subways and other such persons who deal in nickels and dimes and quarters. Recently, in Bermuda, I saw a woman hand the conductor on the little railway there a bill of such huge denomination that I was utterly unfamiliar with it. I was sitting too far away to see exactly what it was, but I had the feeling that it was a five-hundred-dollar bill. The conductor merely ignored it and stood there waiting—the fare was just one shilling. Eventually, scrabbling around in her handbag, the woman found a shilling. All the men on the train who witnessed the transaction tightened up inside; that's what a woman with a ten-dollar bill or a twenty or a five-hundred does to a man in such situations —she tightens him up inside. The episode gives him the feeling that some monstrous triviality is threatening the whole structure of civilization. It is difficult to analyze this feeling, but there it is.

[5] Another spectacle that depresses the male and makes him fear women,

and therefore hate them, is that of a woman looking another woman up and down, to see what she is wearing. The cold, flat look that comes into a woman's eyes when she does this, the swift coarsening of her countenance, and the immediate evaporation from it of all humane quality make the male shudder. He is likely to go to his stateroom or his den or his private office and lock himself in for hours. I know one man who surprised that look in his wife's eyes and never afterward would let her come near him. If she started toward him, he would dodge behind a table or a sofa, as if he were engaging in some unholy game of tag. That look, I believe, is one reason men disappear, and turn up in Tahiti or the Arctic or the United States Navy.

[6] I (to quit hiding behind the generalization of "the male") hate women because they almost never get anything exactly right. They say, "I have been faithful to thee, Cynara, after my fashion" instead of "in my fashion." They will bet you that Alfred Smith's middle name is Aloysius, instead of Emanuel. They will tell you to take the 2:57 train, on a day that the 2:57 does not run, or, if it does run, does not stop at the station where you are supposed to get off. Many men, separated from a woman by this particular form of imprecision, have never showed up in her life again. Nothing so embitters a man as to end up in Bridgeport when he was supposed to get off at Westport.

[7] I hate women because they have brought into the currency of our language such expressions as "all righty" and "yes indeedy" and hundreds of others. I hate women because they throw baseballs (or plates or vases) with the wrong foot advanced. I marvel that more of them have not broken their backs. I marvel that women, who coordinate so well in languorous motion, look uglier and sillier than a goose-stepper when they attempt any form of violent activity.

[8] I had a lot of other notes jotted down about why I hate women, but I seem to have lost them all, except one. That one is to the effect that I hate women because, while they never lose old snapshots or anything of that sort, they invariably lose one glove. I believe that I have never gone anywhere with any woman in my whole life who did not lose one glove. I have searched for single gloves under tables in crowded restaurants and under the feet of people in darkened movie theatres. I have spent some part of every day or night hunting for a woman's glove. If there were no other reason in the world for hating women, that one would be enough. In fact, you can leave all the others out.

VOCABULARY

Define the following words as they are used in the selection: *fixed, subconsciously* [1]; *blush, perverse, churlish* [2]; *languishes, reiterates* [3]; *spectacle, coarsening, countenance, unholy* [5]; *currency* [7].

QUESTIONS FOR STUDY AND DISCUSSION

1. Although Thurber's humorous essay has the obvious purpose of listing the reasons he personally hates women, the title of the selection suggests that his broader purpose is to make an indictment against women in general. Assuming for the purposes of discussion and analysis that he is serious, do you think that his arguments are effective? Are they based upon sufficient evidence?

2. Thurber gives seven reasons for hating women. List them in sentence form.

3. Thurber admits that the first reason, which is the most fully developed one in the essay, initially seems to be a little consequence. But how does a woman's knowledge of where everything is reflect on the man? How does it make him appear to other people? What is the "certain nameless fear" that Thurber describes in paragraph 3?

4. Fear is also at the basis of the reason discussed in paragraph 4. Thurber says that he is unable to analyze the feeling, but it seems to stem from a threat to the whole structure of civilization. In what way could such an apparently trivial characteristic of women have such significant implications?

5. In paragraph 5 Thurber again says that fear is the direct result in men of another characteristic of women. Are the exaggerated responses Thurber describes effective in showing the importance of this characteristic of women? Explain your answer.

6. The next three reasons, in paragraphs 6 and 7, have more than trivial implications. What areas of human existence are threatened by the characteristics described here?

7. The final reason, Thurber says, is the most important one. Why? What is the effect, other than annoyance and inconvenience, on the man?

8. In summary, how do the reasons Thurber gives suggest that women destroy a man's image of himself, the sense of order, harmony, and beauty that he wishes to believe are present in the world, and his enjoyment of simple pleasures?

9. Although Thurber employs the methods of enumeration and example rather than logical process, there is an implicit syllogism in each of the reasons he discusses. For instance, in paragraphs 2 and 3, the major premise is that men hate people who reveal them to be inadequate. The minor premise is that women do

make men appear inadequate. Hence, men hate women. Set up syllogisms based on the other reasons.

10. What qualities of the woman who asked Thurber the question in paragraph 1 can be related to the reasons developed in the essay?

11. The quotation in paragraph 6 is from the poem "Non Sum Qualis Eram Bonæ Sub Regno Cynaræ" (I Am Not What Once I Was in Kind Cynara's Day") by Ernest Dowson, a nineteenth-century poet. The speaker in the poem confesses an act of infidelity while remaining true "in my fashion" to Cynara. Why is the quotation a particularly apt one in the essay?

Robert Claiborne

A WASP STINGS BACK

> *Robert Claiborne (b. 1919) started college as a chemistry student but switched to journalism. Since 1957 he has combined scientific and literary interests, editing such journals as* Scientific American *and* Medical World News *and contributing articles to* The Nation, Harper's, *and* Newsweek. *Appointed editor of the* Life Science Library *in 1964, he contributed as collaborator on two books in that series,* Time *and* Drugs. *Free-lancing since 1965, Claiborne has produced two books*: Climate, Man, and History *(1970) and* God or Beast: Evolution and Human Nature *(1974).*

[1]   Over the past few years, American pop culture has acquired a new folk antihero: the Wasp. One slick magazine tells us that the White Anglo-Saxon Protestants rule New York City, while other media gurus credit (or discredit) them with ruling the country—and, by inference, ruining it. A Polish-American declares in a leading newspaper that Wasps have "no sense of honor." *Newsweek* patronizingly describes Chautauqua as a citadel of "Wasp values," while other folklorists characterize these values more explicitly as a compulsive commitment to the work ethic, emotional uptightness and sexual inhibition. The Wasps, in fact, are rapidly becoming the one minority that every other ethnic group—blacks, Italians, chicanos, Jews, Poles and all the rest—feels absolutely free to dump on. I have not yet had a friend greet me with "Did you hear the one about the two Wasps who . . . ?"—but any day now!

[2]   I come of a long line of Wasps; if you disregard my French great-great-grandmother and a couple of putatively Irish ancestors of the same vintage, a

From *Newsweek*, September 30, 1974. Copyright 1974 by Newsweek, Inc. All rights reserved. Reprinted by permission.

rather pure line. My mother has long been one of the Colonial Dames, an organization some of whose members consider the Daughters of the American Revolution rather parvenu. My umpty-umpth Wasp great-grandfather, William Claiborne, founded the first European settlement in what is now Maryland (his farm and trading post were later ripped off by the Catholic Lord Baltimore, Maryland politics being much the same then as now).

[3] As a Wasp, the mildest thing I can say about the stereotype emerging from the current wave of anti-Wasp chic is that I don't recognize myself. As regards emotional uptightness and sexual inhibition, modesty forbids comment—though I dare say various friends and lovers of mine could testify on these points if they cared to. I will admit to enjoying work—because I am lucky enough to be able to work at what I enjoy—but not, I think, to the point of compulsiveness. And so far as ruling America, or even New York, is concerned, I can say flatly that (a) it's a damn lie because (b) if I *did* rule them, both would be in better shape than they are. Indeed I and all my Wasp relatives, taken in a lump, have far less clout with the powers that run this country than any one of the Buckleys or Kennedys (Irish Catholic), the Sulzbergers or Guggenheims (Jewish), or the late A. P. Giannini (Italian) of the Bank of America.

[4] Admittedly, both corporate and (to a lesser extent) political America are dominated by Wasps—just as (let us say) the garment industry is dominated by Jews, and organized crime by Italians. But to conclude from this that The Wasps are the American elite is as silly as to say that The Jews are cloak-and-suiters or The Italians are gangsters. Wasps, like other ethnics, come in all varieties, including criminals—political, corporate and otherwise.

[5] More seriously, I would like to say a word for the maligned "Wasp values," one of them in particular. As a matter of historical fact, it was we Wasps—by which I mean here the English-speaking peoples—who invented the idea of *limited governments*: that there are some things that no king, President or other official is allowed to do. It began more than seven centuries ago, with Magna Carta, and continued (to cite only the high spots) through the wrangles between Parliament and the Stuart kings, the Puritan Revolution of 1640, the English Bill of Rights of 1688, the American Revolution and our own Bill of Rights and Constitution.

[6] The Wasp principle of limited government emerged through protracted struggle with the much older principle of unlimited government. This latter was never more cogently expressed than at the trial of Charles I, when the

hapless monarch informed his judges that, as an anointed king, he was not accountable to any court in the land. A not dissimilar position was taken more recently by another Wasp head of state—and with no more success; Executive privilege went over no better in 1974 than divine right did in 1649. The notion that a king, a President or any other official can do as he damn well pleases has never played in Peoria—or Liverpool or Glasgow, Melbourne or Toronto. For more than 300 years, no Wasp nation has endured an absolute monarchy, dictatorship or any other form of unlimited government—which is something no Frenchman, Italian, German, Pole, Russian or Hispanic can say.

[7] It is perfectly true, of course, that we Wasps have on occasion imposed unlimited governments on other (usually darker) peoples. We have, that is, acted in much the same way as have most other nations that possessed the requisite power and opportunity—including many Third World nations whose leaders delight in lecturing us on political morality (for recent information on this point, consult the files on Biafra, Bangladesh and Brazil, Indian tribes of). Yet even here, Wasp values have played an honorable part. When you start with the idea that Englishmen are entitled to self-government, you end by conceding the same right to Africans and Indians. If you begin by declaring that all (white) men are created equal, you must sooner or later face up to the fact that blacks are also men—and conform your conduct, however reluctantly, to your values.

[8] Keeping the Wasp faith hasn't always been easy. We Wasps, like other people, don't always live up to our own principles, and those of us who don't, if occupying positions of power, can pose formidabe problems to the rest of us. Time after time, in the name of anti-Communism, peace with honor or some other slippery shibboleth, we have been conned or bullied into tolerating government interference with our liberties and privacy in all sorts of covert—and sometimes overt—ways; time after time we have had to relearn the lesson that eternal vigilance is the price of liberty.

[9] It was a Wasp who uttered that last thought. And it was a congress of Wasps who, about the same time, denounced the executive privileges of George III and committed to the cause of liberty their lives, their fortunes and—*pace* my Polish-American compatriot—their sacred honor.

VOCABULARY

Define the following words as they are used in the selection: *gurus* [1]; *putatively, parvenu* [2]; *chic, clout* [3]; *elite* [4]; *maligned* [5]; *cogently, hap-*

less [6]; *shibboleth* [8]. The word *pace* [9] is printed in italics, indicating that it is not an English word; does your dictionary help to define it? (Does your dictionary define the phrase *Requiescat in pace?*)

QUESTIONS FOR STUDY AND DISCUSSION

1. Claiborne's essay, as its title suggests, is a counterattack. He tries to show that denunciations of White Anglo-Saxon Protestants, like denunciations of other ethnic groups, rest upon fallacies. What specific attacks upon Wasps does he cite in paragraph 1?

2. What is the basic fallacy, according to Claiborne (see paragraph 3), of the popular charges against Wasps? (See pp. 257–259 for a discussion of false reasoning.)

3. In paragraph 4 Claiborne develops an argument in almost syllogistic statements, trying to show that such an argument is fallacious. Can you put that argument into full syllogistic form with major premise, minor premise, and conclusion? What is the fallacy in the argument?

4. Why does Claiborne use the phrase "More seriously . . ." to begin paragraph 5? Does he mean that his arguments up to that point have not been serious?

5. Beginning with paragraph 5, Claiborne turns to the contribution of Wasps to the world's recognition of human rights. What is the central contribution that he cites?

6. Claiborne uses contemporary allusions in paragraph 2 ("Maryland politics being much the same then as now") and paragraph 6 ("Executive privilege went over no better in 1974 than divine right did in 1649"). To what persons and events of *now* and *1974* does he allude? What do these allusions and the many other references to specific dates (1640, 1688, the Magna Carta) contribute to the essay?

7. Claiborne admits (paragraph 7) that Wasps on occasion have not fostered human rights but have "acted in much the same way as have most other nations that possessed the requisite power and opportunity." Is his argument—that Wasps, when not true to principles, were no worse than others—a logical argument or an emotional one?

8. To whom does Claiborne refer as "my Polish-American compatriot" (paragraph 9)? How does that phrase help the over-all structure of the essay?

9. "What we need is a mixed diction," said Aristotle. Sheridan Baker, an American professor, agrees: "What we need is a diction that marries the popular with the dignified, the clear current with the sedgy margins of language and thought." Does the Claiborne article live up to that requirement for diction? Make a brief list of words from his essay to show that Claiborne mixes formal words with slang.

10. "The notion that a king, a President or any other official can do as he damn well pleases has never *played* in Peoria," says Claiborne. What does *played* mean in that context? And what does *Peoria* mean? Does it suggest more than a city in Illinois?

11. Why does Claiborne list the cities of Peoria, Liverpool, Glasgow, Melbourne, and Toronto? Why would Berlin, Paris, and Rome not have fit into the list for Claiborne's purpose?

12. Says Claiborne in paragraph 6, "For more than 300 years, no Wasp nation has endured an absolute monarchy, dictatorship or any other form of unlimited government—which is something no Frenchman, Italian, German, Pole, Russian or Hispanic can say." Is he right? What is the purpose of that statement in the essay? Does the statement help to make a valid point in his counterattack upon those who feel "absolutely free to dump on" Wasps?

Thomas Jefferson

THE DECLARATION OF INDEPENDENCE

On July 4, 1776, the Continental Congress adopted "The Unanimous Declaration of the Thirteen United States of America," whereby the United Colonies of America declared themselves to be "Free and Independent States." The composition of the Declaration was principally the work of Thomas Jefferson (1743–1826), though the rough draft bears emendations in the handwriting of John Adams and Benjamin Franklin. These three men, with Roger Sherman and Robert Livingston, constituted a committee to draw up the Declaration. The present text follows the form of the Parchment Copy, which was signed on August 2 by the delegates of the Congress.

[1] When in the Course of human events, it becomes necessary for one people to dissolve the political bands which have connected them with another, and to assume among the powers of the earth, the separate and equal station to which the Laws of Nature and of Nature's God entitle them, a decent respect to the opinions of mankind requires that they should declare the causes which impel them to the separation.—We hold these truths to be self-evident, that all men are created equal, that they are endowed by their Creator with certain unalienable Rights, that among these are Life, Liberty, and the pursuit of Happiness.—That to secure these rights, Governments are instituted among Men, deriving their just powers from the consent of the gov-

erned,—That whenever any Form of Government becomes destructive of these ends, it is the Right of the People to alter or to abolish it, and to institute new Government, laying its foundation on such principles and organizing its powers in such form, as to them shall seem most likely to effect their Safety and Happiness. Prudence, indeed, will dictate that Governments long established should not be changed for light and transient causes; and accordingly all experience hath shewn, that mankind are more disposed to suffer, while evils are sufferable, than to right themselves by abolishing the forms to which they are accustomed. But when a long train of abuses and usurpations, pursuing invariably the same Object evinces a design to reduce them under absolute Despotism, it is their right, it is their duty, to throw off such Government, and to provide Guards for their future security.—Such has been the patient sufferance of these Colonies; and such is now the necessity which constrains them to alter their former Systems of Government. The history of the present King of Great Britain is a history of repeated injuries and usurpations, all having in direct object the establishment of an absolute Tyranny over these States. To prove this, let Facts be submitted to a candid world.—He has refused his Assent to Laws, the most wholesome and necessary to the public good.—He has forbidden his Governors to pass Laws of immediate and pressing importance, unless suspended in their operation till his Assent should be obtained; and when so suspended, he has utterly neglected to attend to them. —He has refused to pass other Laws for the accommodation of large districts of people, unless those people would relinquish the right of Representation in the Legislature, a right inestimable to them and formidable to tyrants only.— He has called together legislative bodies at places unusual, uncomfortable, and distant from the depository of their public Records, for the sole purpose of fatiguing them into compliance with his measures.—He has dissolved Representative Houses repeatedly, for opposing with manly firmness his invasions on the right of the people.—He has refused for a long time, after such dissolutions, to cause others to be elected; whereby the Legislative powers, incapable of Annihilation, have returned to the People at large for their exercise; the State remaining in the mean time exposed to all the dangers of invasion from without, and convulsions within.—He has endeavoured to prevent the population of these States; for that purpose obstructing the Laws for Naturalization of Foreigners; refusing to pass others to encourage their migrations hither, and raising the conditions of new Appropriations of Lands.—He has obstructed the Administration of Justice, by refusing his Assent to Laws for establishing Judiciary powers.—He has made Judges dependent on his Will alone, for the tenure of their offices, and the amount and payment of their salaries.—He has erected a multitude of New Offices, and sent hither swarms of Officers to harass our people, and eat out their substance.—He has kept among us, in times of peace, Standing Armies without the Consent of our legislatures.—He has affected to render the Military independent of and superior to the Civil power.—He has combined with others to subject us to a jurisdiction foreign to our constitution, and unacknowledged by our laws; giving his Assent to their Acts of pretended Legislation:—For quartering large bodies of armed troops among us:—For protecting them, by a mock Trial, from punishment for any Murders which they should commit on the Inhabitants of these States:—For cutting off our Trade with all parts of the world:—For imposing Taxes on us without our Consent:—For depriving us in many cases, of the benefits of Trial by Jury:—For transporting us beyond Seas to be tried for pretended offences:—For abolishing the free System of English Laws in a neighbouring Province, establishing therein an Arbitrary government, and enlarging its Boundaries so as to render it at once an example and fit instrument for introducing the same absolute rule into these Colonies:—For taking away our Charters, abolishing our most valuable Laws, and altering fundamentally the Forms of our Governments:—For suspending our own Legislatures, and declaring themselves invested with power to legislate for us in all cases whatsoever.—He has abdicated Government here, by declaring us out of his Protection and waging War against us.—He has plundered our seas, ravaged our Coasts, burnt our towns, and destroyed the lives of our people.—He is at this time transporting large Armies of foreign Mercenaries to complete the works of death, desolation and tyranny, already begun with circumstances of Cruelty & perfidy scarcely paralleled in the most barbarous ages, and totally unworthy the Head of a civilized nation.—He has constrained our fellow Citizens taken Captive on the high Seas to bear Arms against their Country, to become the executioners of their friends and Brethren, or to fall themselves by their Hands.—He has excited domestic insurrections amongst us, and has endeavoured to bring on the inhabitants of our frontiers, the merciless Indian Savages, whose known rule of warfare, is an undistinguished destruction of all ages, sexes and conditions. In every stage of these Oppressions We have Petitioned for Redress in the most humble terms. Our repeated Petitions have been answered only by repeated injury. A Prince, whose character is thus marked by every act which may define a Tyrant, is unfit to be the ruler of a free people. Nor have We been wanting in attentions to our British brethren. We have warned them from time to time of attempts by their legislature to extend an unwarrantable jurisdiction over us. We have reminded them of the circumstances of our emigration and settlement here. We have appealed to their native justice and magnanimity, and we have conjured them by the ties of our common kindred to disavow these usurpations, which would inevitably interrupt our connections and correspondence. They too have been deaf to the voice of justice and of consanguinity. We must, therefore, acquiesce in the necessity, which denounces our Separation, and hold them, as we hold the rest of mankind, Enemies in War, in Peace Friends.—

[2] We, therefore, the Representatives of the united States of America, in General Congress, Assembled, appealing to the Supreme Judge of the world for the rectitude of our intentions, do, in the Name, and by the Authority of the good People of these Colonies, solemnly publish and declare, That these United Colonies are, and of Right ought to be Free and Independent States; that they are Absolved from all Allegiance to the British Crown, and that all political connection between them and the State of Great Britain, is and ought to be totally dissolved; and that as Free and Independent States, they have full Power to levy War, conclude Peace, contract Alliances, establish Commerce, and to do all other Acts and Things which Independent States may of right do.—And for the support of this Declaration, with a firm reliance on the protection of divine Providence, we mutually pledge to each other our Lives, our Fortunes, and our sacred Honor.

VOCABULARY

Define the following words as they are used in the selection: *unalienable, prudence, transient, usurpations, evinces, formidable, harass, perfidy, constrained, magnanimity, conjured, consanguinity, acquiesce* [1]; *rectitude, absolved* [2].

QUESTIONS FOR STUDY AND DISCUSSION

1. The basic organization of the Declaration of Independence is syllogistic and therefore divides into three principal sections. The first sets forth the major premise—the truths that are self-evident: government is formed by men to preserve certain rights and may be abolished if it does not preserve those rights. In other words, tyrants should be deposed. The minor premise establishes that King George III is a tyrant. The conclusion is obvious. Set up this syllogism in conventional form. Indicate in the Declaration where the divisions occur.

2. The major premise of the syllogism speaks of self-evident truths. Should Jefferson have attempted to prove them? Are these truths self-evident to all men in all times, or are they self-evident in that they are the ideals of the founding fathers and still, supposedly, of the American people? Is the language in which these truths are couched of a type to invite dispute? Does it carry conviction?

3. The major premise is based upon the social-compact theory of John Locke, which holds that men relinquish certain rights (such as the right of self-help, a part of their natural liberty) in return for the protection by government of the greater rights of life, liberty, and the security of property. Does the argument of some historians that man has never existed except in some form of society which defined his individual rights materially weaken the major premise?

4. John Locke, in his treatise *Of Civil Government* (1690), defines tyranny as "the exercise of power beyond right." Jefferson does not use Locke's phrase, but he does imply the definition of a tyrant. Where?

5. The second part of the Declaration is an overwhelming enumeration of instances of "the exercise of power beyond right." Naturally they are chosen as examples of the king's tyranny, but the Declaration is so phrased in places that the efforts of the colonists are by implication placed in the best possible light. At the time, the British regarded the founding fathers as despicable rebels against authority, but Jefferson speaks of their "manly firmness," thereby further slanting the Declaration for the colonists and against the king. What other examples of such phrases can you point out?

6. Each charge against the king begins "He has . . ." Jefferson obviously knew that he was violating a rhetorical principle in not varying the sentence structure or the sentence length. What justification for this deliberately extensive parallelism can you suggest? How does the very form of the charges against the king help to build the case against him?

7. Contrast the language and tone of the list of grievances with the language and tone of the three sentences beginning "Prudence, indeed"; "But when a long train of abuses"; and "Such has been the patient sufferance." What contrast between the colonists and their ruler do the language and tone suggest? What adjectives can be used to describe the attitude of the colonists?

8. Parliament, of course, as well as the king, contributed to the grievances of the colonists. Why is Parliament all but ignored in the Declaration? What reference is made to it? How would an attack upon it confuse the syllogism on which the Declaration is based?

9. What further justification for the breaking away from England does Jefferson offer at the end of paragraph 1 (section beginning "In every stage of these Oppressions")? Does this section of the Declaration contribute to the contrast referred to in question 7? How?

10. To what is the over-all appeal of the Declaration addressed—the mind or the heart, or both? If you feel that the appeal is to both the mind and the heart, to which aspects of it does the mind respond, and to which ones the heart?

11. Comment on the following statement by Carl L. Becker:

The closing sentence . . . is perfection itself. Congress amended the sentence by including the phrase, "with a firm reliance upon the protection of divine Providence." It may be that Providence always welcomes the responsibilities thrust upon it in times of war and revolution; but personally, I like the sentence better as Jefferson wrote it. "And for the support of this Declaration we mutually pledge to each other our lives, our fortunes, and our sacred honor." It is true (assuming that men value life more than property, which is doubtful) that the statement violates the rhetorical rule of climax; but it was a sure sense that made Jefferson place 'lives' first and 'fortunes' second. How much weaker if he had written "our fortunes, our lives, and our sacred honor"! Or suppose him to have used the word 'property' instead of 'fortunes'! Or suppose him to have omitted 'sacred'! Consider the effect of omitting any of the words, such as the last two 'ours'—

"our lives, fortunes, and sacred honor." No, the sentence can hardly be improved.*

Henry David Thoreau

GOVERNMENT AND THE MORAL SENSE

Henry David Thoreau's famous essay "Civil Disobedience" first appeared under the title "Resistance to Civil Government" in an 1849 anthology, Aesthetic Papers, published in Boston. A passionately democratic essay, it argues that when government, an instrument of the people, responds to majority pressure and infringes upon the freedom of thought and moral action of the individual or the minority, the individual or minority must take the course of passive resistance, or "civil disobedience." Through the essay Thoreau (1817–1862) influenced Mahatma Gandhi and the cause of independence in India, as well as Martin Luther King, Jr., and the cause of racial equality in the United States. The following selection comprises the opening paragraphs of the essay. The motto quoted was that of the United States Magazine and Democratic Review, a literary-political periodical of Thoreau's time.

[1] I heartily accept the motto, "That government is best which governs least"; and I should like to see it acted up to more rapidly and systematically. Carried out, it finally amounts to this, which also I believe—"That government is best which governs not at all"; and when men are prepared for it, that will be the kind of government which they will have. Government is at best but an expedient; but most governments are usually, and all governments are sometimes, inexpedient. The objections which have been brought against a standing army, and they are many and weighty, and deserve to prevail, may also at last be brought against a standing government. The government itself, which is only the mode which the people have chosen to execute their will, is equally liable to be abused and perverted before the people can act through it. Witness the present Mexican war, the work of comparatively a few individuals using the standing government as their tool; for, in the outset, the people would not have consented to this measure.

* Carl Becker, The Declaration of Independence: A Study in the History of Political Ideas (New York: Peter Smith, 1933), p. 197.

[2] This American government—what is it but a tradition, though a recent one, endeavoring to transmit itself unimpaired to posterity, but each instant losing some of its integrity? It has not the vitality and force of a single living man; for a single man can bend it to his will. It is a sort of wooden gun to the people themselves. But it is not the less necessary for this; for the people must have some complicated machinery or other, and hear its din, to satisfy that idea of government which they have. Governments show thus how successfully men can be imposed on, even impose on themselves, for their own advantage. It is excellent, we must all allow. Yet this government never of itself furthered any enterprise, but by the alacrity with which it got out of its way. *It* does not keep the country free. *It* does not settle the West. *It* does not educate. The character inherent in the American people has done all that has been accomplished; and it would have done somewhat more, if the government had not got in its way. For government is an expedient by which men would fain succeed in letting one another alone; and, as has been said, when it is most expedient, the governed are most let alone by it. Trade and commerce, if they were not made of india-rubber, would never manage to bounce over the obstacles which legislators are continually putting in their way; and, if one were to judge these men wholly by the effects of their actions and not partly by their intentions, they would deserve to be classed and punished with those mischievous persons who put obstructions on the railroads.

[3] But, to speak practically and as a citizen, unlike those who call themselves no-government men, I ask for, not at once no government, but *at once* a better government. Let every man make known what kind of government would command his respect, and that will be one step toward obtaining it.

[4] After all, the practical reason why, when the power is once in the hands of the people, a majority are permitted, and for a long period continue, to rule is not because they are most likely to be in the right, nor because this seems fairest to the minority, but because they are physically the strongest. But a government in which the majority rule in all cases cannot be based on justice, even as far as men understand it. Can there not be a government in which majorities do not virtually decide right and wrong, but conscience?—in which majorities decide only those questions to which the rule of expediency is applicable? Must the citizen ever for a moment, or in the least degree, resign his conscience to the legislator? Why has every man a conscience, then? I think that we should be men first, and subjects afterward. It is not desirable to cultivate a respect for the law, so much as for the right. The only obligation which I have a right to assume is to do at any time what I think right. It is truly enough said that a corporation has no conscience; but a corporation of conscientious men is a corporation *with* a conscience. Law never made men

a whit more just; and, by means of their respect for it, even the well-disposed are daily made the agents of injustice. A common and natural result of an undue respect for law is, that you may see a file of soldiers, colonel, captain, corporal, privates, powder-monkeys, and all, marching in admirable order over hill and dale to the wars, against their wills, ay, against their common sense and consciences, which makes it very steep marching indeed, and produces a palpitation of the heart. They have no doubt that it is a damnable business in which they are concerned; they are all peaceably inclined. Now, what are they? Men at all? or small movable forts and magazines, at the service of some unscrupulous man in power? Visit the Navy Yard, and behold a marine, such a man as an American government can make, or such as it can make a man with its black arts—a mere shadow and reminiscence of humanity, a man laid out alive and standing, and already, as one may say, buried under arms with funeral accompaniments, though it may be,

> "Not a drum was heard, not a funeral note,
> As his corse to the rampart we hurried;
> Not a soldier discharged his farewell shot
> O'er he grave where our hero we buried."

[5] The mass of men serve the state thus, not as men mainly, but as machines, with their bodies. They are the standing army, and the militia, jailers, constables, *posse comitatus*, etc. In most cases there is no free exercise whatever of the judgment or of the moral sense; but they put themselves on a level with wood and earth and stones; and wooden men can perhaps be manufactured that will serve the purpose as well. Such command no more respect than men of straw or a lump of dirt. They have the same sort of worth only as horses and dogs. Yet such as these even are commonly esteemd good citizens. Others—as most legislators, politicians, lawyers, ministers, and office-holders—serve the state chiefly with their heads; and, as they rarely make any moral distinctions, they are as likely to serve the devil, without *intending* it, as God. A very few—as heroes, patriots, martyrs, reformers in the great sense, and *men* —serve the state with their consciences also, and so necessarily resist it for the most part; and they are commonly treated as enemies by it. A wise man will only be useful as a man, and will not submit to be "clay," and "stop a hole to keep the wind away," but leave that office to his dust at least:

> "I am too high-born to be propertied,
> To be a secondary at control,
> Or useful serving-man and instrument
> To any sovereign state throughout the world."

[6] He who gives himself entirely to his fellow men appears to them useless and selfish; but he who gives himself partially to them is pronounced a benefactor and philanthropist.

VOCABULARY

Define the following words as they are used in the selection: *expedient, inexpedient, mode* [1]; *india-rubber* [2]; *powder-monkeys, corse* [4]; *posse comitatus* [5]; *philanthropist* [6].

QUESTIONS FOR STUDY AND DISCUSSION

1. Thoreau opens his essay with an assertion that is pointed, brief, pithy. At first glance it seems startlingly radical; yet it is firmly in the American democratic tradition. What assumption in the Declaration of Independence parallels or justifies Thoreau's assertion?

2. Thoreau begins his argument with the second sentence of paragraph 1, drawing a syllogistic conclusion ("That government is best which governs not at all") from his major premise ("That government is best which governs least"). What is the implied minor premise? Is the syllogism valid? Do you find any basis for disagreement with the syllogism?

3. What attitude toward man does Thoreau imply in the second clause of the second sentence? Do you think he is realistic or idealistic in his expectations?

4. In what sense is government an expedient? When is a government inexpedient? Do Thoreau's statements about expediency support his initial assertion?

5. In the second half of paragraph 1 Thoreau makes a brief analogy between a standing government and a standing army. What parallels does he find between the two institutions? How do paragraphs 4 and 5 strengthen the analogy?

6. Northern critics of the Mexican War (1846–1848), such as Thoreau, viewed the war as a means by which southern politicians and northern cotton merchants were attempting to extend slave territory. How does this example illustrate Thoreau's contention that governments are sometimes inexpedient?

7. What is the topic idea of paragraph 2? Which sentence in the paragraph best expresses the topic idea?

8. What are the implications of the metaphorical description of government as "a sort of wooden gun to the people"? What attitudes toward his fellow Americans does Thoreau project in paragraph 2? Point out an example of the verbal irony in this paragraph.

9. In the concluding sentence of paragraph 2 Thoreau draws an analogy between legislators and revolutionists. Upon what similarity is the analogy based?

10. What purpose does paragraph 3 serve? How do Thoreau's observations in paragraphs 1 and 2 justify his speaking "practically"?

11. What is the topic idea of paragraph 4? What statement of paragraph 3 is developed in this paragraph? How does this paragraph elaborate and support Thoreau's argument that the best government governs least?

12. In the second half of paragraph 4 Thoreau employs emotionally charged language and imagery. Which phrases and images owe their power to their emotional connotations rather than to their argumentative value?

13. The word *thus* in the first sentence of paragraph 5 signals that a logical conclusion has been reached. Trace the argument leading to this conclusion. Can it be set up as a syllogism?

14. Paragraph 5 presents an analysis of the types of citizens. What three categories does Thoreau describe? How does he employ emotionally charged imagery and language to help characterize these three types of citizens?

15. Does the assertive statement that comprises paragraph 6 follow logically from the argument that Thoreau has presented? What attitude toward the government does Thoreau imply to be the only attitude proper for the person whom he considers to be a really good citizen?

16. Paragraph 4 concludes with a quotation from a once-famous poem by Charles Wolfe, an Irish poet; paragraph 4 concludes with two allusions to Shakespeare's plays—*Hamlet*, Act V, Scene 1, lines 236–237, and *King John*, Act V, Scene 2, lines 79–82. What does Thoreau gain by employing these literary allusions? Is their use an effective argumentative or persuasive technique?

Ralph Waldo Emerson

THE MIND OF THE PAST

In its entirety, the "American Scholar" address by Emerson (1803–1882), delivered in 1837 as the Phi Beta Kappa Address at Harvard University, has been termed "our intellectual Declaration of Independence." Not for the first time, but at the right time, Emerson asked that Americans sever the intellectual strings that bound them to Europe (and to the past) and that the American scholars (not students, or bookworms, but "Man Thinking") assume a more active and important role in the leadership of their country. The American Scholar ("Man Thinking") is subjected, Emerson says, to three principal influences: nature, which reveals to the scholar the underlying unity of the universe; the past, which is discussed in this present excerpt; and action, or life itself, in which the scholar makes use of his knowledge and genius and also finds "the raw material out of which the intellect moulds her splendid products."

[1] The next great influence into the spirit of the scholar is the mind of the Past,—in whatever form, whether of literature, of art, of institutions, that mind is inscribed. Books are the best type of the influence of the past, and perhaps we shall get at the truth,—learn the amount of this influence more conveniently,—by considering their value alone.

[2] The theory of books is noble. The scholar of the first age received into him the world around; brooded thereon; gave it the new arrangement of his own mind, and uttered it again. It came into him life; it went out from him truth. It came to him short-lived actions; it went out from him immortal thoughts. It came to him business; it went from him poetry. It was a dead fact; now, it is quick thought. It can stand, and it can go. It now endures, it now flies, it now inspires. Precisely in proportion to the depth of mind from which it issued, so high does it soar, so long does it sing.

[3] Or, I might say, it depends on how far the process had gone, of transmuting life into truth. In proportion to the completeness of the distillation, so will the purity and imperishableness of the product be. But none is quite perfect. As no air-pump can by any means make a perfect vacuum, so neither can any artist entirely exclude the conventional, the local, the perishable from his book, or write a book of pure thought, that shall be as efficient, in all respects, to a remote posterity, as to contemporaries, or rather to the second age. Each age, it is found, must write its own books; or rather, each generation for the next succeeding. The books of an older period will not fit this.

[4] Yet hence arrives a grave mischief. The sacredness which attaches to the act of creation, the act of thought, is transferred to the record. The poet chanting was felt to be a divine man: henceforth the chant is divine also. The writer was a just and wise spirit: henceforward it is settled the book is perfect; as love of the hero corrupts into worship of his statue. Instantly the book becomes noxious: the guide is a tyrant. The sluggish and perverted mind of the multitude, slow to open to the incursions of Reason, having once so opened, having once received this book, stands upon it, and makes an outcry if it is disparaged. Colleges are built on it. Books are written on it by thinkers, not by Man Thinking; by men of talent, that is, who start wrong, who set out from accepted dogmas, not from their own sight of principles. Meek young men grow up in libraries, believing it their duty to accept the views which Cicero, which Locke, which Bacon, have given; forgetful that Cicero, Locke, and Bacon were only young men in libraries when they wrote these books.

[5] Hence, instead of Man Thinking, we have the bookworm. Hence the book-learned class, who value books, as such; not as related to nature and the

human constitution, but as making a sort of Third Estate with the world and the soul. Hence the restorers of readings, the emendators, the bibliomaniacs of all degrees.

[6] Books are the best of things, well used; abused, among the worst. What is the right use? What is the one end which all means go to effect? They are for nothing but to inspire. I had better never see a book than to be warped by its attraction clean out of my own orbit, and made a satellite instead of a system. The one thing in the world, of value, is the active soul. This every man is entitled to; this every man contains within him, although in almost all men obstructed, and as yet unborn. The soul active sees absolute truth and utters truth, or creates. In this action it is genius; not the privilege of here and there a favorite, but the sound estate of every man. In its essence, it is progressive. The book, the college, the school of art, the institution of any kind, stop with some past utterance of genius. This is good, say they,—let us hold by this. They pin me down. They look backward and not forward. But genius looks forward: the eyes of man are set in his forehead, not in his hindhead: man hopes: genius creates. Whatever talents may be, if the man create not, the pure efflux of the Deity is not his;—cinders and smoke there may be, but not yet flame. There are creative manners, there are creative actions, and creative words; manners, actions, words, that is, indicative of no custom or authority, but springing spontaneous from the mind's own sense of good and fair.

[7] On the other part, instead of being its own seer, let it receive from another mind its truth, though it were in torrents of light, without periods of solitude, inquest, and self-recovery, and a fatal disservice is done. Genius is always sufficiently the enemy of genius by over-influence. The literature of every nation bears me witness. The English dramatic poets have Shakespearized now for two hundred years.

[8] Undoubtedly there is a right way of reading, so it be sternly subordinated. Man Thinking must not be subdued by his instruments. Books are for the scholar's idle times. When he can read God directly, the hour is too precious to be wasted in other men's transcripts of their readings. But when the intervals of darkness come, as come they must,—when the sun is hid and the stars withdraw their shining,—we repair to the lamps which were kindled by their ray, to guide our steps to the East again, where the dawn is. We hear, that we may speak. The Arabian proverb says, "A fig tree, looking on a fig tree, becometh fruitful."

[9] It is remarkable, the character of the pleasure we derive from the best books. They impress us with the conviction that one nature wrote and the

same reads. We read the verses of one of the great English poets, of Chaucer, of Marvell, of Dryden, with the most modern joy,—with a pleasure, I mean, which is in great part caused by the abstraction of all *time* from their verses. There is some awe mixed with the joy of our surprise, when this poet, who lived in some past world, two or there hundred years ago, says that which lies close to my own soul, that which I also had well-nigh thought and said. But for the evidence thence afforded to the philosophical doctrine of the identity of all minds, we should suppose some preëstablished harmony, some foresight of souls that were to be, and some preparation of stores for their future wants, like the fact observed in insects, who lay up food before death for the young grub they shall never see.

[10] I would not be hurried by any love of system, by any exaggeration of instincts, to underrate the Book. We all know, that as the human body can be nourished on any food, though it were boiled grass and the broth of shoes, so the human mind can be fed by any knowledge. And great and heroic men have existed who had almost no other information than by the printed page. I only would say that it needs a strong head to bear that diet. One must be an inventor to read well. As the proverb says, "He that would bring home the wealth of the Indies, must carry out the wealth of the Indies." There is then creative reading as well as creative writing. When the mind is braced by labor and invention, the page of whatever book we read becomes luminous with manifold allusion. Every sentence is doubly significant, and the sense of our author is as broad as the world. We then see, what is always true, that as the seer's hour of vision is short and rare among heavy days and months, so is its record, perchance the least part of his volume. The discerning will read, in his Plato or Shakespeare, only that least part,—only the authentic utterances of the oracle;—all the rest he rejects, were it never so many times Plato's and Shakespeare's.

[11] Of course there is a portion of reading quite indispensable to a wise man. History and exact science he must learn by laborious reading. Colleges, in like manner, have their indispensable office,—to teach elements. But they can only highly serve us when they aim not to drill, but to create; when they gather from far every ray of various genius to their hospitable halls, and by the concentrated fires, set the hearts of their youth on flame. Thought and knowledge are natures in which apparatus and pretension avail nothing. Gowns and pecuniary foundations, though of towns of gold, can never countervail the least sentence or syllable of wit. Forget this, and our American colleges will recede in their public importance, whilst they grow richer every year.

VOCABULARY

1. By using your dictionary, identify the following: *Cicero, Locke, Bacon, Chaucer, Marvell, Dryden, Plato*.
2. Define the following words as they are used in the selection: *transmuting* [3]; *noxious, incursions, disparaged, dogmas* [4]; *Third Estate, emendators, bibliomaniacs* [5]; *efflux* [6]; *seer, Shakespearized* [7]; *pecuniary, countervail, wit* [11].

QUESTIONS FOR STUDY AND DISCUSSION

1. What, specifically, is the purpose of Emerson's remarks? What particular attitude toward books does he oppose? What attitude toward books does he advocate?

2. Divide the essay by paragraphs into its over-all organizational pattern. What constitutes the introduction? What is the main point of the introduction? Which paragraphs are concerned with Emerson's attack? Which are concerned with the attitude toward books that he is advocating?

3. Trace the line of argument in paragraphs 2 through 5. In paragraph 2 Emerson describes "the theory of books," but in paragraph 3 he assesses the theory to reveal its limitations. The result of the mistaken attitude is discussed in paragraphs 4 through 5.

4. Do the second and third sentences of paragraph 4 effectively summarize paragraphs 2 through 5? Emerson has here created two syllogisms (with the major premises omitted), but he disagrees with the conclusions:

Major premise: _____
Minor premise: This poem is written by a divine poet.
Conclusion: Thus, this poem is divine.

Major premise: _____
Minor premise: This writer is just and wise.
Conclusion: Thus, this book is perfect (i.e., just and wise).

What are the omitted major premises? Are they true?

5. Point out the uses of analogy in paragraphs 3 through 4. Are they convincing? Do they illustrate or prove the points that Emerson is writing about?

6. What words in paragraph 4 are slanted to indicate Emerson's attitude toward what he considers to be the mistaken use of books?

7. Summarize Emerson's statements about the right use of books. What arguments does he advance to support his statements? Are they convincing?

8. What, according to Emerson, is the source of significant knowledge? How does the reverence for books hamper this knowledge?

9. After describing the theory of books, attacking this theory, and advancing his own ideas about their proper use, Emerson concedes that books do have value, even though they are overrated. Where does the concession to the value of books begin in the essay? Enumerate the values that books have. Does the concession weaken Emerson's argument?

10. What further uses of the device of analogy do you find after paragraph 4? Comment on their effectiveness.

11. What is the meaning of the "cinders and smoke" metaphor in paragraph 6?

12. Do the proverbs in paragraphs 8 and 10 give substantial support to Emerson's statements?

13. How effective is the sentence rhythm of the essay? Note particularly the lyrical sentences of paragraph 2.

14. Emerson is noted for his aphoristic sentences. What examples of readily quotable statements can you point out?

EMOTIONAL APPEALS

Since logical argument may be subordinate in an emotionally persuasive statement, one of the most important features of an emotional appeal is the language in which it is couched. The writer attempts to move his audience through his use of words and their arrangement. The patterned repetition of phrases (as in the second paragraph of Martin Luther King's "I Have a Dream," in which he four times refers to the present as "one hundred years later" than the signing of the Emancipation Proclamation); the emphatic repetition of a single word (as with the insistent *Now* in the fifth paragraph of that speech); alliteration (such as Dr. King's phrase "this sweltering summer"); and figurative language (". . . we will not be satisfied until justice rolls down like waters and righteousness like a mighty stream") produce the same effect as poetry; and appeal to the emotions and the imagination, as well as to the intellect.

Individual words, too, have importance. Each connotation must be considered carefully for its value and for its consistency with the tone and intent of the appeal. The speaker delivers an "address"; his opponent makes a "campaign speech." The soldiers on the writer's side make "willing sacrifices to their ideals"; the enemy soldiers are "fanatics." His side "withdraws"; the other "retreats." In "A Giant's Dead Body," Nathaniel Hawthorne's young rebel replies to his friend Phoebe, who has accused him of hating everything "old," that he certainly loves nothing "mouldy." When Holgrave uses the connotative *mouldy* rather than the denotative *old*, he is employing language with emotional rather than only intellectual impact.

In his discussion of the color of words, Paul Roberts (p. 33) distinguishes three types of words. The writer of emotional appeals makes most frequent use of Roberts's second category of words: those that are "colored—that is, loaded with associations, good or bad." In order to gain support for his cause, the writer will couch his argument in language with good connotations. Roberts lists, as examples, *mother, home, liberty, fireside, patriot*. On the other hand, words with bad connotations—Roberts mentions *liberal, reactionary, Communist, socialist, capitalist*—can, in some contexts, "convey contempt on the part of the speaker." It will be worthwhile to reread Roberts's selection with respect to the use of language in emotional persuasion. Loaded language has its place, but its place should always be to strengthen arguments that may be logically defended. Emotionally colored language cannot replace facts and logic for the intelligent reader. It will, of course, appeal to him if it buttresses a defensible argument; but it will only repel him if it stands alone.

The ideals that the writer places on his side attach to his own arguments. Words and ideas that suggest patriotic or spiritual imagery are extremely valuable to the writer of persuasion. The ideals of the forefathers, their hardships, and the blood they shed can, unfortunately, be invoked to support causes which these forefathers would view not only without sympathy but probably with contempt. The prevailing deity of the time is assumed to bless the writer's cause. Honestly used, however, historically allusive language adds emotional strength to a statement. Standing in front of the Lincoln Memorial in 1963, Martin Luther King, Jr., opened his moving "I Have a Dream" speech with the observation that "Five score years ago, a great American, in whose symbolic shadow we now stand, signed the Emancipation Proclamation." Dr. King effectively invokes both the language and symbolic presence of Lincoln to give emotional coloration to his own message.

The writer of an emotionally persuasive statement must squarely face two questions and answer them as honestly as his knowledge of the circumstances permits. First, *is the statement ethically defensible?* The effusions of the writers of advertising copy and political-campaign literature and speeches provide inexhaustible examples of the ability of writers to appeal to an audience and present their products or their candidates in an enticing light without saying anything substantial about them. "My party stands for the American way of life," declares the platform speaker, leaving the listener to conjure in his own imagination what he considers to be the ideals of America democracy suggested by the phrase "American way of life." The orator has said nothing substantial about his political position; and he has implied that the opposing party is somehow against the "American way of life." Or, he may announce, "I stand firm for patriotism"—deliberately not clarifying whether the patriotism he upholds is the unassailable screen that Samuel Johnson called "the last refuge of the scoundrel," the thoughtless chauvinism of Stephen Decatur's "My country, right or wrong," or the humble and selfless commitment to the still unrealized ideals which the founders of the country asserted in the Declaration of Independence and attempted to legislate in the Constitution and the Bill of Rights.

Second, *does the emotional appeal support a logical argument, or does it replace one?* The Devil's indictment of Man in Shaw's play can be supported by the evidence of history, but the denunciation in its dramatic context is perhaps a more stern reminder of Man's inherent nature than any calendar of facts and figures. In "The Pool," the poet Allan Planz evokes the image of a formerly pure watering place, frequented by buffalo, geese, and pioneers, now corrupted with rusted iron, oil, and sewage. This reminder of what man has done to his environment persuasively supplements the facts and figures and the dire predictions of scientific ecologists. Hawthorne's Holgrave attacks, through richly evocative images, the power of the past to act as a curse upon the present. Holgrave—an artist—gives emotional support to arguments advanced more logically by both Thomas Jefferson and Ralph Waldo Emerson. William Faulkner's Nobel Prize Acceptance Speech is not intended primarily to stir an audience to action but, rather, to examine anew its spiritual values, which in a time of international unrest have been overshadowed by fear. Martin Luther King, Jr., describes again the dream of human dignity and mutual toleration and love that is expressed in both the legal and the sentimental documents of the United States. The argument he builds from needs no further proof; but the social implications of that argument, he reminds us, need yet to be realized.

All of the selections below are emotional appeals to support actions or beliefs that can be defended, though perhaps less effectively, intellectually.

A final point should be remembered. The characteristics of emotional appeals—such as sensitivity to sentence rhythm and the connotations of words—are in large measure the mark of good writing of any type; it is the ability of emotionally persuasive language to replace argument that makes it at times treacherous and objectionable.

Allan Planz

THE POOL

> *Allan Planz (b. 1937) is both a poet and a writer of prose. He has contributed prose and poetry to* The Nation, *of which he is Poetry Editor; and his poems have appeared in other periodicals, such as* Poetry *and* The Chicago Review. *His first volume of poetry,* A Night for Rioting (1969), *has been described as a "haunting volume" which "registers desolation" and "compasses the guts and horror and tenderness of America." The following prose sketch conveys these same qualities.*

[1] On the west bank of brown river there is a place where the wildness of nature mingles savagely with the wildness of civilization. Bare rocks have shouldered the rain into a sunken meadow, and more than a dozen autobodies

From *Ecotactics: Sierra Club Handbook.* Copyright © 1970, by the Sierra Club. Reprinted by permission of Pocket Books/division of Simon & Schuster, Inc.

create a ring of metallic resonance around the small pond, from which all life, even the mosquito wriggler, has been choked by chemical stasis. Sunlight sickens on rust and purpled alloys, glints on the black water and shimmers on oil-stained sand. This was a watering place once, a ford, a concourse, and one of many thousands of departure points. Buffalo rested by the rocks, heads to the wind, and geese held back the encroaching swamp for centuries, until guns killed off the geese and later gasoline killed the weeds. The erosion gulley was a stream when lush grasses upcountry sifted the rain through their roots. Now every drizzle means sudden flood. Here Indians made camp near the bank, and watched the fire shape and shadow the waters. The pioneer paused to collect his forces for the plunge farther into the west on the trail which, under moonlight, stirred faintly above the dark. A family settled here, and built a homestead, of which only a few rectangular depressions remain. This land was overgrazed, overfarmed, and abandoned, then assumed a civilized function as a dumping-ground for vandalized carwrecks from the highway a mile off. Though doubtless title to it is jealously guarded, nobody possesses it now, nobody watches over it, and it is nameless. One can come across it hiking and descend the rocks to the black pond and rest among the junked cars and among the slaughtered beasts. Locusts skid in the sand or sing, entombed, in the sticky sludge spilled from crankcases. The river with its machined flow scours the pocked bank. The shadows inside and under the cars are bruises of blue air. Dustdevils snake in the fine grit and whirl flakes of rusted metal. One may calculate and possess again all the miles he has traveled, all the cities and towns that he has called home and that irresistibly erupted him back on the road. One may calculate all those whom money had bought, or killed. One may do nothing, wish nothing. If the hot breeze stirs, it brings only the hands of buried men, and bears no witness to the riposte of osprey and eagle above terraces of clear water. And the night comes on, upside down, gaining on the earth a darkness it never has in the sky. The air smells of heated iron, rancid oils, and of water thickened with sewage. Voices in the blood begin talking of the blood's cessation. One picks up a theme, then, of the splendor of empire weighted against the dust of the people who built it.

[2] And gives it to the heaviness of the night through which one has lived each night, getting drunk under stars arranged in patterns long since prefigured in the fears of men. And with the geophysics of the night in one hand, a bottle in the other, invokes that theme, so that, when the dawn splays the broken figure of man or beast on a hilltop, the wind may come again, if ever it comes again, singing not requiem but revolution.

VOCABULARY

Define the following words as they are used in the selection: *resonance, stasis, concourse, dustdevils, riposte* [1]; *splays, requiem* [2].

QUESTIONS FOR STUDY AND DISCUSSION

1. This description of a pool is developed largely by means of contrasts. What is the principal contrast employed in paragraph 1? Does the first sentence suggest this contrast?

2. What was the pool once? Identify all of the functions it served. What words and images are most effective in suggesting what the pool once was?

3. What is the pool now? What words and images best connote the present state of the pool?

4. Point out the contrasts connoted by the distinction between *stasis* and the italicized words in the following phrases: "Buffalo *rested* by the rocks," "Here Indians *made camp*," "The pioneer *paused*," and "A family *settled* here."

5. If paragraph 1 were divided, where would be a logical point for the break? Why?

6. What are the alternatives available to the hiker who happens upon this pool? What is suggested by the statement "One may do nothing, wish nothing"?

7. What train of thought does the pool ultimately suggest for the writer? Do the present functions of the pool and the language used to describe its functions and appearance warrant this ultimate suggestion?

8. What is the understood grammatical subject of the fragmentary sentences in paragraph 2?

9. Which feeling—hope or despair—does the concluding sentence most prominently suggest? Or does the sentence convey some other feeling or possibility? If so, what one?

10. What is Planz's persuasive intention in this essay? To what action or realization does Planz perhaps hope to move the reader?

Nathaniel Hawthorne

A GIANT'S DEAD BODY

> A great-grandson of a judge at the Salem witchcraft trials and a descendant of generations of Puritans, Nathaniel Hawthorne (1804–1864) had a personal as well as an artistic interest in the influences of the past. The house that gives its name to the title of his novel The House of the Seven Gables (1851) is a symbol of the dark past of Salem life. Blighted by a curse placed upon it when old Colonel Pyncheon of Salem obtained it by falsely convicting its rightful owner of witchcraft, it is inhabited by the colonel's descendants, among them a country cousin, Phoebe Pyncheon. The artist and writer Holgrave, a descendant of the man convicted of witchcraft, also lives there as a lodger. In the words of young Holgrave, Hawthorne presents an eloquent attack upon the corrosive influences of the past. The conversation between Holgrave and Phoebe appears in Chapter 12 of the novel.

[1] At length, something was said by Holgrave that made it apposite for Phoebe to inquire what had first brought him acquainted with her cousin Hepzibah, and why he now chose to lodge in the desolate old Pyncheon House. Without directly answering her, he turned from the Future, which had heretofore been the theme of his discourse, and began to speak of the influences of the Past. One subject, indeed, is but the reverberation of the other.

[2] "Shall we never, never get rid of this Past?" cried he, keeping up the earnest tone of his preceding conversation. "It lies upon the Present like a giant's dead body! In fact, the case is just as if a young giant were compelled to waste all his strength in carrying about the corpse of the old giant, his grandfather, who died a long while ago, and only needs to be decently buried. Just think a moment, and it will startle you to see what slaves we are to bygone times,—to Death, if we give the matter the right word!"

[3] "But I do not see it," observed Phoebe.

[4] "For example, then," continued Holgrave: "a dead man, if he happen to have made a will, disposes of wealth no longer his own; or, if he die intestate, it is distributed in accordance with the notions of men much longer dead than he. A dead man sits on all our judgment-seats; and living judges do but search out and repeat his decisions. We read in dead men's books! We laugh at dead men's jokes, and cry at dead men's pathos! We are sick of dead men's

diseases, physical and moral, and die of the same remedies with which dead doctors killed their patients! We worship the living Deity according to dead men's forms and creeds. Whatever we seek to do, of our own free motion, a dead man's icy hand obstructs us! Turn our eyes to what point we may, a dead man's white, immitigable face encounters them, and freezes our very heart! And we must be dead ourselves before we can begin to have our proper influence on our own world, which will then be no longer our world, but the world of another generation, with which we shall have no shadow of a right to interfere. I ought to have said, too, that we live in dead men's houses; as, for instance, in this of the Seven Gables!"

[5]   "And why not," said Phoebe, "so long as we can be comfortable in them?"

[6]   "But we shall live to see the day, I trust," went on the artist, "when no man shall build his house for posterity. Why should he? He might just as reasonably order a durable suit of clothes,—leather, or gutta-percha, or whatever else lasts longest,—so that his great-grandchildren should have the benefit of them, and cut precisely the same figure in the world that he himself does. If each generation were allowed and expected to build its own houses, that single change, comparatively unimportant in itself, would imply almost every reform which society is now suffering for. I doubt whether even our public edifices—our capitols, state-houses, courthouses, city-hall, and churches—ought to be built of such permanent materials as stone or brick. It were better that they should crumble to ruin once in twenty years, or thereabouts, as a hint to the people to examine into and reform the institutions which they symbolize."

[7]   "How you hate everything old!" said Phoebe, in dismay. "It makes me dizzy to think of such a shifting world!"

[8]   "I certainly love nothing mouldy," answered Holgrave. "Now, this old Pyncheon House! Is it a wholesome place to live in, with its black shingles, and the green moss that shows how damp they are?—its dark, low-studded rooms?—its grime and sordidness, which are the crystallization on its walls of the human breath, that has been drawn and exhaled here in discontent and anguish? The house ought to be purified with fire,—purified till only its ashes remain!"

[9]   "Then why do you live in it?" asked Phoebe, a little piqued.

[10]   "Oh, I am pursuing my studies here; not in books, however," replied Holgrave. "The house, in my view, is expressive of that odious and abominable Past, with all its bad influences, against which I have just been declaiming. I

EMOTIONAL APPEALS

dwell in it for a while, that I may know the better how to hate it. By the by, did you ever hear the story of Maule, the wizard, and what happened between him and your immeasurably great-grandfather?"

[11] "Yes, indeed!" said Phoebe; "I heard it long ago, from my father, and two or three times from my cousin Hepzibah, in the month that I have been here. She seems to think that all the calamities of the Pyncheons began from that quarrel with the wizard, as you call him. And you, Mr. Holgrave, look as if you thought so too! How singular, that you should believe what is so very absurd, when you reject many things that are a great deal worthier of credit!"

[12] "I do believe it," said the artist, seriously; "not as a superstition, however, but as proved by unquestionable facts, and as exemplifying a theory. Now, see: under those seven gables, at which we now look up,—and which old Colonel Pyncheon meant to be the house of his descendants, in prosperity and happiness, down to an epoch far beyond the present,—under that roof, through a portion of three centuries, there has been perpetual remorse of conscience, a constantly defeated hope, strife amongst kindred, various misery, a strange form of death, dark suspicion, unspeakable disgrace,—all, or most of which calamity I have the means of tracing to the old Puritan's inordinate desire to plant and endow a family. To plant a family! This idea is at the bottom of most of the wrong and mischief which men do. The truth is, that, once in every half-century, at longest, a family should be merged into the great, obscure mass of humanity, and forget all about its ancestors. Human blood, in order to keep its freshness, should run in hidden streams, as the water of an aqueduct is conveyed in subterranean pipes. In the family existence of these Pyncheons, for instance,—forgive me, Phoebe; but I cannot think of you as one of them,—in their brief New England pedigree, there has been time enough to infect them all with one kind of lunacy or another!"

VOCABULARY

Define the following words as they are used in the selection: *apposite, discourse, reverberation* [1]; *intestate, pathos, immitigable* [4]; *gutta-percha* [6]; *epoch, inordinate, subterranean, pedigree* [12].

QUESTIONS FOR STUDY AND DISCUSSION

1. Though they are not presented as an essay, Holgrave's words, divorced from the exposition provided by Hawthorne as novelist and the brief remarks by

Phoebe, have the organization and development of ideas of an essay. What purpose do the remarks of Phoebe have?

2. What does Hawthorne mean when he says that the subjects of the past and the future are reverberations of each other? What effect is gained by capitalizing *Past* and *Future*?

3. What quality or characteristic of the past is the topic of paragraph 2? In developing his point Holgrave uses a simile, an analogy, and a metaphor. Point out these devices. Are they successful in illustrating the topic idea of the paragraph?

4. What purpose does paragraph 4 serve in relation to paragraph 2? How is the transition between the two paragraphs effected?

5. Make a list of the areas of human existence mentioned in the first half of paragraph 4. Are they randomly presented, or is their order based upon any pattern? Do they encompass sufficient areas of life to warrant Holgrave's generalization of "whatever we seek to do"?

6. In the two sentences of paragraph 4 beginning with "Whatever we seek to do," Holgrave develops contrasts between the living and the dead. Give attention to the language he employs in these two sentences. What words and phrases connote life? Which ones connote death? Is the language of these sentences intended to produce any emotional response?

7. Is there an orderly development of ideas in paragraph 4? Why is the next-to-last sentence more effective at the end of the paragraph than at the beginning? What is achieved by the mention of houses in the final sentence, rather than earlier in the paragraph?

8. Is the comparison in paragraph 6 between clothes and buildings a convincing argument? Does it seem to you to be based upon logical reasoning?

9. Point out the emotionally connotative words in paragraph 8. What contrast does this paragraph enforce?

10. What figure of speech does Holgrave employ in paragraph 12 to support his point? How does the language in which it is couched appeal to the emotions as well as to the imagination?

11. Go through the selection and draw up a list of the qualities Holgrave attributes to the past. What is the cumulative effect, according to Holgrave, of the characteristics of the past?

12. The arguments advanced by Holgrave, revolutionary though they seem, were being entertained by—and had been entertained by—highly respectable thinkers of the time. Consider the following words of Thomas Jefferson, quoted from a letter of 6 September 1789 to James Madison:

> The question, whether one generation of men has a right to bind another, seems never to have been started either on this or our side of the water. Yet it is a question of such consequences as not only to merit decision, but place also among the fundamental principles of every government. The course of reflection in which we are immersed here, on the elementary principles of society, has presented this question to my mind; and that no such

obligation can be transmitted, I think very capable of proof. I set out on this ground, which I suppose to be self-evident, that the *earth belongs in usufruct to the living;* that the dead have neither powers nor rights over it. . . .

 . . . No society can make a perpetual constitution, or even a perpetual law. The earth belongs always to the living generation: they may manage it, then, and what proceeds from it, as they please, during their usufruct. They are masters, too, of their own persons, and consequently may govern them as they please. But persons and property make the sum of the objects of government. The constitution and the laws of their predecessors are extinguished then, in their natural course, with those whose will gave them being. This could preserve that being, till it ceased to be itself, and no longer. Every constitution, then, and every law, naturally expires at the end of thirty-four years. If it be enforced longer, it is an act of force, and not of right. It may be said, that the succeeding generation exercising, in fact, the power of repeal, this leaves them as free as if the constitution or law had been expressly limited to thirty-four years only. In the first place, this objection admits the right, in proposing an equivalent. But the power of repeal is not an equivalent. It might be, indeed, if every form of government were so perfectly contrived, that the will of the majority could always be obtained, fairly and without impediment. But this is true of no form. The people cannot assemble themselves; their representation is unequal and vicious. Various checks are opposed to every legislative proposition. Factions get possession of the public councils, bribery corrupts them, personal interests lead them astray from the general interests of their constituents; and other impediments arise, so as to prove to every practical man, that a law of limited duration is much more manageable than one which needs a repeal.

This principle, that the earth belongs to the living and not to the dead, is of very extensive application and consequences in every country. . . .

Jefferson bases his argument on assertion, which he says is self-evident; Holgrave employs language that is figurative and emotionally connotative. Which of the methods is the more convincing? How do the methods and language of the two statements correspond to the roles of the two speakers?

William Faulkner

THE STOCKHOLM ADDRESS

On December 10, 1950, in Stockholm, Sweden, William Faulkner (1897–1962) delivered his brief speech of acceptance upon the award of the Nobel Prize for Literature, the world's most coveted prize for literary excellence. His words define his exalted conception of the writer's obligation and at the same time present an eloquent image of mankind. Faulkner's ideals—"the old universal verities"—are illustrated, often negatively or indirectly, in such novels as The Sound and the Fury *(1929),* As I Lay Dying *(1930),* Light in August *(1932),* Absalom, Absalom! *(1936),* The Hamlet *(1940), and* Intruder in the Dust *(1948).*

[1] I feel that this award was not made to me as a man, but to my work—a life's work in the agony and sweat of the human spirit, not for glory and least of all for profit, but to create out of the materials of the human spirit something which did not exist before. So this award is only mine in trust. It will not be difficult to find a dedication for the money part of it commensurate with the purpose and significance of its origin. But I would like to do the same with the acclaim too, by using this moment as a pinnacle from which I might be listened to by the young men and women already dedicated to the same anguish and travail, among whom is already that one who will some day stand here where I am standing.

[2] Our tragedy today is a general and universal physical fear so long sustained by now that we can even bear it. There are no longer problems of the spirit. There is only the question: When will I be blown up? Because of this, the young man or woman writing today has forgotten the problems of the human heart in conflict with itself which alone can make good writing because only that is worth writing about, worth the agony and the sweat.

[3] He must learn them again. He must teach himself that the basest of all things is to be afraid; and, teaching himself that, forget it forever, leaving no room in his workshop for anything but the old verities and truths of the heart, the old universal truths lacking which any story is ephemeral and doomed—love and honor and pity and pride and compassion and sacrifice. Until he

Reprinted from *The Faulkner Reader* (New York: Random House, Inc., 1954).

does so, he labors under a curse. He writes not of love but of lust, of defeats in which nobody loses anything of value, of victories without hope and, worst of all, without pity or compassion. His griefs grieve on no universal bones, leaving no scars. He writes not of the heart but of the glands.

[4] Until he relearns these things, he will write as though he stood among and watched the end of man. I decline to accept the end of man. It is easy enough to say that man is immortal simply because he will endure: that when the last ding-dong of doom has clanged and faded from the last worthless rock hanging tideless in the last red and dying evening, that even then there will still be one more sound: that of his puny inexhaustible voice, still talking. I refuse to accept this. I believe that man will not merely endure: he will prevail. He is immortal, not because he alone among creatures has an inexhaustible voice, but because he has a soul, a spirit capable of compassion and sacrifice and endurance. The poet's, the writer's, duty is to write about these things. It is his privilege to help man endure by lifting his heart, by reminding him of the courage and honor and hope and pride and compassion and pity and sacrifice which have been the glory of his past. The poet's voice need not merely be the record of man, it can be one of the props, the pillars to help him endure and prevail.

VOCABULARY

1. Define the following words as they are used in the selection: *commensurate, anguish, travail* [1]; *sustained* [2]; *ephemeral* [3].

2. What are the denotative and connotative meanings of the "old verities" that Faulkner lists: *love, honor, pity, pride, compassion, sacrifice, courage, hope?*

QUESTIONS FOR STUDY AND DISCUSSION

1. What is the tone of Faulkner's acceptance speech? Does it seem appropriate to the occasion? How does the occasion lend significance and value to Faulkner's words?

2. Describe the effect that Faulkner's message has upon you. Is the style or the substance of the statement primarily responsible for the effect?

3. Which part of the statement is concerned with what might be called the occasional content, the comments relating to the acceptance of the honor and

the monetary award? Is this part of the statement expressed in the same tone as the remainder of the address?

4. At what point does it become clear that the address will be a persuasive statement? To whom is the statement addressed? What, in summary form, is the paraphrasable content of the speech?

5. What are the principal points of paragraph 1?

6. Is there any formal transition between the first two paragraphs? Does the second logically follow the first? What repeated phrases provide suitable links between the two paragraphs?

7. Does the first word of paragraph 2 refer to "the young men and women" of the present, or does it refer to mankind?

8. The "today" of paragraph 2 (first sentence) suggests the end of World War II only five years before, the threat of nuclear weapons, and the outbreak in 1950 of the Korean War. Does the current "today" present similar bases of fear? What does Faulkner mean when he says that the fear is "so long sustained by now that we can even bear it"?

9. With paragraph 3 Faulkner announces his credo and elaborates on paragraph 2. How does he achieve transition from paragraph 2? What pronouns or phrases refer to the previous paragraph?

10. To what does *it* (in the second sentence of paragraph 3) refer? What is the meaning of Faulkner's statement about fear in this paragraph?

11. Faulkner illustrates the failure of the writer to concern himself with "the old universal truths" by presenting alternative possibilities. What is the difference between love and lust? In what kind of defeat does man lose nothing of value? What kind of victory would be one without hope, pity, or compassion? What kind of grief would leave no scars? What contrast exists between the heart and the glands? What do all of these alternative possibilities have in common?

12. Point out the transition from paragraph 3 to paragraph 4. The first five words of the first sentence illustrate three types of transition (repetition, parallelism, and pronoun reference).

13. With paragraph 4 Faulkner extends his persuasive message, from a statement about the role of the writer to an assertion of his own view of man, and concludes by relating the two ideas. Point out the principal divisions of the paragraph.

14. The three central words of paragraph 4—of the whole address, in fact —are *immortal,* *endure,* and *prevail.* Can you define the words and discuss the differences? How can endurance lead to immortality? Why is the immortality of man through his enduring not so desirable as his immortality through his prevailing?

15. Does Faulkner seem to be using the words *immortal* and *soul* in paragraph 4 in the traditional religious sense? Is traditional religious faith a requisite for agreement with Faulkner's ideals?

16. Two images emerge from paragraph 4: one of man's last day upon this

planet; one of the task of the poet, the writer, in uplifting the human heart. In the first, point out the repetition and the words that contribute to an image of utter finality. In the second, point out the use of alliteration and explain its general effect.

17. The over-all organization of paragraphs 2 through 4 turns in large measure upon the concept of time: the glory of man's past, when man addressed his attention to the old verities; man's present condition of fear and materialistic endurance; and the future, which can continue the present state of endurance or be transformed into a period of man's prevailing through his adherence to the truths of the heart. Trace this concept of time through these three paragraphs.

George Bernard Shaw

THE DEVIL SPEAKS

In a kind of dream sequence within his play Man and Superman *George Bernard Shaw (1856–1950) presents a whimsical picture of Hell—and a Devil much more talkative than menacing. The "Don Juan in Hell" scene of the play leads to some biting criticisms of man by the prince of disillusionment. Though he marshals some easily recognizable facts, the Devil's language is nonetheless that of emotional appeal as he holds a mirror up to man—and to himself.*

THE DEVIL. And is Man any the less destroying himself for all this boasted brain of his? Have you walked up and down upon the earth lately? I have; and I have examined Man's wonderful inventions. And I tell you that in the arts of life man invents nothing; but in the arts of death he outdoes Nature herself, and produces by chemistry and machinery all the slaughter of plague, pestilence, and famine. The peasant I tempt today eats and drinks what was eaten and drunk by the peasants of ten thousand years ago; and the house he lives in has not altered as much in a thousand centuries as the fashion of a lady's bonnet in a score of weeks. But when he goes out to slay, he carries a marvel of mechanism that lets loose at the touch of his finger all the hidden molecular energies, and leaves the javelin, the arrow, the blowpipe of his fathers far behind. In the arts of peace Man is a bungler. I have seen his cotton factories and the like, with machinery that a greedy dog could have invented if it had wanted money instead of food. I know his clumsy typewriters and bungling

From *Man and Superman* from *Seven Plays* by George Bernard Shaw. Reprinted by permission of The Society of Authors on behalf of the Bernard Shaw Estate.

locomotives and tedious bicycles: they are toys compared to the Maxim gun, the submarine torpedo boat. There is nothing in Man's industrial machinery but his greed and sloth: his heart is in his weapons. This marvellous force of Life of which you boast is a force of Death: Man measures his strength by his destructiveness. What is his religion? An excuse for hating me. What is his law? An excuse for hanging you. What is his morality? Gentility! an excuse for consuming without producing. What is his art? An excuse for gloating over pictures of slaughter. What are his politics? Either the worship of a despot because a despot can kill, or parliamentary cockfighting. I spent an evening lately in a certain celebrated legislature, and heard the pot lecturing the kettle for its blackness, and ministers answering questions. When I left I chalked up on the door the old nursery saying "Ask no questions and you will be told no lies." I bought a sixpenny family magazine, and found it full of pictures of young men shooting and stabbing one another. I saw a man die: he was a London bricklayer's laborer with seven children. He left seventeen pounds club money; and his wife spent it all on his funeral and went into the workhouse with the children next day. She would not have spent sevenpence on her children's schooling: the law had to force her to let them be taught gratuitously; but on death she spent all she had. Their imagination glows, their energies rise up at the idea of death, these people: they love it; and the more horrible it is the more they enjoy it. Hell is a place far above their comprehension: they derive their notion of it from two of the greatest fools that ever lived, an Italian and an Englishman. The Italian described it as a place of mud, frost, filth, fire, and venomous serpents: all torture. This ass, when he was not lying about me, was maundering about some woman whom he saw once in the street. The Englishman described me as being expelled from Heaven by cannons and gunpowder; and to this day every Briton believes that the whole of his silly story is in the Bible. What else he says I do not know; for it is all in a long poem which neither I nor anyone else ever succeeded in wading through. It is the same in everything. The highest form of literature is the tragedy, a play in which everybody is murdered at the end. In the old chronicles you read of earthquakes and pestilences, and are told that these shewed the power and majesty of God and the littleness of Man. Nowadays the chronicles describe battles. In a battle two bodies of men shoot at one another with bullets and explosive shells until one body runs away, when the others chase the fugitives on horseback and cut them to pieces as they fly. And this, the chronicle concludes, shews the greatness and majesty of empires, and the littleness of the vanquished. Over such battles the people run about the streets yelling with delight, and egg their Governments on to spend hundreds of millions of money in the slaughter, whilst the strongest Ministers dare not spend an extra penny in the pound against the poverty and pestilence through which they themselves daily walk. I could give you a thousand instances; but they all come to the same thing: the power that governs the earth is not the power of Life but of Death; and the inner need that has nerved Life to the effort of organizing itself into the human being is not the need for higher life but for a more efficient engine of destruction. The plague, the famine, the earthquake, the tempest were too spasmodic in their action; the tiger and crocodile were too easily satiated and not cruel enough: something more constantly, more ruthlessly, more ingeniously destructive was needed; and that something was Man, the inventor of the rack, the stake, the gallows, the electric chair; of sword and gun and poison gas: above all, of justice, duty, patriotism, and all the other isms by which even those who are clever enough to be humanely disposed are persuaded to become the most destructive of all the destroyers.

VOCABULARY

Define the following words as they are used in the selection: *gratuitously, chronicles, pestilences, engine, spasmodic, satiated.*

QUESTIONS FOR STUDY AND DISCUSSION

1. What sentence in the selection could serve as a topic sentence for the paragraph? Why is the selection not broken into several paragraphs?

2. In this passage, as in many others, Shaw achieves much of the power of his prose through *antithesis*, the balancing of opposites. An example early in the passage: "And I tell you that *in the arts of life* man invents nothing; but *in the arts of death* he outdoes Nature herself. . . ." Find and mark several other examples of antithesis in the passage.

3. Devices of sound repetition lend strength to a prose style if they are carefully handled and not overdone. Shaw uses considerable *alliteration,* or repetition of initial sounds in the words of a sentence. An example: ". . . the strongest Ministers dare not spend an extra *penny* in the *pound* against the *poverty* and *pestilence* through which they themselves daily walk." Find and mark several other examples of alliteration in the passage. Do they seem to contribute to the emphasis of the argument?

4. Identify the poets whom Shaw's Devil describes as "two of the greatest fools that ever lived, an Italian and an Englishman." What are their works that the Devil alludes to? Why should the Devil not admire those works?

5. Shaw spends most of the passage developing the idea of man's destructive weapons such as guns, the rack, the stake, the gallows, the sword, and poison gas. But he builds to the climax of the speech and turns to other devices by

which men "become the most destructive of all the destroyers." What are those devices?

6. Does the strength of the Devil's argument come wholly from the words and their arrangement in Shaw's passage? Do you find that he cites sufficient evidence so that a logical basis for the argument exists?

7. In view of the fact that these words are written to be spoken by the Devil, do you find any reason to believe that Shaw did not himself believe what he has the Devil say? Explain your answer.

8. What is the underlying irony in this passage—again considering that it is spoken by the Devil?

9. Notice that destruction is the unifying idea in the passage, appearing in the seventh word of the speech and again in the fifth word from the end. What, according to the Devil, is man destroying?

Martin Luther King, Jr.

I HAVE A DREAM

On August 28, 1963, a quarter of a million people of all races marched on Washington, D.C., in a civil rights demonstration. This March for Freedom culminated at the Lincoln Memorial, where leaders of the civil rights movement spoke the hopes of most Americans. It was Dr. Martin Luther King, Jr. (1929–1968), however, who made the most eloquent statement of the Negroes' dreams and aspirations. Seven years before, he rose to international prominence as organizer of the year-long boycott of local bus companies in Montgomery, Alabama, which ended in the desegregation of the buses. The year after the march on Washington, Dr. King received the Nobel Prize for Peace. In his last speech he said, "I've seen the promised land," but added, "I may not get there with you." The next day, April 4, 1968, in Memphis, he was assassinated.

[1] I am happy to join with you today in what will go down in history as the greatest demonstration for freedom in the history of our nation.

[2] Five score years ago, a great American, in whose symbolic shadow we stand today, signed the Emancipation Proclamation. This momentous decree came as a great beacon light of hope to millions of Negro slaves who had been

Reprinted by permission of Joan Daves. Copyright © 1963 by Martin Luther King, Jr.

seared in the flames of withering injustice. It came as a joyous daybreak to end the long night of their captivity. But one hundred years later, the Negro still is not free. One hundred years later, the life of the Negro is still sadly crippled by the manacles of segregation and the chains of discrimination. One hundred years later, the Negro lives on a lonely island of poverty in the midst of a vast ocean of material prosperity. One hundred years later, the Negro is still anguished in the corners of American society and finds himself in exile in his own land. And so we have come here today to dramatize a shameful condition.

[3] In a sense we have come to our nation's capital to cash a check. When the architects of our republic wrote the magnificent words of the Constitution and the Declaration of Independence, they were signing a promissory note to which every American was to fall heir. This note was the promise that all men —yes, Black men as well as white men—would be guaranteed the inalienable rights of life, liberty, and the pursuit of happiness.

[4] It is obvious today that America has defaulted on this promissory note insofar as her citizens of color are concerned. Instead of honoring this sacred obligation, America has given the Negro people a bad check, a check which has come back marked "insufficient funds." But we refuse to believe that the bank of justice is bankrupt. We refuse to believe that there are insufficient funds in the great vaults of opportunity of this nation; and so we have come to cash this check, a check that will give us upon demand the riches of freedom and the security of justice.

[5] We have also come to this hallowed spot to remind America of the fierce urgency of *now*. This is no time to engage in the luxury of cooling off or to take the tranquilizing drug of gradualism. *Now* is the time to make real the promises of democracy. *Now* is the time to rise from the dark and desolate valley of segregation to the sunlit path of racial justice. *Now* is the time to lift our nation from the quicksands of racial injustice to the solid rock of brotherhood. *Now* is the time to make justice a reality for all of God's children.

[6] It would be fatal for the nation to overlook the urgency of the moment. This sweltering summer of the Negro's legitimate discontent will not pass until there is an invigorating autumn of freedom and equality. Nineteen Sixty-three is not an end, but a beginning. And those who hope that the Negro needed to blow off steam and will now be content will have a rude awakening if the nation returns to business as usual. There will be neither rest nor tranquility in America until the Negro is granted his citizenship rights. The whirlwinds of revolt will continue to shake the foundations of our nation until the bright day of justice emerges.

[7] But there is something that I must say to my people who stand on the warm threshold which leads into the palace of justice. In the process of gaining our rightful place, we must not be guilty of wrongful deeds. Let us not seek to satisfy our thirst for freedom by drinking from the cup of bitterness and hatred. We must forever conduct our struggle on the high plane of dignity and discipline. We must not allow our creative protest to degenerate into physical violence. Again and again we must rise to the majestic heights of meeting physical force with soul force. And the marvelous new militancy which has engulfed the Negro community must not lead us to a distrust of all white people; for many of our white brothers, as evidenced by their presence here today, have come to realize that their destiny is tied up with our destiny, and they have come to realize that their freedom is inextricably bound to our freedom.

[8] We cannot walk alone. And as we walk we must make the pledge that we shall always march ahead. We cannot turn back. There are those who are asking the devotees of civil rights, "When will you be satisfied?" We can never be satisfied as long as the Negro is the victim of the unspeakable horrors of police brutality. We can never be satisfied as long as our bodies, heavy with the fatigue of travel, cannot gain lodging in the motels of the highways and the hotels of the cities. We cannot be satisfied as long as the Negro's basic mobility is from a smaller ghetto to a larger one. We can never be satisfied as long as our children are stripped of their selfhood and robbed of their dignity by signs stating "For Whites Only." We cannot be satisfied as long as the Negro in Mississippi cannot vote and a Negro in New York believes he has nothing for which to vote. No, no, we are not satisfied, and we will not be satisfied until justice rolls down like waters and righteousness like a mighty stream.

[9] I am not unmindful that some of you have come here out of great trials and tribulations. Some of you have come fresh from narrow jail cells. Some of you have come from areas where your quest for freedom left you battered by the storms of persecution and staggered by the winds of police brutality. You have been the veterans of creative suffering. Continue to work with the faith that unearned suffering is redemptive.

[10] Go back to Mississippi, and go back to Alabama. Go back to South Carolina. Go back to Georgia. Go back to Louisiana. Go back to the slums and ghettos of our Northern cities, knowing that somehow this situation can and will be changed. Let us not wallow in the valley of despair.

[11] I say to you today, my friends, even though we face the difficulties of

today and tomorrow, I still have a dream. It is a dream deeply rooted in the American dream. I have a dream that one day this nation will rise up and live out the true meaning of its creed: "We hold these truths to be self-evident, that all men are created equal." I have a dream that one day, on the red hills of Georgia, sons of former slaves and the sons of former slave owners will be able to sit down together at the table of brotherhood. I have a dream that one day even the state of Mississippi, a state sweltering with the heat of injustice, sweltering with the heat of oppression, will be transformed into an oasis of freedom and justice. I have a dream that my four little children will one day live in a nation where they will not be judged by the color of their skin, but by the content of their character.

[12] I have a dream today. I have a dream that one day down in Alabama—with its vicious racists, with its governor's lips dripping with the words of interposition and nullification—one day right there in Alabama, little Black boys and Black girls will be able to join hands with little white boys and white girls as sisters and brothers.

[13] I have a dream today. I have a dream that one day every valley shall be exalted and every hill and mountain shall be made low, the rough places will be made plain and the crooked places will be made straight, and the glory of the Lord shall be revealed, and all flesh shall see it together.

[14] This is our hope. This is the faith that I go back to the South with. And with this faith we will be able to hew out of the mountain of despair a stone of hope. With this faith we will be able to transform the jangling discords of our nation into a beautiful symphony of brotherhood. With this faith we will be able to work together, to play together, to struggle together, to go to jail together, to stand up for freedom together, knowing that we will be free one day.

[15] And this will be the day—this will be the day when all of God's children will be able to sing with new meaning:

> My country, 'tis of thee,
> Sweet land of liberty,
>   Of thee I sing;
> Land where my fathers died,
> Land of the Pilgrims' pride,
> From every mountainside
>   Let freedom ring.

And if America is to be a great nation, this must become true.

[16]   And so let freedom ring from the prodigious hilltops of New Hampshire. Let freedom ring from the mighty mountains of New York. Let freedom ring from the heightening Alleghenies of Pennsylvania. Let freedom ring from the snow-capped Rockies of Colorado. Let freedom ring from the curvaceous slopes of California.

[17]   But not only that. Let freedom ring from Stone Mountain of Georgia. Let freedom ring from Lookout Mountain of Tennessee. Let freedom ring from every hill and molehill of Mississippi. "From every mountainside let freedom ring."

[18]   And when this happens—when we allow freedom to ring, when we let it ring from every village and every hamlet, from every state and every city—we will be able to speed up that day when all of God's children, Black men and white men, Jews and Gentiles, Protestants and Catholics, will be able to join hands and sing in the words of the old Negro spiritual: "Free at last! Free at last! Thank God Almighty. We are free at last!"

VOCABULARY

Define the following words as they are used in the selection: *inalienable* [3]; *hallowed, gradualism* [5]; *devotees* [8]; *redemptive* [9]; *interposition, nullification* [12]; *exalted* [13]; *discords* [14]; *prodigious* [16].

QUESTIONS FOR STUDY AND DISCUSSION

1. Though this speech depends for its cumulative effect on the eloquence of the language and the power of the vision Dr. King creates, its assumptions are essentially argumentative rather than emotional. Trace the allusions to a promissory note in the opening paragraphs and point out how these paragraphs are based upon the following line of reasoning:

> A promise was made.
> It has not been kept.
> Therefore, it is still owed.

2. Paragraph 4 continues the logical argument, in the form of a syllogism, with a major premise of "America honors its promises" and a minor premise of "America has made a promise to us." What is the logical conclusion? Though the major premise is an expression of an ideal, the conclusion is a demand for action. How does Dr. King make the transition in this paragraph from social idealism to a sense of immediate social reality?

3. Several of the images of the speech are based upon contrasts suggesting the conditions of the American Negro. In paragraph 2, for instance, Dr. King contrasts "a joyous daybreak" and "the long night of captivity." Point out similar contrasting images in the speech. Discuss their appropriateness and effectiveness.

4. Look for the images associated with the ideal of justice. What are the various connotations of these images?

5. One of the most effective rhetorical devices in the speech is the use of repetition of a phrase or a word to give both unity and climax to the statements. What examples of this technique do you find? Trace the development of some of these examples to see how, through both sentence length and the power of the imagery, Dr. King builds to climactic statements.

6. Dr. King makes much use of adjectives to communicate emotion. In paragraph 2, for example, the evocative adjectives are *great* (used twice), *symbolic, momentous, withering,* and *joyous.* Read the paragraph without these adjectives. Does the paragraph lose effectiveness? What further examples of evocative adjectives do you find?

7. Since the speech turns on contrasts of time, verbs denoting tense are very significant. In paragraph 8, for example, most of the statements are in present tense, and the change in tense is thus dramatic. Where does the change occur? What other effective uses of tense differences do you find?

8. In what ways does Dr. King make use of the setting of the speech? Do you find any words or phrases suggested by the association with Lincoln?

9. Dr. King quotes from and alludes to several famous American documents. What is the effect of these references and allusions? What is the basis of their appeal?

10. What, specifically, is the argumentative content of the speech? What is Dr. King advising his listeners to do? Do you see any inconsistency between his expression of urgency in paragraph 5 and his advice in paragraph 10? How are the statements in these paragraphs related to the warning in paragraph 7?

11. The present text of the speech is taken from a transcription that does not indicate paragraph divisions. Can you suggest improvements in paragraphing?

FOR FURTHER ANALYSIS

Tom Bethell

DARWIN'S MISTAKE

> Tom Bethell studied philosophy at Oxford. In this essay of argumentation he asks readers to give reconsideration to an old controversy between religion and science, then shows that more recent controversy among scientists themselves has led to some revaluations of the theory of natural selection. Says Bethell, "Darwin's idea of natural selection was quietly abandoned, even by his most ardent supporters, some years ago."

[1] How do we come to have horses and tigers and things? There are at least a million species in existence today, according to the paleontologist George Gaylord Simpson, and for every one extant, perhaps 100 are extinct. Such profusion! Such variety! How did it come about? The old answer was that they are created by God. But with the increasingly scientific temper of the eighteenth and nineteenth centuries, this explanation began to look insufficient. God was invisible, and so could not be part of any scientific explanation.

[2] So an alternative explanation was proposed by a number of savants, among them Jean Baptiste Lamarck and Erasmus Darwin: the various forms of life did not just appear (as at the tip of a magician's wand), but evolved by a process of gradual transformation. Horses came from something slightly less horselike, tigers from something slightly less tigerlike, and so on back, until finally, if you went back far enough in time, you would come to a primitive blob of life which itself got started (perhaps) by lightning striking the primeval soup.

[3] "Either each species of crocodile has been specially created," said Thomas Henry Huxley, "or it has arisen out of some pre-existing form by the operation of natural causes. Choose your hypothesis; I have chosen mine."

Copyright 1976 by *Harper's* magazine. Reprinted from the February 1976 issue by special permission.

[4] That's all very well, replied more conservative thinkers. If all of this life got here by evolution from more primitive life, then how did evolution occur? No answer was immediately forthcoming. Genesis prevailed. Then Charles Darwin (grandson of Erasmus) furnished what looked like the solution. He proposed the machinery of evolution, and claimed that it existed in nature. Natural selection, he called it.

[5] His idea was accepted with great rapidity. Once stated it seemed only too obvious. The survival of the fittest—of course! Some types are fitter than others, and given the competition—the "struggle for existence"—the fitter ones will survive to propagate their kind. And so animals, plants, all life in fact, will tend to get better and better. They would have to, with the fitter ones inevitably replacing those that are less fit. Nature itself, then, had evolving machinery built into it. "How extremely stupid not to have thought of that!" Huxley commented, after reading the *Origin of Species*. Huxley had coined the term *agnostic*, and he remained one. Meanwhile, the Genesis version didn't entirely fade away, but it inevitably took on a slightly superfluous air.

[6] That was a little over 100 years ago. By the time of the Darwin Centennial Celebrations at the University of Chicago in 1959, Darwinism was triumphant. At a panel discussion Sir Julian Huxley (grandson of Thomas Henry) affirmed that "the evolution of life is no longer a theory; it is a fact." He added sternly: "We do not intend to get bogged down in semantics and definitions." At about the same time, Sir Gavin de Beer of the British Museum remarked that if a layman sought to "impugn" Darwin's conclusions, it must be the result of "ignorance or effrontery." Garrett Hardin of the California Institute of Technology asserted that anyone who did not honor Darwin "inevitably attracts the speculative psychiatric eye to himself." Sir Julian Huxley saw the need for "true belief."

[7] So that was it, then. The whole matter was settled—as I assumed, and as I imagined most people must. Darwin had won. No doubt there were backward folk tucked away in the remoter valleys of Appalachia who still clung to their comforting beliefs, but they, of course, lacked education. Not everyone was enlightened—goodness knows the Scopes trial had proved that, if nothing else. And some of them still wouldn't let up, apparently—they were trying to change the textbooks and get the Bible back into biology. Well, there are always diehards.

[8] So it was only casually, about a year ago, that I picked up a copy of *Darwin Retried*, a slim volume by one Norman Macbeth, a Harvard-trained lawyer. An odd field for a lawyer, certainly. But an endorsement on the cover

by Karl Popper caught my eye. "I regard the book as . . . a really important contribution to the debate," Popper had written.

[9] The debate? What debate? This interested me. I had studied philosophy, and in my undergraduate days Popper was regarded as one of the top philosophers—especially important for having set forth "rules" for discriminating between genuine and pseudo science. And Popper evidently thought there had been a "debate" worth mentioning. In his bibliography Macbeth listed a few articles that had appeared in academic philosophy journals in recent years and evidently were a part of this debate.

[10] That was, as I say, a year ago, and by now I have read these articles and a good many others. In fact, I have spent a good portion of the last year familiarizing myself with this debate. It is surprising that so little word of it has leaked out, because it seems to have been one of the most important academic debates of the 1960s, and as I see it the conclusion is pretty staggering: Darwin's theory, I believe, is on the verge of collapse. In his famous book, *On the Origin of Species by Means of Natural Selection, or The Preservation of Favored Races in the Struggle for Life,* Darwin made a mistake sufficiently serious to undermine his theory. And that mistake has only recently been recognized as such. The machinery of evolution that he supposedly discovered has been challenged, and it is beginning to look as though what he really discovered was nothing more than the Victorian propensity to believe in progress. At one point in his argument, Darwin was misled. I shall try to elucidate here precisely where Darwin went wrong.

[11] What was it, then, that Darwin discovered? What was this mechanism of natural selection? Here it comes as a slight shock to learn that Darwin really didn't "discover" anything at all, certainly not in the same way that Kepler, for example, discovered the laws of planetary motion. The *Origin of Species* was not a demonstration but an argument—"one long argument," Darwin himself said at the end of the book—and natural selection was an idea, not a discovery. It was an idea that occurred to him in London in the late 1830s which he then pondered in the Home Counties over the next twenty years. As we now know, several other thinkers came up with the same or a very similar idea at about the same time. The most famous of these was Alfred Russel Wallace, but there were several others.

[12] The British philosopher Herbert Spencer was one who came within a hair's breadth of the idea of natural selection, in an essay called "The Theory of Population" published in the *Westminster Review* seven years before the *Origin of Species* came out. In this article Spencer used the phrase "the sur-

vival of the fittest" for the first time. Darwin then appropriated the phrase in the fifth edition of the *Origin of Species*, considering it an admirable summation of his argument. This argument was in fact an analogy, as follows:

[13] While in his country retreat Darwin spent a good deal of time with pigeon fanciers and animal breeders. He even bred pigeons himself. Of particular relevance to him was that breeders bred for certain characteristics (length of feather, length of wool, coloring), and that the offspring of the selected mates often tended to have the desired characteristics more abundantly, or more noticeably, than its parents. Thus, it could perhaps be said, a small amount of "evolution" had occurred between one generation and the next.

[14] By analogy, then, the same process occurred in nature, Darwin thought. As he wrote in the *Origin of Species*: "How fleeting are the wishes of man! how short his time! and consequently how poor will his productions be, compared with those accumulated by nature during whole geological periods. Can we wonder, then, that nature's productions should be far 'truer' in character than man's productions?"

[15] Just as the breeders selected those individuals best suited to the breeders' needs to be the parents of the next generation, so, Darwin argued, nature selected those organisms that were best fitted to survive the struggle for existence. In that way evolution would inevitably occur. And so there it was: a sort of improving machine inevitably at work in nature, "daily and hourly scrutinizing," Darwin wrote, "silently and insensibly working . . . at the improvement of each organic being." In this way, Darwin thought, one type of organism could be transformed into another—for instance, he suggested, bears into whales. So that was how we came to have horses and tigers and things—by natural selection.

[16] For quite some time Darwin's mechanism was not seriously examined, until the renowned geneticist T. H. Morgan, winner of the Nobel Prize for his work in mapping the chromosomes of fruit flies, suggested that the whole thing looked suspiciously like a tautology. "For, it may appear little more than a truism," he wrote, "to state that the individuals that are the best adapted to survive have a better chance of surviving than those not so well adapted to survive."

[17] The philosophical debate of the past ten to fifteen years has focused on precisely this point. The survival of the fittest? Any way of identifying the fittest other than by looking at the survivors? The preservation of "favored" races? Any way of identifying them other than by looking at the preserved

ones? If not, then Darwin's theory is reduced from the status of scientific theory to that of tautology.

[18] Philosophers have ranged on both sides of this critical question: are there criteria of fitness that are independent of survival? In one corner we have Darwin himself, who assumed that the answer was yes, and his supporters, prominent among them David Hull of the University of Wisconsin. In the other corner are those who say no, among whom may be listed A. G. N. Flew, A. R. Manser, and A. D. Barker. In a nutshell here is how the debate has gone:

[19] Darwin, as I say, just assumed that there really were independent criteria of fitness. For instance, it seemed obvious to him that extra speed would be useful for a wolf in an environment where prey was scarce, and only those wolves first on the scene of a kill would get enough to eat and, therefore, survive. David Hull has supported this line of reasoning, giving the analogous example of a creature that was better able than its mates to withstand desiccation in an arid environment.

[20] The riposte has been as follows: a mutation that enables a wolf to run faster than the pack only enables the wolf to survive better if it does, in fact, survive better. But such a mutation could also result in the wolf outrunning the pack a couple of times and getting first crack at the food, and then abruptly dropping dead of a heart attack, because the extra power in its legs placed an extra strain on its heart. Fitness must be identified with survival, because it is the overall animal that survives, or does not survive, not individual parts of it.

[21] However, we don't have to worry too much about umpiring this dispute, because a look at the biology books shows us that the evolutionary biologists themselves, perhaps in anticipation of this criticism, retreated to a fortified position some time ago, and conceded that "the survival of the fittest" was in truth a tautology. Here is C. H. Waddington, a prominent geneticist, speaking at the aforementioned Darwin Centennial in Chicago:

[22] "Natural selection, which was at first considered as though it were a hypothesis that was in need of experimental or observational confirmation turns out on closer inspection to be a tautology, a statement of an inevitable although previously unrecognized relation. It states that the fittest individuals in a population (defined as those which leave most offspring) will leave most offspring."

[23] The admission that Darwin's theory of natural selection was tautologi-

EMOTIONAL APPEALS 311

cal did not greatly bother the evolutionary theorists, however, because they had already taken the precaution of redefining natural selection to mean something quite different from what Darwin had in mind. Like the philosophical debate of the past decade, this remarkable development went largely unnoticed. In its new form, natural selection meant nothing more than that some organisms have more offspring than others: in the argot, differential reproduction. This indeed was an empirical fact about the world, not just something true by definition, as was the case with the claim that the fittest survive.

[24] The bold act of redefining selection was made by the British statistician and geneticist R. A. Fisher in a widely heralded book called *The Genetical Theory of Natural Selection*. Moreover, by making certain assumptions about birth and death rates, and combining them with Mendelian genetics, Fisher was able to qualify the resulting rates at which population ratios changed. This was called population genetics, and it brought great happiness to the hearts of many biologists, because the mathematical formulae looked so deliciously scientific and seemed to enhance the status of biology, making it more like physics. But here is what Waddington recently said about *this* development:

[25] "The theory of neo-Darwinism is a theory of the evolution of the population in respect to leaving offspring and not in respect to anything else. . . . Everybody has it in the back of his mind that the animals that leave the largest number of offspring are going to be those best adapted also for eating peculiar vegetation, or something of this sort, but this is not explicit in the theory. . . . There you do come to what is, in effect, a vacuous statement: Natural selection is that some things leave more offspring than others; and, you ask, which leave more offspring than others; and it is those that leave more offspring, and there is nothing more to it than that. *The whole real guts of evolution—which is how do you come to have horses and tigers and things —is outside the mathematical theory* [my italics]."

[26] Here, then, was the problem. Darwin's theory was supposed to have answered this question about horses and tigers. They had gradually developed, bit by bit, as it were, over the eons, through the good offices of an agency called natural selection. But now, in its new incarnation, natural selection was only able to explain how horses and tigers became more (or less) numerous— that is, by "differential reproduction." This failed to solve the question of how they came into existence in the first place.

[27] This was no good at all. As T. H. Morgan had remarked, with great clarity: "Selection, then, has not produced anything new, but only more of

certain kinds of individuals. Evolution, however, means producing new things, not more of what already exists."

[28] One more quotation should be enough to convince most people that Darwin's idea of natural selection was quietly abandoned, even by his most ardent supporters, some years ago. The following comment, by the geneticist H. J. Muller, another Nobel Prize winner, appeared in the Proceedings of the American Philosophical Society in 1949. It represents a direct admission by one of Darwin's greatest admirers that, however we come to have horses and tigers and things, it is not by natural selection. "We have just seen," Muller wrote, "that if selection could be somehow dispensed with, so that all variants survived and multiplied, the higher forms would nevertheless have arisen."

[29] I think it should now be abundantly clear that Darwin made a mistake in proposing his natural-selection theory, and it is fairly easy to detect the mistake. We have seen that what the theory so grievously lacks is a criterion of fitness that is independent of survival. If only there were some way of identifying the fittest beforehand, without always having to wait and see which ones survive, Darwin's theory would be testable rather than tautological.

[30] But as almost everyone now seems to agree, fittest inevitably means "those that survive best." Why, then, did Darwin assume that there were independent criteria? And the answer is, because in the case of artificial selection, from which he worked by analogy, *there really are independent criteria*. Darwin went wrong in thinking that this aspect of his analogy was valid. In our sheep example, remember, long wool was the "desirable" feature—the independent criterion. The lambs of woolly parental sheep may possess this feature even more than their parents, and so be "more evolved"—more in the desired direction.

[31] In nature, on the other hand, the offspring may differ from their parents in any direction whatsoever and be considered "more evolved" than their parents, provided only that they survive and leave offspring themselves. There is, then, no "selection" by nature at all. Nor does nature "act," as it is so often said to do in biology books. One organism may indeed be "fitter" than another from an evolutionary point of view, but the only event that determines this fitness is death (or infertility). This, of course, is not something which helps *create* the organism, but is something that terminates it. It occurs at the end, not the beginning of life.

[32] Darwin seems to have made the mistake of just assuming that there were independent criteria of fitness because he lived in a society in which change

was nearly always perceived as being for the good. R. C. Lewontin, Agassiz Professor of Zoology at Harvard, has written on this point: "The bourgeois revolution not only established change as the characteristic element of the cosmos, but added direction and progress as well. A world in which a man could rise from humble origins must have seemed, to him at least, a good world. Change per se was a moral quality. In this light, Spencer's assertion that change *is* progress is not surprising." One may note also James D. Watson's remark in *The Double Helix* that "cultural traditions play major roles" in the development of science.

[33] Lewontin goes on to point out that "the bourgeois revolution gave way to a period of consolidation, a period in which we find ourselves now." Perhaps that is why only relatively recently has the concept of natural selection come under strong attack.

[34] There is, in a way, a remarkable conclusion to this brief history of natural selection. The idea started out as a way of explaining how one type of animal gradually changed into another, but then it was redefined to be an explanation of how a given type of animal became more numerous. But wasn't natural selection supposed to have a *creative* role? the evolutionary theorists were asked. Darwin had thought so, after all. Now watch how they responded to this:

[35] The geneticist Theodosius Dobzhansky compared natural selection to "a human activity such as performing or composing music." Sir Gavin de Beer described it as a "master of ceremonies." George Gaylord Simpson at one point likened selection to a poet, at another to a builder. Ernst Mayr, Lewontin's predecessor at Harvard, compared selection to a sculptor. Sir Julian Huxley topped them all, however, by comparing natural selection to William Shakespeare.

[36] Life on Earth, initially thought to constitute a sort of prima facie case for a creator, was, as a result of Darwin's idea, envisioned merely as being the outcome of a process and a process that was, according to Dobzhansky, "blind, mechanical, automatic, impersonal," and, according to de Beer, was "wasteful, blind, and blundering." But as soon as these criticisms were leveled at natural selection, the "blind process" itself was compared to a poet, a composer a sculptor, Shakespeare—to the very notion of creativity that the idea of natural selection had originally replaced. It is clear, I think, that there was something very, very wrong with such an idea.

[37] I have not been surprised to read, therefore, in Lewontin's recent book,

The Genetic Basis of Evolutionary Change (1974), that in some of the latest evolutionary theories "natural selection plays no role at all." Darwin, I suggest, is in the process of being discarded, but perhaps in deference to the venerable old gentleman, resting comfortably in Westminster Abbey next to Sir Isaac Newton, it is being done as discreetly and gently as possible, with a minimum of publicity.

SUGGESTIONS FOR WRITING

1. Human imperfections and weaknesses make both sexes—of all ages, of all occupations, of all degrees of merit and virtue—vulnerable to such an attack as Thurber levels against women. Write an essay making a case against a single group: men, wives, husbands, younger brothers or sisters, older brothers or sisters, twin brothers or sisters, mothers, fathers, parents, teacher, students, movie actors, mechanics, politicians, farmers, folk singers, and so on. You will surely have your favorite group to inveigh against and your private list of reasons.

2. Write an essay on "The Case *for* Women," countering the arguments *against* women in Thurber's essay.

3. Since there are very few majorities these days, you are probably a member of some "minority" group that has been attacked or joked about. Following the method of Claiborne, write a rebuttal citing facts to show that your group deserves better treatment than it has sometimes received.

4. Parallels to the situation that motivated Thoreau to write "Civil Disobedience" are evident today. Write an essay on a contemporary issue, arguing a minority or anti-government position.

5. Select a current issue of local, campus, state, or national concern. As an individual or as a member of a group, write a statement of position or beliefs on the issue. Typically, such statements summarize the issue, set forth a list of reasons or arguments (often including grievances), and conclude with a strong statement of intention or belief. Follow the method of Jefferson in the Declaration of Independence.

6. Using the persuasive pattern of concession (as used by Emerson—see question 9, p. 283), write an essay discussing a subject that has something good to be said on both sides, but more to be said (as you see it) on one side than the other. For instance, you will find these topics suitable: the uses of television, labor unions, the volunteer army, movie censorship, athletic scholarships, social security, required college courses. Avoid the use of pro-and-con arguments; identify yourself with one set of arguments, state them, concede that there are other views, but show that the opposing arguments are not, in the final analysis, as significant or as valid as your own.

7. As did Planz, describe a place which is a testimony to "the wildness of civilization": a polluted river, stream, lake, or bay; a vacant lot, beach, or shoreline filled with debris; an abandoned play yard or vandalized park; even a housing

ARGUMENTATION

development or commercial area that was once an orchard or a farm or a wilderness. Use contrasts and descriptive language as instruments of persuasion.

8. Faulkner, especially in his last three paragraphs, presents a situation confronting the writer of today and places himself on record with advice about what the writer should do. Write an essay discussing the problems confronting one of these occupational groups: the teacher (faced with narrowing academic freedom and inadequate salary); the minister (faced with an increasingly sophisticated and secular congregation); the doctor (faced with high insurance fees and the threat of socialized medicine); the employer (faced with strong labor unions and the demand for employee fringe benefits); the worker (faced with inflation and a tight job market). You may, of course, select some other person or situation that you understand and feel strongly about. Indicate what the person should do about his situation.

9. Assume that you have just heard the Devil deliver the speech written for him by Shaw. Write a response countering his arguments indicting mankind. You may point out that the Devil has ignored man's accomplishments that could be considered beneficial—and cite a few of them. Try to use Shaw's device of antithesis in developing your essay (see question 2, p. 299).

10. Write an essay opposing an activity (a hobby, a sport, a laboratory assignment) or a medium of communication or entertainment (television, radio, newspapers, family magazines, news magazines, X-rated movies). Establish your position; do not cite evidence in favor of your subject. This is an assignment in the setting forth of evidence, not in objectivity.

11. "It is not desirable," says Thoreau, "to cultivate a respect for the law, so much as for the right. The only obligation which I have a right to assume is to do at any time what I think is right." Write an essay either defending or attacking Thoreau's statement. A concern with the definition of "right"—its nature and one's source of knowledge of it—should be central to the essay, whichever position is taken.

12. Write an essay in which you persuade the reader to do something by dwelling upon the fearful consequences of inaction or of following the opposite course of action. Show what will happen, for example, if he fails to vote at election time, take injections for immunity to a disease, keep up his grades, set a life goal and work toward it, provide for his old age, get a good education, get regular physical examinations, take care of his general health, or stop polluting the environment.

13. Plan an essay in which you show (in the manner of Bethell's "Darwin's Mistake") that a widely known theory of science, economics, or psychology may be attacked and abandoned one day. It will be helpful to use the *Readers' Guide to Periodical Literature* or other indexes to find articles revealing recent thought or discovery bearing upon your topic.

14. Using Dr. King's speech as a model, write an emotionally persuasive appeal, to be delivered at a site of appropriate historical significance, urging and encouraging your fellow man to adopt a course of action or to assume an attitude of mind that you believe necessary. Subjects that readily come to mind bear on such issues as segregation, civil rights, the environment, overpopulation, peace, women's liberation, mobilization and preparedness, and justice.

INDEX

This index includes terminology and explanations, names of authors of selections, and titles of selections. It does not include references to the contents of the selections or to the incidental names of authors in the introductory material and other apparatus.

Abstractions, defining, 109
Accuracy, in cause and effect, 79
Adequacy, in cause and effect, 79
Ad hominem arguments, 258–259
Alliteration, 136, 284
Allusions, historical, 285
The American, 162–166
Americanism, 116–119
Analogy: *see also* Comparison
   in argumentation, 259
   in definition, 109–110
   in the process, 6
Analysis: *see* Classification
". . . And I Hungered for Books,"
   243–251
Anecdotes, 236, 241–243
   in autobiography and biography, 197
   in descriptions of persons, 156
Angels on a Pin, 217–220
Appearance, in descriptions of persons, 156
Argumentation, 2, 80, 253–315
   emotional persuasion, 254–255, 284–305
   logical, 254–255, 255–283
   purposes of, 253–254
   types of, 254–255
Asimov, Isaac, 21–29
Assertions, in argumentation, 259–260
Assonance, 136
Authority, in cause and effect, 79
Autobiography, 196–214
   extended, 197

"Baby," 124–126
Bacon, Francis, 37–40

Becker, Carl L., 110–113, 113–115
Beginnings, in narration, 195
Berne, Eric, 43–46
Bethell, Tom, 306–314
Biography, 196–214
Birthday Party, 240–241
Bloomfield, Morton W., 121–124
Brackman, Jacob, 65–67
Brown, Claude, 124–126
Brush, Katharine, 240–241

Caen, Herb, 152–155
Calandra, Alexander, 217–220
Can People Be Judged by Their Appearance?, 43–46
Captain Ahab, 166–168
The Case against Women, 260–265
Categories, in classification, 30–31
Cause and effect, 78–108
   in factual narration, 216
   in logical argument, 258
   in paragraph development, 3
"A Child Went Forth," 202–205
Chronological development, in exposition, 3–4
Chronological tracing, in definition, 109
Chronology:
   in factual and historical narration, 216
   in narration, 195–196
   in the process, 4–5
Claiborne, Robert, 265–269
Classification, 30–55
Clemens, Samuel L.: *see* Twain, Mark
Colonizing the Heavens, 21–29

Colorful, Colored, and Colorless Words, 33–37
Comparison: *see also* Contrast
  in classification, 31, 56
  in definition, 56, 109–110
  in description, 135–136
  in exposition, 3
  in the process, 6
Comparison and contrast, 55–78
  defined, 55–56
  purposes of, 56
Concession, in argumentation, 260
Conclusion:
  in cause and effect, 79
  in narration, 195
  in syllogisms, 257–258
Confessions of a Female Chauvinist Sow, 72–77
Conflict, in fiction, 234
Connotation, 284–285
Consistency of tone, 236
Consonance, 136–137
Contrast: *see also* Comparison
  in classification, 31
  in definition, 109
  in description, 138
  in exposition, 3
Coordination, in the process, 5
Crane, Stephen, 182–185
Criteria, in classification, 30–31

Darwin's Mistake, 306–314
The Declaration of Independence, 269–274
Deduction:
  in argumentation, 256–257
  in definition, 110
Definition, 2, 3, 108–132
  defined, 108–109
  in paragraph development, 3
  types of, 108–109
Democracy, 113–115
Description, 133–192
  defined, 133–134
  impressionistic, 134
  of persons, 155–173
  of places, 137–155
  of sights, sounds, sensations, 173–185
  realistic, 134

Details:
  in autobiography, 196–197
  in description, 134–135, 137–138, 156, 174
  in narration, 194
  in paragraph development, 3
Development, methods of, 2–4, 31
  in definition, 110
The Devil Speaks, 297–300
Devoe, Alan, 9–13
Dialogue, in narration, 194, 195
Differentiae, in definition, 109
Documentation, 215–216
Dramatized narration, 194

Eastman, Max, 40–43
Effect, in description, 135
Emerson, Ralph Waldo, 279–283
Emotional appeals, 284–305
Empty Houses, 176–178
Enumeration, in classification, 31
Enumeration of details, in exposition, 3
Etymology, in definition, 109
Events, in narration, 215–216
Evidence:
  in argumentation, 255–256
  in cause and effect, 78–79
Examples:
  in classification, 31
  in definition, 109–110
  in exposition, 2–3
Exclusion:
  in classification, 30–31
  in definition, 110
  in exposition, 3
Explanation of a process, 2, 4–30
Exposition, 1–132
  classification, 30–55
  defined, 1
  definition, 108–132
  the process, 4–30
  types of, 2
Extended autobiography, 197
Extended definitions, 109, 110

Factual and historical narration, 215–233
Fallacies, logical, 79, 257–258
False analogy, 259

INDEX

Faulkner, William, 294–297
Fiction, 233–243
Figurative language, in description, 135–136. *See also* Imagery
Footnotes, 215
Formal definition, 108–109
Four Men in a Boat, 182–185
Four Types of Students, 31–33
Franklin, Benjamin, 6–8, 241–243
Frederic, Harold, 169–173
Fuller, Thomas, 31–33

Generalizations:
   hasty, 256
   in descriptions of persons, 156
   in induction, 256
Generalized narration, 194–195
Genus, in definition, 109
A Giant's Dead Body, 289–293
Golding, William, 47–54
Government and the Moral Sense, 274–278
Guilt by association, 257–258

A Hanging, 220–226
Hasty generalization, 256
Hawthorne, Nathaniel, 289–293
Hersey, John, 229–233
Historical narration, 215–233
Historical tracing, in definition, 109
History, 110–113
The House of Babbitt, 150–152
Huffaker, Clair, 209–214
Hughes, Langston, 198–201
Huntley, Chet, 178–181

I Have a Dream, 300–305
Imagery, in emotional appeals, 284, 285. *See also* Figurative language
Impressionistic description, 134, 156
In Business, 206–209
Induction:
   in argumentation, 256
   in cause and effect, 78
   in definition, 110
Informal definition, 109

James, Henry, 162–166

Jefferson, Thomas, 269–274

King, Martin Luther, Jr., 300–305

Lacy, Dan, 80–84
Langer, Susanne, 67–72
Language, 119–121
Language, in emotional appeals, 284–285
Learning to Write, 6–8
Lewis, Sinclair, 150–152
The Libido for the Ugly, 185–188
Life and Death of a Worm, 9–13
Logical argument, 254–255, 255–283
Logical definition, 108–109
Logical fallacies, 79, 257–258
London, Jack, 146–149
The Lord of Creation, 67–72

Major premise, 257–258
Melville, Herman, 166–168
Mencken, H. L., 185–188
Men's Words; Women's Roles, 80–84
Merwin, W. S., 17–21
Metaphor, 136
The Mind of the Past, 279–283
Minor premise, 257–258
Mood, in description, 134, 137
Morison, Samuel Eliot, 226–229
Muhammad Ali, 157–162

Narration, 193–252
   anecdotes, 236, 241–243
   autobiography and biography, 196–214
   defined, 193
   dramatized, 194
   factual and historical, 215–233
   fictional, 233–243
   generalized, 194–195
   structure of, 195–196
   summarized, 194–195
   types of, 193
Negation, in exposition, 3
Newmark, Leonard, 121–124
A Noiseless Flash, 229–233
Non sequitur, 79, 258
Norris, Frank, 139–142
Nouns, concrete, 109

Objectivity:
  in cause and effect, 78
  in description, 134, 156
  in factual and historical narration, 216
  in the process, 4
Of Babalawos and Shamans, 57–59
Of Studies, 37–40
Omniscient observer, 235
On Making Camp, 13–17
On Owning a Farm, 92–96
Onomatopoeia, 137
Organization:
  in exposition, 3
  in factual and historical narration, 216
Orwell, George, 96–107, 220–226
Outlining, 4–5

Paragraph development, 2–4
Personification, 136
Persuasion: *see* Argumentation
Pines, Maya, 57–59
Planz, Allan, 286–288
The Plastic Fantastic, 152–155
Plot, in fiction, 234–235
Point of view:
  in description, 135, 137, 156
  in fiction, 235–236
  in the process, 5–6
Politics and the English Language, 96–107
Polk Street, 139–142
Pony Boy, 209–214
The Pool, 286–288
Post hoc ergo propter hoc, 79, 258
Practical and Poetic People, 40–43
Preliminary Sketches, 171–173
Premises, in syllogisms, 257–258
Probability, 78–79
The process, 4–30
The Put-on, 65–67

Realistic description, 134
Repetition of phrases, 284
Restatement, in definition, 110
Richardson, Jack, 60–64
Roberts, Paul, 33–37
Roiphe, Anne, 72–77

The Salem Witchcraft Frenzy, 226–229
Salvation, 198–201
Science Has Spoiled My Supper, 85–92
Shaw, George Bernard, 297–300
Shecter, Leonard, 157–162
Simile, 135–136
Six O'Clock Prayers, 60–64
Slang, 121–124
The Song of the Land, 178–181
Sorting, in classification, 30–31
The Speckled Ax, 241–243
Steamboat Town, 143–145
Steinbeck, John, 176–178, 237–239
The Stockholm Address, 294–297
Storm on Jackson's Island, 174–176
Student Quarters, 146–149
Sturtevant, E. H., 119–121
Subjectivity, in description, 134
Subordination, in the process, 5
Summarized narration, 194–195
Syllogism, 257–258

Term, in definition, 108–109
Testimony, in argumentation, 256
Theme, in fiction, 234
Thinking as a Hobby, 47–54
Thomas, Piri, 206–209
Thoreau, Henry David, 92–96, 274–278
The Three Trustees, 169–173
Thurber, James, 260–265
Time sequence: *see* Chronology
Tone:
  in cause and effect, 79, 80
  in description, 135
  in fiction, 236
Topic sentences:
  in classification, 31
  in the process, 5
Transitions:
  in classification, 31
  in the process, 4–5
Truth:
  in cause and effect, 78–79
  in logical argument, 255–258
  in narration, 215, 233–234
  in syllogisms, 257
The Turtle, 237–239
Twain, Mark, 143–145, 174–176
Typicality, in cause and effect, 79

INDEX

Unchopping a Tree, 17–21

Validity:
   in logical argument, 255–258
   in syllogisms, 257
Van Doren, Mark, 127–130

A *Wasp Stings Back*, 265–269
What Is a Poet?, 127–130
White, Stewart Edward, 13–17
White, William Allen, 202–205
Wilson, Edmund, 116–119
Wright, Richard, 243–251
Wylie, Philip, 85–92

Morning Mastery
Journal

Volume ∞

Master Your Mornings, Master Your Life.

Created with love by
Amir Atighehchi, Ari Banayan, & Mikey Ahdoot

Copyright ©2019 Every Damn Day, LLC
All rights reserved.
Published by Every Damn Day, LLC.

No part of this publication may be reproduced, or stored in a retrieval system, or transmitted in any form or by any means, electronic, mechanical, recording, photocopying, scanning or otherwise, without express written permission of the publisher.

For information about permission to reproduce elections from this book, email team@habitnest.com
Visit our website at www.HabitNest.com

PUBLISHER'S DISCLAIMER

While the publisher and author have used their best efforts in preparing this book, they make no representations or warranties with respect to the accuracy or completeness of the contents of this book. The advice and strategies contained herein may not be suitable for your situation. You should consult with a professional where appropriate. Neither the publisher nor the author shall be liable for any loss of profit or any other commercial damages, including but not limited to special, incidental, consequential, or other damages.

The company, product, and service names used in this book are for identification purposes only. All trademarks and registered trademarks are the property of their respective owners.

SPECIAL THANKS

We'd like to extend a wholehearted, sincere thank you to Skyler Wolpert and Lindsay McDermott for formatting + editing help. We love ya!

ISBN: 9780998656199

SECOND EDITION

Our Mission

We are a team of people **obsessed with taking ACTION** and **learning new things** as quickly as possible.

We love finding the **fastest, most effective ways** to build a new skill, then **systemizing that process for others**.

With building new habits, we empathize with others every step of the way *because we go through the same process ourselves.* We live and breathe everything in our company.

We use our hard-earned intuition to outline **beautifully designed, intuitive products** to help people live **happier, more fulfilled lives.**

Everything we create comes with a mix of **bite-sized information, strategy, and accountability.** This hands you a simple yet **drastically effective roadmap** to build **any skill** or habit with.

We take this a step further by diving into **published scientific studies**, the opinions of subject-matter **experts**, and the **feedback we get from customers** to further enhance all the products we create.

Ultimately, Habit Nest is a **practical, action-oriented startup** aimed at helping others take back decisional authority over every action they take. We're here to help people live **wholesome, rewarding lives** at the **brink of their potential!**

– *Amir Atighehchi, Ari Banayan, & Mikey Ahdoot*
Cofounders of Habit Nest

Table of Contents

1 The 'Why' Revisited
- *Understanding Your Why*

7 The 'What'
- *Daily Tracking*

9 The 'How'
- *Make Your Mind Work for You*
- *The Power of Accountability*
- *A Simple Idea*
- *Commit*

16 Sprints
- *Sprint 7 - Gratitude. Days 1-31.*
- *Sprint 8 - Self-Care. Days 32-61.*
- *Sprint 9 - Mindset. Days 62-92.*
- *Sprint 10 - Optimism. Days 93-122.*
- *Sprint 11 - Exploration. Days 123-153.*
- *Sprint 12 - Authenticity. Days 154-183.*

227 Fin
- *Continuing the Habit… Maybe?*
- *Meet the Habit Nest Team*
- *What Habit Will You Conquer Next?*
- *Share the Love*
- *Bonus Free-writing Space*

The 'Why,' Revisited

Understanding Your Why

No matter what path we take on in life, our purpose and reasoning will serve as our guiding point throughout it. Our 'why' is the closest connection we have to our mental strength and power, and spending time to clarify it over and over as we grow throughout our journey is incredibly valuable.

You'll remember the emphasis we placed on this section in Volumes I - III of The *Morning Sidekick Journal*, and this time around is no different.

As your needs change, your values evolve, and your sense of drive continues to grow, re-establishing your 'Why' will help you throughout this new journal and keep you on a steady track to winning your mornings and winning your days.

Here are a few simple questions that <u>you should take your time to answer sincerely before moving on</u>.

These questions are aimed at getting to the root of what drives you, what gets you up every single morning.

The point of this is to guide you to make concrete decisions about how to set up your morning to fit the beautiful vision you have for your perfect life.

If you're going to continue doing this habit, you had better stay clear on why you're doing it in the first place.

Seriously. Take the time to define your dream life.

1. What did your life look like **before** beginning your last Morning Sidekick Journal? How did your life change afterwards?

_____
_____
_____
_____
_____

2. What sort of ripple effect would doing a morning routine have on other areas of my life? On other people's lives around me?

_____
_____
_____

3. What would my life look like if I do not do this? What would I be missing out on? How would missing those make me feel?

4. What life goals do I consistently avoid making time for? Can I implement taking action on these goals into my morning routine?

Bonus Question: What new hurdles am I facing in this new adventure that were not existent in my previous go at building my morning routine? How can I be extra vigilant about these?

_____

_____

_____

_____

_____

Bookmark this section and flip back here the next time you're struggling to stay consistent with this habit.

This section is your SOS Lifeline.

What to Expect

Daily Tracking
New Themed Sprints.

The tracking found in the Morning Mastery Journal revisits the themed sprints found in Volumes 2-3. The sprints will be extended to 30 days and will alternate between the ones found in Volume 2 and Volume 3. The breakdown is as follows:

Days 01-31: *Gratitude*
Days 31-62: *Self-Care*
Days 63-92: *Mindset*
Days 93-122: Optimism
Days 123-153: Exploration
Days 154-183: Authenticity

Having a different question throughout each sprint will set for a different mental focus on different parts of life that you can improve upon, while adding enough variety to keep the process interesting as you continue growing.

The chosen questions can be answered a multitude of times and, depending on what you are dealing with each day, will provide a different perspective on thinking further about your day.

The 'How'

Make Your Mind Work for You

Building habits vs. maintaining habits are two very different things.

At this point, you have done such a fantastic job with the former — it's time to set our sites on the latter. There are a few things to keep in mind with maintaining a habit in the long-term.

1. *Maintain a mindset of adaptability.*

    Just because doing a certain morning routine was useful for you at a certain point does not mean it should be something you must do every single day you for the rest of your life. In fact, exploration — either with different types of routines to set you up for your day, or with completely different types of activities — is something that should be experimented with continually as your life goals and focuses evolve.

    It's important to keep an eye on whether the ways you are starting your day are giving you an element of useful structure, a burst of energy, and a sense of fulfillment. If they do not anymore, that's a great sign to experiment with variability. Maybe reading a book became too static and you want to try consuming more content via podcasts or videos. Maybe you watch too much content daily and want a break from all the media, leading you back to books. Your exercise routine may completely change based on something your friend showed you last month.

    Double down on experimentation and adaptability. This is

something that will serve you for the rest of your life.

2. ***Remove all guilt associated in comparing your current self with your past self.***

If your life shifts into a phase where you are not doing a morning routine consistently, it can be very easy to compare yourself to the past 'you' where things were going perfectly.

Although learning from the past to see where you want to set your standard can be a useful thing, any emotional baggage over the past only detracts from your life.

*The beauty of all the work you put into building this as a habit is the ability of **shifting** from a place of not doing a routine, to a place where you are... NOT to be perfect all the time.*

Remember this and practice it as your life will call for different habits from you at different times. You can ALWAYS go back to where you were, it just **takes a few days of building the momentum.**

No, you did not 'lose your edge.' Your life just called for different things from you and now you get the ability to shift it in a direction that works for your needs NOW.

The Power of Accountability

Think about yourself over the last month — how many of those days could you say you lived as the absolute best version of yourself?

For many of us, the answer to that question is not as great as it could be. We all have ways of improving this over time, though having a source of external accountability can make ALL the difference in staying consistent with our goals.

It's so much easier to give in to our emotional needs and our shifting desires than it is to be disciplined, at all times.

However, this completely changes if we have somebody else checking in on us and specifically asking about the decisions we're making. Not in a guilt-inducing way whatsoever, but much more as a mirror reflecting the best version of ourselves and what we're capable of… as a real-world reminder that letting yourself down is something that you will have to think about and face later.

This is why we created our own accountability service, *Accountability Nest*, where a military veteran will hold you accountable to your goals every day.
Our coaches are people who have not only built discipline in their own life to a large degree, but who at the same time, are incredibly empathetic about other people and working with their individualized needs.

They'll reverse-engineer whether you're the type of person who thrives better under tough-love, under a more supportive environment, or a mix of the two.

They're very passionate to build up the discipline in yourself so you won't need to work with them for the long-run.

If this is something that interests you, you can learn more here: **habitnest.com/accountability**

A Simple Idea

We hope that after reading the introductory pages, you're motivated and ready to tackle tomorrow morning with every ounce of energy you have.

We'll leave you to it with one simple idea.

Tomorrow, you will be exactly who you are **today**.

The rest of your life is a future projection of who you are today.

If you **change** today, tomorrow will be **different**.

If you **don't change** today, the rest of your life is **pre-determined**.

Commit.

Although I've seen great growth already...

I know true warriors stay consistent on their path.

I know what needs to be done,
And I WILL stick with it.

I **<u>will</u>** do my morning
routine for the next week.

My word is like **gold**.

I will do whatever it takes
to make this happen.

I **<u>will</u>** do my morning routine this week (circle one):

(On Weekdays Only)   (Every Damn Day)

_____   _____
Signature   Date

(Note: We added 20 blank, lined pages with free-writing room at the end of the journal as an optional resource for you to use at anytime).

SPRINT 7:
DAYS 1-31

Sprint 7 **Gratitude.** Sprint 8 Self-Care. Sprint 9 Mindset. Sprint 10 Optimism. Sprint 11 Exploration. Sprint 12 Authenticity.

Sprint 7
Theme: *Gratitude.*

The theme for Sprint 7 is **GRATITUDE**. The quality of being grateful for one or another aspect of your life. Feeling grateful doesn't have to be something we experience by chance.

Gratitude is a choice that we can make by looking differently at our own life circumstances. It can be built as a muscle through practice. And that's one of the primary goals for this sprint.

For 21 days, you'll alternate through three questions that will encourage you to think about what you can be grateful for in your life.

Our recommendation? Don't simply say the first thing that comes to mind (the easy thing). Take a few minutes to really sit with the question and think about it. Try to find the feeling of gratitude as you write, rather than simply answering the question with something you know you 'should' be grateful for.

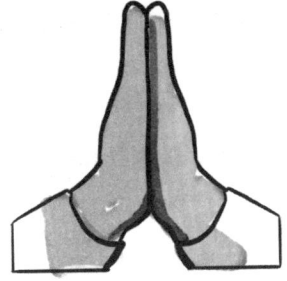

DATE

Night 00

TONIGHT I'LL SLEEP AT: _____ & TOMORROW I'LL WAKE UP AT: _____

🎁 WHAT AM I MOST GRATEFUL FOR TODAY?

_____
_____
_____

🤝 WHAT IS A CHALLENGE - BIG OR SMALL - I'VE SUCCESSFULLY MOVED PAST TODAY?

_____
_____

☀️ MY MORNING RITUAL TOMORROW WILL BE: *Completed?*

1. _____ ☐
2. _____ ☐
3. _____ ☐
4. _____ ☐
5. _____ ☐

Day 01

LAST NIGHT I SLEPT AT: _____ & WOKE UP TODAY AT: _____

🐸 MY MOST IMPORTANT TASK FOR TODAY IS:

_____

⏱ WHAT IS AN AREA OF WEAKNESS I HAVE IN MY LIFE THAT I WANT TO IMPROVE ON?

_____

DATE _____

Night 01

TONIGHT I'LL SLEEP AT: _____ & TOMORROW I'LL WAKE UP AT: _____

WHAT'S BEEN ONE BLESSING IN DISGUISE IN MY LIFE?

_____
_____
_____

WHAT IS A SKILL I'VE BUILT IN MY LIFE THAT I USED TO MY BENEFIT TODAY?

_____

MY MORNING RITUAL TOMORROW WILL BE: *Completed?*

1. _____ ☐
2. _____ ☐
3. _____ ☐
4. _____ ☐
5. _____ ☐

Day 02

LAST NIGHT I SLEPT AT: _____ & WOKE UP TODAY AT: _____

MY MOST IMPORTANT TASK FOR TODAY IS:

_____

WHO IS ONE PERSON I CAN GIVE EXTRA CARE AND ATTENTION TO TODAY?

_____

DATE

Night 02

TONIGHT I'LL SLEEP AT: _____ & TOMORROW I'LL WAKE UP AT: _____

WHAT'S ONE THING I CAN GIVE TO THE WORLD WITH NO EXPECTATION OF ANYTHING IN RETURN?

_____
_____
_____

WHAT IS ONE THING I DID TODAY THAT WILL HAVE A CHAIN-EFFECT OF SPREADING POSITIVITY?

_____

MY MORNING RITUAL TOMORROW WILL BE: *Completed?*

1. _____ ☐
2. _____ ☐
3. _____ ☐
4. _____ ☐
5. _____ ☐

Day 03

LAST NIGHT I SLEPT AT: _____ & WOKE UP TODAY AT: _____

MY MOST IMPORTANT TASK FOR TODAY IS:

_____

IF I WERE LIVING AS THE ABSOLUTE BEST VERSION OF MYSELF, WHAT COULD I CHANGE ABOUT MY ACTIONS TODAY?

_____

DATE _____

Night 03

TONIGHT I'LL SLEEP AT: _____ & TOMORROW I'LL WAKE UP AT: _____

WHAT AM I MOST GRATEFUL FOR TODAY?

_____
_____

IF A CLOSE FRIEND SAW HOW I HANDLED MY DAY TODAY, WHAT WOULD THEY TELL ME?

_____

Completed?

MY MORNING RITUAL TOMORROW WILL BE:

1. _____ ☐
2. _____ ☐
3. _____ ☐
4. _____ ☐
5. _____ ☐

Day 04

LAST NIGHT I SLEPT AT: _____ & WOKE UP TODAY AT: _____

MY MOST IMPORTANT TASK FOR TODAY IS:

_____

WHAT CAUSES ME STRESS AND HOW COULD I BETTER RESPOND TO IT?

_____

DATE _____

Night 04

TONIGHT I'LL SLEEP AT: _____ & TOMORROW I'LL WAKE UP AT: _____

🎁 WHAT'S BEEN ONE BLESSING IN DISGUISE IN MY LIFE?

_____
_____
_____

🤝 WHAT AM I GREAT AT THAT I DON'T GIVE MYSELF ENOUGH CREDIT FOR?

_____

☀ MY MORNING RITUAL TOMORROW WILL BE: *Completed?*

1. _____ ☐
2. _____ ☐
3. _____ ☐
4. _____ ☐
5. _____ ☐

Day 05

LAST NIGHT I SLEPT AT: _____ & WOKE UP TODAY AT: _____

🐎 MY MOST IMPORTANT TASK FOR TODAY IS:

_____

⏱ IF I WERE TO MAKE NO EXCUSES FOR MY LIFE, WHAT WOULD I DO DIFFERENTLY?

_____

DATE

Night 05

TONIGHT I'LL SLEEP AT: _____ & TOMORROW I'LL WAKE UP AT: _____

WHAT'S ONE THING I CAN GIVE TO THE WORLD WITH NO EXPECTATION OF ANYTHING IN RETURN?

_____
_____
_____

HOW HAVE I POSITIVELY IMPACTED SOMEONE'S LIFE TODAY?

_____

MY MORNING RITUAL TOMORROW WILL BE: *Completed?*

1. _____ ☐
2. _____ ☐
3. _____ ☐
4. _____ ☐
5. _____ ☐

Day 06

LAST NIGHT I SLEPT AT: _____ & WOKE UP TODAY AT: _____

MY MOST IMPORTANT TASK FOR TODAY IS:

_____

WHERE IS ONE PLACE I AM SPENDING TIME THAT DOES NOT BRING ME REAL HAPPINESS?

_____

Night 06

TONIGHT I'LL SLEEP AT: _____ & TOMORROW I'LL WAKE UP AT: _____

DATE

WHAT AM I MOST GRATEFUL FOR TODAY?

_____
_____
_____

WHAT IS SOMETHING I SPENT TIME ON TODAY THAT COULD POSITIVELY IMPACT MY FUTURE?

_____

MY MORNING RITUAL TOMORROW WILL BE: *Completed?*

1. _____ ☐
2. _____ ☐
3. _____ ☐
4. _____ ☐
5. _____ ☐

Day 07

LAST NIGHT I SLEPT AT: _____ & WOKE UP TODAY AT: _____

MY MOST IMPORTANT TASK FOR TODAY IS:

_____

WHO IS ONE CONTENT CREATOR OR AUTHOR I CAN REVISIT OR LEARN MORE FROM TO IMPROVE MY LIFE?

_____

DATE

Night 07

TONIGHT I'LL SLEEP AT: _____ & TOMORROW I'LL WAKE UP AT: _____

WHAT'S BEEN ONE BLESSING IN DISGUISE IN MY LIFE?

_____
_____
_____

WHAT IS ONE EMOTIONAL RESPONSE I HAD TODAY THAT I AM PROUD OF?

_____

MY MORNING RITUAL TOMORROW WILL BE: *Completed?*

1. _____ ☐
2. _____ ☐
3. _____ ☐
4. _____ ☐
5. _____ ☐

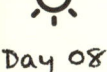

Day 08

LAST NIGHT I SLEPT AT: _____ & WOKE UP TODAY AT: _____

 ### MY MOST IMPORTANT TASK FOR TODAY IS:

_____

WHAT IS ONE TIME I WANT TO BE MORE PRESENT AND LESS DISTRACTED DURING MY DAY?

_____
_____

DATE

Night 08

TONIGHT I'LL SLEEP AT: _____ & TOMORROW I'LL WAKE UP AT: _____

WHAT'S ONE THING I CAN GIVE TO THE WORLD WITH NO EXPECTATION OF ANYTHING IN RETURN?

_____

_____

_____

HOW HAS MY OUTLOOK ON LIFE IMPROVED MY DAY?

_____

MY MORNING RITUAL TOMORROW WILL BE: *Completed?*

1. _____ ☐
2. _____ ☐
3. _____ ☐
4. _____ ☐
5. _____ ☐

Day 09

LAST NIGHT I SLEPT AT: _____ & WOKE UP TODAY AT: _____

MY MOST IMPORTANT TASK FOR TODAY IS:

_____

WHEN WAS THE LAST TIME I DID NOT STICK TO MY WORD? HOW CAN I AVOID DOING SO AGAIN?

_____

DATE _____

Night 09

TONIGHT I'LL SLEEP AT: _____ & TOMORROW I'LL WAKE UP AT: _____

WHAT AM I MOST GRATEFUL FOR TODAY?

_____
_____
_____

HOW HAVE I SET MY FUTURE SELF UP FOR SUCCESS TODAY?

_____

MY MORNING RITUAL TOMORROW WILL BE: *Completed?*

1. _____ ☐
2. _____ ☐
3. _____ ☐
4. _____ ☐
5. _____ ☐

Day 10

LAST NIGHT I SLEPT AT: _____ & WOKE UP TODAY AT: _____

MY MOST IMPORTANT TASK FOR TODAY IS:

_____

WHAT IS ONE AREA I CAN APPROACH WITH MORE ENTHUSIASM AND ENERGY TODAY?

_____
_____

DATE

Night 10

TONIGHT I'LL SLEEP AT: _____ & TOMORROW I'LL WAKE UP AT: _____

WHAT'S BEEN ONE BLESSING IN DISGUISE IN MY LIFE?

_____
_____
_____

WHAT IS A CHALLENGE - BIG OR SMALL - I'VE SUCCESSFULLY MOVED PAST TODAY?

_____

MY MORNING RITUAL TOMORROW WILL BE: *Completed?*

1. _____ ☐
2. _____ ☐
3. _____ ☐
4. _____ ☐
5. _____ ☐

Day 11

LAST NIGHT I SLEPT AT: _____ & WOKE UP TODAY AT: _____

MY MOST IMPORTANT TASK FOR TODAY IS:

_____

WHAT IS AN AREA OF WEAKNESS I HAVE IN MY LIFE THAT I WANT TO IMPROVE ON?

_____

DATE _____

Night 11

TONIGHT I'LL SLEEP AT: _____ & TOMORROW I'LL WAKE UP AT: _____

WHAT'S ONE THING I CAN GIVE TO THE WORLD WITH NO EXPECTATION OF ANYTHING IN RETURN?

_____
_____
_____

WHAT IS A SKILL I'VE BUILT IN MY LIFE THAT I USED TO MY BENEFIT TODAY?

_____

MY MORNING RITUAL TOMORROW WILL BE: *Completed?*

1. _____ ☐
2. _____ ☐
3. _____ ☐
4. _____ ☐
5. _____ ☐

Day 12

LAST NIGHT I SLEPT AT: _____ & WOKE UP TODAY AT: _____

MY MOST IMPORTANT TASK FOR TODAY IS:

_____

WHO IS ONE PERSON I CAN GIVE EXTRA CARE AND ATTENTION TO TODAY?

_____

DATE _____

Night 12

TONIGHT I'LL SLEEP AT: _____ & TOMORROW I'LL WAKE UP AT: _____

WHAT AM I MOST GRATEFUL FOR TODAY?

_____
_____
_____

WHAT IS ONE THING I DID TODAY THAT WILL HAVE A CHAIN-EFFECT OF SPREADING POSITIVITY?

_____

MY MORNING RITUAL TOMORROW WILL BE: *Completed?*

1. _____ ☐
2. _____ ☐
3. _____ ☐
4. _____ ☐
5. _____ ☐

Day 13

LAST NIGHT I SLEPT AT: _____ & WOKE UP TODAY AT: _____

MY MOST IMPORTANT TASK FOR TODAY IS:

_____

IF I WERE LIVING AS THE ABSOLUTE BEST VERSION OF MYSELF, WHAT COULD I CHANGE ABOUT MY ACTIONS TODAY?

_____

DATE _____

Night 13

TONIGHT I'LL SLEEP AT: _____ & TOMORROW I'LL WAKE UP AT: _____

🎁 WHAT'S BEEN ONE BLESSING IN DISGUISE IN MY LIFE?

_____

_____

_____

🤝 IF A CLOSE FRIEND SAW HOW I HANDLED MY DAY TODAY, WHAT WOULD THEY TELL ME?

_____

☀ MY MORNING RITUAL TOMORROW WILL BE: *Completed?*

1. _____ ☐
2. _____ ☐
3. _____ ☐
4. _____ ☐
5. _____ ☐

Day 14

LAST NIGHT I SLEPT AT: _____ & WOKE UP TODAY AT: _____

🐎 MY MOST IMPORTANT TASK FOR TODAY IS:

_____

🎯 WHAT CAUSES ME STRESS AND HOW COULD I BETTER RESPOND TO IT?

_____

DATE _____

Night 14

TONIGHT I'LL SLEEP AT: _____ & TOMORROW I'LL WAKE UP AT: _____

WHAT'S ONE THING I CAN GIVE TO THE WORLD WITH NO EXPECTATION OF ANYTHING IN RETURN?

_____
_____
_____

WHAT AM I GREAT AT THAT I DON'T GIVE MYSELF ENOUGH CREDIT FOR?

_____

MY MORNING RITUAL TOMORROW WILL BE: *Completed?*

1. _____ ☐
2. _____ ☐
3. _____ ☐
4. _____ ☐
5. _____ ☐

Day 15

LAST NIGHT I SLEPT AT: _____ & WOKE UP TODAY AT: _____

MY MOST IMPORTANT TASK FOR TODAY IS:

_____

IF I WERE TO MAKE NO EXCUSES FOR MY LIFE, WHAT WOULD I DO DIFFERENTLY?

_____

DATE

Night 15

TONIGHT I'LL SLEEP AT: _____ & TOMORROW I'LL WAKE UP AT: _____

WHAT AM I MOST GRATEFUL FOR TODAY?

_____
_____
_____

HOW HAVE I POSITIVELY IMPACTED SOMEONE'S LIFE TODAY?

_____

MY MORNING RITUAL TOMORROW WILL BE: *Completed?*

1. _____ ☐
2. _____ ☐
3. _____ ☐
4. _____ ☐
5. _____ ☐

Day 16

LAST NIGHT I SLEPT AT: _____ & WOKE UP TODAY AT: _____

MY MOST IMPORTANT TASK FOR TODAY IS:

_____

WHERE IS ONE PLACE I AM SPENDING TIME THAT DOES NOT BRING ME REAL HAPPINESS?

_____

Night 16

DATE: _____

TONIGHT I'LL SLEEP AT: _____ & TOMORROW I'LL WAKE UP AT: _____

🎁 WHAT'S BEEN ONE BLESSING IN DISGUISE IN MY LIFE?

_____

_____

_____

🤝 WHAT IS SOMETHING I SPENT TIME ON TODAY THAT COULD POSITIVELY IMPACT MY FUTURE?

_____

☀ MY MORNING RITUAL TOMORROW WILL BE: *Completed?*

1. _____ ☐
2. _____ ☐
3. _____ ☐
4. _____ ☐
5. _____ ☐

Day 17

LAST NIGHT I SLEPT AT: _____ & WOKE UP TODAY AT: _____

🐎 MY MOST IMPORTANT TASK FOR TODAY IS:

_____

⏰ WHO IS ONE CONTENT CREATOR OR AUTHOR I CAN REVISIT OR LEARN MORE FROM TO IMPROVE MY LIFE?

_____

DATE _____

Night 17

TONIGHT I'LL SLEEP AT: _____ & TOMORROW I'LL WAKE UP AT: _____

WHAT'S ONE THING I CAN GIVE TO THE WORLD WITH NO EXPECTATION OF ANYTHING IN RETURN?

_____
_____
_____

WHAT IS ONE EMOTIONAL RESPONSE I HAD TODAY THAT I AM PROUD OF?

_____

MY MORNING RITUAL TOMORROW WILL BE: *Completed?*

1. _____ ☐
2. _____ ☐
3. _____ ☐
4. _____ ☐
5. _____ ☐

Day 18

LAST NIGHT I SLEPT AT: _____ & WOKE UP TODAY AT: _____

MY MOST IMPORTANT TASK FOR TODAY IS:

_____

WHAT IS ONE TIME I WANT TO BE MORE PRESENT AND LESS DISTRACTED DURING MY DAY?

_____

DATE _____

Night 18

TONIGHT I'LL SLEEP AT: _____ & TOMORROW I'LL WAKE UP AT: _____

🎁 WHAT AM I MOST GRATEFUL FOR TODAY?

_____
_____
_____

🤝 HOW HAS MY OUTLOOK ON LIFE IMPROVED MY DAY?

_____

☀️ MY MORNING RITUAL TOMORROW WILL BE: *Completed?*

1. _____ ☐
2. _____ ☐
3. _____ ☐
4. _____ ☐
5. _____ ☐

Day 19

LAST NIGHT I SLEPT AT: _____ & WOKE UP TODAY AT: _____

🐸 MY MOST IMPORTANT TASK FOR TODAY IS:

_____

⏱ WHEN WAS THE LAST TIME I DID NOT STICK TO MY WORD? HOW CAN I AVOID DOING SO AGAIN?

_____

DATE _____

Night 19

TONIGHT I'LL SLEEP AT: _____ & TOMORROW I'LL WAKE UP AT: _____

🎁 WHAT'S BEEN ONE BLESSING IN DISGUISE IN MY LIFE?

_____
_____
_____

🤝 HOW HAVE I SET MY FUTURE SELF UP FOR SUCCESS TODAY?

_____

☀ MY MORNING RITUAL TOMORROW WILL BE: Completed?

1. _____ ☐
2. _____ ☐
3. _____ ☐
4. _____ ☐
5. _____ ☐

Day 20

LAST NIGHT I SLEPT AT: _____ & WOKE UP TODAY AT: _____

🐸 MY MOST IMPORTANT TASK FOR TODAY IS:

_____

🎯 WHAT IS ONE AREA I CAN APPROACH WITH MORE ENTHUSIASM AND ENERGY TODAY?

_____

DATE _____

Night 20

TONIGHT I'LL SLEEP AT: _____ & TOMORROW I'LL WAKE UP AT: _____

WHAT'S ONE THING I CAN GIVE TO THE WORLD WITH NO EXPECTATION OF ANYTHING IN RETURN?

_____
_____
_____

WHAT IS A CHALLENGE - BIG OR SMALL - I'VE SUCCESSFULLY MOVED PAST TODAY?

_____

MY MORNING RITUAL TOMORROW WILL BE: *Completed?*

1. _____ ☐
2. _____ ☐
3. _____ ☐
4. _____ ☐
5. _____ ☐

Day 21

LAST NIGHT I SLEPT AT: _____ & WOKE UP TODAY AT: _____

MY MOST IMPORTANT TASK FOR TODAY IS:

_____

WHAT IS AN AREA OF WEAKNESS I HAVE IN MY LIFE THAT I WANT TO IMPROVE ON?

_____

DATE _____

Night 21

TONIGHT I'LL SLEEP AT: _____ & TOMORROW I'LL WAKE UP AT: _____

WHAT AM I MOST GRATEFUL FOR TODAY?

_____
_____
_____

WHAT IS A SKILL I'VE BUILT IN MY LIFE THAT I USED TO MY BENEFIT TODAY?

_____

MY MORNING RITUAL TOMORROW WILL BE: *Completed?*

1. _____ ☐
2. _____ ☐
3. _____ ☐
4. _____ ☐
5. _____ ☐

Day 22

LAST NIGHT I SLEPT AT: _____ & WOKE UP TODAY AT: _____

MY MOST IMPORTANT TASK FOR TODAY IS:

_____

WHO IS ONE PERSON I CAN GIVE EXTRA CARE AND ATTENTION TO TODAY?

_____

DATE _____

Night 22

TONIGHT I'LL SLEEP AT: _____ & TOMORROW I'LL WAKE UP AT: _____

WHAT'S BEEN ONE BLESSING IN DISGUISE IN MY LIFE?

_____
_____
_____

WHAT IS ONE THING I DID TODAY THAT WILL HAVE A CHAIN-EFFECT OF SPREADING POSITIVITY?

_____

MY MORNING RITUAL TOMORROW WILL BE: *Completed?*

1. _____ ☐
2. _____ ☐
3. _____ ☐
4. _____ ☐
5. _____ ☐

Day 23

LAST NIGHT I SLEPT AT: _____ & WOKE UP TODAY AT: _____

MY MOST IMPORTANT TASK FOR TODAY IS:

_____

IF I WERE LIVING AS THE ABSOLUTE BEST VERSION OF MYSELF, WHAT COULD I CHANGE ABOUT MY ACTIONS TODAY?

_____

DATE _____

Night 23

TONIGHT I'LL SLEEP AT: _____ & TOMORROW I'LL WAKE UP AT: _____

WHAT'S ONE THING I CAN GIVE TO THE WORLD WITH NO EXPECTATION OF ANYTHING IN RETURN?

_____
_____
_____

IF A CLOSE FRIEND SAW HOW I HANDLED MY DAY TODAY, WHAT WOULD THEY TELL ME?

_____

MY MORNING RITUAL TOMORROW WILL BE: *Completed?*

1. _____ ☐
2. _____ ☐
3. _____ ☐
4. _____ ☐
5. _____ ☐

Day 24

LAST NIGHT I SLEPT AT: _____ & WOKE UP TODAY AT: _____

MY MOST IMPORTANT TASK FOR TODAY IS:

_____

WHAT CAUSES ME STRESS AND HOW COULD I BETTER RESPOND TO IT?

_____

DATE _____

Night 24

TONIGHT I'LL SLEEP AT: _____ & TOMORROW I'LL WAKE UP AT: _____

🎁 WHAT AM I MOST GRATEFUL FOR TODAY?

_____
_____
_____

🤝 WHAT AM I GREAT AT THAT I DON'T GIVE MYSELF ENOUGH CREDIT FOR?

_____

☀ MY MORNING RITUAL TOMORROW WILL BE:

Completed?

1. _____ ☐
2. _____ ☐
3. _____ ☐
4. _____ ☐
5. _____ ☐

Day 25

LAST NIGHT I SLEPT AT: _____ & WOKE UP TODAY AT: _____

🐸 MY MOST IMPORTANT TASK FOR TODAY IS:

_____

⊕ IF I WERE TO MAKE NO EXCUSES FOR MY LIFE, WHAT WOULD I DO DIFFERENTLY?

_____

DATE _____

Night 25

TONIGHT I'LL SLEEP AT: _____ & TOMORROW I'LL WAKE UP AT: _____

WHAT'S BEEN ONE BLESSING IN DISGUISE IN MY LIFE?

_____
_____
_____

HOW HAVE I POSITIVELY IMPACTED SOMEONE'S LIFE TODAY?

_____

MY MORNING RITUAL TOMORROW WILL BE: *Completed?*

1. _____ ☐
2. _____ ☐
3. _____ ☐
4. _____ ☐
5. _____ ☐

Day 26

LAST NIGHT I SLEPT AT: _____ & WOKE UP TODAY AT: _____

MY MOST IMPORTANT TASK FOR TODAY IS:

_____

WHERE IS ONE PLACE I AM SPENDING TIME THAT DOES NOT BRING ME REAL HAPPINESS?

_____

DATE

Night 26

TONIGHT I'LL SLEEP AT: _____ & TOMORROW I'LL WAKE UP AT: _____

WHAT'S ONE THING I CAN GIVE TO THE WORLD WITH NO EXPECTATION OF ANYTHING IN RETURN?

_____
_____
_____

WHAT IS SOMETHING I SPENT TIME ON TODAY THAT COULD POSITIVELY IMPACT MY FUTURE?

_____

MY MORNING RITUAL TOMORROW WILL BE: *Completed?*

1. _____ ☐
2. _____ ☐
3. _____ ☐
4. _____ ☐
5. _____ ☐

Day 27

LAST NIGHT I SLEPT AT: _____ & WOKE UP TODAY AT: _____

MY MOST IMPORTANT TASK FOR TODAY IS:

_____

WHO IS ONE CONTENT CREATOR OR AUTHOR I CAN REVISIT OR LEARN MORE FROM TO IMPROVE MY LIFE?

_____

DATE _____

Night 27

TONIGHT I'LL SLEEP AT: _____ & TOMORROW I'LL WAKE UP AT: _____

🎁 WHAT AM I MOST GRATEFUL FOR TODAY?

_____
_____
_____

🤝 WHAT IS ONE EMOTIONAL RESPONSE I HAD TODAY THAT I AM PROUD OF?

_____

☀ MY MORNING RITUAL TOMORROW WILL BE: *Completed?*

1. _____ ☐
2. _____ ☐
3. _____ ☐
4. _____ ☐
5. _____ ☐

Day 28

LAST NIGHT I SLEPT AT: _____ & WOKE UP TODAY AT: _____

🦌 MY MOST IMPORTANT TASK FOR TODAY IS:

_____

⏲ WHAT IS ONE TIME I WANT TO BE MORE PRESENT AND LESS DISTRACTED DURING MY DAY?

_____

DATE _____

Night 28

TONIGHT I'LL SLEEP AT: _____ & TOMORROW I'LL WAKE UP AT: _____

🎁 WHAT'S BEEN ONE BLESSING IN DISGUISE IN MY LIFE?

_____
_____
_____

🤝 HOW HAS MY OUTLOOK ON LIFE IMPROVED MY DAY?

_____

☀ MY MORNING RITUAL TOMORROW WILL BE: *Completed?*

1. _____ ☐
2. _____ ☐
3. _____ ☐
4. _____ ☐
5. _____ ☐

Day 29

LAST NIGHT I SLEPT AT: _____ & WOKE UP TODAY AT: _____

🐎 MY MOST IMPORTANT TASK FOR TODAY IS:

_____

🕐 WHEN WAS THE LAST TIME I DID NOT STICK TO MY WORD? HOW CAN I AVOID DOING SO AGAIN?

_____

DATE _____

Night 29

TONIGHT I'LL SLEEP AT: _____ & TOMORROW I'LL WAKE UP AT: _____

WHAT'S ONE THING I CAN GIVE TO THE WORLD WITH NO EXPECTATION OF ANYTHING IN RETURN?

_____
_____
_____

WHAT MEMORABLE MOMENT(S) DID I EXPERIENCE RECENTLY?

_____

MY MORNING RITUAL TOMORROW WILL BE: *Completed?*

1. _____ ☐
2. _____ ☐
3. _____ ☐
4. _____ ☐
5. _____ ☐

Day 30

LAST NIGHT I SLEPT AT: _____ & WOKE UP TODAY AT: _____

MY MOST IMPORTANT TASK FOR TODAY IS:

_____

WHAT IS ONE SMALL WAY I CAN IMPROVE MY LIFE?

_____

(Sprint 7 Complete!)   DATE

Night 30

TONIGHT I'LL SLEEP AT: _____ & TOMORROW I'LL WAKE UP AT: _____

WHAT AM I MOST GRATEFUL FOR TODAY?
_____
_____
_____

HOW HAVE I SHOWN MYSELF SELF-LOVE AND CARE TODAY?
_____
_____

MY MORNING RITUAL TOMORROW WILL BE: Completed?

1. _____ ☐
2. _____ ☐
3. _____ ☐
4. _____ ☐
5. _____ ☐

Day 31

LAST NIGHT I SLEPT AT: _____ & WOKE UP TODAY AT: _____

MY MOST IMPORTANT TASK FOR TODAY IS:
_____

WHO IS SOMEONE THAT WILL HAVE A POSITIVE EFFECT IN MY LIFE THAT I SHOULD SPEND MORE TIME WITH?
_____

~~SPRINT 7.~~ COMPLETED.

Sprint 7 Recap: Days 1-31

1. What have I learned about gratitude in the last 31 days?

_____

_____

2. What are some of the aspects of my life I realized I can be grateful for that I don't usually think about?

_____

_____

3. How does gratitude and positive thinking impact my day?

_____

_____

4. What am I grateful for in myself that I don't give myself enough credit for?

_____

_____

_____

5. How does an attitude of gratitude impact others around me?

_____

_____

_____

SPRINT 8:
DAYS 32-61

~~Sprint 7 Gratitude.~~ **Sprint 8 Self-Care.** Sprint 9 Mindset. Sprint 10 Optimism. Sprint 11 Exploration. Sprint 12 Authenticity.

Sprint 8
Theme: <u>Self-Care.</u>

This sprint's theme is self-care. Not self-care in the sense of actions you can do to take care of yourself, but rather how you change your way of looking at yourself and the events of your life to make you feel better about yourself.

For example, judging yourself less, closely examining how your actions and desires may contradict, learning to get over little things that cause emotional uproars in you, etc.

It's all about developing a sense of care and love for yourself by realizing you don't have to be so critical of yourself or others. We'll help you do this with questions that hopefully get you to look at very specific events in your life you can try to practice more self-care with.

(Sprint 7 Medal Earned!)   DATE _____

Night 31

TONIGHT I'LL SLEEP AT: _____ & TOMORROW I'LL WAKE UP AT: _____

🧘 IN WHAT WAYS AM I OVERLY CRITICAL OF MYSELF? HOW COULD I BE A BETTER BEST FRIEND TO MYSELF?

_____

_____

_____

🤝 WHAT IS A CHALLENGE - BIG OR SMALL - I'VE SUCCESSFULLY MOVED PAST TODAY?

_____

☀️ MY MORNING RITUAL TOMORROW WILL BE: *Completed?*

1. _____ ☐
2. _____ ☐
3. _____ ☐
4. _____ ☐
5. _____ ☐

Day 32

LAST NIGHT I SLEPT AT: _____ & WOKE UP TODAY AT: _____

🐸 MY MOST IMPORTANT TASK FOR TODAY IS:

_____

🎯 WHAT IS AN AREA OF WEAKNESS I HAVE IN MY LIFE THAT I WANT TO IMPROVE ON?

_____

DATE _____

Night 32

TONIGHT I'LL SLEEP AT: _____ & TOMORROW I'LL WAKE UP AT: _____

HOW AM I EMOTIONALLY RESPONDING TO CERTAIN SITUATIONS THAT I COULD PERCEIVE DIFFERENTLY TO BETTER SERVE MYSELF AND OTHERS?

_____
_____
_____

WHAT IS A SKILL I'VE BUILT IN MY LIFE THAT I USED TO MY BENEFIT TODAY?

_____

MY MORNING RITUAL TOMORROW WILL BE: *Completed?*

1. _____ ☐
2. _____ ☐
3. _____ ☐
4. _____ ☐
5. _____ ☐

Day 33

LAST NIGHT I SLEPT AT: _____ & WOKE UP TODAY AT: _____

MY MOST IMPORTANT TASK FOR TODAY IS:

_____

WHO IS ONE PERSON I CAN GIVE EXTRA CARE AND ATTENTION TO TODAY?

_____

Night 33

DATE

TONIGHT I'LL SLEEP AT: _____ & TOMORROW I'LL WAKE UP AT: _____

WHAT COULD I DO TO HELP MEET MY EMOTIONAL DESIRES MORE CONSISTENTLY?

_____

_____

_____

WHAT IS ONE THING I DID TODAY THAT WILL HAVE A CHAIN-EFFECT OF SPREADING POSITIVITY?

_____

MY MORNING RITUAL TOMORROW WILL BE: *Completed?*

1. _____ ☐
2. _____ ☐
3. _____ ☐
4. _____ ☐
5. _____ ☐

Day 34

LAST NIGHT I SLEPT AT: _____ & WOKE UP TODAY AT: _____

MY MOST IMPORTANT TASK FOR TODAY IS:

_____

IF I WERE LIVING AS THE ABSOLUTE BEST VERSION OF MYSELF, WHAT COULD I CHANGE ABOUT MY ACTIONS TODAY?

_____

DATE _____

Night 34

TONIGHT I'LL SLEEP AT: _____ & TOMORROW I'LL WAKE UP AT: _____

IN WHAT WAYS AM I OVERLY CRITICAL OF MYSELF? HOW COULD I BE A BETTER BEST FRIEND TO MYSELF?

_____
_____
_____

IF A CLOSE FRIEND SAW HOW I HANDLED MY DAY TODAY, WHAT WOULD THEY TELL ME?

_____

MY MORNING RITUAL TOMORROW WILL BE: *Completed?*

1. _____ ☐
2. _____ ☐
3. _____ ☐
4. _____ ☐
5. _____ ☐

Day 35

LAST NIGHT I SLEPT AT: _____ & WOKE UP TODAY AT: _____

MY MOST IMPORTANT TASK FOR TODAY IS:

_____

WHAT CAUSES ME STRESS AND HOW COULD I BETTER RESPOND TO IT?

_____

DATE _____

Night 35

TONIGHT I'LL SLEEP AT: _____ & TOMORROW I'LL WAKE UP AT: _____

HOW AM I EMOTIONALLY RESPONDING TO CERTAIN SITUATIONS THAT I COULD PERCEIVE DIFFERENTLY TO BETTER SERVE MYSELF AND OTHERS?

_____
_____
_____

WHAT AM I GREAT AT THAT I DON'T GIVE MYSELF ENOUGH CREDIT FOR?

_____

MY MORNING RITUAL TOMORROW WILL BE: *Completed?*

1. _____ ☐
2. _____ ☐
3. _____ ☐
4. _____ ☐
5. _____ ☐

Day 36

LAST NIGHT I SLEPT AT: _____ & WOKE UP TODAY AT: _____

MY MOST IMPORTANT TASK FOR TODAY IS:

_____

IF I WERE TO MAKE NO EXCUSES FOR MY LIFE, WHAT WOULD I DO DIFFERENTLY?

_____

DATE: _____

Night 36

TONIGHT I'LL SLEEP AT: _____ & TOMORROW I'LL WAKE UP AT: _____

WHAT COULD I DO TO HELP MEET MY EMOTIONAL DESIRES MORE CONSISTENTLY?

_____
_____
_____

HOW HAVE I POSITIVELY IMPACTED SOMEONE'S LIFE TODAY?

_____

MY MORNING RITUAL TOMORROW WILL BE: *Completed?*

1. _____ ☐
2. _____ ☐
3. _____ ☐
4. _____ ☐
5. _____ ☐

Day 37

LAST NIGHT I SLEPT AT: _____ & WOKE UP TODAY AT: _____

MY MOST IMPORTANT TASK FOR TODAY IS:

_____

WHERE IS ONE PLACE I AM SPENDING TIME THAT DOES NOT BRING ME REAL HAPPINESS?

_____

DATE

Night 37

TONIGHT I'LL SLEEP AT: _____ & TOMORROW I'LL WAKE UP AT: _____

**IN WHAT WAYS AM I OVERLY CRITICAL OF MYSELF?
HOW COULD I BE A BETTER BEST FRIEND TO MYSELF?**

_____
_____
_____

**WHAT IS SOMETHING I SPENT TIME ON TODAY
THAT COULD POSITIVELY IMPACT MY FUTURE?**

_____

MY MORNING RITUAL TOMORROW WILL BE: *Completed?*

1. _____ ☐
2. _____ ☐
3. _____ ☐
4. _____ ☐
5. _____ ☐

Day 38

LAST NIGHT I SLEPT AT: _____ & WOKE UP TODAY AT: _____

MY MOST IMPORTANT TASK FOR TODAY IS:

_____

**WHO IS ONE CONTENT CREATOR OR AUTHOR I CAN REVISIT
OR LEARN MORE FROM TO IMPROVE MY LIFE?**

_____

DATE _____

Night 38

TONIGHT I'LL SLEEP AT: _____ & TOMORROW I'LL WAKE UP AT: _____

HOW AM I EMOTIONALLY RESPONDING TO CERTAIN SITUATIONS THAT I COULD PERCEIVE DIFFERENTLY TO BETTER SERVE MYSELF AND OTHERS?

_____
_____
_____

WHAT IS ONE EMOTIONAL RESPONSE I HAD TODAY THAT I AM PROUD OF?

_____

MY MORNING RITUAL TOMORROW WILL BE: *Completed?*

1. _____ ☐
2. _____ ☐
3. _____ ☐
4. _____ ☐
5. _____ ☐

Day 39

LAST NIGHT I SLEPT AT: _____ & WOKE UP TODAY AT: _____

MY MOST IMPORTANT TASK FOR TODAY IS:

_____

WHAT IS ONE TIME I WANT TO BE MORE PRESENT AND LESS DISTRACTED DURING MY DAY?

_____

DATE

Night 39

TONIGHT I'LL SLEEP AT: _____ & TOMORROW I'LL WAKE UP AT: _____

WHAT COULD I DO TO HELP MEET MY EMOTIONAL DESIRES MORE CONSISTENTLY?

_____
_____
_____

HOW HAS MY OUTLOOK ON LIFE IMPROVED MY DAY?

_____

MY MORNING RITUAL TOMORROW WILL BE:

Completed?

1. _____ ☐
2. _____ ☐
3. _____ ☐
4. _____ ☐
5. _____ ☐

Day 40

LAST NIGHT I SLEPT AT: _____ & WOKE UP TODAY AT: _____

MY MOST IMPORTANT TASK FOR TODAY IS:

_____

WHEN WAS THE LAST TIME I DID NOT STICK TO MY WORD? HOW CAN I AVOID DOING SO AGAIN?

_____

DATE _____

Night 40

TONIGHT I'LL SLEEP AT: _____ & TOMORROW I'LL WAKE UP AT: _____

IN WHAT WAYS AM I OVERLY CRITICAL OF MYSELF? HOW COULD I BE A BETTER BEST FRIEND TO MYSELF?

_____
_____
_____

HOW HAVE I SET MY FUTURE SELF UP FOR SUCCESS TODAY?

_____

MY MORNING RITUAL TOMORROW WILL BE: *Completed?*

1. _____ ☐
2. _____ ☐
3. _____ ☐
4. _____ ☐
5. _____ ☐

Day 41

LAST NIGHT I SLEPT AT: _____ & WOKE UP TODAY AT: _____

MY MOST IMPORTANT TASK FOR TODAY IS:

_____

WHAT IS ONE AREA I CAN APPROACH WITH MORE ENTHUSIASM AND ENERGY TODAY?

_____

DATE _____

Night 41

TONIGHT I'LL SLEEP AT: _____ & TOMORROW I'LL WAKE UP AT: _____

HOW AM I EMOTIONALLY RESPONDING TO CERTAIN SITUATIONS THAT I COULD PERCEIVE DIFFERENTLY TO BETTER SERVE MYSELF AND OTHERS?

_____
_____
_____

WHAT IS A CHALLENGE - BIG OR SMALL - I'VE SUCCESSFULLY MOVED PAST TODAY?

_____

MY MORNING RITUAL TOMORROW WILL BE: *Completed?*

1. _____ ☐
2. _____ ☐
3. _____ ☐
4. _____ ☐
5. _____ ☐

Day 42

LAST NIGHT I SLEPT AT: _____ & WOKE UP TODAY AT: _____

MY MOST IMPORTANT TASK FOR TODAY IS:

_____

WHAT IS AN AREA OF WEAKNESS I HAVE IN MY LIFE THAT I WANT TO IMPROVE ON?

_____

DATE _____

Night 42

TONIGHT I'LL SLEEP AT: _____ & TOMORROW I'LL WAKE UP AT: _____

WHAT COULD I DO TO HELP MEET MY EMOTIONAL DESIRES MORE CONSISTENTLY?

_____
_____
_____

WHAT IS A SKILL I'VE BUILT IN MY LIFE THAT I USED TO MY BENEFIT TODAY?

_____

MY MORNING RITUAL TOMORROW WILL BE: *Completed?*

1. _____ ☐
2. _____ ☐
3. _____ ☐
4. _____ ☐
5. _____ ☐

Day 43

LAST NIGHT I SLEPT AT: _____ & WOKE UP TODAY AT: _____

MY MOST IMPORTANT TASK FOR TODAY IS:

_____

WHO IS ONE PERSON I CAN GIVE EXTRA CARE AND ATTENTION TO TODAY?

_____

Night 43

DATE _____

TONIGHT I'LL SLEEP AT: _____ & TOMORROW I'LL WAKE UP AT: _____

IN WHAT WAYS AM I OVERLY CRITICAL OF MYSELF? HOW COULD I BE A BETTER BEST FRIEND TO MYSELF?

_____
_____
_____

WHAT IS ONE THING I DID TODAY THAT WILL HAVE A CHAIN-EFFECT OF SPREADING POSITIVITY?

_____

MY MORNING RITUAL TOMORROW WILL BE: *Completed?*

1. _____ ☐
2. _____ ☐
3. _____ ☐
4. _____ ☐
5. _____ ☐

Day 44

LAST NIGHT I SLEPT AT: _____ & WOKE UP TODAY AT: _____

MY MOST IMPORTANT TASK FOR TODAY IS:

_____

IF I WERE LIVING AS THE ABSOLUTE BEST VERSION OF MYSELF, WHAT COULD I CHANGE ABOUT MY ACTIONS TODAY?

_____

DATE _____

Night 44

TONIGHT I'LL SLEEP AT: _____ & TOMORROW I'LL WAKE UP AT: _____

HOW AM I EMOTIONALLY RESPONDING TO CERTAIN SITUATIONS THAT I COULD PERCEIVE DIFFERENTLY TO BETTER SERVE MYSELF AND OTHERS?

_____
_____
_____

IF A CLOSE FRIEND SAW HOW I HANDLED MY DAY TODAY, WHAT WOULD THEY TELL ME?

_____

MY MORNING RITUAL TOMORROW WILL BE: *Completed?*

1. _____ ☐
2. _____ ☐
3. _____ ☐
4. _____ ☐
5. _____ ☐

Day 45

LAST NIGHT I SLEPT AT: _____ & WOKE UP TODAY AT: _____

MY MOST IMPORTANT TASK FOR TODAY IS:

_____

WHAT CAUSES ME STRESS AND HOW COULD I BETTER RESPOND TO IT?

_____

Night 45

DATE

TONIGHT I'LL SLEEP AT: _____ & TOMORROW I'LL WAKE UP AT: _____

WHAT COULD I DO TO HELP MEET MY EMOTIONAL DESIRES MORE CONSISTENTLY?

_____
_____
_____

WHAT AM I GREAT AT THAT I DON'T GIVE MYSELF ENOUGH CREDIT FOR?

_____

MY MORNING RITUAL TOMORROW WILL BE:

Completed?

1. _____ ☐
2. _____ ☐
3. _____ ☐
4. _____ ☐
5. _____ ☐

Day 46

LAST NIGHT I SLEPT AT: _____ & WOKE UP TODAY AT: _____

MY MOST IMPORTANT TASK FOR TODAY IS:

_____

IF I WERE TO MAKE NO EXCUSES FOR MY LIFE, WHAT WOULD I DO DIFFERENTLY?

_____

DATE _____

Night 46

TONIGHT I'LL SLEEP AT: _____ & TOMORROW I'LL WAKE UP AT: _____

IN WHAT WAYS AM I OVERLY CRITICAL OF MYSELF? HOW COULD I BE A BETTER BEST FRIEND TO MYSELF?

_____
_____
_____

HOW HAVE I POSITIVELY IMPACTED SOMEONE'S LIFE TODAY?

_____

MY MORNING RITUAL TOMORROW WILL BE: *Completed?*

1. _____ ☐
2. _____ ☐
3. _____ ☐
4. _____ ☐
5. _____ ☐

Day 47

LAST NIGHT I SLEPT AT: _____ & WOKE UP TODAY AT: _____

MY MOST IMPORTANT TASK FOR TODAY IS:

_____

WHERE IS ONE PLACE I AM SPENDING TIME THAT DOES NOT BRING ME REAL HAPPINESS?

_____

DATE _____

Night 47

TONIGHT I'LL SLEEP AT: _____ & TOMORROW I'LL WAKE UP AT: _____

HOW AM I EMOTIONALLY RESPONDING TO CERTAIN SITUATIONS THAT I COULD PERCEIVE DIFFERENTLY TO BETTER SERVE MYSELF AND OTHERS?

_____
_____
_____

WHAT IS SOMETHING I SPENT TIME ON TODAY THAT COULD POSITIVELY IMPACT MY FUTURE?

_____

MY MORNING RITUAL TOMORROW WILL BE: *Completed?*

1. _____ ☐
2. _____ ☐
3. _____ ☐
4. _____ ☐
5. _____ ☐

Day 48

LAST NIGHT I SLEPT AT: _____ & WOKE UP TODAY AT: _____

MY MOST IMPORTANT TASK FOR TODAY IS:

_____

WHO IS ONE CONTENT CREATOR OR AUTHOR I CAN REVISIT OR LEARN MORE FROM TO IMPROVE MY LIFE?

_____

DATE

Night 48

TONIGHT I'LL SLEEP AT: _____ & TOMORROW I'LL WAKE UP AT: _____

WHAT COULD I DO TO HELP MEET MY EMOTIONAL DESIRES MORE CONSISTENTLY?

_____

_____

_____

WHAT IS ONE EMOTIONAL RESPONSE I HAD TODAY THAT I AM PROUD OF?

_____

MY MORNING RITUAL TOMORROW WILL BE: *Completed?*

1. _____ ☐
2. _____ ☐
3. _____ ☐
4. _____ ☐
5. _____ ☐

Day 49

LAST NIGHT I SLEPT AT: _____ & WOKE UP TODAY AT: _____

MY MOST IMPORTANT TASK FOR TODAY IS:

_____

WHAT IS ONE TIME I WANT TO BE MORE PRESENT AND LESS DISTRACTED DURING MY DAY?

_____

Night 49

DATE

TONIGHT I'LL SLEEP AT: _____ & TOMORROW I'LL WAKE UP AT: _____

**IN WHAT WAYS AM I OVERLY CRITICAL OF MYSELF?
HOW COULD I BE A BETTER BEST FRIEND TO MYSELF?**

_____

_____

_____

HOW HAS MY OUTLOOK ON LIFE IMPROVED MY DAY?

_____

MY MORNING RITUAL TOMORROW WILL BE: *Completed?*

1. _____ ☐
2. _____ ☐
3. _____ ☐
4. _____ ☐
5. _____ ☐

Day 50

LAST NIGHT I SLEPT AT: _____ & WOKE UP TODAY AT: _____

MY MOST IMPORTANT TASK FOR TODAY IS:

_____

**WHEN WAS THE LAST TIME I DID NOT STICK TO MY WORD?
HOW CAN I AVOID DOING SO AGAIN?**

_____

DATE _____

Night 50

TONIGHT I'LL SLEEP AT: _____ & TOMORROW I'LL WAKE UP AT: _____

HOW AM I EMOTIONALLY RESPONDING TO CERTAIN SITUATIONS THAT I COULD PERCEIVE DIFFERENTLY TO BETTER SERVE MYSELF AND OTHERS?

_____
_____
_____

HOW HAVE I SET MY FUTURE SELF UP FOR SUCCESS TODAY?

_____

MY MORNING RITUAL TOMORROW WILL BE: *Completed?*

1. _____ ☐
2. _____ ☐
3. _____ ☐
4. _____ ☐
5. _____ ☐

Day 51

LAST NIGHT I SLEPT AT: _____ & WOKE UP TODAY AT: _____

MY MOST IMPORTANT TASK FOR TODAY IS:

_____

WHAT IS ONE AREA I CAN APPROACH WITH MORE ENTHUSIASM AND ENERGY TODAY?

_____

Night 51

TONIGHT I'LL SLEEP AT: _____ & TOMORROW I'LL WAKE UP AT: _____

WHAT COULD I DO TO HELP MEET MY EMOTIONAL DESIRES MORE CONSISTENTLY?

_____
_____
_____

WHAT IS A CHALLENGE - BIG OR SMALL - I'VE SUCCESSFULLY MOVED PAST TODAY?

_____

MY MORNING RITUAL TOMORROW WILL BE:

Completed?

1. _____ ☐
2. _____ ☐
3. _____ ☐
4. _____ ☐
5. _____ ☐

Day 52

LAST NIGHT I SLEPT AT: _____ & WOKE UP TODAY AT: _____

MY MOST IMPORTANT TASK FOR TODAY IS:

_____

WHAT IS AN AREA OF WEAKNESS I HAVE IN MY LIFE THAT I WANT TO IMPROVE ON?

_____

DATE _____

Night 52

TONIGHT I'LL SLEEP AT: _____ & TOMORROW I'LL WAKE UP AT: _____

**IN WHAT WAYS AM I OVERLY CRITICAL OF MYSELF?
HOW COULD I BE A BETTER BEST FRIEND TO MYSELF?**

_____
_____
_____

**WHAT IS A SKILL I'VE BUILT IN MY LIFE
THAT I USED TO MY BENEFIT TODAY?**

_____

MY MORNING RITUAL TOMORROW WILL BE: *Completed?*

1. _____ ☐
2. _____ ☐
3. _____ ☐
4. _____ ☐
5. _____ ☐

Day 53

LAST NIGHT I SLEPT AT: _____ & WOKE UP TODAY AT: _____

MY MOST IMPORTANT TASK FOR TODAY IS:

_____

**WHO IS ONE PERSON I CAN GIVE EXTRA
CARE AND ATTENTION TO TODAY?**

_____

DATE

Night 53

TONIGHT I'LL SLEEP AT: _____ & TOMORROW I'LL WAKE UP AT: _____

HOW AM I EMOTIONALLY RESPONDING TO CERTAIN SITUATIONS THAT I COULD PERCEIVE DIFFERENTLY TO BETTER SERVE MYSELF AND OTHERS?

_____
_____
_____

WHAT IS ONE THING I DID TODAY THAT WILL HAVE A CHAIN-EFFECT OF SPREADING POSITIVITY?

_____

MY MORNING RITUAL TOMORROW WILL BE: *Completed?*

1. _____ ☐
2. _____ ☐
3. _____ ☐
4. _____ ☐
5. _____ ☐

Day 54

LAST NIGHT I SLEPT AT: _____ & WOKE UP TODAY AT: _____

MY MOST IMPORTANT TASK FOR TODAY IS:

_____

IF I WERE LIVING AS THE ABSOLUTE BEST VERSION OF MYSELF, WHAT COULD I CHANGE ABOUT MY ACTIONS TODAY?

_____

DATE

Night 54

TONIGHT I'LL SLEEP AT: _____ & TOMORROW I'LL WAKE UP AT: _____

WHAT COULD I DO TO HELP MEET MY EMOTIONAL DESIRES MORE CONSISTENTLY?

_____
_____
_____

IF A CLOSE FRIEND SAW HOW I HANDLED MY DAY TODAY, WHAT WOULD THEY TELL ME?

_____

MY MORNING RITUAL TOMORROW WILL BE: *Completed?*

1. _____ ☐
2. _____ ☐
3. _____ ☐
4. _____ ☐
5. _____ ☐

Day 55

LAST NIGHT I SLEPT AT: _____ & WOKE UP TODAY AT: _____

MY MOST IMPORTANT TASK FOR TODAY IS:

_____

WHAT CAUSES ME STRESS AND HOW COULD I BETTER RESPOND TO IT?

_____

DATE _____

Night 55

TONIGHT I'LL SLEEP AT: _____ & TOMORROW I'LL WAKE UP AT: _____

**IN WHAT WAYS AM I OVERLY CRITICAL OF MYSELF?
HOW COULD I BE A BETTER BEST FRIEND TO MYSELF?**

_____
_____
_____

WHAT AM I GREAT AT THAT I DON'T GIVE MYSELF ENOUGH CREDIT FOR?

_____

MY MORNING RITUAL TOMORROW WILL BE: *Completed?*

1. _____ ☐
2. _____ ☐
3. _____ ☐
4. _____ ☐
5. _____ ☐

Day 56

LAST NIGHT I SLEPT AT: _____ & WOKE UP TODAY AT: _____

MY MOST IMPORTANT TASK FOR TODAY IS:

_____

**IF I WERE TO MAKE NO EXCUSES FOR MY LIFE,
WHAT WOULD I DO DIFFERENTLY?**

_____

DATE _____

Night 56

TONIGHT I'LL SLEEP AT: _____ & TOMORROW I'LL WAKE UP AT: _____

HOW AM I EMOTIONALLY RESPONDING TO CERTAIN SITUATIONS THAT I COULD PERCEIVE DIFFERENTLY TO BETTER SERVE MYSELF AND OTHERS?

_____
_____
_____

HOW HAVE I POSITIVELY IMPACTED SOMEONE'S LIFE TODAY?

_____

MY MORNING RITUAL TOMORROW WILL BE: *Completed?*

1. _____ ☐
2. _____ ☐
3. _____ ☐
4. _____ ☐
5. _____ ☐

Day 57

LAST NIGHT I SLEPT AT: _____ & WOKE UP TODAY AT: _____

MY MOST IMPORTANT TASK FOR TODAY IS:

_____

WHERE IS ONE PLACE I AM SPENDING TIME THAT DOES NOT BRING ME REAL HAPPINESS?

_____

DATE _____

Night 57

TONIGHT I'LL SLEEP AT: _____ & TOMORROW I'LL WAKE UP AT: _____

 WHAT COULD I DO TO HELP MEET MY EMOTIONAL DESIRES MORE CONSISTENTLY?

_____
_____
_____

WHAT IS SOMETHING I SPENT TIME ON TODAY THAT COULD POSITIVELY IMPACT MY FUTURE?

_____

MY MORNING RITUAL TOMORROW WILL BE: *Completed?*

1. _____ ☐
2. _____ ☐
3. _____ ☐
4. _____ ☐
5. _____ ☐

Day 58

LAST NIGHT I SLEPT AT: _____ & WOKE UP TODAY AT: _____

MY MOST IMPORTANT TASK FOR TODAY IS:

_____

WHO IS ONE CONTENT CREATOR OR AUTHOR I CAN REVISIT OR LEARN MORE FROM TO IMPROVE MY LIFE?

_____

DATE _____

Night 58

TONIGHT I'LL SLEEP AT: _____ & TOMORROW I'LL WAKE UP AT: _____

**IN WHAT WAYS AM I OVERLY CRITICAL OF MYSELF?
HOW COULD I BE A BETTER BEST FRIEND TO MYSELF?**

_____
_____
_____

WHAT IS ONE EMOTIONAL RESPONSE I HAD TODAY THAT I AM PROUD OF?

_____

MY MORNING RITUAL TOMORROW WILL BE: *Completed?*

1. _____ ☐
2. _____ ☐
3. _____ ☐
4. _____ ☐
5. _____ ☐

Day 59

LAST NIGHT I SLEPT AT: _____ & WOKE UP TODAY AT: _____

MY MOST IMPORTANT TASK FOR TODAY IS:

_____

**WHAT IS ONE TIME I WANT TO BE MORE PRESENT
AND LESS DISTRACTED DURING MY DAY?**

_____

DATE _____

Night 59

TONIGHT I'LL SLEEP AT: _____ & TOMORROW I'LL WAKE UP AT: _____

HOW AM I EMOTIONALLY RESPONDING TO CERTAIN SITUATIONS THAT I COULD PERCEIVE DIFFERENTLY TO BETTER SERVE MYSELF AND OTHERS?

_____
_____
_____

HOW HAS MY OUTLOOK ON LIFE IMPROVED MY DAY?

_____

MY MORNING RITUAL TOMORROW WILL BE: *Completed?*

1. _____ ☐
2. _____ ☐
3. _____ ☐
4. _____ ☐
5. _____ ☐

Day 60

LAST NIGHT I SLEPT AT: _____ & WOKE UP TODAY AT: _____

MY MOST IMPORTANT TASK FOR TODAY IS:

_____

WHEN WAS THE LAST TIME I DID NOT STICK TO MY WORD? HOW CAN I AVOID DOING SO AGAIN?

_____

(Sprint 8 Complete!)   DATE _____

Night 60

TONIGHT I'LL SLEEP AT: _____ & TOMORROW I'LL WAKE UP AT: _____

WHAT COULD I DO TO HELP MEET MY EMOTIONAL DESIRES MORE CONSISTENTLY?

_____
_____
_____

WHAT IS ONE UNIQUE THING ABOUT ME THAT MAKES ME INCREDIBLY SPECIAL?

_____

MY MORNING RITUAL TOMORROW WILL BE:

Completed?

1. _____ ☐
2. _____ ☐
3. _____ ☐
4. _____ ☐
5. _____ ☐

Day 61

LAST NIGHT I SLEPT AT: _____ & WOKE UP TODAY AT: _____

MY MOST IMPORTANT TASK FOR TODAY IS:

_____

WHAT IS ONE WAY I AM NOT FULLY LIVING UP TO MY POTENTIAL?

_____

SPRINT 8: COMPLETED.

Sprint 8 Recap: Days 31-61

1. In what ways was I beating myself up emotionally?

_____

_____

2. Which of my own needs can I take better care of?

_____

_____

3. What is something I can do for myself consistently that will provide me with a sense of joy?

_____

_____

4. How does taking care of myself better affect the rest of my life?

_____

_____

5. How does taking care of myself impact others around me?

_____

_____

SPRINT 9:
DAYS 62-92

Sprint 7 Gratitude. | Sprint 8 Self-Care. | **Sprint 9 Mindset.** | Sprint 10 Optimism. | Sprint 11 Exploration. | Sprint 12 Authenticity.

Sprint 9
Theme: <u>Mindset.</u>

The way we approach any part of our lives - what we think about it - our ideas and beliefs around it - determine our experience with it.

The goal for this theme is to begin to become more aware of what your day-to-day mindset currently is and how you can alter your system of ideas and beliefs. You'll be taking the mental space you ordinarily step into every day and shift it to better satisfy your image for the life you want to live.

You'll rotate through three questions as a guide to help you think more critically about your mindset to help you understand how powerful and important it is to try to choose your mindset rather than let it dictate your days.

(Sprint 8 Medal Earned!)   DATE _____

Night 61

TONIGHT I'LL SLEEP AT: _____ & TOMORROW I'LL WAKE UP AT: _____

IF I HAD A CONFIDENT, UNBREAKABLE MINDSET TODAY, HOW WOULD MY DAY TURN OUT?

_____

_____

_____

WHAT IS A CHALLENGE - BIG OR SMALL - I'VE SUCCESSFULLY MOVED PAST TODAY?

_____

MY MORNING RITUAL TOMORROW WILL BE: *Completed?*

1. _____ ☐
2. _____ ☐
3. _____ ☐
4. _____ ☐
5. _____ ☐

Day 62

LAST NIGHT I SLEPT AT: _____ & WOKE UP TODAY AT: _____

MY MOST IMPORTANT TASK FOR TODAY IS:

_____

WHAT IS AN AREA OF WEAKNESS I HAVE IN MY LIFE THAT I WANT TO IMPROVE ON?

_____

DATE _____

Night 62

TONIGHT I'LL SLEEP AT: _____ & TOMORROW I'LL WAKE UP AT: _____

WHAT WOULD THE STRONGEST VERSION OF MYSELF GUIDE ME IN DOING TODAY?

_____
_____
_____

WHAT IS A SKILL I'VE BUILT IN MY LIFE THAT I USED TO MY BENEFIT TODAY?

_____

MY MORNING RITUAL TOMORROW WILL BE: *Completed?*

1. _____ ☐
2. _____ ☐
3. _____ ☐
4. _____ ☐
5. _____ ☐

Day 63

LAST NIGHT I SLEPT AT: _____ & WOKE UP TODAY AT: _____

MY MOST IMPORTANT TASK FOR TODAY IS:

_____

WHO IS ONE PERSON I CAN GIVE EXTRA CARE AND ATTENTION TO TODAY?

_____

Night 63

TONIGHT I'LL SLEEP AT: _____ & TOMORROW I'LL WAKE UP AT: _____

WHAT IS A SEEMINGLY DIFFICULT MOMENT I COULD APPROACH WITH A DIFFERENT PERSPECTIVE TODAY?

_____
_____
_____

WHAT IS ONE THING I DID TODAY THAT WILL HAVE A CHAIN-EFFECT OF SPREADING POSITIVITY?

_____

MY MORNING RITUAL TOMORROW WILL BE: *Completed?*

1. _____ ☐
2. _____ ☐
3. _____ ☐
4. _____ ☐
5. _____ ☐

Day 64

LAST NIGHT I SLEPT AT: _____ & WOKE UP TODAY AT: _____

MY MOST IMPORTANT TASK FOR TODAY IS:

_____

IF I WERE LIVING AS THE ABSOLUTE BEST VERSION OF MYSELF, WHAT COULD I CHANGE ABOUT MY ACTIONS TODAY?

_____

DATE

DATE _____

Night 64

TONIGHT I'LL SLEEP AT: _____ & TOMORROW I'LL WAKE UP AT: _____

IF I HAD A CONFIDENT, UNBREAKABLE MINDSET TODAY, HOW WOULD MY DAY TURN OUT?

_____
_____
_____

IF A CLOSE FRIEND SAW HOW I HANDLED MY DAY TODAY, WHAT WOULD THEY TELL ME?

_____

MY MORNING RITUAL TOMORROW WILL BE: *Completed?*

1. _____ ☐
2. _____ ☐
3. _____ ☐
4. _____ ☐
5. _____ ☐

Day 65

LAST NIGHT I SLEPT AT: _____ & WOKE UP TODAY AT: _____

MY MOST IMPORTANT TASK FOR TODAY IS:

_____

WHAT CAUSES ME STRESS AND HOW COULD I BETTER RESPOND TO IT?

_____

DATE _____

Night 65

TONIGHT I'LL SLEEP AT: _____ & TOMORROW I'LL WAKE UP AT: _____

WHAT WOULD THE STRONGEST VERSION OF MYSELF GUIDE ME IN DOING TODAY?

_____
_____
_____

WHAT AM I GREAT AT THAT I DON'T GIVE MYSELF ENOUGH CREDIT FOR?

_____

MY MORNING RITUAL TOMORROW WILL BE: *Completed?*

1. _____ ☐
2. _____ ☐
3. _____ ☐
4. _____ ☐
5. _____ ☐

Day 66

LAST NIGHT I SLEPT AT: _____ & WOKE UP TODAY AT: _____

MY MOST IMPORTANT TASK FOR TODAY IS:

_____

IF I WERE TO MAKE NO EXCUSES FOR MY LIFE, WHAT WOULD I DO DIFFERENTLY?

_____

DATE _____

Night 66

TONIGHT I'LL SLEEP AT: _____ & TOMORROW I'LL WAKE UP AT: _____

WHAT IS A SEEMINGLY DIFFICULT MOMENT I COULD APPROACH WITH A DIFFERENT PERSPECTIVE TODAY?

_____
_____
_____

HOW HAVE I POSITIVELY IMPACTED SOMEONE'S LIFE TODAY?

_____

MY MORNING RITUAL TOMORROW WILL BE: *Completed?*

1. _____ ☐
2. _____ ☐
3. _____ ☐
4. _____ ☐
5. _____ ☐

Day 67

LAST NIGHT I SLEPT AT: _____ & WOKE UP TODAY AT: _____

MY MOST IMPORTANT TASK FOR TODAY IS:

_____

WHERE IS ONE PLACE I AM SPENDING TIME THAT DOES NOT BRING ME REAL HAPPINESS?

_____

DATE _____

Night 67

TONIGHT I'LL SLEEP AT: _____ & TOMORROW I'LL WAKE UP AT: _____

IF I HAD A CONFIDENT, UNBREAKABLE MINDSET TODAY, HOW WOULD MY DAY TURN OUT?

_____
_____
_____

WHAT IS SOMETHING I SPENT TIME ON TODAY THAT COULD POSITIVELY IMPACT MY FUTURE?

_____

MY MORNING RITUAL TOMORROW WILL BE: *Completed?*

1. _____ ☐
2. _____ ☐
3. _____ ☐
4. _____ ☐
5. _____ ☐

Day 68

LAST NIGHT I SLEPT AT: _____ & WOKE UP TODAY AT: _____

MY MOST IMPORTANT TASK FOR TODAY IS:

_____

WHO IS ONE CONTENT CREATOR OR AUTHOR I CAN REVISIT OR LEARN MORE FROM TO IMPROVE MY LIFE?

_____

DATE _____

Night 68

TONIGHT I'LL SLEEP AT: _____ & TOMORROW I'LL WAKE UP AT: _____

WHAT WOULD THE STRONGEST VERSION OF MYSELF GUIDE ME IN DOING TODAY?

_____
_____
_____

WHAT IS ONE EMOTIONAL RESPONSE I HAD TODAY THAT I AM PROUD OF?

_____

MY MORNING RITUAL TOMORROW WILL BE: Completed?

1. _____ ☐
2. _____ ☐
3. _____ ☐
4. _____ ☐
5. _____ ☐

Day 69

LAST NIGHT I SLEPT AT: _____ & WOKE UP TODAY AT: _____

MY MOST IMPORTANT TASK FOR TODAY IS:

_____

WHAT IS ONE TIME I WANT TO BE MORE PRESENT AND LESS DISTRACTED DURING MY DAY?

_____

DATE _____

Night 69

TONIGHT I'LL SLEEP AT: _____ & TOMORROW I'LL WAKE UP AT: _____

WHAT IS A SEEMINGLY DIFFICULT MOMENT I COULD APPROACH WITH A DIFFERENT PERSPECTIVE TODAY?

_____

_____

_____

HOW HAS MY OUTLOOK ON LIFE IMPROVED MY DAY?

_____

MY MORNING RITUAL TOMORROW WILL BE:

Completed?

1. _____ ☐
2. _____ ☐
3. _____ ☐
4. _____ ☐
5. _____ ☐

Day 70

LAST NIGHT I SLEPT AT: _____ & WOKE UP TODAY AT: _____

MY MOST IMPORTANT TASK FOR TODAY IS:

_____

WHEN WAS THE LAST TIME I DID NOT STICK TO MY WORD? HOW CAN I AVOID DOING SO AGAIN?

_____

DATE _____

Night 70

TONIGHT I'LL SLEEP AT: _____ & TOMORROW I'LL WAKE UP AT: _____

IF I HAD A CONFIDENT, UNBREAKABLE MINDSET TODAY, HOW WOULD MY DAY TURN OUT?

_____
_____
_____

HOW HAVE I SET MY FUTURE SELF UP FOR SUCCESS TODAY?

_____

MY MORNING RITUAL TOMORROW WILL BE: *Completed?*

1. _____ ☐
2. _____ ☐
3. _____ ☐
4. _____ ☐
5. _____ ☐

Day 71

LAST NIGHT I SLEPT AT: _____ & WOKE UP TODAY AT: _____

MY MOST IMPORTANT TASK FOR TODAY IS:

_____

WHAT IS ONE AREA I CAN APPROACH WITH MORE ENTHUSIASM AND ENERGY TODAY?

_____

DATE

Night 71

TONIGHT I'LL SLEEP AT: _____ & TOMORROW I'LL WAKE UP AT: _____

WHAT WOULD THE STRONGEST VERSION OF MYSELF GUIDE ME IN DOING TODAY?

_____
_____
_____

WHAT IS A CHALLENGE - BIG OR SMALL - I'VE SUCCESSFULLY MOVED PAST TODAY?

_____

MY MORNING RITUAL TOMORROW WILL BE: *Completed?*

1. _____ ☐
2. _____ ☐
3. _____ ☐
4. _____ ☐
5. _____ ☐

Day 72

LAST NIGHT I SLEPT AT: _____ & WOKE UP TODAY AT: _____

MY MOST IMPORTANT TASK FOR TODAY IS:

_____

WHAT IS AN AREA OF WEAKNESS I HAVE IN MY LIFE THAT I WANT TO IMPROVE ON?

_____

DATE _____

Night 72

TONIGHT I'LL SLEEP AT: _____ & TOMORROW I'LL WAKE UP AT: _____

WHAT IS A SEEMINGLY DIFFICULT MOMENT I COULD APPROACH WITH A DIFFERENT PERSPECTIVE TODAY?

_____
_____
_____

WHAT IS A SKILL I'VE BUILT IN MY LIFE THAT I USED TO MY BENEFIT TODAY?

_____
_____

MY MORNING RITUAL TOMORROW WILL BE: *Completed?*

1. _____ ☐
2. _____ ☐
3. _____ ☐
4. _____ ☐
5. _____ ☐

Day 73

LAST NIGHT I SLEPT AT: _____ & WOKE UP TODAY AT: _____

MY MOST IMPORTANT TASK FOR TODAY IS:

_____

WHO IS ONE PERSON I CAN GIVE EXTRA CARE AND ATTENTION TO TODAY?

_____

DATE _____

Night 73

TONIGHT I'LL SLEEP AT: _____ & TOMORROW I'LL WAKE UP AT: _____

IF I HAD A CONFIDENT, UNBREAKABLE MINDSET TODAY, HOW WOULD MY DAY TURN OUT?

_____
_____
_____

WHAT IS ONE THING I DID TODAY THAT WILL HAVE A CHAIN-EFFECT OF SPREADING POSITIVITY?

_____

MY MORNING RITUAL TOMORROW WILL BE: Completed?

1. _____ ☐
2. _____ ☐
3. _____ ☐
4. _____ ☐
5. _____ ☐

Day 74

LAST NIGHT I SLEPT AT: _____ & WOKE UP TODAY AT: _____

MY MOST IMPORTANT TASK FOR TODAY IS:

_____

IF I WERE LIVING AS THE ABSOLUTE BEST VERSION OF MYSELF, WHAT COULD I CHANGE ABOUT MY ACTIONS TODAY?

_____

Night 74

TONIGHT I'LL SLEEP AT: _____ & TOMORROW I'LL WAKE UP AT: _____

WHAT WOULD THE STRONGEST VERSION OF MYSELF GUIDE ME IN DOING TODAY?

_____
_____
_____

IF A CLOSE FRIEND SAW HOW I HANDLED MY DAY TODAY, WHAT WOULD THEY TELL ME?

_____

MY MORNING RITUAL TOMORROW WILL BE: *Completed?*

1. _____ ☐
2. _____ ☐
3. _____ ☐
4. _____ ☐
5. _____ ☐

Day 75

LAST NIGHT I SLEPT AT: _____ & WOKE UP TODAY AT: _____

MY MOST IMPORTANT TASK FOR TODAY IS:

_____

WHAT CAUSES ME STRESS AND HOW COULD I BETTER RESPOND TO IT?

_____

DATE

Night 75

TONIGHT I'LL SLEEP AT: _____ & TOMORROW I'LL WAKE UP AT: _____

WHAT IS A SEEMINGLY DIFFICULT MOMENT I COULD APPROACH WITH A DIFFERENT PERSPECTIVE TODAY?

_____
_____
_____

WHAT AM I GREAT AT THAT I DON'T GIVE MYSELF ENOUGH CREDIT FOR?

_____

MY MORNING RITUAL TOMORROW WILL BE: *Completed?*

1. _____ ☐
2. _____ ☐
3. _____ ☐
4. _____ ☐
5. _____ ☐

Day 76

LAST NIGHT I SLEPT AT: _____ & WOKE UP TODAY AT: _____

MY MOST IMPORTANT TASK FOR TODAY IS:

_____

IF I WERE TO MAKE NO EXCUSES FOR MY LIFE, WHAT WOULD I DO DIFFERENTLY?

_____

DATE _____

Night 76

TONIGHT I'LL SLEEP AT: _____ & TOMORROW I'LL WAKE UP AT: _____

IF I HAD A CONFIDENT, UNBREAKABLE MINDSET TODAY, HOW WOULD MY DAY TURN OUT?

_____

_____

_____

HOW HAVE I POSITIVELY IMPACTED SOMEONE'S LIFE TODAY?

_____

MY MORNING RITUAL TOMORROW WILL BE: *Completed?*

1. _____ ☐
2. _____ ☐
3. _____ ☐
4. _____ ☐
5. _____ ☐

Day 77

LAST NIGHT I SLEPT AT: _____ & WOKE UP TODAY AT: _____

MY MOST IMPORTANT TASK FOR TODAY IS:

_____

WHERE IS ONE PLACE I AM SPENDING TIME THAT DOES NOT BRING ME REAL HAPPINESS?

_____

Night 77

DATE _____

TONIGHT I'LL SLEEP AT: _____ & TOMORROW I'LL WAKE UP AT: _____

WHAT WOULD THE STRONGEST VERSION OF MYSELF GUIDE ME IN DOING TODAY?

_____
_____
_____

WHAT IS SOMETHING I SPENT TIME ON TODAY THAT COULD POSITIVELY IMPACT MY FUTURE?

_____

MY MORNING RITUAL TOMORROW WILL BE: *Completed?*

1. _____ ☐
2. _____ ☐
3. _____ ☐
4. _____ ☐
5. _____ ☐

Day 78

LAST NIGHT I SLEPT AT: _____ & WOKE UP TODAY AT: _____

MY MOST IMPORTANT TASK FOR TODAY IS:

_____

WHO IS ONE CONTENT CREATOR OR AUTHOR I CAN REVISIT OR LEARN MORE FROM TO IMPROVE MY LIFE?

_____

DATE

Night 78

TONIGHT I'LL SLEEP AT: _____ & TOMORROW I'LL WAKE UP AT: _____

WHAT IS A SEEMINGLY DIFFICULT MOMENT I COULD APPROACH WITH A DIFFERENT PERSPECTIVE TODAY?

_____
_____
_____

WHAT IS ONE EMOTIONAL RESPONSE I HAD TODAY THAT I AM PROUD OF?

_____

MY MORNING RITUAL TOMORROW WILL BE: *Completed?*

1. _____ ☐
2. _____ ☐
3. _____ ☐
4. _____ ☐
5. _____ ☐

Day 79

LAST NIGHT I SLEPT AT: _____ & WOKE UP TODAY AT: _____

MY MOST IMPORTANT TASK FOR TODAY IS:

_____

WHAT IS ONE TIME I WANT TO BE MORE PRESENT AND LESS DISTRACTED DURING MY DAY?

_____

Night 79

DATE

TONIGHT I'LL SLEEP AT: _____ & TOMORROW I'LL WAKE UP AT: _____

IF I HAD A CONFIDENT, UNBREAKABLE MINDSET TODAY, HOW WOULD MY DAY TURN OUT?

_____
_____
_____

HOW HAS MY OUTLOOK ON LIFE IMPROVED MY DAY?

_____

MY MORNING RITUAL TOMORROW WILL BE: *Completed?*

1. _____ ☐
2. _____ ☐
3. _____ ☐
4. _____ ☐
5. _____ ☐

Day 80

LAST NIGHT I SLEPT AT: _____ & WOKE UP TODAY AT: _____

MY MOST IMPORTANT TASK FOR TODAY IS:

_____

WHEN WAS THE LAST TIME I DID NOT STICK TO MY WORD? HOW CAN I AVOID DOING SO AGAIN?

_____

DATE

Night 80

TONIGHT I'LL SLEEP AT: _____ & TOMORROW I'LL WAKE UP AT: _____

WHAT WOULD THE STRONGEST VERSION OF MYSELF GUIDE ME IN DOING TODAY?

_____
_____
_____

HOW HAVE I SET MY FUTURE SELF UP FOR SUCCESS TODAY?

_____

MY MORNING RITUAL TOMORROW WILL BE:

Completed?

1. _____ ☐
2. _____ ☐
3. _____ ☐
4. _____ ☐
5. _____ ☐

Day 81

LAST NIGHT I SLEPT AT: _____ & WOKE UP TODAY AT: _____

MY MOST IMPORTANT TASK FOR TODAY IS:

_____

WHAT IS ONE AREA I CAN APPROACH WITH MORE ENTHUSIASM AND ENERGY TODAY?

_____

DATE

Night 81

TONIGHT I'LL SLEEP AT: _____ & TOMORROW I'LL WAKE UP AT: _____

WHAT IS A SEEMINGLY DIFFICULT MOMENT I COULD APPROACH WITH A DIFFERENT PERSPECTIVE TODAY?

_____
_____
_____

WHAT IS A CHALLENGE - BIG OR SMALL - I'VE SUCCESSFULLY MOVED PAST TODAY?

_____

MY MORNING RITUAL TOMORROW WILL BE: *Completed?*

1. _____ ☐
2. _____ ☐
3. _____ ☐
4. _____ ☐
5. _____ ☐

Day 82

LAST NIGHT I SLEPT AT: _____ & WOKE UP TODAY AT: _____

MY MOST IMPORTANT TASK FOR TODAY IS:

_____

WHAT IS AN AREA OF WEAKNESS I HAVE IN MY LIFE THAT I WANT TO IMPROVE ON?

_____

DATE _____

Night 82

TONIGHT I'LL SLEEP AT: _____ & TOMORROW I'LL WAKE UP AT: _____

IF I HAD A CONFIDENT, UNBREAKABLE MINDSET TODAY, HOW WOULD MY DAY TURN OUT?

_____
_____
_____

WHAT IS A SKILL I'VE BUILT IN MY LIFE THAT I USED TO MY BENEFIT TODAY?

_____

MY MORNING RITUAL TOMORROW WILL BE: *Completed?*

1. _____ ☐
2. _____ ☐
3. _____ ☐
4. _____ ☐
5. _____ ☐

Day 83

LAST NIGHT I SLEPT AT: _____ & WOKE UP TODAY AT: _____

MY MOST IMPORTANT TASK FOR TODAY IS:

_____

WHO IS ONE PERSON I CAN GIVE EXTRA CARE AND ATTENTION TO TODAY?

_____

DATE

Night 83

TONIGHT I'LL SLEEP AT: _____ & TOMORROW I'LL WAKE UP AT: _____

WHAT WOULD THE STRONGEST VERSION OF MYSELF GUIDE ME IN DOING TODAY?

_____
_____
_____

WHAT IS ONE THING I DID TODAY THAT WILL HAVE A CHAIN-EFFECT OF SPREADING POSITIVITY?

_____

MY MORNING RITUAL TOMORROW WILL BE: *Completed?*

1. _____ ☐
2. _____ ☐
3. _____ ☐
4. _____ ☐
5. _____ ☐

Day 84

LAST NIGHT I SLEPT AT: _____ & WOKE UP TODAY AT: _____

MY MOST IMPORTANT TASK FOR TODAY IS:

_____

IF I WERE LIVING AS THE ABSOLUTE BEST VERSION OF MYSELF, WHAT COULD I CHANGE ABOUT MY ACTIONS TODAY?

_____

DATE _____

Night 84

TONIGHT I'LL SLEEP AT: _____ & TOMORROW I'LL WAKE UP AT: _____

WHAT IS A SEEMINGLY DIFFICULT MOMENT I COULD APPROACH WITH A DIFFERENT PERSPECTIVE TODAY?

_____
_____
_____

IF A CLOSE FRIEND SAW HOW I HANDLED MY DAY TODAY, WHAT WOULD THEY TELL ME?

_____

MY MORNING RITUAL TOMORROW WILL BE: *Completed?*

1. _____ ☐
2. _____ ☐
3. _____ ☐
4. _____ ☐
5. _____ ☐

Day 85

LAST NIGHT I SLEPT AT: _____ & WOKE UP TODAY AT: _____

MY MOST IMPORTANT TASK FOR TODAY IS:

_____

WHAT CAUSES ME STRESS AND HOW COULD I BETTER RESPOND TO IT?

_____

DATE _____

Night 85

TONIGHT I'LL SLEEP AT: _____ & TOMORROW I'LL WAKE UP AT: _____

IF I HAD A CONFIDENT, UNBREAKABLE MINDSET TODAY, HOW WOULD MY DAY TURN OUT?

_____
_____
_____

WHAT AM I GREAT AT THAT I DON'T GIVE MYSELF ENOUGH CREDIT FOR?

_____

MY MORNING RITUAL TOMORROW WILL BE: *Completed?*

1. _____ ☐
2. _____ ☐
3. _____ ☐
4. _____ ☐
5. _____ ☐

Day 86

LAST NIGHT I SLEPT AT: _____ & WOKE UP TODAY AT: _____

MY MOST IMPORTANT TASK FOR TODAY IS:

_____

IF I WERE TO MAKE NO EXCUSES FOR MY LIFE, WHAT WOULD I DO DIFFERENTLY?

_____

DATE _____

Night 86

TONIGHT I'LL SLEEP AT: _____ & TOMORROW I'LL WAKE UP AT: _____

WHAT WOULD THE STRONGEST VERSION OF MYSELF GUIDE ME IN DOING TODAY?

_____
_____
_____

HOW HAVE I POSITIVELY IMPACTED SOMEONE'S LIFE TODAY?

_____

MY MORNING RITUAL TOMORROW WILL BE: *Completed?*

1. _____ ☐
2. _____ ☐
3. _____ ☐
4. _____ ☐
5. _____ ☐

Day 87

LAST NIGHT I SLEPT AT: _____ & WOKE UP TODAY AT: _____

MY MOST IMPORTANT TASK FOR TODAY IS:

_____

WHERE IS ONE PLACE I AM SPENDING TIME THAT DOES NOT BRING ME REAL HAPPINESS?

_____

DATE

Night 87

TONIGHT I'LL SLEEP AT: _____ & TOMORROW I'LL WAKE UP AT: _____

WHAT IS A SEEMINGLY DIFFICULT MOMENT I COULD APPROACH WITH A DIFFERENT PERSPECTIVE TODAY?

_____
_____
_____

WHAT IS SOMETHING I SPENT TIME ON TODAY THAT COULD POSITIVELY IMPACT MY FUTURE?

_____

MY MORNING RITUAL TOMORROW WILL BE: *Completed?*

1. _____ ☐
2. _____ ☐
3. _____ ☐
4. _____ ☐
5. _____ ☐

Day 88

LAST NIGHT I SLEPT AT: _____ & WOKE UP TODAY AT: _____

MY MOST IMPORTANT TASK FOR TODAY IS:

_____

WHO IS ONE CONTENT CREATOR OR AUTHOR I CAN REVISIT OR LEARN MORE FROM TO IMPROVE MY LIFE?

_____

DATE _____

Night 88

TONIGHT I'LL SLEEP AT: _____ & TOMORROW I'LL WAKE UP AT: _____

IF I HAD A CONFIDENT, UNBREAKABLE MINDSET TODAY, HOW WOULD MY DAY TURN OUT?

_____
_____
_____

WHAT IS ONE EMOTIONAL RESPONSE I HAD TODAY THAT I AM PROUD OF?

_____

MY MORNING RITUAL TOMORROW WILL BE: *Completed?*

1. _____ ☐
2. _____ ☐
3. _____ ☐
4. _____ ☐
5. _____ ☐

Day 89

LAST NIGHT I SLEPT AT: _____ & WOKE UP TODAY AT: _____

MY MOST IMPORTANT TASK FOR TODAY IS:

_____

WHAT IS ONE TIME I WANT TO BE MORE PRESENT AND LESS DISTRACTED DURING MY DAY?

_____

DATE

Night 89

TONIGHT I'LL SLEEP AT: _____ & TOMORROW I'LL WAKE UP AT: _____

WHAT WOULD THE STRONGEST VERSION OF MYSELF GUIDE ME IN DOING TODAY?

_____
_____
_____

HOW HAS MY OUTLOOK ON LIFE IMPROVED MY DAY?

_____

MY MORNING RITUAL TOMORROW WILL BE: *Completed?*

1. _____ ☐
2. _____ ☐
3. _____ ☐
4. _____ ☐
5. _____ ☐

Day 90

LAST NIGHT I SLEPT AT: _____ & WOKE UP TODAY AT: _____

MY MOST IMPORTANT TASK FOR TODAY IS:

_____

WHEN WAS THE LAST TIME I DID NOT STICK TO MY WORD? HOW CAN I AVOID DOING SO AGAIN?

_____

DATE _____

Night 90

TONIGHT I'LL SLEEP AT: _____ & TOMORROW I'LL WAKE UP AT: _____

WHAT IS A SEEMINGLY DIFFICULT MOMENT I COULD APPROACH WITH A DIFFERENT PERSPECTIVE TODAY?

_____
_____
_____

HOW HAVE I SET MY FUTURE SELF UP FOR SUCCESS TODAY?

_____

MY MORNING RITUAL TOMORROW WILL BE: *Completed?*

1. _____ ☐
2. _____ ☐
3. _____ ☐
4. _____ ☐
5. _____ ☐

Day 91

LAST NIGHT I SLEPT AT: _____ & WOKE UP TODAY AT: _____

MY MOST IMPORTANT TASK FOR TODAY IS:

_____

WHAT IS ONE AREA I CAN APPROACH WITH MORE ENTHUSIASM AND ENERGY TODAY?

_____

(Sprint 9 Complete!)

DATE

Night 91

TONIGHT I'LL SLEEP AT: _____ & TOMORROW I'LL WAKE UP AT: _____

IF I HAD A CONFIDENT, UNBREAKABLE MINDSET TODAY, HOW WOULD MY DAY TURN OUT?

_____
_____
_____

WHAT IS ONE UNIQUE THING ABOUT ME THAT MAKES ME INCREDIBLY SPECIAL?

_____

MY MORNING RITUAL TOMORROW WILL BE: *Completed?*

1. _____ ☐
2. _____ ☐
3. _____ ☐
4. _____ ☐
5. _____ ☐

Day 92

LAST NIGHT I SLEPT AT: _____ & WOKE UP TODAY AT: _____

MY MOST IMPORTANT TASK FOR TODAY IS:

_____

WHAT IS ONE WAY I AM NOT FULLY LIVING UP TO MY POTENTIAL?

_____

~~SPRINT 9.~~ CONQUERED.

Sprint 2 Recap: Days 62-92

1. What is my general daily mindset?

_____
_____

2. If I intentionally could choose my daily mindset, what would it be?

_____
_____

3. How does intentionally choosing how I perceive events in my life impact those events?

_____
_____

4. How does my mindset impact others around me?

_____
_____
_____

5. What else have I learned in the last 30 days?

_____
_____
_____

Sprint 10
Theme: <u>Optimism.</u>

Like most of the other themes you've gone through, this is about how you're mentally and emotionally looking at yourself and the events that take place in your life.

You'll get questions that'll prompt you to feel grateful for yourself by looking at how far you've come along, to look at future events with optimism, and planning optimistic mindsets for difficult situations to come.

Again, mindset is everything. Practicing your mindset intentionally is critically important to living the life you want.

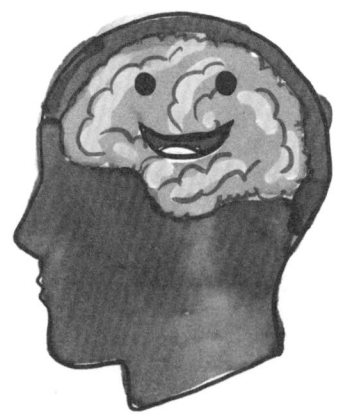

SPRINT 10:
DAYS 93-122

Sprint 7
Gratitude.

Sprint 8
Self-Care.

Sprint 9
Mindset.

**Sprint 10
Optimism.**

Sprint 11
Exploration.

Sprint 12
Authenticity.

(Sprint 9 Medal Earned!)

DATE _____

Night 92

TONIGHT I'LL SLEEP AT: _____ & TOMORROW I'LL WAKE UP AT: _____

WHAT AM I EXCITED FOR IN THE NEAR FUTURE? HOW CAN I MAKE THAT EXPERIENCE EVEN BETTER?

_____
_____
_____

WHAT IS A CHALLENGE - BIG OR SMALL - I'VE SUCCESSFULLY MOVED PAST TODAY?

_____

MY MORNING RITUAL TOMORROW WILL BE: *Completed?*

1. _____ ☐
2. _____ ☐
3. _____ ☐
4. _____ ☐
5. _____ ☐

Day 93

LAST NIGHT I SLEPT AT: _____ & WOKE UP TODAY AT: _____

MY MOST IMPORTANT TASK FOR TODAY IS:

_____

WHAT IS AN AREA OF WEAKNESS I HAVE IN MY LIFE THAT I WANT TO IMPROVE ON?

_____

Night 93

TONIGHT I'LL SLEEP AT: _____ & TOMORROW I'LL WAKE UP AT: _____

WHAT DID I VIEW AS A BIG CHALLENGE IN LIFE THAT I EVENTUALLY OVERCAME? WHAT DOES THAT SHOW ME ABOUT MYSELF?

_____
_____
_____

WHAT IS A SKILL I'VE BUILT IN MY LIFE THAT I USED TO MY BENEFIT TODAY?

_____

MY MORNING RITUAL TOMORROW WILL BE: *Completed?*

1. _____ ☐
2. _____ ☐
3. _____ ☐
4. _____ ☐
5. _____ ☐

Day 94

LAST NIGHT I SLEPT AT: _____ & WOKE UP TODAY AT: _____

MY MOST IMPORTANT TASK FOR TODAY IS:

_____

WHO IS ONE PERSON I CAN GIVE EXTRA CARE AND ATTENTION TO TODAY?

_____

DATE _____

Night 94

TONIGHT I'LL SLEEP AT: _____ & TOMORROW I'LL WAKE UP AT: _____

WHAT IS A DIFFICULT SITUATION I MAY FACE IN MY FUTURE? WHAT IS AN OPTIMISTIC MINDSET I COULD APPLY SHOULD I FACE IT?

_____
_____
_____

WHAT IS ONE THING I DID TODAY THAT WILL HAVE A CHAIN-EFFECT OF SPREADING POSITIVITY?

_____

MY MORNING RITUAL TOMORROW WILL BE: *Completed?*

1. _____ ☐
2. _____ ☐
3. _____ ☐
4. _____ ☐
5. _____ ☐

Day 95

LAST NIGHT I SLEPT AT: _____ & WOKE UP TODAY AT: _____

MY MOST IMPORTANT TASK FOR TODAY IS:

_____

IF I WERE LIVING AS THE ABSOLUTE BEST VERSION OF MYSELF, WHAT COULD I CHANGE ABOUT MY ACTIONS TODAY?

_____

DATE _____

Night 95

TONIGHT I'LL SLEEP AT: _____ & TOMORROW I'LL WAKE UP AT: _____

**WHAT AM I EXCITED FOR IN THE NEAR FUTURE?
HOW CAN I MAKE THAT EXPERIENCE EVEN BETTER?**

_____
_____
_____

**IF A CLOSE FRIEND SAW HOW I HANDLED MY
DAY TODAY, WHAT WOULD THEY TELL ME?**

_____

MY MORNING RITUAL TOMORROW WILL BE: *Completed?*

1. _____ ☐
2. _____ ☐
3. _____ ☐
4. _____ ☐
5. _____ ☐

Day 96

LAST NIGHT I SLEPT AT: _____ & WOKE UP TODAY AT: _____

MY MOST IMPORTANT TASK FOR TODAY IS:

_____

WHAT CAUSES ME STRESS AND HOW COULD I BETTER RESPOND TO IT?

_____

DATE _____

Night 96

TONIGHT I'LL SLEEP AT: _____ & TOMORROW I'LL WAKE UP AT: _____

WHAT DID I VIEW AS A BIG CHALLENGE IN LIFE THAT I EVENTUALLY OVERCAME? WHAT DOES THAT SHOW ME ABOUT MYSELF?

_____
_____
_____

WHAT AM I GREAT AT THAT I DON'T GIVE MYSELF ENOUGH CREDIT FOR?

_____

MY MORNING RITUAL TOMORROW WILL BE: *Completed?*

1. _____ ☐
2. _____ ☐
3. _____ ☐
4. _____ ☐
5. _____ ☐

Day 97

LAST NIGHT I SLEPT AT: _____ & WOKE UP TODAY AT: _____

MY MOST IMPORTANT TASK FOR TODAY IS:

_____

IF I WERE TO MAKE NO EXCUSES FOR MY LIFE, WHAT WOULD I DO DIFFERENTLY?

_____

DATE _____

Night 97

TONIGHT I'LL SLEEP AT: _____ & TOMORROW I'LL WAKE UP AT: _____

WHAT IS A DIFFICULT SITUATION I MAY FACE IN MY FUTURE? WHAT IS AN OPTIMISTIC MINDSET I COULD APPLY SHOULD I FACE IT?

_____
_____
_____

HOW HAVE I POSITIVELY IMPACTED SOMEONE'S LIFE TODAY?

_____

MY MORNING RITUAL TOMORROW WILL BE: *Completed?*

1. _____ ☐
2. _____ ☐
3. _____ ☐
4. _____ ☐
5. _____ ☐

Day 98

LAST NIGHT I SLEPT AT: _____ & WOKE UP TODAY AT: _____

MY MOST IMPORTANT TASK FOR TODAY IS:

_____

WHERE IS ONE PLACE I AM SPENDING TIME THAT DOES NOT BRING ME REAL HAPPINESS?

_____

DATE

Night 98

TONIGHT I'LL SLEEP AT: _____ & TOMORROW I'LL WAKE UP AT: _____

**WHAT AM I EXCITED FOR IN THE NEAR FUTURE?
HOW CAN I MAKE THAT EXPERIENCE EVEN BETTER?**

_____
_____
_____

**WHAT IS SOMETHING I SPENT TIME ON TODAY
THAT COULD POSITIVELY IMPACT MY FUTURE?**

_____

MY MORNING RITUAL TOMORROW WILL BE: *Completed?*

1. _____ ☐
2. _____ ☐
3. _____ ☐
4. _____ ☐
5. _____ ☐

Day 99

LAST NIGHT I SLEPT AT: _____ & WOKE UP TODAY AT: _____

 MY MOST IMPORTANT TASK FOR TODAY IS:

_____

**WHO IS ONE CONTENT CREATOR OR AUTHOR I CAN REVISIT
OR LEARN MORE FROM TO IMPROVE MY LIFE?**

_____

DATE _____

Night 99

TONIGHT I'LL SLEEP AT: _____ & TOMORROW I'LL WAKE UP AT: _____

WHAT DID I VIEW AS A BIG CHALLENGE IN LIFE THAT I EVENTUALLY OVERCAME? WHAT DOES THAT SHOW ME ABOUT MYSELF?

_____
_____
_____

WHAT IS ONE EMOTIONAL RESPONSE I HAD TODAY THAT I AM PROUD OF?

_____

MY MORNING RITUAL TOMORROW WILL BE: *Completed?*

1. _____ ☐
2. _____ ☐
3. _____ ☐
4. _____ ☐
5. _____ ☐

Day 100

LAST NIGHT I SLEPT AT: _____ & WOKE UP TODAY AT: _____

MY MOST IMPORTANT TASK FOR TODAY IS:

_____

WHAT IS ONE TIME I WANT TO BE MORE PRESENT AND LESS DISTRACTED DURING MY DAY?

_____

DATE

Night 100

TONIGHT I'LL SLEEP AT: _____ & TOMORROW I'LL WAKE UP AT: _____

**WHAT IS A DIFFICULT SITUATION I MAY FACE IN MY FUTURE?
WHAT IS AN OPTIMISTIC MINDSET I COULD APPLY SHOULD I FACE IT?**

_____

_____

_____

HOW HAS MY OUTLOOK ON LIFE IMPROVED MY DAY?

_____

MY MORNING RITUAL TOMORROW WILL BE: *Completed?*

1. _____ ☐
2. _____ ☐
3. _____ ☐
4. _____ ☐
5. _____ ☐

Day 101

LAST NIGHT I SLEPT AT: _____ & WOKE UP TODAY AT: _____

MY MOST IMPORTANT TASK FOR TODAY IS:

_____

**WHEN WAS THE LAST TIME I DID NOT STICK TO MY WORD?
HOW CAN I AVOID DOING SO AGAIN?**

_____

DATE _____

Night 101

TONIGHT I'LL SLEEP AT: _____ & TOMORROW I'LL WAKE UP AT: _____

WHAT AM I EXCITED FOR IN THE NEAR FUTURE? HOW CAN I MAKE THAT EXPERIENCE EVEN BETTER?

_____
_____
_____

HOW HAVE I SET MY FUTURE SELF UP FOR SUCCESS TODAY?

_____

MY MORNING RITUAL TOMORROW WILL BE: *Completed?*

1. _____ ☐
2. _____ ☐
3. _____ ☐
4. _____ ☐
5. _____ ☐

Day 102

LAST NIGHT I SLEPT AT: _____ & WOKE UP TODAY AT: _____

MY MOST IMPORTANT TASK FOR TODAY IS:

_____

WHAT IS ONE AREA I CAN APPROACH WITH MORE ENTHUSIASM AND ENERGY TODAY?

_____

DATE _____

Night 102

TONIGHT I'LL SLEEP AT: _____ & TOMORROW I'LL WAKE UP AT: _____

WHAT DID I VIEW AS A BIG CHALLENGE IN LIFE THAT I EVENTUALLY OVERCAME? WHAT DOES THAT SHOW ME ABOUT MYSELF?

_____
_____
_____

WHAT IS A CHALLENGE - BIG OR SMALL - I'VE SUCCESSFULLY MOVED PAST TODAY?

_____

MY MORNING RITUAL TOMORROW WILL BE: *Completed?*

1. _____ ☐
2. _____ ☐
3. _____ ☐
4. _____ ☐
5. _____ ☐

Day 103

LAST NIGHT I SLEPT AT: _____ & WOKE UP TODAY AT: _____

MY MOST IMPORTANT TASK FOR TODAY IS:

_____

WHAT IS AN AREA OF WEAKNESS I HAVE IN MY LIFE THAT I WANT TO IMPROVE ON?

_____

DATE _____

Night 103

TONIGHT I'LL SLEEP AT: _____ & TOMORROW I'LL WAKE UP AT: _____

WHAT IS A DIFFICULT SITUATION I MAY FACE IN MY FUTURE? WHAT IS AN OPTIMISTIC MINDSET I COULD APPLY SHOULD I FACE IT?

_____
_____
_____

WHAT IS A SKILL I'VE BUILT IN MY LIFE THAT I USED TO MY BENEFIT TODAY?

_____

MY MORNING RITUAL TOMORROW WILL BE: *Completed?*

1. _____ ☐
2. _____ ☐
3. _____ ☐
4. _____ ☐
5. _____ ☐

Day 104

LAST NIGHT I SLEPT AT: _____ & WOKE UP TODAY AT: _____

MY MOST IMPORTANT TASK FOR TODAY IS:

_____

WHO IS ONE PERSON I CAN GIVE EXTRA CARE AND ATTENTION TO TODAY?

_____

DATE _____

Night 104

TONIGHT I'LL SLEEP AT: _____ & TOMORROW I'LL WAKE UP AT: _____

WHAT AM I EXCITED FOR IN THE NEAR FUTURE? HOW CAN I MAKE THAT EXPERIENCE EVEN BETTER?

_____
_____
_____

WHAT IS ONE THING I DID TODAY THAT WILL HAVE A CHAIN-EFFECT OF SPREADING POSITIVITY?

_____

MY MORNING RITUAL TOMORROW WILL BE: *Completed?*

1. _____ ☐
2. _____ ☐
3. _____ ☐
4. _____ ☐
5. _____ ☐

Day 105

LAST NIGHT I SLEPT AT: _____ & WOKE UP TODAY AT: _____

MY MOST IMPORTANT TASK FOR TODAY IS:

_____

IF I WERE LIVING AS THE ABSOLUTE BEST VERSION OF MYSELF, WHAT COULD I CHANGE ABOUT MY ACTIONS TODAY?

_____

DATE _____

Night 105

TONIGHT I'LL SLEEP AT: _____ & TOMORROW I'LL WAKE UP AT: _____

WHAT DID I VIEW AS A BIG CHALLENGE IN LIFE THAT I EVENTUALLY OVERCAME? WHAT DOES THAT SHOW ME ABOUT MYSELF?

_____
_____
_____

IF A CLOSE FRIEND SAW HOW I HANDLED MY DAY TODAY, WHAT WOULD THEY TELL ME?

_____

MY MORNING RITUAL TOMORROW WILL BE: *Completed?*

1. _____ ☐
2. _____ ☐
3. _____ ☐
4. _____ ☐
5. _____ ☐

Day 106

LAST NIGHT I SLEPT AT: _____ & WOKE UP TODAY AT: _____

MY MOST IMPORTANT TASK FOR TODAY IS:

_____

WHAT CAUSES ME STRESS AND HOW COULD I BETTER RESPOND TO IT?

_____

DATE

Night 106

TONIGHT I'LL SLEEP AT: _____ & TOMORROW I'LL WAKE UP AT: _____

WHAT IS A DIFFICULT SITUATION I MAY FACE IN MY FUTURE? WHAT IS AN OPTIMISTIC MINDSET I COULD APPLY SHOULD I FACE IT?

_____
_____
_____

WHAT AM I GREAT AT THAT I DON'T GIVE MYSELF ENOUGH CREDIT FOR?

_____

MY MORNING RITUAL TOMORROW WILL BE: *Completed?*

1. _____ ☐
2. _____ ☐
3. _____ ☐
4. _____ ☐
5. _____ ☐

Day 107

LAST NIGHT I SLEPT AT: _____ & WOKE UP TODAY AT: _____

MY MOST IMPORTANT TASK FOR TODAY IS:

_____

IF I WERE TO MAKE NO EXCUSES FOR MY LIFE, WHAT WOULD I DO DIFFERENTLY?

_____

Night 107

DATE

TONIGHT I'LL SLEEP AT: _____ & TOMORROW I'LL WAKE UP AT: _____

**WHAT AM I EXCITED FOR IN THE NEAR FUTURE?
HOW CAN I MAKE THAT EXPERIENCE EVEN BETTER?**

_____
_____
_____

HOW HAVE I POSITIVELY IMPACTED SOMEONE'S LIFE TODAY?

_____

MY MORNING RITUAL TOMORROW WILL BE: *Completed?*

1. _____ ☐
2. _____ ☐
3. _____ ☐
4. _____ ☐
5. _____ ☐

Day 108

LAST NIGHT I SLEPT AT: _____ & WOKE UP TODAY AT: _____

MY MOST IMPORTANT TASK FOR TODAY IS:

_____

**WHERE IS ONE PLACE I AM SPENDING TIME THAT
DOES NOT BRING ME REAL HAPPINESS?**

_____

DATE

Night 108

TONIGHT I'LL SLEEP AT: _____ & TOMORROW I'LL WAKE UP AT: _____

WHAT DID I VIEW AS A BIG CHALLENGE IN LIFE THAT I EVENTUALLY OVERCAME? WHAT DOES THAT SHOW ME ABOUT MYSELF?

_____
_____
_____

WHAT IS SOMETHING I SPENT TIME ON TODAY THAT COULD POSITIVELY IMPACT MY FUTURE?

_____

MY MORNING RITUAL TOMORROW WILL BE: *Completed?*

1. _____ ☐
2. _____ ☐
3. _____ ☐
4. _____ ☐
5. _____ ☐

Day 109

LAST NIGHT I SLEPT AT: _____ & WOKE UP TODAY AT: _____

MY MOST IMPORTANT TASK FOR TODAY IS:

_____

WHO IS ONE CONTENT CREATOR OR AUTHOR I CAN REVISIT OR LEARN MORE FROM TO IMPROVE MY LIFE?

_____

DATE _____

Night 109

TONIGHT I'LL SLEEP AT: _____ & TOMORROW I'LL WAKE UP AT: _____

WHAT IS A DIFFICULT SITUATION I MAY FACE IN MY FUTURE? WHAT IS AN OPTIMISTIC MINDSET I COULD APPLY SHOULD I FACE IT?

_____
_____
_____

WHAT IS ONE EMOTIONAL RESPONSE I HAD TODAY THAT I AM PROUD OF?

_____

MY MORNING RITUAL TOMORROW WILL BE: *Completed?*

1. _____ ☐
2. _____ ☐
3. _____ ☐
4. _____ ☐
5. _____ ☐

Day 110

LAST NIGHT I SLEPT AT: _____ & WOKE UP TODAY AT: _____

MY MOST IMPORTANT TASK FOR TODAY IS:

_____

WHAT IS ONE TIME I WANT TO BE MORE PRESENT AND LESS DISTRACTED DURING MY DAY?

_____

Night 110

DATE _____

TONIGHT I'LL SLEEP AT: _____ & TOMORROW I'LL WAKE UP AT: _____

WHAT AM I EXCITED FOR IN THE NEAR FUTURE? HOW CAN I MAKE THAT EXPERIENCE EVEN BETTER?

_____
_____
_____

HOW HAS MY OUTLOOK ON LIFE IMPROVED MY DAY?

_____

MY MORNING RITUAL TOMORROW WILL BE: *Completed?*

1. _____ ☐
2. _____ ☐
3. _____ ☐
4. _____ ☐
5. _____ ☐

Day 111

LAST NIGHT I SLEPT AT: _____ & WOKE UP TODAY AT: _____

MY MOST IMPORTANT TASK FOR TODAY IS:

_____

WHEN WAS THE LAST TIME I DID NOT STICK TO MY WORD? HOW CAN I AVOID DOING SO AGAIN?

_____

DATE _____

Night 111

TONIGHT I'LL SLEEP AT: _____ & TOMORROW I'LL WAKE UP AT: _____

WHAT DID I VIEW AS A BIG CHALLENGE IN LIFE THAT I EVENTUALLY OVERCAME? WHAT DOES THAT SHOW ME ABOUT MYSELF?

_____
_____
_____

HOW HAVE I SET MY FUTURE SELF UP FOR SUCCESS TODAY?

_____

MY MORNING RITUAL TOMORROW WILL BE: *Completed?*

1. _____ ☐
2. _____ ☐
3. _____ ☐
4. _____ ☐
5. _____ ☐

Day 112

LAST NIGHT I SLEPT AT: _____ & WOKE UP TODAY AT: _____

MY MOST IMPORTANT TASK FOR TODAY IS:

_____

WHAT IS ONE AREA I CAN APPROACH WITH MORE ENTHUSIASM AND ENERGY TODAY?

_____

DATE _____

Night 112

TONIGHT I'LL SLEEP AT: _____ & TOMORROW I'LL WAKE UP AT: _____

WHAT IS A DIFFICULT SITUATION I MAY FACE IN MY FUTURE? WHAT IS AN OPTIMISTIC MINDSET I COULD APPLY SHOULD I FACE IT?

_____
_____
_____

WHAT IS A CHALLENGE - BIG OR SMALL - I'VE SUCCESSFULLY MOVED PAST TODAY?

_____

MY MORNING RITUAL TOMORROW WILL BE: *Completed?*

1. _____ ☐
2. _____ ☐
3. _____ ☐
4. _____ ☐
5. _____ ☐

Day 113

LAST NIGHT I SLEPT AT: _____ & WOKE UP TODAY AT: _____

MY MOST IMPORTANT TASK FOR TODAY IS:

_____

WHAT IS AN AREA OF WEAKNESS I HAVE IN MY LIFE THAT I WANT TO IMPROVE ON?

_____

DATE _____

Night 113

TONIGHT I'LL SLEEP AT: _____ & TOMORROW I'LL WAKE UP AT: _____

WHAT AM I EXCITED FOR IN THE NEAR FUTURE? HOW CAN I MAKE THAT EXPERIENCE EVEN BETTER?

_____
_____
_____

WHAT IS A SKILL I'VE BUILT IN MY LIFE THAT I USED TO MY BENEFIT TODAY?

_____

MY MORNING RITUAL TOMORROW WILL BE: *Completed?*

1. _____ ☐
2. _____ ☐
3. _____ ☐
4. _____ ☐
5. _____ ☐

Day 114

LAST NIGHT I SLEPT AT: _____ & WOKE UP TODAY AT: _____

MY MOST IMPORTANT TASK FOR TODAY IS:

_____

WHO IS ONE PERSON I CAN GIVE EXTRA CARE AND ATTENTION TO TODAY?

_____

DATE _____

Night 114

TONIGHT I'LL SLEEP AT: _____ & TOMORROW I'LL WAKE UP AT: _____

WHAT DID I VIEW AS A BIG CHALLENGE IN LIFE THAT I EVENTUALLY OVERCAME? WHAT DOES THAT SHOW ME ABOUT MYSELF?

_____
_____
_____

WHAT IS ONE THING I DID TODAY THAT WILL HAVE A CHAIN-EFFECT OF SPREADING POSITIVITY?

_____

MY MORNING RITUAL TOMORROW WILL BE: *Completed?*

1. _____ ☐
2. _____ ☐
3. _____ ☐
4. _____ ☐
5. _____ ☐

Day 115

LAST NIGHT I SLEPT AT: _____ & WOKE UP TODAY AT: _____

MY MOST IMPORTANT TASK FOR TODAY IS:

_____

IF I WERE LIVING AS THE ABSOLUTE BEST VERSION OF MYSELF, WHAT COULD I CHANGE ABOUT MY ACTIONS TODAY?

_____

DATE _____

Night 115

TONIGHT I'LL SLEEP AT: _____ & TOMORROW I'LL WAKE UP AT: _____

WHAT IS A DIFFICULT SITUATION I MAY FACE IN MY FUTURE? WHAT IS AN OPTIMISTIC MINDSET I COULD APPLY SHOULD I FACE IT?

_____
_____
_____

IF A CLOSE FRIEND SAW HOW I HANDLED MY DAY TODAY, WHAT WOULD THEY TELL ME?

_____

MY MORNING RITUAL TOMORROW WILL BE: *Completed?*

1. _____ ☐
2. _____ ☐
3. _____ ☐
4. _____ ☐
5. _____ ☐

Day 116

LAST NIGHT I SLEPT AT: _____ & WOKE UP TODAY AT: _____

MY MOST IMPORTANT TASK FOR TODAY IS:

_____

WHAT CAUSES ME STRESS AND HOW COULD I BETTER RESPOND TO IT?

_____

DATE

Night 116

TONIGHT I'LL SLEEP AT: _____ & TOMORROW I'LL WAKE UP AT: _____

**WHAT AM I EXCITED FOR IN THE NEAR FUTURE?
HOW CAN I MAKE THAT EXPERIENCE EVEN BETTER?**

_____
_____
_____

WHAT AM I GREAT AT THAT I DON'T GIVE MYSELF ENOUGH CREDIT FOR?

_____

MY MORNING RITUAL TOMORROW WILL BE: *Completed?*

1. _____ ☐
2. _____ ☐
3. _____ ☐
4. _____ ☐
5. _____ ☐

Day 117

LAST NIGHT I SLEPT AT: _____ & WOKE UP TODAY AT: _____

MY MOST IMPORTANT TASK FOR TODAY IS:

_____

**IF I WERE TO MAKE NO EXCUSES FOR MY LIFE,
WHAT WOULD I DO DIFFERENTLY?**

_____

DATE _____

Night 117

TONIGHT I'LL SLEEP AT: _____ & TOMORROW I'LL WAKE UP AT: _____

WHAT DID I VIEW AS A BIG CHALLENGE IN LIFE THAT I EVENTUALLY OVERCAME? WHAT DOES THAT SHOW ME ABOUT MYSELF?

_____
_____
_____

HOW HAVE I POSITIVELY IMPACTED SOMEONE'S LIFE TODAY?

_____

MY MORNING RITUAL TOMORROW WILL BE: *Completed?*

1. _____   ☐
2. _____   ☐
3. _____   ☐
4. _____   ☐
5. _____   ☐

Day 118

LAST NIGHT I SLEPT AT: _____ & WOKE UP TODAY AT: _____

MY MOST IMPORTANT TASK FOR TODAY IS:

_____

WHERE IS ONE PLACE I AM SPENDING TIME THAT DOES NOT BRING ME REAL HAPPINESS?

_____

DATE

Night 118

TONIGHT I'LL SLEEP AT: _____ & TOMORROW I'LL WAKE UP AT: _____

**WHAT IS A DIFFICULT SITUATION I MAY FACE IN MY FUTURE?
WHAT IS AN OPTIMISTIC MINDSET I COULD APPLY SHOULD I FACE IT?**

_____

_____

_____

**WHAT IS SOMETHING I SPENT TIME ON TODAY
THAT COULD POSITIVELY IMPACT MY FUTURE?**

_____

MY MORNING RITUAL TOMORROW WILL BE: *Completed?*

1. _____ ☐
2. _____ ☐
3. _____ ☐
4. _____ ☐
5. _____ ☐

Day 119

LAST NIGHT I SLEPT AT: _____ & WOKE UP TODAY AT: _____

MY MOST IMPORTANT TASK FOR TODAY IS:

_____

**WHO IS ONE CONTENT CREATOR OR AUTHOR I CAN REVISIT
OR LEARN MORE FROM TO IMPROVE MY LIFE?**

_____

DATE _____

Night 119

TONIGHT I'LL SLEEP AT: _____ & TOMORROW I'LL WAKE UP AT: _____

WHAT AM I EXCITED FOR IN THE NEAR FUTURE? HOW CAN I MAKE THAT EXPERIENCE EVEN BETTER?

_____
_____
_____

WHAT IS ONE EMOTIONAL RESPONSE I HAD TODAY THAT I AM PROUD OF?

_____

MY MORNING RITUAL TOMORROW WILL BE: *Completed?*

1. _____ ☐
2. _____ ☐
3. _____ ☐
4. _____ ☐
5. _____ ☐

Day 120

LAST NIGHT I SLEPT AT: _____ & WOKE UP TODAY AT: _____

MY MOST IMPORTANT TASK FOR TODAY IS:

_____

WHAT IS ONE TIME I WANT TO BE MORE PRESENT AND LESS DISTRACTED DURING MY DAY?

_____

Night 120

TONIGHT I'LL SLEEP AT: _____ & TOMORROW I'LL WAKE UP AT: _____

DATE

WHAT DID I VIEW AS A BIG CHALLENGE IN LIFE THAT I EVENTUALLY OVERCAME? WHAT DOES THAT SHOW ME ABOUT MYSELF?

_____

_____

_____

HOW HAS MY OUTLOOK ON LIFE IMPROVED MY DAY?

_____

MY MORNING RITUAL TOMORROW WILL BE: *Completed?*

1. _____ ☐
2. _____ ☐
3. _____ ☐
4. _____ ☐
5. _____ ☐

Day 121

LAST NIGHT I SLEPT AT: _____ & WOKE UP TODAY AT: _____

MY MOST IMPORTANT TASK FOR TODAY IS:

_____

WHEN WAS THE LAST TIME I DID NOT STICK TO MY WORD? HOW CAN I AVOID DOING SO AGAIN?

_____

(Sprint 10 Complete!)

DATE

Night 121

TONIGHT I'LL SLEEP AT: _____ & TOMORROW I'LL WAKE UP AT: _____

WHAT IS A DIFFICULT SITUATION I MAY FACE IN MY FUTURE? WHAT IS AN OPTIMISTIC MINDSET I COULD APPLY SHOULD I FACE IT?

_____
_____
_____

HOW HAVE I SHOWN MYSELF SELF-LOVE AND CARE TODAY?

_____

MY MORNING RITUAL TOMORROW WILL BE: *Completed?*

1. _____ ☐
2. _____ ☐
3. _____ ☐
4. _____ ☐
5. _____ ☐

Day 122

LAST NIGHT I SLEPT AT: _____ & WOKE UP TODAY AT: _____

MY MOST IMPORTANT TASK FOR TODAY IS:

_____

WHO IS SOMEONE THAT WILL HAVE A POSITIVE EFFECT IN MY LIFE THAT I SHOULD SPEND MORE TIME WITH?

_____

SPRINT 10: DESTROYED.

Sprint 10 Recap: Days 93-122

1. What situations do I regularly bring a 'negative' mindset to?

_____
_____

2. How can I remind myself to let go of negative thinking more often?

_____
_____

3. What are my negative preconceived notions of myself?

_____
_____

4. Do I enjoy life more when I have a positive mindset?

_____
_____
_____

5. How does my mindset impact others around me?

_____
_____
_____

SPRINT 11:
DAYS 123-153

Sprint 7
Gratitude.

Sprint 8
Self-Care.

Sprint 9
Mindset.

Sprint 10
Optimism.

**Sprint 11
Exploration.**

Sprint 12
Authenticity.

Sprint 11
Theme: *Exploration.*

As we go through life, the tendency is to become more static and less flexible in our belief about ourselves - the things we like, the things we don't like, the things we do, the things we don't do, who we are, why we're here, what's important in life, etc.

The goal for this theme is to become aware of the ways your ideas about yourself are limiting, and to try to open to new ways of thinking about yourself, and new things you can do in you life that will help expand your idea of who you are. That includes new ways of thinking, trying new activities, and really pondering what it means to grow as a person.

You'll rotate through three questions as a guide to help facilitate the theme of exploration.

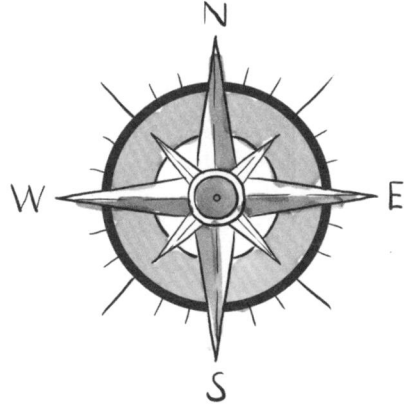

(Sprint 10 Medal Earned!)   DATE

Night 122

TONIGHT I'LL SLEEP AT: _____ & TOMORROW I'LL WAKE UP AT: _____

🔍 BIG OR SMALL, WHAT IS SOMETHING NEW I WANT TO TRY OR LEARN ABOUT IN LIFE?

_____

_____

_____

🤝 WHAT IS A CHALLENGE - BIG OR SMALL - I'VE SUCCESSFULLY MOVED PAST TODAY?

_____

☀ MY MORNING RITUAL TOMORROW WILL BE: *Completed?*

1. _____ ☐
2. _____ ☐
3. _____ ☐
4. _____ ☐
5. _____ ☐

Day 123

LAST NIGHT I SLEPT AT: _____ & WOKE UP TODAY AT: _____

🐸 MY MOST IMPORTANT TASK FOR TODAY IS:

_____

🧭 WHAT IS AN AREA OF WEAKNESS I HAVE IN MY LIFE THAT I WANT TO IMPROVE ON?

_____

DATE _____

Night 123

TONIGHT I'LL SLEEP AT: _____ & TOMORROW I'LL WAKE UP AT: _____

HOW CAN I GROW EXPONENTIALLY IN WHO I AM AS A PERSON AND REACH A NEW LEVEL OF POTENTIAL?

_____

_____

_____

WHAT IS A SKILL I'VE BUILT IN MY LIFE THAT I USED TO MY BENEFIT TODAY?

_____

MY MORNING RITUAL TOMORROW WILL BE: — *Completed?*

1. _____ ☐
2. _____ ☐
3. _____ ☐
4. _____ ☐
5. _____ ☐

Day 124

LAST NIGHT I SLEPT AT: _____ & WOKE UP TODAY AT: _____

MY MOST IMPORTANT TASK FOR TODAY IS:

_____

WHO IS ONE PERSON I CAN GIVE EXTRA CARE AND ATTENTION TO TODAY?

_____

DATE _____

Night 124

TONIGHT I'LL SLEEP AT: _____ & TOMORROW I'LL WAKE UP AT: _____

WHAT IS A NEW MINDSET OR PERSPECTIVE I COULD EXPLORE FURTHER INCORPORATING INTO MY LIFE? HOW WOULD THIS IMPACT ME?

_____
_____
_____

WHAT IS ONE THING I DID TODAY THAT WILL HAVE A CHAIN-EFFECT OF SPREADING POSITIVITY?

_____

MY MORNING RITUAL TOMORROW WILL BE: *Completed?*

1. _____ ☐
2. _____ ☐
3. _____ ☐
4. _____ ☐
5. _____ ☐

Day 125

LAST NIGHT I SLEPT AT: _____ & WOKE UP TODAY AT: _____

MY MOST IMPORTANT TASK FOR TODAY IS:

_____

IF I WERE LIVING AS THE ABSOLUTE BEST VERSION OF MYSELF, WHAT COULD I CHANGE ABOUT MY ACTIONS TODAY?

_____

DATE _____

Night 125

TONIGHT I'LL SLEEP AT: _____ & TOMORROW I'LL WAKE UP AT: _____

BIG OR SMALL, WHAT IS SOMETHING NEW I WANT TO TRY OR LEARN ABOUT IN LIFE?

_____
_____
_____

IF A CLOSE FRIEND SAW HOW I HANDLED MY DAY TODAY, WHAT WOULD THEY TELL ME?

_____

MY MORNING RITUAL TOMORROW WILL BE: *Completed?*

1. _____ ☐
2. _____ ☐
3. _____ ☐
4. _____ ☐
5. _____ ☐

Day 126

LAST NIGHT I SLEPT AT: _____ & WOKE UP TODAY AT: _____

MY MOST IMPORTANT TASK FOR TODAY IS:

_____

WHAT CAUSES ME STRESS AND HOW COULD I BETTER RESPOND TO IT?

_____

DATE _____

Night 126

TONIGHT I'LL SLEEP AT: _____ & TOMORROW I'LL WAKE UP AT: _____

HOW CAN I GROW EXPONENTIALLY IN WHO I AM AS A PERSON AND REACH A NEW LEVEL OF POTENTIAL?

_____
_____
_____

WHAT AM I GREAT AT THAT I DON'T GIVE MYSELF ENOUGH CREDIT FOR?

_____

MY MORNING RITUAL TOMORROW WILL BE: *Completed?*

1. _____ ☐
2. _____ ☐
3. _____ ☐
4. _____ ☐
5. _____ ☐

Day 127

LAST NIGHT I SLEPT AT: _____ & WOKE UP TODAY AT: _____

MY MOST IMPORTANT TASK FOR TODAY IS:

_____

IF I WERE TO MAKE NO EXCUSES FOR MY LIFE, WHAT WOULD I DO DIFFERENTLY?

_____

DATE _____

Night 127

TONIGHT I'LL SLEEP AT: _____ & TOMORROW I'LL WAKE UP AT: _____

WHAT IS A NEW MINDSET OR PERSPECTIVE I COULD EXPLORE FURTHER INCORPORATING INTO MY LIFE? HOW WOULD THIS IMPACT ME?

_____
_____
_____

HOW HAVE I POSITIVELY IMPACTED SOMEONE'S LIFE TODAY?

_____

MY MORNING RITUAL TOMORROW WILL BE: *Completed?*

1. _____ ☐
2. _____ ☐
3. _____ ☐
4. _____ ☐
5. _____ ☐

Day 128

LAST NIGHT I SLEPT AT: _____ & WOKE UP TODAY AT: _____

MY MOST IMPORTANT TASK FOR TODAY IS:

_____

WHERE IS ONE PLACE I AM SPENDING TIME THAT DOES NOT BRING ME REAL HAPPINESS?

_____

DATE

Night 128

TONIGHT I'LL SLEEP AT: _____ & TOMORROW I'LL WAKE UP AT: _____

BIG OR SMALL, WHAT IS SOMETHING NEW I WANT TO TRY OR LEARN ABOUT IN LIFE?

_____
_____
_____

WHAT IS SOMETHING I SPENT TIME ON TODAY THAT COULD POSITIVELY IMPACT MY FUTURE?

_____

MY MORNING RITUAL TOMORROW WILL BE: *Completed?*

1. _____ ☐
2. _____ ☐
3. _____ ☐
4. _____ ☐
5. _____ ☐

Day 129

LAST NIGHT I SLEPT AT: _____ & WOKE UP TODAY AT: _____

MY MOST IMPORTANT TASK FOR TODAY IS:

_____

WHO IS ONE CONTENT CREATOR OR AUTHOR I CAN REVISIT OR LEARN MORE FROM TO IMPROVE MY LIFE?

_____

DATE _____

Night 129

TONIGHT I'LL SLEEP AT: _____ & TOMORROW I'LL WAKE UP AT: _____

HOW CAN I GROW EXPONENTIALLY IN WHO I AM AS A PERSON AND REACH A NEW LEVEL OF POTENTIAL?

_____
_____
_____

WHAT IS ONE EMOTIONAL RESPONSE I HAD TODAY THAT I AM PROUD OF?

_____

MY MORNING RITUAL TOMORROW WILL BE: *Completed?*

1. _____ ☐
2. _____ ☐
3. _____ ☐
4. _____ ☐
5. _____ ☐

Day 130

LAST NIGHT I SLEPT AT: _____ & WOKE UP TODAY AT: _____

MY MOST IMPORTANT TASK FOR TODAY IS:

_____

WHAT IS ONE TIME I WANT TO BE MORE PRESENT AND LESS DISTRACTED DURING MY DAY?

_____

DATE _____

Night 130

TONIGHT I'LL SLEEP AT: _____ & TOMORROW I'LL WAKE UP AT: _____

WHAT IS A NEW MINDSET OR PERSPECTIVE I COULD EXPLORE FURTHER INCORPORATING INTO MY LIFE? HOW WOULD THIS IMPACT ME?

_____

_____

HOW HAS MY OUTLOOK ON LIFE IMPROVED MY DAY?

_____

MY MORNING RITUAL TOMORROW WILL BE: *Completed?*

1. _____ ☐
2. _____ ☐
3. _____ ☐
4. _____ ☐
5. _____ ☐

Day 131

LAST NIGHT I SLEPT AT: _____ & WOKE UP TODAY AT: _____

MY MOST IMPORTANT TASK FOR TODAY IS:

_____

WHEN WAS THE LAST TIME I DID NOT STICK TO MY WORD? HOW CAN I AVOID DOING SO AGAIN?

_____

DATE _____

Night 131

TONIGHT I'LL SLEEP AT: _____ & TOMORROW I'LL WAKE UP AT: _____

BIG OR SMALL, WHAT IS SOMETHING NEW I WANT TO TRY OR LEARN ABOUT IN LIFE?

_____
_____
_____

HOW HAVE I SET MY FUTURE SELF UP FOR SUCCESS TODAY?

_____

MY MORNING RITUAL TOMORROW WILL BE: *Completed?*

1. _____ ☐
2. _____ ☐
3. _____ ☐
4. _____ ☐
5. _____ ☐

Day 132

LAST NIGHT I SLEPT AT: _____ & WOKE UP TODAY AT: _____

MY MOST IMPORTANT TASK FOR TODAY IS:

_____

WHAT IS ONE AREA I CAN APPROACH WITH MORE ENTHUSIASM AND ENERGY TODAY?

_____

DATE

Night 132

TONIGHT I'LL SLEEP AT: _____ & TOMORROW I'LL WAKE UP AT: _____

HOW CAN I GROW EXPONENTIALLY IN WHO I AM AS A PERSON AND REACH A NEW LEVEL OF POTENTIAL?

_____

_____

WHAT IS A CHALLENGE - BIG OR SMALL - I'VE SUCCESSFULLY MOVED PAST TODAY?

_____

MY MORNING RITUAL TOMORROW WILL BE: *Completed?*

1. _____ ☐
2. _____ ☐
3. _____ ☐
4. _____ ☐
5. _____ ☐

Day 133

LAST NIGHT I SLEPT AT: _____ & WOKE UP TODAY AT: _____

MY MOST IMPORTANT TASK FOR TODAY IS:

_____

WHAT IS AN AREA OF WEAKNESS I HAVE IN MY LIFE THAT I WANT TO IMPROVE ON?

_____

DATE _____

Night 133

TONIGHT I'LL SLEEP AT: _____ & TOMORROW I'LL WAKE UP AT: _____

WHAT IS A NEW MINDSET OR PERSPECTIVE I COULD EXPLORE FURTHER INCORPORATING INTO MY LIFE? HOW WOULD THIS IMPACT ME?

_____
_____
_____

WHAT IS A SKILL I'VE BUILT IN MY LIFE THAT I USED TO MY BENEFIT TODAY?

_____

MY MORNING RITUAL TOMORROW WILL BE: *Completed?*

1. _____ ☐
2. _____ ☐
3. _____ ☐
4. _____ ☐
5. _____ ☐

Day 134

LAST NIGHT I SLEPT AT: _____ & WOKE UP TODAY AT: _____

MY MOST IMPORTANT TASK FOR TODAY IS:

_____

WHO IS ONE PERSON I CAN GIVE EXTRA CARE AND ATTENTION TO TODAY?

_____

DATE

Night 134

TONIGHT I'LL SLEEP AT: _____ & TOMORROW I'LL WAKE UP AT: _____

🔍 BIG OR SMALL, WHAT IS SOMETHING NEW I WANT TO TRY OR LEARN ABOUT IN LIFE?

_____
_____
_____

🤝 WHAT IS ONE THING I DID TODAY THAT WILL HAVE A CHAIN-EFFECT OF SPREADING POSITIVITY?

_____

☀ MY MORNING RITUAL TOMORROW WILL BE: *Completed?*

1. _____ ☐
2. _____ ☐
3. _____ ☐
4. _____ ☐
5. _____ ☐

Day 135

LAST NIGHT I SLEPT AT: _____ & WOKE UP TODAY AT: _____

🐸 MY MOST IMPORTANT TASK FOR TODAY IS:

_____

⬆ IF I WERE LIVING AS THE ABSOLUTE BEST VERSION OF MYSELF, WHAT COULD I CHANGE ABOUT MY ACTIONS TODAY?

_____

DATE _____

Night 135

TONIGHT I'LL SLEEP AT: _____ & TOMORROW I'LL WAKE UP AT: _____

HOW CAN I GROW EXPONENTIALLY IN WHO I AM AS A PERSON AND REACH A NEW LEVEL OF POTENTIAL?

_____
_____
_____

IF A CLOSE FRIEND SAW HOW I HANDLED MY DAY TODAY, WHAT WOULD THEY TELL ME?

_____

MY MORNING RITUAL TOMORROW WILL BE: *Completed?*

1. _____ ☐
2. _____ ☐
3. _____ ☐
4. _____ ☐
5. _____ ☐

Day 136

LAST NIGHT I SLEPT AT: _____ & WOKE UP TODAY AT: _____

MY MOST IMPORTANT TASK FOR TODAY IS:

_____

WHAT CAUSES ME STRESS AND HOW COULD I BETTER RESPOND TO IT?

_____

DATE _____

Night 136

TONIGHT I'LL SLEEP AT: _____ & TOMORROW I'LL WAKE UP AT: _____

WHAT IS A NEW MINDSET OR PERSPECTIVE I COULD EXPLORE FURTHER INCORPORATING INTO MY LIFE? HOW WOULD THIS IMPACT ME?

_____
_____
_____

WHAT AM I GREAT AT THAT I DON'T GIVE MYSELF ENOUGH CREDIT FOR?

_____

MY MORNING RITUAL TOMORROW WILL BE: *Completed?*

1. _____ ☐
2. _____ ☐
3. _____ ☐
4. _____ ☐
5. _____ ☐

Day 137

LAST NIGHT I SLEPT AT: _____ & WOKE UP TODAY AT: _____

MY MOST IMPORTANT TASK FOR TODAY IS:

_____

IF I WERE TO MAKE NO EXCUSES FOR MY LIFE, WHAT WOULD I DO DIFFERENTLY?

_____

DATE _____

Night 137

TONIGHT I'LL SLEEP AT: _____ & TOMORROW I'LL WAKE UP AT: _____

BIG OR SMALL, WHAT IS SOMETHING NEW I WANT TO TRY OR LEARN ABOUT IN LIFE?

_____
_____
_____

HOW HAVE I POSITIVELY IMPACTED SOMEONE'S LIFE TODAY?

_____

MY MORNING RITUAL TOMORROW WILL BE:

Completed?

1. _____ ☐
2. _____ ☐
3. _____ ☐
4. _____ ☐
5. _____ ☐

Day 138

LAST NIGHT I SLEPT AT: _____ & WOKE UP TODAY AT: _____

MY MOST IMPORTANT TASK FOR TODAY IS:

_____

WHERE IS ONE PLACE I AM SPENDING TIME THAT DOES NOT BRING ME REAL HAPPINESS?

_____

DATE _____

Night 138

TONIGHT I'LL SLEEP AT: _____ & TOMORROW I'LL WAKE UP AT: _____

HOW CAN I GROW EXPONENTIALLY IN WHO I AM AS A PERSON AND REACH A NEW LEVEL OF POTENTIAL?

_____
_____
_____

WHAT IS SOMETHING I SPENT TIME ON TODAY THAT COULD POSITIVELY IMPACT MY FUTURE?

_____

MY MORNING RITUAL TOMORROW WILL BE: *Completed?*

1. _____ ☐
2. _____ ☐
3. _____ ☐
4. _____ ☐
5. _____ ☐

Day 139

LAST NIGHT I SLEPT AT: _____ & WOKE UP TODAY AT: _____

MY MOST IMPORTANT TASK FOR TODAY IS:

_____

WHO IS ONE CONTENT CREATOR OR AUTHOR I CAN REVISIT OR LEARN MORE FROM TO IMPROVE MY LIFE?

_____

DATE _____

Night 139

TONIGHT I'LL SLEEP AT: _____ & TOMORROW I'LL WAKE UP AT: _____

WHAT IS A NEW MINDSET OR PERSPECTIVE I COULD EXPLORE FURTHER INCORPORATING INTO MY LIFE? HOW WOULD THIS IMPACT ME?

_____
_____
_____

WHAT IS ONE EMOTIONAL RESPONSE I HAD TODAY THAT I AM PROUD OF?

_____

MY MORNING RITUAL TOMORROW WILL BE: *Completed?*

1. _____ ☐
2. _____ ☐
3. _____ ☐
4. _____ ☐
5. _____ ☐

Day 140

LAST NIGHT I SLEPT AT: _____ & WOKE UP TODAY AT: _____

MY MOST IMPORTANT TASK FOR TODAY IS:

_____

WHAT IS ONE TIME I WANT TO BE MORE PRESENT AND LESS DISTRACTED DURING MY DAY?

_____

DATE

Night 140

TONIGHT I'LL SLEEP AT: _____ & TOMORROW I'LL WAKE UP AT: _____

BIG OR SMALL, WHAT IS SOMETHING NEW I WANT TO TRY OR LEARN ABOUT IN LIFE?

_____
_____
_____

HOW HAS MY OUTLOOK ON LIFE IMPROVED MY DAY?

_____

MY MORNING RITUAL TOMORROW WILL BE: *Completed?*

1. _____ ☐
2. _____ ☐
3. _____ ☐
4. _____ ☐
5. _____ ☐

Day 141

LAST NIGHT I SLEPT AT: _____ & WOKE UP TODAY AT: _____

MY MOST IMPORTANT TASK FOR TODAY IS:

_____

WHEN WAS THE LAST TIME I DID NOT STICK TO MY WORD? HOW CAN I AVOID DOING SO AGAIN?

_____

DATE

Night 141

TONIGHT I'LL SLEEP AT: _____ & TOMORROW I'LL WAKE UP AT: _____

HOW CAN I GROW EXPONENTIALLY IN WHO I AM AS A PERSON AND REACH A NEW LEVEL OF POTENTIAL?

_____
_____
_____

HOW HAVE I SET MY FUTURE SELF UP FOR SUCCESS TODAY?

_____

MY MORNING RITUAL TOMORROW WILL BE: *Completed?*

1. _____ ☐
2. _____ ☐
3. _____ ☐
4. _____ ☐
5. _____ ☐

Day 142

LAST NIGHT I SLEPT AT: _____ & WOKE UP TODAY AT: _____

MY MOST IMPORTANT TASK FOR TODAY IS:

_____

WHAT IS ONE AREA I CAN APPROACH WITH MORE ENTHUSIASM AND ENERGY TODAY?

_____

DATE

Night 142

TONIGHT I'LL SLEEP AT: _____ & TOMORROW I'LL WAKE UP AT: _____

WHAT IS A NEW MINDSET OR PERSPECTIVE I COULD EXPLORE FURTHER INCORPORATING INTO MY LIFE? HOW WOULD THIS IMPACT ME?

_____
_____
_____

WHAT IS A CHALLENGE - BIG OR SMALL - I'VE SUCCESSFULLY MOVED PAST TODAY?

_____

MY MORNING RITUAL TOMORROW WILL BE: *Completed?*

1. _____ ☐
2. _____ ☐
3. _____ ☐
4. _____ ☐
5. _____ ☐

Day 143

LAST NIGHT I SLEPT AT: _____ & WOKE UP TODAY AT: _____

MY MOST IMPORTANT TASK FOR TODAY IS:

_____

WHAT IS AN AREA OF WEAKNESS I HAVE IN MY LIFE THAT I WANT TO IMPROVE ON?

_____

DATE: _____

Night 143

TONIGHT I'LL SLEEP AT: _____ & TOMORROW I'LL WAKE UP AT: _____

BIG OR SMALL, WHAT IS SOMETHING NEW I WANT TO TRY OR LEARN ABOUT IN LIFE?

_____
_____
_____

WHAT IS A SKILL I'VE BUILT IN MY LIFE THAT I USED TO MY BENEFIT TODAY?

_____

MY MORNING RITUAL TOMORROW WILL BE: *Completed?*

1. _____ ☐
2. _____ ☐
3. _____ ☐
4. _____ ☐
5. _____ ☐

Day 144

LAST NIGHT I SLEPT AT: _____ & WOKE UP TODAY AT: _____

MY MOST IMPORTANT TASK FOR TODAY IS:

_____

WHO IS ONE PERSON I CAN GIVE EXTRA CARE AND ATTENTION TO TODAY?

_____

Night 144

DATE _____

TONIGHT I'LL SLEEP AT: _____ & TOMORROW I'LL WAKE UP AT: _____

HOW CAN I GROW EXPONENTIALLY IN WHO I AM AS A PERSON AND REACH A NEW LEVEL OF POTENTIAL?

_____
_____
_____

WHAT IS ONE THING I DID TODAY THAT WILL HAVE A CHAIN-EFFECT OF SPREADING POSITIVITY?

_____

MY MORNING RITUAL TOMORROW WILL BE: *Completed?*

1. _____ ☐
2. _____ ☐
3. _____ ☐
4. _____ ☐
5. _____ ☐

Day 145

LAST NIGHT I SLEPT AT: _____ & WOKE UP TODAY AT: _____

MY MOST IMPORTANT TASK FOR TODAY IS:

_____

IF I WERE LIVING AS THE ABSOLUTE BEST VERSION OF MYSELF, WHAT COULD I CHANGE ABOUT MY ACTIONS TODAY?

_____

DATE _____

Night 145

TONIGHT I'LL SLEEP AT: _____ & TOMORROW I'LL WAKE UP AT: _____

WHAT IS A NEW MINDSET OR PERSPECTIVE I COULD EXPLORE FURTHER INCORPORATING INTO MY LIFE? HOW WOULD THIS IMPACT ME?

_____
_____
_____

IF A CLOSE FRIEND SAW HOW I HANDLED MY DAY TODAY, WHAT WOULD THEY TELL ME?

_____

MY MORNING RITUAL TOMORROW WILL BE: *Completed?*

1. _____ ☐
2. _____ ☐
3. _____ ☐
4. _____ ☐
5. _____ ☐

Day 146

LAST NIGHT I SLEPT AT: _____ & WOKE UP TODAY AT: _____

MY MOST IMPORTANT TASK FOR TODAY IS:

_____

WHAT CAUSES ME STRESS AND HOW COULD I BETTER RESPOND TO IT?

_____

DATE _____

Night 146

TONIGHT I'LL SLEEP AT: _____ & TOMORROW I'LL WAKE UP AT: _____

BIG OR SMALL, WHAT IS SOMETHING NEW I WANT TO TRY OR LEARN ABOUT IN LIFE?

_____
_____
_____

WHAT AM I GREAT AT THAT I DON'T GIVE MYSELF ENOUGH CREDIT FOR?

_____

MY MORNING RITUAL TOMORROW WILL BE:　　　*Completed?*

1. _____ ☐
2. _____ ☐
3. _____ ☐
4. _____ ☐
5. _____ ☐

Day 147

LAST NIGHT I SLEPT AT: _____ & WOKE UP TODAY AT: _____

MY MOST IMPORTANT TASK FOR TODAY IS:

_____

IF I WERE TO MAKE NO EXCUSES FOR MY LIFE, WHAT WOULD I DO DIFFERENTLY?

_____

Night 147

DATE

TONIGHT I'LL SLEEP AT: _____ & TOMORROW I'LL WAKE UP AT: _____

HOW CAN I GROW EXPONENTIALLY IN WHO I AM AS A PERSON AND REACH A NEW LEVEL OF POTENTIAL?

_____
_____
_____

HOW HAVE I POSITIVELY IMPACTED SOMEONE'S LIFE TODAY?

_____

MY MORNING RITUAL TOMORROW WILL BE: *Completed?*

1. _____ ☐
2. _____ ☐
3. _____ ☐
4. _____ ☐
5. _____ ☐

Day 148

LAST NIGHT I SLEPT AT: _____ & WOKE UP TODAY AT: _____

MY MOST IMPORTANT TASK FOR TODAY IS:

_____

WHERE IS ONE PLACE I AM SPENDING TIME THAT DOES NOT BRING ME REAL HAPPINESS?

_____

DATE _____

Night 148

TONIGHT I'LL SLEEP AT: _____ & TOMORROW I'LL WAKE UP AT: _____

WHAT IS A NEW MINDSET OR PERSPECTIVE I COULD EXPLORE FURTHER INCORPORATING INTO MY LIFE? HOW WOULD THIS IMPACT ME?

_____
_____
_____

WHAT IS SOMETHING I SPENT TIME ON TODAY THAT COULD POSITIVELY IMPACT MY FUTURE?

_____

MY MORNING RITUAL TOMORROW WILL BE: *Completed?*

1. _____ ☐
2. _____ ☐
3. _____ ☐
4. _____ ☐
5. _____ ☐

Day 149

LAST NIGHT I SLEPT AT: _____ & WOKE UP TODAY AT: _____

MY MOST IMPORTANT TASK FOR TODAY IS:

_____

WHO IS ONE CONTENT CREATOR OR AUTHOR I CAN REVISIT OR LEARN MORE FROM TO IMPROVE MY LIFE?

_____

DATE _____

Night 149

TONIGHT I'LL SLEEP AT: _____ & TOMORROW I'LL WAKE UP AT: _____

BIG OR SMALL, WHAT IS SOMETHING NEW I WANT TO TRY OR LEARN ABOUT IN LIFE?

_____
_____
_____

WHAT IS ONE EMOTIONAL RESPONSE I HAD TODAY THAT I AM PROUD OF?

_____

MY MORNING RITUAL TOMORROW WILL BE: *Completed?*

1. _____ ☐
2. _____ ☐
3. _____ ☐
4. _____ ☐
5. _____ ☐

Day 150

LAST NIGHT I SLEPT AT: _____ & WOKE UP TODAY AT: _____

MY MOST IMPORTANT TASK FOR TODAY IS:

_____

WHAT IS ONE TIME I WANT TO BE MORE PRESENT AND LESS DISTRACTED DURING MY DAY?

_____

DATE

Night 150

TONIGHT I'LL SLEEP AT: _____ & TOMORROW I'LL WAKE UP AT: _____

HOW CAN I GROW EXPONENTIALLY IN WHO I AM AS A PERSON AND REACH A NEW LEVEL OF POTENTIAL?

_____
_____
_____

HOW HAS MY OUTLOOK ON LIFE IMPROVED MY DAY?

_____

MY MORNING RITUAL TOMORROW WILL BE: *Completed?*

1. _____ ☐
2. _____ ☐
3. _____ ☐
4. _____ ☐
5. _____ ☐

Day 151

LAST NIGHT I SLEPT AT: _____ & WOKE UP TODAY AT: _____

MY MOST IMPORTANT TASK FOR TODAY IS:

_____

WHEN WAS THE LAST TIME I DID NOT STICK TO MY WORD? HOW CAN I AVOID DOING SO AGAIN?

_____

DATE _____

Night 151

TONIGHT I'LL SLEEP AT: _____ & TOMORROW I'LL WAKE UP AT: _____

WHAT IS A NEW MINDSET OR PERSPECTIVE I COULD EXPLORE FURTHER INCORPORATING INTO MY LIFE? HOW WOULD THIS IMPACT ME?

_____
_____
_____

HOW HAVE I SET MY FUTURE SELF UP FOR SUCCESS TODAY?

_____

MY MORNING RITUAL TOMORROW WILL BE: *Completed?*

1. _____ ☐
2. _____ ☐
3. _____ ☐
4. _____ ☐
5. _____ ☐

Day 152

LAST NIGHT I SLEPT AT: _____ & WOKE UP TODAY AT: _____

MY MOST IMPORTANT TASK FOR TODAY IS:

_____

WHAT IS ONE AREA I CAN APPROACH WITH MORE ENTHUSIASM AND ENERGY TODAY?

_____

(Sprint 11 Complete!)

DATE

Night 152

TONIGHT I'LL SLEEP AT: _____ & TOMORROW I'LL WAKE UP AT: _____

BIG OR SMALL, WHAT IS SOMETHING NEW I WANT TO TRY OR LEARN ABOUT IN LIFE?

_____

_____

_____

HOW HAVE I SHOWN SELF-LOVE AND CARE TO MYSELF TODAY?

_____

MY MORNING RITUAL TOMORROW WILL BE: *Completed?*

1. _____ ☐
2. _____ ☐
3. _____ ☐
4. _____ ☐
5. _____ ☐

Day 153

LAST NIGHT I SLEPT AT: _____ & WOKE UP TODAY AT: _____

MY MOST IMPORTANT TASK FOR TODAY IS:

_____

WHO IS SOMEONE THAT WILL HAVE A POSITIVE EFFECT IN MY LIFE THAT I SHOULD SPEND MORE TIME WITH?

_____

SPRINT 11: DESTROYED.

Sprint 11 Recap: Days 123-153 ✓

1. What have I learned about myself in the last 30 days?

_____
_____
_____

2. What are some new things I've found I want to explore or learn about?

_____
_____
_____
_____

3. In what way does fear hold me back?

_____
_____
_____

4. What am I proud of myself for?

_____
_____

SPRINT 12:
DAYS 154-183

 Sprint 7 Gratitude.
 Sprint 8 Self-Care.
 Sprint 9 Mindset.
 Sprint 10 Optimism.
 Sprint 11 Exploration.
 **Sprint 12 Authenticity.**

Sprint 12
Theme: <u>Authenticity.</u>

The last themed spring of this journal is 'Authenticity'.

The goal for this theme is to really bring attention to the ways in which you're limited by wanting to be accepted, along with ways in which you're proud of yourself for being 'you.'

We all worry about what people think - whether its friends, family, or society, we want to be accepted and loved. That causes us to conform on some level out of fear of judgment or rejection.

That's not necessarily a horrible thing, but starting to look at the ways in which you conform can be enlightening and it gives you the opportunity to re-evaluate things about the way you show yourself to others.

AUTHENTICITY

(Sprint 11 Medal Earned!)   DATE

Night 153

TONIGHT I'LL SLEEP AT: _____ & TOMORROW I'LL WAKE UP AT: _____

WHAT WOULD I DO DIFFERENTLY IF I WASN'T WORRIED ABOUT OTHER PEOPLE'S JUDGEMENT?

_____
_____
_____

WHAT IS A CHALLENGE - BIG OR SMALL - I'VE SUCCESSFULLY MOVED PAST TODAY?

_____

MY MORNING RITUAL TOMORROW WILL BE: *Completed?*

1. _____ ☐
2. _____ ☐
3. _____ ☐
4. _____ ☐
5. _____ ☐

Day 154

LAST NIGHT I SLEPT AT: _____ & WOKE UP TODAY AT: _____

MY MOST IMPORTANT TASK FOR TODAY IS:

_____

WHAT IS AN AREA OF WEAKNESS I HAVE IN MY LIFE THAT I WANT TO IMPROVE ON?

_____

Night 154

DATE: _____

TONIGHT I'LL SLEEP AT: _____ & TOMORROW I'LL WAKE UP AT: _____

WHERE DO MY BIGGEST INSECURITIES STEM FROM? HOW CAN I WORK TOWARDS GETTING OVER THEM?

_____
_____
_____

WHAT IS A SKILL I'VE BUILT IN MY LIFE THAT I USED TO MY BENEFIT TODAY?

_____

MY MORNING RITUAL TOMORROW WILL BE: *Completed?*

1. _____ ☐
2. _____ ☐
3. _____ ☐
4. _____ ☐
5. _____ ☐

Day 155

LAST NIGHT I SLEPT AT: _____ & WOKE UP TODAY AT: _____

MY MOST IMPORTANT TASK FOR TODAY IS:

_____

WHO IS ONE PERSON I CAN GIVE EXTRA CARE AND ATTENTION TO TODAY?

_____

DATE _____

Night 155

TONIGHT I'LL SLEEP AT: _____ & TOMORROW I'LL WAKE UP AT: _____

WHAT ARE SOME OF THE QUALITIES I HAVE THAT I'M MOST PROUD OF AND STAND BY UNWAVERINGLY? HOW CAN I EMBODY THESE PROUDLY?

_____

_____

_____

WHAT IS ONE THING I DID TODAY THAT WILL HAVE A CHAIN-EFFECT OF SPREADING POSITIVITY?

_____

MY MORNING RITUAL TOMORROW WILL BE: *Completed?*

1. _____ ☐
2. _____ ☐
3. _____ ☐
4. _____ ☐
5. _____ ☐

Day 156

LAST NIGHT I SLEPT AT: _____ & WOKE UP TODAY AT: _____

MY MOST IMPORTANT TASK FOR TODAY IS:

_____

IF I WERE LIVING AS THE ABSOLUTE BEST VERSION OF MYSELF, WHAT COULD I CHANGE ABOUT MY ACTIONS TODAY?

_____

DATE _____

Night 156

TONIGHT I'LL SLEEP AT: _____ & TOMORROW I'LL WAKE UP AT: _____

WHAT WOULD I DO DIFFERENTLY IF I WASN'T WORRIED ABOUT OTHER PEOPLE'S JUDGEMENT?

_____
_____
_____

IF A CLOSE FRIEND SAW HOW I HANDLED MY DAY TODAY, WHAT WOULD THEY TELL ME?

_____

MY MORNING RITUAL TOMORROW WILL BE: *Completed?*

1. _____ ☐
2. _____ ☐
3. _____ ☐
4. _____ ☐
5. _____ ☐

Day 157

LAST NIGHT I SLEPT AT: _____ & WOKE UP TODAY AT: _____

MY MOST IMPORTANT TASK FOR TODAY IS:

_____

WHAT CAUSES ME STRESS AND HOW COULD I BETTER RESPOND TO IT?

_____

Night 157

TONIGHT I'LL SLEEP AT: _____ & TOMORROW I'LL WAKE UP AT: _____

WHERE DO MY BIGGEST INSECURITIES STEM FROM? HOW CAN I WORK TOWARDS GETTING OVER THEM?

_____
_____
_____

WHAT AM I GREAT AT THAT I DON'T GIVE MYSELF ENOUGH CREDIT FOR?

_____

MY MORNING RITUAL TOMORROW WILL BE: *Completed?*

1. _____ ☐
2. _____ ☐
3. _____ ☐
4. _____ ☐
5. _____ ☐

Day 158

LAST NIGHT I SLEPT AT: _____ & WOKE UP TODAY AT: _____

MY MOST IMPORTANT TASK FOR TODAY IS:

_____

IF I WERE TO MAKE NO EXCUSES FOR MY LIFE, WHAT WOULD I DO DIFFERENTLY?

_____

DATE _____

Night 158

TONIGHT I'LL SLEEP AT: _____ & TOMORROW I'LL WAKE UP AT: _____

WHAT ARE SOME OF THE QUALITIES I HAVE THAT I'M MOST PROUD OF AND STAND BY UNWAVERINGLY? HOW CAN I EMBODY THESE PROUDLY?

_____

_____

_____

HOW HAVE I POSITIVELY IMPACTED SOMEONE'S LIFE TODAY?

_____

MY MORNING RITUAL TOMORROW WILL BE: *Completed?*

1. _____ ☐
2. _____ ☐
3. _____ ☐
4. _____ ☐
5. _____ ☐

Day 159

LAST NIGHT I SLEPT AT: _____ & WOKE UP TODAY AT: _____

MY MOST IMPORTANT TASK FOR TODAY IS:

_____

WHERE IS ONE PLACE I AM SPENDING TIME THAT DOES NOT BRING ME REAL HAPPINESS?

_____

DATE

Night 159

TONIGHT I'LL SLEEP AT: _____ & TOMORROW I'LL WAKE UP AT: _____

WHAT WOULD I DO DIFFERENTLY IF I WASN'T WORRIED ABOUT OTHER PEOPLE'S JUDGEMENT?

_____
_____
_____

WHAT IS SOMETHING I SPENT TIME ON TODAY THAT COULD POSITIVELY IMPACT MY FUTURE?

_____

MY MORNING RITUAL TOMORROW WILL BE: *Completed?*

1. _____ ☐
2. _____ ☐
3. _____ ☐
4. _____ ☐
5. _____ ☐

Day 160

LAST NIGHT I SLEPT AT: _____ & WOKE UP TODAY AT: _____

MY MOST IMPORTANT TASK FOR TODAY IS:

_____

WHO IS ONE CONTENT CREATOR OR AUTHOR I CAN REVISIT OR LEARN MORE FROM TO IMPROVE MY LIFE?

_____

DATE _____

Night 160

TONIGHT I'LL SLEEP AT: _____ & TOMORROW I'LL WAKE UP AT: _____

WHERE DO MY BIGGEST INSECURITIES STEM FROM? HOW CAN I WORK TOWARDS GETTING OVER THEM?

_____
_____
_____

WHAT IS ONE EMOTIONAL RESPONSE I HAD TODAY THAT I AM PROUD OF?

_____

MY MORNING RITUAL TOMORROW WILL BE: *Completed?*

1. _____ ☐
2. _____ ☐
3. _____ ☐
4. _____ ☐
5. _____ ☐

Day 161

LAST NIGHT I SLEPT AT: _____ & WOKE UP TODAY AT: _____

MY MOST IMPORTANT TASK FOR TODAY IS:

_____

WHAT IS ONE TIME I WANT TO BE MORE PRESENT AND LESS DISTRACTED DURING MY DAY?

_____

DATE _____

Night 161

TONIGHT I'LL SLEEP AT: _____ & TOMORROW I'LL WAKE UP AT: _____

WHAT ARE SOME OF THE QUALITIES I HAVE THAT I'M MOST PROUD OF AND STAND BY UNWAVERINGLY? HOW CAN I EMBODY THESE PROUDLY?

_____

_____

_____

HOW HAS MY OUTLOOK ON LIFE IMPROVED MY DAY?

_____

MY MORNING RITUAL TOMORROW WILL BE: *Completed?*

1. _____ ☐
2. _____ ☐
3. _____ ☐
4. _____ ☐
5. _____ ☐

Day 162

LAST NIGHT I SLEPT AT: _____ & WOKE UP TODAY AT: _____

MY MOST IMPORTANT TASK FOR TODAY IS:

_____

WHEN WAS THE LAST TIME I DID NOT STICK TO MY WORD? HOW CAN I AVOID DOING SO AGAIN?

_____

Night 162

DATE _____

TONIGHT I'LL SLEEP AT: _____ & TOMORROW I'LL WAKE UP AT: _____

WHAT WOULD I DO DIFFERENTLY IF I WASN'T WORRIED ABOUT OTHER PEOPLE'S JUDGEMENT?

_____
_____
_____

HOW HAVE I SET MY FUTURE SELF UP FOR SUCCESS TODAY?

_____

MY MORNING RITUAL TOMORROW WILL BE:　　　*Completed?*

1. _____ ☐
2. _____ ☐
3. _____ ☐
4. _____ ☐
5. _____ ☐

Day 163

LAST NIGHT I SLEPT AT: _____ & WOKE UP TODAY AT: _____

MY MOST IMPORTANT TASK FOR TODAY IS:

_____

WHAT IS ONE AREA I CAN APPROACH WITH MORE ENTHUSIASM AND ENERGY TODAY?

_____

Night 163

DATE _____

TONIGHT I'LL SLEEP AT: _____ & TOMORROW I'LL WAKE UP AT: _____

WHERE DO MY BIGGEST INSECURITIES STEM FROM? HOW CAN I WORK TOWARDS GETTING OVER THEM?

_____
_____
_____

WHAT IS A CHALLENGE - BIG OR SMALL - I'VE SUCCESSFULLY MOVED PAST TODAY?

_____

MY MORNING RITUAL TOMORROW WILL BE: *Completed?*

1. _____ ☐
2. _____ ☐
3. _____ ☐
4. _____ ☐
5. _____ ☐

Day 164

LAST NIGHT I SLEPT AT: _____ & WOKE UP TODAY AT: _____

MY MOST IMPORTANT TASK FOR TODAY IS:

_____

WHAT IS AN AREA OF WEAKNESS I HAVE IN MY LIFE THAT I WANT TO IMPROVE ON?

_____

DATE _____

Night 164

TONIGHT I'LL SLEEP AT: _____ & TOMORROW I'LL WAKE UP AT: _____

WHAT ARE SOME OF THE QUALITIES I HAVE THAT I'M MOST PROUD OF AND STAND BY UNWAVERINGLY? HOW CAN I EMBODY THESE PROUDLY?

_____
_____
_____

WHAT IS A SKILL I'VE BUILT IN MY LIFE THAT I USED TO MY BENEFIT TODAY?

_____

MY MORNING RITUAL TOMORROW WILL BE: *Completed?*

1. _____ ☐
2. _____ ☐
3. _____ ☐
4. _____ ☐
5. _____ ☐

Day 165

LAST NIGHT I SLEPT AT: _____ & WOKE UP TODAY AT: _____

MY MOST IMPORTANT TASK FOR TODAY IS:

_____

WHO IS ONE PERSON I CAN GIVE EXTRA CARE AND ATTENTION TO TODAY?

_____

Night 165

(11) _____ DATE

TONIGHT I'LL SLEEP AT: _____ & TOMORROW I'LL WAKE UP AT: _____

WHAT WOULD I DO DIFFERENTLY IF I WASN'T WORRIED ABOUT OTHER PEOPLE'S JUDGEMENT?

_____
_____
_____

WHAT IS ONE THING I DID TODAY THAT WILL HAVE A CHAIN-EFFECT OF SPREADING POSITIVITY?

_____

MY MORNING RITUAL TOMORROW WILL BE: *Completed?*

1. _____ ☐
2. _____ ☐
3. _____ ☐
4. _____ ☐
5. _____ ☐

Day 166

LAST NIGHT I SLEPT AT: _____ & WOKE UP TODAY AT: _____

MY MOST IMPORTANT TASK FOR TODAY IS:

_____

IF I WERE LIVING AS THE ABSOLUTE BEST VERSION OF MYSELF, WHAT COULD I CHANGE ABOUT MY ACTIONS TODAY?

_____

DATE _____

Night 166

TONIGHT I'LL SLEEP AT: _____ & TOMORROW I'LL WAKE UP AT: _____

WHERE DO MY BIGGEST INSECURITIES STEM FROM? HOW CAN I WORK TOWARDS GETTING OVER THEM?

_____
_____
_____

IF A CLOSE FRIEND SAW HOW I HANDLED MY DAY TODAY, WHAT WOULD THEY TELL ME?

_____

MY MORNING RITUAL TOMORROW WILL BE: *Completed?*

1. _____ ☐
2. _____ ☐
3. _____ ☐
4. _____ ☐
5. _____ ☐

Day 167

LAST NIGHT I SLEPT AT: _____ & WOKE UP TODAY AT: _____

MY MOST IMPORTANT TASK FOR TODAY IS:

_____

WHAT CAUSES ME STRESS AND HOW COULD I BETTER RESPOND TO IT?

_____

DATE _____

Night 167

TONIGHT I'LL SLEEP AT: _____ & TOMORROW I'LL WAKE UP AT: _____

WHAT ARE SOME OF THE QUALITIES I HAVE THAT I'M MOST PROUD OF AND STAND BY UNWAVERINGLY? HOW CAN I EMBODY THESE PROUDLY?

_____
_____
_____

WHAT AM I GREAT AT THAT I DON'T GIVE MYSELF ENOUGH CREDIT FOR?

_____

MY MORNING RITUAL TOMORROW WILL BE: *Completed?*

1. _____ ☐
2. _____ ☐
3. _____ ☐
4. _____ ☐
5. _____ ☐

Day 168

LAST NIGHT I SLEPT AT: _____ & WOKE UP TODAY AT: _____

MY MOST IMPORTANT TASK FOR TODAY IS:

_____

IF I WERE TO MAKE NO EXCUSES FOR MY LIFE, WHAT WOULD I DO DIFFERENTLY?

_____

DATE _____

Night 168

TONIGHT I'LL SLEEP AT: _____ & TOMORROW I'LL WAKE UP AT: _____

WHAT WOULD I DO DIFFERENTLY IF I WASN'T WORRIED ABOUT OTHER PEOPLE'S JUDGEMENT?

_____
_____
_____

HOW HAVE I POSITIVELY IMPACTED SOMEONE'S LIFE TODAY?

_____

MY MORNING RITUAL TOMORROW WILL BE: *Completed?*

1. _____ ☐
2. _____ ☐
3. _____ ☐
4. _____ ☐
5. _____ ☐

Day 169

LAST NIGHT I SLEPT AT: _____ & WOKE UP TODAY AT: _____

MY MOST IMPORTANT TASK FOR TODAY IS:

_____

WHERE IS ONE PLACE I AM SPENDING TIME THAT DOES NOT BRING ME REAL HAPPINESS?

_____

DATE _____

Night 169

TONIGHT I'LL SLEEP AT: _____ & TOMORROW I'LL WAKE UP AT: _____

WHERE DO MY BIGGEST INSECURITIES STEM FROM? HOW CAN I WORK TOWARDS GETTING OVER THEM?

_____
_____
_____

WHAT IS SOMETHING I SPENT TIME ON TODAY THAT COULD POSITIVELY IMPACT MY FUTURE?

_____

MY MORNING RITUAL TOMORROW WILL BE: *Completed?*

1. _____ ☐
2. _____ ☐
3. _____ ☐
4. _____ ☐
5. _____ ☐

Day 170

LAST NIGHT I SLEPT AT: _____ & WOKE UP TODAY AT: _____

MY MOST IMPORTANT TASK FOR TODAY IS:

_____

WHO IS ONE CONTENT CREATOR OR AUTHOR I CAN REVISIT OR LEARN MORE FROM TO IMPROVE MY LIFE?

_____

DATE _____

Night 170

TONIGHT I'LL SLEEP AT: _____ & TOMORROW I'LL WAKE UP AT: _____

WHAT ARE SOME OF THE QUALITIES I HAVE THAT I'M MOST PROUD OF AND STAND BY UNWAVERINGLY? HOW CAN I EMBODY THESE PROUDLY?

_____
_____
_____

WHAT IS ONE EMOTIONAL RESPONSE I HAD TODAY THAT I AM PROUD OF?

_____

MY MORNING RITUAL TOMORROW WILL BE: *Completed?*

1. _____ ☐
2. _____ ☐
3. _____ ☐
4. _____ ☐
5. _____ ☐

Day 171

LAST NIGHT I SLEPT AT: _____ & WOKE UP TODAY AT: _____

MY MOST IMPORTANT TASK FOR TODAY IS:

_____

WHAT IS ONE TIME I WANT TO BE MORE PRESENT AND LESS DISTRACTED DURING MY DAY?

_____

Night 171

DATE: _____

TONIGHT I'LL SLEEP AT: _____ & TOMORROW I'LL WAKE UP AT: _____

WHAT WOULD I DO DIFFERENTLY IF I WASN'T WORRIED ABOUT OTHER PEOPLE'S JUDGEMENT?

_____

_____

_____

HOW HAS MY OUTLOOK ON LIFE IMPROVED MY DAY?

_____

MY MORNING RITUAL TOMORROW WILL BE: *Completed?*

1. _____ ☐
2. _____ ☐
3. _____ ☐
4. _____ ☐
5. _____ ☐

Day 172

LAST NIGHT I SLEPT AT: _____ & WOKE UP TODAY AT: _____

MY MOST IMPORTANT TASK FOR TODAY IS:

_____

WHEN WAS THE LAST TIME I DID NOT STICK TO MY WORD? HOW CAN I AVOID DOING SO AGAIN?

_____

Night 172

DATE _____

TONIGHT I'LL SLEEP AT: _____ & TOMORROW I'LL WAKE UP AT: _____

WHERE DO MY BIGGEST INSECURITIES STEM FROM? HOW CAN I WORK TOWARDS GETTING OVER THEM?

_____
_____
_____

HOW HAVE I SET MY FUTURE SELF UP FOR SUCCESS TODAY?

_____

MY MORNING RITUAL TOMORROW WILL BE: *Completed?*

1. _____ ☐
2. _____ ☐
3. _____ ☐
4. _____ ☐
5. _____ ☐

Day 173

LAST NIGHT I SLEPT AT: _____ & WOKE UP TODAY AT: _____

MY MOST IMPORTANT TASK FOR TODAY IS:

_____

WHAT IS ONE AREA I CAN APPROACH WITH MORE ENTHUSIASM AND ENERGY TODAY?

_____

DATE

Night 173

TONIGHT I'LL SLEEP AT: _____ & TOMORROW I'LL WAKE UP AT: _____

WHAT ARE SOME OF THE QUALITIES I HAVE THAT I'M MOST PROUD OF AND STAND BY UNWAVERINGLY? HOW CAN I EMBODY THESE PROUDLY?

_____
_____
_____

WHAT IS A CHALLENGE - BIG OR SMALL - I'VE SUCCESSFULLY MOVED PAST TODAY?

_____

MY MORNING RITUAL TOMORROW WILL BE: *Completed?*

1. _____ ☐
2. _____ ☐
3. _____ ☐
4. _____ ☐
5. _____ ☐

Day 174

LAST NIGHT I SLEPT AT: _____ & WOKE UP TODAY AT: _____

MY MOST IMPORTANT TASK FOR TODAY IS:

_____

WHAT IS AN AREA OF WEAKNESS I HAVE IN MY LIFE THAT I WANT TO IMPROVE ON?

_____

Night 174

TONIGHT I'LL SLEEP AT: _____ & TOMORROW I'LL WAKE UP AT: _____

WHAT WOULD I DO DIFFERENTLY IF I WASN'T WORRIED ABOUT OTHER PEOPLE'S JUDGEMENT?

_____
_____
_____

WHAT IS A SKILL I'VE BUILT IN MY LIFE THAT I USED TO MY BENEFIT TODAY?

_____

MY MORNING RITUAL TOMORROW WILL BE: *Completed?*

1. _____ ☐
2. _____ ☐
3. _____ ☐
4. _____ ☐
5. _____ ☐

Day 175

LAST NIGHT I SLEPT AT: _____ & WOKE UP TODAY AT: _____

MY MOST IMPORTANT TASK FOR TODAY IS:

_____

WHO IS ONE PERSON I CAN GIVE EXTRA CARE AND ATTENTION TO TODAY?

_____

DATE _____

Night 175

TONIGHT I'LL SLEEP AT: _____ & TOMORROW I'LL WAKE UP AT: _____

WHERE DO MY BIGGEST INSECURITIES STEM FROM? HOW CAN I WORK TOWARDS GETTING OVER THEM?

_____
_____
_____

WHAT IS ONE THING I DID TODAY THAT WILL HAVE A CHAIN-EFFECT OF SPREADING POSITIVITY?

_____

MY MORNING RITUAL TOMORROW WILL BE:

Completed?

1. _____ ☐
2. _____ ☐
3. _____ ☐
4. _____ ☐
5. _____ ☐

Day 176

LAST NIGHT I SLEPT AT: _____ & WOKE UP TODAY AT: _____

MY MOST IMPORTANT TASK FOR TODAY IS:

_____

IF I WERE LIVING AS THE ABSOLUTE BEST VERSION OF MYSELF, WHAT COULD I CHANGE ABOUT MY ACTIONS TODAY?

_____

DATE _____

Night 176

TONIGHT I'LL SLEEP AT: _____ & TOMORROW I'LL WAKE UP AT: _____

WHAT ARE SOME OF THE QUALITIES I HAVE THAT I'M MOST PROUD OF AND STAND BY UNWAVERINGLY? HOW CAN I EMBODY THESE PROUDLY?

_____
_____
_____

IF A CLOSE FRIEND SAW HOW I HANDLED MY DAY TODAY, WHAT WOULD THEY TELL ME?

_____

MY MORNING RITUAL TOMORROW WILL BE: *Completed?*

1. _____ ☐
2. _____ ☐
3. _____ ☐
4. _____ ☐
5. _____ ☐

Day 177

LAST NIGHT I SLEPT AT: _____ & WOKE UP TODAY AT: _____

MY MOST IMPORTANT TASK FOR TODAY IS:

_____

WHAT CAUSES ME STRESS AND HOW COULD I BETTER RESPOND TO IT?

_____

DATE _____

Night 177

TONIGHT I'LL SLEEP AT: _____ & TOMORROW I'LL WAKE UP AT: _____

WHAT WOULD I DO DIFFERENTLY IF I WASN'T WORRIED ABOUT OTHER PEOPLE'S JUDGEMENT?

_____
_____
_____

WHAT AM I GREAT AT THAT I DON'T GIVE MYSELF ENOUGH CREDIT FOR?

_____

MY MORNING RITUAL TOMORROW WILL BE: *Completed?*

1. _____ ☐
2. _____ ☐
3. _____ ☐
4. _____ ☐
5. _____ ☐

Day 178

LAST NIGHT I SLEPT AT: _____ & WOKE UP TODAY AT: _____

MY MOST IMPORTANT TASK FOR TODAY IS:

_____

IF I WERE TO MAKE NO EXCUSES FOR MY LIFE, WHAT WOULD I DO DIFFERENTLY?

_____

DATE _____

Night 178

TONIGHT I'LL SLEEP AT: _____ & TOMORROW I'LL WAKE UP AT: _____

WHERE DO MY BIGGEST INSECURITIES STEM FROM? HOW CAN I WORK TOWARDS GETTING OVER THEM?

_____
_____
_____

HOW HAVE I POSITIVELY IMPACTED SOMEONE'S LIFE TODAY?

_____

MY MORNING RITUAL TOMORROW WILL BE: *Completed?*

1. _____ ☐
2. _____ ☐
3. _____ ☐
4. _____ ☐
5. _____ ☐

Day 179

LAST NIGHT I SLEPT AT: _____ & WOKE UP TODAY AT: _____

MY MOST IMPORTANT TASK FOR TODAY IS:

_____

WHERE IS ONE PLACE I AM SPENDING TIME THAT DOES NOT BRING ME REAL HAPPINESS?

_____

DATE

Night 179

TONIGHT I'LL SLEEP AT: _____ & TOMORROW I'LL WAKE UP AT: _____

WHAT ARE SOME OF THE QUALITIES I HAVE THAT I'M MOST PROUD OF AND STAND BY UNWAVERINGLY? HOW CAN I EMBODY THESE PROUDLY?

_____
_____
_____

WHAT IS SOMETHING I SPENT TIME ON TODAY THAT COULD POSITIVELY IMPACT MY FUTURE?

_____

MY MORNING RITUAL TOMORROW WILL BE: *Completed?*

1. _____ ☐
2. _____ ☐
3. _____ ☐
4. _____ ☐
5. _____ ☐

Day 180

LAST NIGHT I SLEPT AT: _____ & WOKE UP TODAY AT: _____

MY MOST IMPORTANT TASK FOR TODAY IS:

_____

WHO IS ONE CONTENT CREATOR OR AUTHOR I CAN REVISIT OR LEARN MORE FROM TO IMPROVE MY LIFE?

_____

DATE _____

Night 180

TONIGHT I'LL SLEEP AT: _____ & TOMORROW I'LL WAKE UP AT: _____

WHAT WOULD I DO DIFFERENTLY IF I WASN'T WORRIED ABOUT OTHER PEOPLE'S JUDGEMENT?

_____
_____
_____

WHAT IS ONE EMOTIONAL RESPONSE I HAD TODAY THAT I AM PROUD OF?

_____

MY MORNING RITUAL TOMORROW WILL BE: *Completed?*

1. _____ ☐
2. _____ ☐
3. _____ ☐
4. _____ ☐
5. _____ ☐

Day 181

LAST NIGHT I SLEPT AT: _____ & WOKE UP TODAY AT: _____

MY MOST IMPORTANT TASK FOR TODAY IS:

_____

WHAT IS ONE TIME I WANT TO BE MORE PRESENT AND LESS DISTRACTED DURING MY DAY?

_____

DATE _____

Night 181

TONIGHT I'LL SLEEP AT: _____ & TOMORROW I'LL WAKE UP AT: _____

WHERE DO MY BIGGEST INSECURITIES STEM FROM? HOW CAN I WORK TOWARDS GETTING OVER THEM?

_____

_____

_____

HOW HAS MY OUTLOOK ON LIFE IMPROVED MY DAY?

_____

MY MORNING RITUAL TOMORROW WILL BE: *Completed?*

1. _____ ☐
2. _____ ☐
3. _____ ☐
4. _____ ☐
5. _____ ☐

Day 182

LAST NIGHT I SLEPT AT: _____ & WOKE UP TODAY AT: _____

MY MOST IMPORTANT TASK FOR TODAY IS:

_____

WHEN WAS THE LAST TIME I DID NOT STICK TO MY WORD? HOW CAN I AVOID DOING SO AGAIN?

_____

(All Medals Earned!! You're Incredible!)

DATE _____

Night 182

TONIGHT I'LL SLEEP AT: _____ & TOMORROW I'LL WAKE UP AT: _____

WHAT ARE SOME OF THE QUALITIES I HAVE THAT I'M MOST PROUD OF AND STAND BY UNWAVERINGLY? HOW CAN I EMBODY THESE PROUDLY?

_____
_____
_____

WHAT IS ONE UNIQUE THING ABOUT ME THAT MAKES ME INCREDIBLY SPECIAL?

_____

MY MORNING RITUAL TOMORROW WILL BE: *Completed?*

1. _____ ☐
2. _____ ☐
3. _____ ☐
4. _____ ☐
5. _____ ☐

Day 183

LAST NIGHT I SLEPT AT: _____ & WOKE UP TODAY AT: _____

MY MOST IMPORTANT TASK FOR TODAY IS:

_____

WHAT IS ONE WAY I AM NOT FULLY LIVING UP TO MY POTENTIAL?

_____

SPRINT 12. COMPLETED.

Journal Recap: Days 1-183

1. Think about what your life looked like before you began this journal — what are you doing differently now? How do you feel?

   _____
   _____
   _____
   _____
   _____
   _____

2. What unforeseen effects has your life gained from all this?

   _____
   _____
   _____
   _____
   _____
   _____

3. What would your life look like if you did a morning routine filled with incredible habits every single day for the next 183 days?

   _____
   _____

4. What would your life look like if you do not do this? What would you be missing out on? How would missing those make you feel?

5. Whether it's this journal or not, what daily tracking and accountability systems can you employ going forward to maintain the momentum you've built here?

- *Fin* -

Continuing The Habit... Maybe?

This is INCREDIBLE!!! You've completed the entire *Morning Sidekick Journal* series!!

- ~~*The Morning Sidekick Journal - Volume I*~~
- ~~*The Morning Sidekick Journal - Volume II*~~
- ~~*The Morning Sidekick Journal - Volume III*~~
- ~~*The Morning Mastery Journal*~~ - Volume ∞

You've officially tracked 366 days (take that, leap year!) of your morning routines. You have demonstrated unbelievable amounts of discipline and are part of the very few people who have been able to stay this consistent with a singular practice.

Take some time to reflect on what you want out of this practice for your future.

Would it benefit you to keep going? Do you want to continue varying your routine? Do you want to take a step back and explore other habits?

There is no right answer, and an eye for experimentation (as always) will serve you very well here.

Meet The Habit Nest Team

Amir Atighehchi graduated from USC's Marshall School of Business in 2013. He got his first taste of entrepreneurship during college with Mikey when they co-founded a bicycle lock company called *Nutlock*. It wasn't until after college when he opened his eyes to the world of personal development and healthy habits. Amir is fascinated by creative challenges and entrepreneurship.

Mikey Ahdoot transformed his life from a 200+ pound video game addict to someone who was completing 17 daily habits consistently at one point. From ice cold showers to brainstorming 10 ideas a day (shoutout to James Altucher) to celebrating life every single day, he is first-hand becoming a habit routine machine that sets himself up for success daily. He is a graduate of USC's Marshall School of Business and a proud Trojan.

Ari Banayan graduated from the University of Southern California Gould School of Law in 2016. Through his own life experience, he understands how important it is to take care of ourselves mentally, physically and emotionally to operate at maximum capacity. He uses waking up early, reading, meditation, exercise, and a healthy diet to create a solid foundation for his everyday life.

Read all of our full stories here:
habitnest.com/aboutus

Shop Habit Nest Products

Meditation Sidekick
Journal

The Meditation Sidekick Journal is built to help two types of people:

1. To help **newcomers or past strugglers** to easily own the practice of meditation.

2. To help **constant meditators** push their practice to another level.

Layout of the Journal

1. **Building the foundation** - get a quick insight into the *science behind meditation* and clarity of what you're likely to experience during it.

2. **Accountability** - track your practice daily to see your progress and hold yourself accountable in staying consistent.

3. **Learn in bite-sized chunks** - get daily exposure to different types of meditations (e.g. transcendental, gratitude, physical body, etc.) and see which ones impact your life the most.

One thing we love: The journal is not just designed to help you meditate effectively, but more importantly, to **help you reach the end goal of consistently living mindfully every day.**

Get yours at habitnest.com/meditation

Sample Journal Page

DATE _____

 TODAY I WILL MEDITATE AT: **FOR AT LEAST:**

7:30 a.m. ✓   5 minutes ✓

♡ **ONE UPCOMING MENTAL OR EMOTIONAL HURDLE TO BE MINDFUL OF:**

My presentation for my boss at work - own it!

✓ **BENEFITS I FELT TODAY (CIRCLE):**

Feel Happier   More Creative   Increased Willpower   Improved Focus   More Energized   Reduced Stress

 WHAT DOES MY INTERNAL DIALOGUE CONSIST OF?

I realize that I think about my appearance A LOT... and I immediately assume people judge me for it.

 ONE SMALL WAY I CAN IMPROVE MY INTERNAL DIALOGUE:

I could be more understanding when I'm feeling self-conscious and willingly accept myself for how I look.

✎ **OPENING UP ABOUT MY DAY:**

Today was a rollercoaster. I realize that when I'm working with others, I prefer not to rely on them to get things done. It's something I want to work on improving because I make myself feel anxious when it happens.

Nutrition Sidekick
Journal

The Nutrition Sidekick Journal has a similar layout to *The Morning Sidekick Journal*. It's designed to be flexible and adaptable to whatever food goals you may have. It can be used to successfully implement:

- Calorie counting
- Weight management and/or muscle building
- General healthy eating
- Paleo / vegan / IIFYM / ketosis / other custom diets

The journal serves as your personal trainer for losing weight and **regaining control over your eating habits** quickly and effectively.

It allows you to **perfectly track** all that you need for YOUR body's optimum nutrition. These include:

- Daily caloric intake goal
- Water drinking goal
- Exercise goal
- Planned vs. actual meals, (& caloric intake for each)
- Snacks, alcohol, and other intake
- Upcoming big meals to watch out for

One thing we love: A lot of the tips are designed to help you **break the association** that may exist between **your confidence / happiness** and **your body weight.**

Get yours at **habitnest.com/nutrition**

Sample Journal Page

DATE _____

⊕ **TODAY'S NUTRITION GOAL**

_____ 2,100 calories _____ ☑

💧 **WATER DRINKING GOAL**   🚶 **EXERCISE GOAL**

__ Two 500mL bottles __ ☑   __ 2 mile jog __ ☐

🍽 **TODAY'S MEALS**

📅 Planned	✓ Actual	Calories	Protein / Carbs / Fat
3 eggs w/ 2 rice cakes	3 eggs w/ 2 rice cakes	340	18g
Chicken + Broccoli + cauliflower	Burrito (tortilla, avocado, tomatoes, chicken)	800	1.5g
Salmon w/ asparagus	Salmon w/ asparagus	500	51g

🍎 SNACKS, DRINKS, & OTHER

30 almonds	210	9g
One snickerdoodle cookie	250	2.5g

TODAY'S TOTALS: **2,100** **82g**

🏃 **POTENTIAL FOOD OBSTACLE(S) TO LOOK OUT FOR TOMORROW:**

__ Resist the cookies at lunch! __

⊕ **ONE SMALL WAY I CAN IMPROVE MY NUTRITION TOMORROW IS:**

__ If I bring a snack to work, I can eat that instead of sweets. __

The Weightlifting Gym Buddy
Journal

The Weightlifting Gym Buddy Journal is a complete 12-week personal training program.

No thinking required, just open the journal, follow the workouts, and track your progress. The journal is designed to accompany you to the gym, to help you track your weight/reps for each workout, and to help you compete against yourself every workout.

- **Contains 60 guided workouts for you to follow**

- **Each day's workout targets 2 muscle groups**

- **For lifters of all levels to push themselves to the next level and maximize competition with themselves**

- **Each workout takes 45-60 minutes**

- **Number of reps to aim for is already set for you**

- **Built with a pyramid weight/rep format to intensify each exercise dramatically**

- **No thinking required - just open the journal and follow along for amazing results**

- **Alternative exercises are listed in the case your gym is missing a specific machine**

Get yours at habitnest.com/weightlifting

 (You'll see links to exercise guides here each day)

Sample Workout: Biceps & Triceps

DATE _____

1. PREACHER CURL
(ALTERNATIVE: SEATED DUMBBELL CURL)

PREVIOUS BEST	REPS: __5__		WEIGHT: __60__
SET 1	REPS: __14__	(GOAL: 10-15)	WEIGHT: __40__
SET 2	REPS: __10__	(GOAL: 8-12)	WEIGHT: __50__
SET 3	REPS: __7__	(GOAL: 6-8)	WEIGHT: __60__
SET 4 (OPTIONAL)	REPS: __6__	(GOAL: 4-6)	WEIGHT: __60__

2. CLOSE GRIP BENCH PRESS

(By having your 'Previous Best' reps and weight values listed for each specific exercise, you'll have a clear target to beat weekly.)

PREVIOUS BEST	REPS: __5__		WEIGHT: __50__
SET 1	REPS: __13__	(GOAL: 10-15)	WEIGHT: __30__
SET 2	REPS: __10__	(GOAL: 8-12)	WEIGHT: __40__
SET 3	REPS: __8__	(GOAL: 6-8)	WEIGHT: __50__
SET 4 (OPTIONAL)	REPS: __5__	(GOAL: 4-6)	WEIGHT: __50__

3. ROPE HAMMER CURL

(The fourth set on each exercise is optional but highly recommended..)

PREVIOUS BEST	REPS: __6__		WEIGHT: __50__
SET 1	REPS: __11__	(GOAL: 10-15)	WEIGHT: __35__
SET 2	REPS: __11__	(GOAL: 8-12)	WEIGHT: __45__
SET 3	REPS: __7__	(GOAL: 6-8)	WEIGHT: __50__
SET 4 (OPTIONAL)	REPS: __-__	(GOAL: 4-6)	WEIGHT: __-__

4. OVERHEAD DUMBBELL EXTENSION

PREVIOUS BEST	REPS: __4__		WEIGHT: __55__
SET 1	REPS: __14__	(GOAL: 10-15)	WEIGHT: __35__
SET 2	REPS: __12__	(GOAL: 8-12)	WEIGHT: __45__
SET 3	REPS: __6__	(GOAL: 6-8)	WEIGHT: __45__
SET 4 (OPTIONAL)	REPS: __5__	(GOAL: 4-6)	WEIGHT: __55__

 TODAY'S WORKOUT INTENSITY: __8.5__ / 10

The Badass Body Goals Booty Shaping & Resistance Training
Journal

The Badass Body Goals Booty Shaping & Resistance Training Journal is a full 10-week personal training program which includes 50 guided workouts that are each unique, engaging, and challenging.

The journal is co-written by fitness expert Jennifer Cohen and has a large focus on circuit training (60% of the journal) with a variety of weight training for the remainder.

- The journal is designed to be done at home or in the gym with weights if you want to use more resistance.

- Every journal comes with a timed video guide that allows you to do the workout from beginning to end by simply following along each day.

- Track your results by filling in certain important variables as you complete each workout. As a result, you'll be getting constant encouragement by seeing first-hand how quickly you're improving.

- The journal contains an optimal mix of 4-3-2-1 interval circuits and resistance training workouts workout days. The two are designed to keep you engaged with different movements for short periods which will optimize fat loss and muscle development at the same time.

Get yours at **habitnest.com/badass**

https://HabitNest.link/booty01

Workout 1: 4-3-2-1

DATE _____

GLUTE ACTIVATION WARMUP
 30s EACH

a. Clam Opener

(30s Each Leg)

b. Glute Bridge w/ Band Flutter

c. Fire Hydrant

(30s Each Side)

d. Lateral Leg Raise

- 30s Each Leg (w/ Foot Flexed)
- 30s Each Leg (w/ Toes Pointing Down)

---— 30 SECOND BREAK ———

 60s EACH
CIRCUIT 1

1a. Curtsy Lunge

REPS: _____ (Left Leg) →

1b. Curtsy Lunge

REPS: _____ (Right Leg) →

1c. Boxing Jab

REPS: _____ →

1d. Side to Side Squat

REPS: _____

---— 30 SECOND BREAK ———

 50s EACH
CIRCUIT 2

2a. 180° Jump Twist to Floor Tap
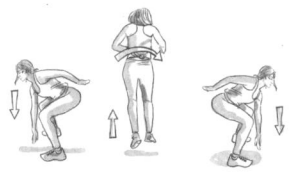
SET 1 REPS: _____ →
SET 2 REPS: _____ →

2b. Squat to Overhead Press

SET 1 REPS: _____ →
SET 2 REPS: _____ →

2c. Plie Jump Squat

SET 1 REPS: _____
SET 2 REPS: _____

Share the Love

If you're reading this, that means you've come pretty far from where you were when starting. You should be extremely proud of yourself!

If you believe this journal has had a positive impact on your life, we invite you to consider gifting a new one to a friend.

Is there a holiday coming up? Is there a special birthday around the corner? Or do you just want to put a smile on someone's face and do something incredible for them?

Gifting this journal is the absolute best way to show any gratitude you may have for what we've written here, as well as serving as a force of good through giving back to others. And you can rest assured that you're helping improve another person's life at the same time.

We created a discount code for getting this far that can be used for any Morning Sidekick Journal reorder (make sure to use the same email address you placed the order with).

If you decide to, feel free to re-order here:
habitnest.com/morning

Use code **MorningChamp15** for 15% off!

Bonus Free-Writing Space

Page 1 of 20   DATE OR DAY #

DATE OR DAY #

DATE OR DAY #

DATE OR DAY #

DATE OR DAY #

DATE OR DAY #

DATE OR DAY #

DATE OR DAY #

DATE OR DAY #

DATE OR DAY #